HORACE WALPOLE

a reference guide

*A
Reference
Publication
in
Literature*

Arthur Weitzman
Editor

HORACE WALPOLE

a reference guide

PETER SABOR

G.K.HALL&CO.

70 LINCOLN STREET, BOSTON, MASS.

Copyright © 1984 by Peter Sabor

Library of Congress Cataloging in Publication Data

Sabor, Peter.
  Horace Walpole : a reference guide.

  (A Reference guide to literature)
  Bibliography: p.
  Includes indexes.
    1. Walpole, Horace, 1717-1797—Bibliography.   I.   Title.
II.   Series.
Z8947.9.S23   1984   [PR3757.W2]   016.828′609   84-6748
ISBN 0-8161-8578-6 (alk. paper)

This publication is printed on permanent/durable acid-free paper
MANUFACTURED IN THE UNITED STATES OF AMERICA

To my mother, father, and sister
Emmi, Rudolph, and Monika

Contents

The Author

Peter Sabor, Associate Professor of English at Queen's University, Ontario, received his degrees from Cambridge, Queen's and London Universities. He has also taught at the University of Port Harcourt, Nigeria, and at the University of Calgary, where he prepared this Reference Guide. He has edited Richardson's Pamela and published on eighteenth-century and African literature.

Preface

This is the first bibliography of writings on Horace Walpole. The nearest previous approach to such a work is Dan J. McNutt's excellent annotated bibliography of the eighteenth-century Gothic novel (1975.7), with a section on Walpole listing 115 items, necessarily confined to a limited part of his oeuvre.

Thanks, however, to the rich holdings of the Lewis Walpole Library, Farmington, I have had an abundance of material from which to select. As well as the Library's subject catalogue, with its many thousands of entries on Walpole and Strawberry Hill, I could draw on a file of secondary material on Walpole compiled by the late George Lam, and on several other finding lists held by the Library. To keep this work within reasonable bounds (it lists about 1600 items), I have used the following procedures:

1. Passing references to Walpole in works on other subjects are excluded. Discrete sections on Walpole in longer works or works dealing extensively with Walpole are included, as are separate studies of Walpole or of Walpole and other authors.

2. Entries on Walpole in literary histories, encyclopaedias, anthologies, biographical dictionaries and other reference works are treated selectively, with routine listings of Walpole's life and works excluded.

3. The coverage of reviews is comprehensive for the eighteenth and nineteenth centuries, but selective for the twentieth century. For the eighteenth century, I have drawn on Benjamin Nangle's two indexes to the _Monthly Review_ and on James Kuist's recent index to the _Gentleman's Magazine_, as well as on Caroline Pearson's unpublished finding list at the Lewis Walpole Library. The unreliable but indispensable Allibone (1871.1) and Poole, supplemented by the meticulously accurate and orderly Wellesley Index, have been my guides to the mass of reviews in nineteenth-century periodicals. For the twentieth century, only substantial reviews or review articles of works by Walpole and a few major reviews of works on Walpole have been included; the emphasis here is on articles, editions, dissertations and full-length studies.

4. The coverage of works in French and German is reasonably comprehensive; Rex Barrell's two volumes on Walpole and France (1978.1 and 1979.2) provided much information. Items in Spanish, Italian, Danish, Russian and Polish are also listed, but no exhaustive search for writings in these or other foreign languages has been undertaken. Russian listings are taken from a checklist by J.S.G. Simmons at the Lewis Walpole Library. For items in Danish, Russian and Polish, I have provided translations of the titles and indicated the language in question; I have also indicated the language for other entries in which the title might cause confusion.

5. Revisions of items or items reprinted in a different format, such as an article reprinted in another journal, or in a collection of essays, or as part of a book, are given separate listings, with cross-references to and from the original entry. Unrevised reprints of books are excluded.

6. Editions or translations of Walpole's writings containing prefatory or other critical material are included, and a separate list of works by Walpole published during his lifetime is provided. Appearances of works or letters by Walpole in journals or books are not recorded, unless accompanied by critical material on Walpole.

7. Doctoral dissertations, but not master's theses, on Walpole or with discrete sections on Walpole are included, with separate entries for their published versions. I have drawn on such standard sources as Dissertation Abstracts International, the ASLIB indexes, Werner Habicht's lists of German dissertations, and Lawrence McNamee's three volumes on dissertations in English and American literature.

8. Imaginative works, parodies, imitations based on Walpole, or invented dialogues between Walpole and others (a favourite Victorian form) are excluded, as are obiter dicta on Walpole by famous authors. Also excluded are correspondence, diaries, or journal entries on Walpole, and manuscript material of any kind: I have, rather, recorded formal, published criticism.

The authors of works published anonymously, pseudonymously or under initials are identified wherever possible, through standard reference works as well as the resources of the Lewis Walpole Library. Some attributions which have appeared through the signed reprintings of anonymous items are original to the present work. Authors are listed under their real names, with cross-references from the pseudonyms; anonymous works are listed by title.

I have attempted to see every work listed; those that have resisted my searches (24 items) are marked with asterisks. More than half of these are dissertations held by libraries that refuse to participate in the interlibrary loan system, and most of these, regrettably, are in America: it is, for example, easier to obtain a doctoral dissertation from Heidelberg than from Harvard. Annotations of unseen items are included, when possible, from such sources as Dissertation Abstracts International or from works listed in the Reference Guide.

The bibliography ranges chronologically from 1757, when the first reviews of works by Walpole appeared, to May 1983, when my manuscript was sent to the publishers. The entries for 1981-82 were prepared without the benefit of several annual indexes, while only a handful of items for 1983 could be included. Items seen too late to appear under the appropriate year are listed as addenda, but are indexed with the other matter.

Most of the annotations are descriptive rather than evaluative, but attention is drawn to items that are especially significant (such as 1960.3), misleading (1934.1), or even fraudulent (1974.3). The subject index is designed to minimize the need for internal cross-referencing, which is used for reprints, revisions, reviews and responses, rather than for directing the reader to further discussions.

There are, undoubtedly, significant items inadvertently omitted, and others incorrectly listed. I should be grateful to be informed of such lapses.

Acknowledgments

In the early stages of this work, I received welcome assistance from Arthur Weitzman, who invited me to undertake the Reference Guide, and from Ruth McClure, who introduced me to the Walpolians at Yale and Farmington. Most of the research was carried out during two delightful visits to the Lewis Walpole Library, where Catherine Jestin, Karen Peltier and Joan Sussler shared with me their expert knowledge of Walpole and made available the Library's matchless holdings. They have also contributed much information since my stays in Farmington; I am indebted to their generosity.

Librarians at the University of Calgary, especially those in the Interlibrary Loan department, have aided me greatly, as have those at the other libraries where I worked: the British Museum, London University, Freiburg University, Yale University, and Queen's University Libraries. Assistance with foreign-language items was provided by Marie Legroulx (French), Emmi Sabor (German), Luigi Desomma (Italian), Agueda Schubert (Spanish), Valery Markhasin and Nicholas Zekulin (Russian), Liza Potvin (Danish) and Donna Macleod (Polish). Several helpful suggestions and items for inclusions came from former colleagues at the University of Calgary: Robert H. Carnie, Roderick McGillis, Janis Svilpis, and Robert H. Tener.

The late Walter Houghton kindly sent me a list of attributions for anonymous reviews appearing in the forthcoming final volume of the Wellesley Index. I also received aid from Rex Barrell, Loftus Jestin, and Janice Meagher, my editor at G.K. Hall. Sarah Block prepared the manuscript on word processor rapidly and efficiently.

Two former University of Calgary students provided invaluable research assistance. Gleba Zekulin prepared the index of authors and proofread the entire manuscript. Debbie deBruijn has helped me from the outset, verifying entries, purging numerous errors, and attempting to create order out of chaos. I am greatly indebted to her tireless industry and acuity.

Financial support was generously given by the University of Calgary, which furnished two research grants. Support of every other kind was given by my wife Marie, who worked with me at the Lewis Walpole Library and whose love and companionship are with me always.

Introduction

In August 1796, six months before his death, Horace Walpole wrote a memorandum requesting his executors to "cord up strongly and seal" a large chest containing his memoirs, a vast, unpublished manuscript of some three million words. The box was to be opened only by the "first son of Lady Waldegrave who shall attain the age of twenty-five years," the key to be guarded by Lady Waldegrave herself. This oblique form of publication - a key to a box containing manuscripts in search of an editor - is emblematic of Walpole's authorial career. His most famous work, The Castle of Otranto, was first published spuriously as a translation from the Italian of "Onuphrio Muralto." His other principal imaginative writings, The Mysterious Mother and Hieroglyphic Tales, were issued only to a few close friends in private editions at Strawberry Hill. Walpole arranged for his collected works to be published only after his death; his collected correspondence has taken until 1983 to reach complete publication in the forty-eight volumes of the Yale Edition; while the memoirs, duly recovered from the sealed chest, were mangled by incompetent nineteenth-century editors and have not yet been published in full.

Born in London in 1717, the son of Catherine Shorter and Sir Robert Walpole, Walpole was the youngest of five children. Educated at Eton and at King's College, Cambridge, he left university in 1739 without a degree, but armed with sinecures and patent places purchased by his wealthy father that gave him a comfortable income for life. His Grand Tour of Europe with Thomas Gray was marred by a mysterious quarrel between the companions, who returned separately to England in 1741, but were reconciled a few years later. From 1741 to 1767 Walpole was a Member of Parliament, ostensibly representing three boroughs at different times. Despite making occasional speeches in the House, he was more an observer than a leader of the political scene.

In 1747, Walpole first leased and then bought the house at Twickenham that became the centre of his life: Strawberry Hill. Here he undertook the Gothic remodelling that had an extraordinary influence in Europe and North America, set up the first significant private press in England, accumulated a remarkable collection of fine art that threatened to outgrow the modest size of the building, and wrote most of his major works, as well as the bulk of his huge correspondence and memoirs.

During his Grand Tour, Walpole began a friendship with the British Envoy in Florence, Horace Mann, that initiated almost half a century of correspondence, largely on political topics. Walpole's other principal correspondents were likewise associated with particular themes: William Cole with antiquities, George Montagu and the Countess of Upper Ossory with social gossip, Thomas Gray and William Mason with literary affairs. Walpole also maintained an extensive correspondence with the Marquise du Deffand, twenty years his senior, whom he met in 1765, and with the Berry sisters, almost fifty years his junior, whom he met in 1787, seven years after Mme du Deffand's death.

Walpole never married, but he cultivated close friendships with his cousin, Henry Seymour Conway, with Mme du Deffand, and, in the last decade of his life, with his "twin wives," Mary and Agnes Berry. In 1791 he became fourth Earl of Orford on the death of his nephew, but he did not take up his seat in the House of Lords. In 1797, dismayed by the terrors of the French Revolution, embittered by persistent accusations that he was responsible for the death of Chatterton, whom he had never met, and racked by gout, Walpole died in his eightieth year.

Since Walpole's two most significant productions, his correspondence and memoirs, remained unpublished at his death, contemporary responses to his writings were necessarily out of focus. A minor squib published in a London newspaper of 1766, purporting to be a letter from the King of Prussia to Rousseau, aroused attention out of all proportion to its importance; the pseudonymous publication of The Castle of Otranto (1765) understandably baffled and annoyed reviewers; The Mysterious Mother (1768), a drama with a double incest plot, was suppressed by Walpole and could scarcely be noticed at all; while other works that he published anonymously, such as A Letter from Xo Ho (1757) and An Account of the Giants (1766), were not even attributed to Walpole by contemporary reviewers. A Catalogue of Royal and Noble Authors (1758) and Historic Doubts on the Life and Reign of King Richard III (1768) offended many through their tendentiousness and through their cavalier attitude to historical research: Historic Doubts attracted a severe joint review by Gibbon and Hume (1769.2), as well as two highly critical monographs by Robert Masters and "St. Christopher" (1772.1 and 1791.1). The only work by Walpole to elicit widespread admiration in his lifetime was Anecdotes of Painting in England (1762), which received favourable reviews both on its first publication and on subsequent continuations. An anonymous obituary notice in the Gentlemen's Magazine (1797.6) reflects the judgment of Walpole's age: Anecdotes of Painting and Royal and Noble Authors were his two most significant pieces; The Mysterious Mother was beginning to receive guarded attention; Otranto was "miserable trash."

The publication of Walpole's collected works a year after his
death (1798.7) and of Pinkerton's Walpoliana (1799.2), a selection of
Walpole's letters and table talk, caused a brief resurgence of interest in his writings, and The Mysterious Mother attracted notice in
Germany (1797.9; 1798.5) as well as in England. Little was written
on Walpole in the early nineteenth century, however, until the publication of Mme du Deffand's letters, edited by Mary Berry (1810.2),
his own side of their correspondence having been destroyed. Some of
Walpole's letters had been included in the Works and in Walpoliana,
and his reputation as a correspondent was augmented by the publication of his letters to Montagu and Cole (1818.10-11), which elicited
many reviews. The reception of Walpole's letters is characterized by
Hazlitt's review essay (1818.2), depicting them as gossipy, witty but
trivial. Walpole's correspondence was admired for its lively style,
but, in the nineteenth century, his lack of seriousness was a constant source of regret.

When Memoires of the Last Ten Years of the Reign of George the
Second was first published (1822.9), a new aspect of Walpole's personality was revealed. Reviewers deplored the acrimonious tone of
Walpole's judgments of his contemporaries, and considered this "posthumous assassination" (1822.7) a form of cowardice. The reputation
that Walpole had achieved through his correspondence was severely
damaged, and the incompetence of his editor, Lord Holland, made mat-
ters worse. John Croker, who edited Walpole's letters to Francis
Conway (1825.5) and wrote largely favourable reviews of other volumes
of the correspondence, dismissed the Memoires as "slander, malice and
falsehood" (1822.2), a representative condemnation.

Walpole's reputation was further harmed by Macaulay's famous
essay (1833.5). Ostensibly a review of Walpole's letters to Mann
(1833.9), it refined previous analyses of Walpole's shortcomings,
such as D'Israeli's (1812.2) and Hazlitt's, with a dazzling display
of rhetoric and wit. Macaulay's portrait of Walpole as a foppish,
unreliable, whimsical dilettante still has some currency today.
Numerous subsequent critics have disputed his judgment, but none has
succeeded in dispelling it from the popular imagination. Ironically,
the letters to Mann were greeted enthusiastically by other reviewers,
but Macaulay's censure has outlived their applause.

During his lifetime Walpole's collection at Strawberry Hill had
received considerable attention, and the works printed at his press
became collector's items. The sale of his collection and library,
including many Strawberry Hill books, in 1842 aroused extraordinary
interest, heightened by the publicizing talents of George Robins, the
auctioneer, and briefly made Walpole a household name. Much of the
commentary, however, was hostile: the Times, in particular, ridi-
culed Walpole's collection in a series of trenchant articles
(1842.21). Robins's extravagant descriptions of minor items in the
Sale Catalogues (1842.17-18) obscured the merits of more significant

works. The charge of triviality, already frequent in reviews of Walpole's letters, was now applied to his activities as a connoisseur.

The Strawberry Hill Sale was shortly followed by the publication of several further volumes of correspondence and by a second journal, Memoirs of the Reign of King George the Third (1845.14). Again the reviews of the letters were largely positive, but the journal caused renewed offence; Croker's view that it could only lessen Walpole's critical standing was shared by many other critics. Its editor, Denis le Marchant, was as ill qualified for his task as Lord Holland; both tampered extensively with Walpole's text, and both had little regard for the works they were editing.

The first biography of Walpole, Robert Williams's Memoirs of Horace Walpole and his Contemporaries (1851.22), also undermined its subject's reputation. The work appeared anonymously, under the ostensible editorship of Eliot Warburton, and reviewers naturally objected to this devious, quasi-Walpolian form of publication, as well as to Williams's garrulous style and lack of critical insights. Walpole was again unfortunate in his posthumous associations, as he had been with Macaulay and Robins. The publication of his correspondence with Mason (1851.20), the least appealing of his letters, was another unlucky coincidence; several composite reviews of 1851 were strongly critical of both works. Rémusat's often reprinted and translated essay on Walpole (1852.3) provided a fairer assessment of his strengths and weaknesses and enhanced his already considerable reputation in France, where he was best known as Madame du Deffand's principal correspondent, but failed to repair the damages of Macaulay's essay and Williams's biography in England.

Since 1810, Walpole's letters and journals had continued to appear with remarkable frequency; "When will it end?" enquired one bewildered reviewer (1851.2). A temporary respite came with Cunningham's edition of Walpole's collected letters in nine volumes (1857-59), and a final set of journals (1859.10). Editions of the collected letters had already been published (1820.2 and 1840.7), but Cunningham's was the first to print all of Walpole's major correspondences, and it remained the standard edition for the remainder of the century. Reviewers, such as Francis Jacox and Charles Dilke, were impressed by the vast range of Walpole's interests, and Cunningham proved to be a reasonably competent editor. The opposite was true of John Doran, editor of the new journals, who was still more cavalier in his attitude to Walpole's text than his predecessors, and again the memoirs failed to please. Reviewers recognized their "strange, stinging interest" (1859.7), but were disconcerted to find Walpole still savaging his contemporaries sixty years after his own death.

During the last forty years of the nineteenth century, no significant new edition of Walpole's correspondence or other works was published. The Castle of Otranto was occasionally reprinted, but Walter Scott (1811.5) remained a solitary enthusiast; Victorian critics largely dismissed the novel as idle nonsense. Some minor writings were published for the first time, such as marginalia on Bayle (1861.4), Ovid (1862.3), Chesterfield (1867.3), and Pope (1871.3), interest in the Strawberry Hill collection and press continued, and Charles Eastlake wrote a pioneering study of Walpole's Gothic interests (1872.2). In the same year, Leslie Stephen published an influential essay (1872.3) treating Walpole as a serious historian, and strongly contesting Macaulay's criticisms. Walpole's second biography, however, L.B. Seeley's Walpole and his World (1884.3), was another disappointment; attempting to combine an account of Walpole's life with a selection of his letters, it failed to illuminate his overall achievement at all.

Austin Dobson's critical biography (1890.4) marked a turning-point in Walpole scholarship: for the first time, a reliable author systematically explored Walpole's life and writings. Revised and much improved in subsequent editions, the work remains in print today, a model of sobriety, lucidity and good sense. Two selections of Walpole's letters published in the same year (1890.18-19), shortly followed by a revision of Cunningham's edition (1891.9), signalled a revival of interest in Walpole in the 1890s. Memoirs of the Reign of King George the Third was re-edited (1894.8), Walpole's activities at Strawberry Hill were discussed in articles by Dobson and others, and his relationship with the Berrys and Mme du Deffand received renewed attention.

Amidst this flurry of activity, Helen Toynbee's note on a misplaced Walpole letter (1895.4) seems of minor importance. It was, however, the first of a series of studies of the text of Walpole's correspondence that culminated in a major new edition of the letters (1903-5). This edition both reflected and stimulated an intense interest in Walpole in the early twentieth century. It was reviewed extensively, and firmly established Walpole among the great English letter writers: he was frequently compared with his contemporaries Gray and Cowper. Several other significant editions and studies of Walpole were published in the pre-war period, including monographs on the Strawberry Hill Press by Munson Havens (1901.1) and Edward Merritt (1907.1), another monograph by Merritt on the Strawberry Hill Sale Catalogues (1915.4), and Lewis Buddy's editions of the Essay on Modern Gardening (1904.16) and the aphoristic "Detached Thoughts" (1905.12). The collected letters were preceded by an edition of Walpole's letters to his cousin Thomas (1902.11), and rapidly followed by two selections (1904.17-18). Caroline Spurgeon wrote a perceptive and frequently reprinted introduction to The Castle of Otranto (1907.4); the first American doctoral dissertation on Walpole, by Blanche Riggs (1909.9), studied his place in the Gothic Revival; while Hans Möbius, Helene Richter, Alice Killen and Wilhelm Paterna contributed pioneering studies in German and French of

Otranto and of Walpole's Gothic interests (1902.5; 1911.4, 8; 1915.3, 5). The Last Journals were published in a slightly improved edition (1910.7), arousing new interest in Walpole's memoirs. Carl Becker's essay (1911.1) is still influential, although several subsequent historians have disputed its findings.

Walpole's correspondence, however, continued to overshadow his other writings. Further selections appeared, concentrating on particular periods and topics: early letters (1908.3), letters on the American War (1908.4) and on the French Revolution (1913.13). J.H. Edge produced a monograph comparing Walpole as a letter writer with Johnson as a conversationalist (1913.5), Alice Greenwood wrote a study of Walpole's "world" (1913.6) and edited another selection of his letters (1914.10), while Helen Toynbee edited, in French, a major new edition of Walpole's correspondence with Mme du Deffand (1912.2). After Mrs. Toynbee's death in the same year, her place as the leading Walpole scholar was taken by her husband, Paget Toynbee, whose first Walpole study was a preface to the du Deffand letters. There followed an edition of Walpole's correspondence with Gray, West and Ashton (1915.9), and three volumes supplementing Helen Toynbee's collected edition (1918.9 and 1925.19). In addition to his work on the letters, Toynbee produced a stream of articles on Walpole's life and writings and some valuable editions of previously unpublished manuscripts, such as the Journal of the Printing Office (1923.15), Strawberry Hill Accounts (1927.15), and "Journals of Visits to Country Seats" (1928.7).

The Castle of Otranto and The Mysterious Mother also received some critical attention in the period between the wars. Montague Summers prepared an elaborate edition of both works (1924.13), with explanatory and (inaccurate) textual notes, and a characteristically dogmatic introduction; he was one of the few British writers since Scott to take the two works seriously. Another useful edition of Otranto followed, edited by Oswald Doughty (1929.7), while seminal studies of The Mysterious Mother appeared in the same year by Leslie Hanawalt and Karl Holzknecht (1929.3-4).

By far the most important work in this period, however, was Paul Yvon's massive, fully documented French critical biography (1924.14), more comprehensive than any subsequent study of Walpole. Never translated into English, this work has been absurdly neglected by most Walpole scholars. In the same year Yvon published a slighter volume, in English, on Walpole's poetry (1924.15), still the only full-length study of the subject. English biographies lagged well behind Yvon's. Dorothy Stuart's monograph (1927.11) is a breezy survey of Walpole's life and writings; Anna de Koven's study of Walpole and Mme du Deffand (1929.2) is stylish but lightweight and impressionistic; Lewis Benjamin's biography (1930.1) is undocumented and unreliable; and Stephen Gwynn's Life (1932.3) is slanted by its highly questionable assumption that Walpole was the son of Lord Hervey, rather than Sir Robert Walpole.

While Walpole lacked a good English biographer between the wars, he found no shortage of editors. In 1926 alone appeared an edition by Paget Toynbee of Walpole's notes on Mason's satirical poems, the first edition of Hieroglyphic Tales since 1785, and three selections of letters. One of these, the Everyman's Library edition by William Hadley, has been reprinted on numerous occasions, providing many readers with their first introduction to Walpole, as well as furnishing copy for a recent American dissertation (1974.3). The second selection, by Dorothy Stuart, has long since been forgotten; the third is by W.S. Lewis.

Lewis's selection, rapidly outsold by the Everyman edition and eventually succeeded by two further selections by Lewis with more accurate texts and annotations (1951.11 and 1973.23), made a modest beginning to a lifetime's work on Walpole. Lewis continued to edit and write on Walpole for over fifty years, producing much the largest single contribution to Walpole scholarship, while collecting an incomparable library of works by, about and related to Walpole, bequeathed to Yale University on Lewis's death in 1979 as the Lewis Walpole Library. His selection of letters was shortly followed by two articles describing the beginnings of his collection (1927.5 and 1930.6), and by the first of a series of editions of manuscripts in his possession (1927.14). Between 1927 and 1940 Lewis published fourteen such volumes under the title of "Miscellaneous Antiquities," a series founded in 1772 by Walpole himself. Of special significance among these privately printed volumes is an edition of Walpole's verse (1931.16) that complements Yvon's critical study. Much unpublished verse by Walpole has since come to light, but the edition has not been revised or superseded.

As well as editing Walpole, Lewis wrote invaluable critical studies of his adopted author and three full-length accounts of his activities as a Walpole collector: Collector's Progress (1951.6), One Man's Education (1967.14) and Rescuing Horace Walpole (1978.9). Among his most significant essays are those on Walpole as an antiquary (1956.2) and collector (1980.8), Walpole's resemblances to Johnson (1968.12), his iconography (with C. Kingsley Adams, 1970.1), and the genesis of Strawberry Hill (1934.4), all still definitive works on their subjects. A monograph on Walpole's library at Strawberry Hill (1958.2) was revised as an introduction to A.T. Hazen's magisterial catalogue of the library (1969.4). And Lewis's Mellon lectures, printed as Horace Walpole (1960.3), constitute perhaps the single most useful work on Walpole: gracefully written, richly illustrated, and highly informative.

Lewis's primary contribution to Walpole scholarship, however, is the magnificent Yale Edition of the correspondence. Beginning with Walpole's correspondence with Cole (1937.15), the edition was finally completed, four years after Lewis's death, with a volume of addenda and corrigenda and five volumes of index (1983.2-3). As general editor, Lewis assembled an outstanding group of scholars to prepare the various volumes, the chief of whom, Warren H. Smith, has been involved with the project from its beginnings to the final index volumes. Although the Toynbees had intended their edition to be definitive, it suffered from three principal disadvantages: its text was inaccurate and expurgated, as Lytton Strachey (1919.7-8) and several others pointed out, the annotations were inadequate, and the letters of Walpole's correspondents were not included. Furthermore, many unpublished Walpole letters had come to light since Paget Toynbee's final supplementary volume. The Yale Edition, in contrast, is one of the great achievements of twentieth-century scholarship. Its text is meticulously accurate, its annotation is astonishingly informative, and the massive index volumes make readily available the full range of Walpole's multifarious interests. A list of correspondents and a chronological list of letters in the addenda volume afford ready access to any of the edition's seven thousand letters, and the appendices to the various volumes include much previously unpublished material by and about Walpole.

Complementing the Yale Edition are A.T. Hazen's definitive bibliographies of the Strawberry Hill Press (1942.5), Walpole's writings (1948.1), and Walpole's library (1969.4). All three volumes received laudatory reviews and each makes an invaluable contribution to Walpole scholarship, providing an accurate account of all the works printed and written by Walpole, as well as a detailed description of every book in his library, with an account of his marginalia in surviving volumes. Among Hazen's several other bibliographical studies, two on the Strawberry Hill Sale (1947.9 and 1955.2) are of especial interest, solving some hitherto unexplained problems.

Most of the best work on Walpole, including Hazen's, postdates the first volumes of the Yale Edition. The standard English biography by R.W. Ketton-Cremer (1940.10) is a reliable and judicious study, although less thorough than Yvon's and pedestrian in its literary criticism. It was improved in subsequent revisions and supplemented by a series of biographical studies of Walpole's dealings with his remarkable nephew George Walpole (1948.3), Johnson (1948.4), Gray (1955.5) and Cole (1964.6). Both Ketton-Cremer and Hazen contributed to Warren Smith's wide-ranging collection of essays on Walpole as writer, politician and connoisseur (1967.22). The essays on Walpole's writings here are less significant than those on his relations with major contemporaries, such as Joshua Reynolds (by Frederick Hilles), Lady Mary Wortley Montagu (by Robert Halsband), Rousseau and Hume (by Frederick Pottle), and Edmond Malone (James Osborne), and those on his politics by John Brooke, Archibald Foord, George Lam, Romney Sedgwick and Robert Smith. Brooke is also the author of useful essays on Walpole's parliamentary career (1964.1) and attitude to George III (1973.1). When his forthcoming <u>Yale Edition of Horace</u>

Introduction

Walpole's Memoirs is published, reliable texts of a major part of Walpole's oeuvre will become available for the first time, and further research on Walpole's views on contemporary politics will be made possible. There is, meanwhile, an exhaustively annotated edition of the "Journal 1783-91" by Gerrit Judd (1947.12), the introduction to which has been separately published (1959.2), a useful selection from the memoirs edited by Matthew Hodgart (1963.8), a dissertation on Walpole's politics by Joseph Binford (1966.1), and a well annotated edition of one of the notebooks by Lars Troide (1978.15).

Most recent writing on Walpole has been devoted to his correspondence and to his literary and architectural Gothicism: The Castle of Otranto, The Mysterious Mother and Strawberry Hill. Otranto, dismissed as a lightweight romance until the present century, has assumed an ever more important place in Walpole's canon. Many critical editions have been published (four in 1963-64 alone), as well as translations into French (1943.11), Russian (1967.26), Polish (1974. 18), and German (1979.22). The Russian edition, in particular, contains an extensive and informative commentary. Otranto has also been the subject of a monograph by K.K. Mehrotra (1934.7) and a dissertation by G. Massara (1977.8), and numerous recent books and dissertations on the Gothic devote chapters to the novel; those by Devendra Varma (1957.10), Maurice Lévy (1968.11) and Robert Kiely (1972.7) are especially significant. Over half the criticism of Otranto listed in the Reference Guide has appeared in the last twenty years, and in 1977 six of the eight items listed are on the novel.

Considerably less has been written on The Mysterious Mother, but it has been the subject of good articles by Alice Brandenburg (1949.2) and Edward Rose (1965.11), and of an excellent critical edition by Janet Dolan (1970.6). Strawberry Hill has been studied in a Danish monograph by H.P. Rohde (1957.7), a dissertation by Kristine Garrigan (1967.4), and a subtle essay by Dianne Ames (1979.1), as well as in many popular illustrated accounts. The catalogue of a major exhibition on Strawberry Hill held in Twickenham (1980.3) is also of considerable interest, but no definitive work to replace Lewis's articles on the building and the collection has yet appeared.

Walpole's non-Gothic writings have aroused less interest. Royal and Noble Authors, the verse, and the comedy, Nature Will Prevail, have been almost entirely ignored by recent critics. Hieroglyphic Tales, likewise, received virtually no attention until Betsy Harfst's fascinating dissertation on Walpole and the unconscious (1968.3). The recent publication of this work (1980.4), which also contains provocative analyses of Otranto and The Mysterious Mother, of an essay by Stephen Prickett (1979.17), and of an edition by Kenneth Gross (1982.7) should stimulate discussion of one of Walpole's most neglected but intriguing compositions. Paul Kendall's edition of Historic Doubts (1965.14) lacks Walpole's extensive supplementary matter, almost as long as the original text, and many of his notes.

Harold Brown's (1970.3) and Colin Duckworth's (1979.6) are the only two significant critical studies. Between the publication of Isabel Chase's definitive edition of the <u>Modern Taste in Gardening</u> (1943.2) and Richard Quaintance's excellent recent essay (1979.18), little was written on Walpole as a garden theorist. Walpole as an art historian has also created relatively little interest, although some fine scholarly works have been published. Frederick Hilles and Philip Daghlian edited from Walpole's manuscripts a supplementary volume to <u>Ancedotes of Painting</u> (1937.14), containing copious notes on art and artists. They were followed by Francis Taylor (1948.8), Martin Kallich (1968.9), Donnita Rogers (1968.14), Lawrence Lipking (1970.10), and John Riely (1973.17; 1975.8; 1978.12), all of whom have written on Walpole and the visual arts.

The subject index to this Reference Guide will direct readers to numerous specialized studies of Walpole's life and works, including such recondite topics as his goldfish (1919.12) and the precise nature of his quinsy (1957.6), but many readers will seek simply the best general introductions. In addition to Ketton-Cremer's standard biography (1940.10), Hugh Honour's brief monograph (1957.4), F.L. Lucas's well-known essay (1959.4), and Lewis's critical study (1960.3), two more recent works are especially noteworthy. Martin Kallich's <u>Horace Walpole</u> (1971.4) contains a succinct, perceptive overview of Walpole's achievement, with particular emphasis on the historical writings. And Rex Barrell's two volumes on Walpole and France (1978.1 and 1979.2) go well beyond their subject, exploring many of Walpole's major interests, his friendships, and his critical reputation in France and England. That reputation has never been higher than it is today. Macaulay's essay still casts its shadow, but the work of hundreds of subsequent scholars has lifted Walpole's "mask within mask." Despite his disguises and subterfuges, and despite his preference for anonymous, pseudonymous or posthumous publication, Walpole's wish to be known to posterity was, according to Charles Hanbury Williams in a letter to George Selwyn of 1764, "his whole aim. For this he has wrote, printed, and built" (1961.9). The extensive interest that posterity has taken in Horace Walpole shows that his aim has been fulfilled.

Works by Walpole
Published during his Lifetime

This list, based on Hazen's two standard bibliographies (1942.5 and 1948.1), does not include revisions and reprints, contributions by Walpole to periodicals and other works, or his "detached pieces" printed at Strawberry Hill.

1742   The Lessons for the Day. London: W. Webb, 12 pp.
        The second of two political satires is primarily by Walpole.

1746   The Beauties. An Epistle to Mr. Eckardt, the Painter. London: M. Cooper, 8 pp.
        Verse addressed to Eckardt but composed for Lady Caroline Fox.

        Epilogue to Tamerlane, on the Suppression of the Rebellion. London: R. Dodsley, 8 pp.
        An epilogue to Rowe's Tamerlane.

1747   Aedes Walpolianae: or, a Description of the Collection of Pictures at Houghton-Hall in Norfolk. London: privately printed, 122 pp.
        A catalogue of Robert Walpole's collection. Includes Walpole's A Sermon on Painting (1742).

        A Letter to the Whigs. Occasion'd by The Letter to the Tories. London: M. Cooper, 56 pp.
        A political pamphlet, replying to Letter to the Tories.

        A Second and Third Letter to the Whigs. London: M. Cooper, 92 pp.
        A political pamphlet.

1748   The Original Speech of Sir William Stanhope. London: W. Webb, 8 pp.
        A speech attacking the Grenvilles, published under the name of Sir William Stanhope.

1748   The Speech of Richard White-Liver Esq. London: W. Webb, 8
        pp.
                A second speech attacking the Grenvilles.

1757   A Letter from Xo Ho, a Chinese Philosopher at London, to his
        Friend Lien Chi at Peking. London: N. Middleton, 6 pp.
                A satire of English politics by the fictitious Xo Ho.

1758   A Catalogue of the Royal and Noble Authors of England, with
        Lists of their Works. Strawberry Hill, 2 vols.
                Biographies and bibliography.

        Fugitive Pieces in Verse and Prose. Strawberry Hill, 220 pp.
                Verses and essays.

1760   A Dialogue Between Two Great Ladies. London: M. Cooper, 20
        pp.
                A satire on the German war.

        Catalogue of Pictures and Drawings in the Holbein-Chamber, at
        Strawberry-Hill. Strawberry Hill: 8 pp.
                Walpole's first catalogue of part of his collection at
        Strawberry Hill.

1762-   Anecdotes of Painting in England; With some Account of the
1771   principal Artists; And incidental Notes on other Arts.
        Strawberry Hill: 4 vols.
                Art history and iconography.   Includes A Catalogue of
        Engravers and The History of the Modern Taste in Garden-
        ing. The highly complex publication history is studied in
        Hazen (1942.5), pp. 55-68.

1763   The Opposition to the Late Minister Vindicated From the
        Aspersions of a Pamphlet, intitled, Considerations on the
        Present Dangerous Crisis. London: W. Bathoe, 48 pp.
                A political pamphlet, replying to one by Owen Ruffhead.

1764   A Counter-Address to the Public, on the Late Dismission of a
        General Officer. London: J. Almon, 48 pp.
                A political pamphlet in defence of Henry Seymour Con-
        way, replying to one by William Guthrie.

1765   The Castle of Otranto, A Story. London: Tho. Lownds, 200
        pp.
            A novel by "Onuphrio Muralto." The second edition,
        also 1765, contains a preface acknowledging Walpole's
        authorship.

1766   An Account of the Giants Lately Discovered; in a Letter to a
        Friend in the Country. London: F. Noble, 32 pp.
            An epistolary satire.

1768   Historic Doubts on the Life and Reign of King Richard the
        Third. London: J. Dodsley, 136 pp.
            A defence of Richard III; Walpole's most controversial
        work.

        The Mysterious Mother. A Tragedy. Strawberry Hill, 120 pp.
            Drama.

1770   Fugitive Pieces in Verse and Prose. Strawberry Hill, 2 vols.
            An unfinished collection of Walpole's works, containing
        much material not in the 1758 Fugitive Pieces.

        A Reply to the Observations of the Rev. Dr. Milles, Dean of
        Exeter, and President of the Society of Antiquaries, on
        the Ward Robe Account. Strawberry Hill, 24 pp.
            Replies to Dean Milles's criticism of Historic Doubts.

1774   A Description of the Villa of Horace Walpole, Youngest Son of
        Sir Robert Walpole Earl of Orford, at Strawberry-Hill,
        near Twickenham. Strawberry Hill, 148 pp.
            A catalogue of Walpole's collection.

1779   A Letter to the Editor of the Miscellanies of Thomas Chatter-
        ton. Strawberry Hill, 56 pp.
            An apologia for Walpole's dealings with Chatterton.

1785   Hieroglyphic Tales. Strawberry Hill, 52 pp.
            Five fantasies.

1786   Postscript to the Royal and Noble Authors.   Strawberry Hill,
        18 pp.
            Additions to Royal and Noble Authors (1758).

Writings about Walpole

1   Review of A Letter from Xo Ho, a Chinese Philosopher at London,
    to his Friend Lien Chi at Peking. Critical Review 3 (May):
    466-67.
        Commends the "ingenious Xo Ho" for his "strokes of true
    humour," and quotes several extracts. Does not attribute
    the satire to Walpole.

2   Review of A Letter from Xo Ho, a Chinese Philosopher at London,
    to his Friend Lien Chi at Peking. Journal encyclopédique,
    no. 4 (June), pp. 93-103.
        Compares the satire to Montesquieu's Persian Letters,
    translates a substantial extract, and states that the work
    has, deservedly, been very favourably reviewed in England.
    Does not identify Walpole as the author.

3   Review of A Letter from Xo Ho, a Chinese Philosopher at London,
    to his Friend Lien Chi at Peking. Monthly Review 16 (May):
    469.
        A brief notice, comparing this satire on the "inconsis-
    tent disposition of the English nation" to Montesquieu's
    Persian Letters. The Letter, not attributed to Walpole, is
    "ingenious," but Montesquieu's work is finer.

1758

1   [BURKE, EDMUND.] Review of A Catalogue of the Royal and Noble
    Authors of England. Annual Register 1:475-95.
        Lengthy extracts, with a preface praising Walpole's
    ability to make "out of so dry a matter so agreeable an
    entertainment." The works of the royal and noble authors
    are of minor interest, but they are treated with "wit and
    spirit."

2   Review of A Catalogue of the Royal and Noble Authors of Eng-
    land. Critical Review 6 (December):483-90.
        An acerbic review, contending that the Catalogue "abounds
    with the most flagrant prejudices of education and party."

Finds Walpole "singular in many opinions," such as his
dislike for Sidney and Fulke Greville, and often inaccurate,
although his style is "agreeable and entertaining."

3   [RUFFHEAD, OWEN.] Review of A Catalogue of the Royal and Noble
     Authors of England. Monthly Review 19 (December):557-69.
          Copious extracts, with a largely approving running
     commentary. Walpole's style is "sometimes incorrect," but
     generally "easy and elegant." His discussions of the
     authors are of interest, but he has discovered no new
     material. Also commends Walpole's essays in The World and
     his Letter from Xo Ho.

1759

1   [HILL, JOHN.] Observations on the Account Given of the
     Catalogue of the Royal and Noble Authors of England, &c. in
     Article Sixth of the Critical Review, No 35. for December,
     1758. London: H. Woodgate & S. Brooks, 40 pp.
          A response to 1758.2, described by Walpole in "Short
     Notes of the life of Horatio Walpole" as "full of gross
     flattery." Numbers the criticisms in the review and
     provides each with a lengthy refutation, concluding with the
     signature, "A FRIEND of Mr. WALPOLE!"

2   [OSBORN, GEORGE?] Remarks on Mr. Walpole's Catalogue of the
     Royal and Noble Authors of England. London: N. Gibson, 87
     pp.
          A pamphlet ascribed by Walpole to "one Carter" (William
     Cartwright), but probably by George Osborn. Undertakes to
     "vindicate the memories of the dead," and furiously attacks
     the "indecent manner" in which Walpole has criticized his
     authors. A preliminary advertisement announces as forth-
     coming, Walpolian Principles Exposed and Confuted; this was
     never published.

3   Review of A Catalogue of the Royal and Noble Authors of
     England. Journal encyclopédique, no. 4 (June), pp. 60-75;
     (July), pp. 75-96.
          Commends the design and execution of the Catalogue and
     provides lengthy extracts in translation. Believes that
     Walpole will himself have a distinguished place in any sub-
     sequent continuation of the work.

4   Review of Observations on the Account Given of the Catalogue of
     the Royal and Noble Authors . . . in the Critical Review.
     Critical Review 7 (February):179.
          Believes that Walpole "will not think himself much
     obliged to this champion," whose sycophantic writing
     "savours strong of the lick-trencher."

5   Review of <u>Remarks on Mr. Walpole's Catalogue of the Royal and Noble Authors of England</u>. <u>Monthly Review</u> 20 (May):464-65.
    Walpole's <u>Catalogue</u> and the <u>Remarks</u> attacking it are equally futile and constitute a "tedious debate."

6   "Some Account of a Work, intitled <u>A Catalogue of the Royal and Noble Authors of England, with Lists of their Works</u>." <u>Gentleman's Magazine</u> 29 (January):19-23.
    Criticizes the irrelevance and obscurity of many of Walpole's comments on royal and noble authors. He shows "traces of party zeal," seems to favour "mere natural religion," and has an inaccurate and affected style. Prints Walpole's account of the Earl of Surrey, with several annotations pointing out errors and omissions.

7   WYNNE, WILLIAM [M.N., pseud.]. "Letter to the Authors of the <u>Critical Review</u>." <u>Critical Review</u> 7 (May):453-57.
    Vigorously refutes a suggestion by Walpole in his <u>Royal and Noble Authors</u> that Wynne had improperly used Bishop Atterbury's speech at the Bishop's trial for treason in 1723, by reading it before the trial and speaking the substance himself. Reprinted: 1765.5.

                                1760

1   [PYE, JOEL HENRIETTA.] "Mr. Walpole's." In <u>A Short Account of the Principal Seats and Gardens in and about Twickenham</u>. London: privately printed, pp. 12-15.
    A brief, enthusiastic description of Strawberry Hill, where "the Gothic Taste is admirably preserved." Dismissed by Walpole, in a letter to Cole of 25 April 1775, as "a most inaccurate, superficial, blundering account."

2   Review of <u>A Dialogue between Two Great Ladies</u>. <u>Monthly Review</u> 22 (April):346.
    A brief notice of Walpole's pamphlet, without indication of its authorship. Its thesis has often been expressed "by much abler pens than our Author's."

                                1762

1   [BURKE, EDMUND.] Review of <u>Anecdotes of Painting in England</u>. <u>Annual Register</u> 5:252-57.
    Admires Walpole's discernment and his knowledge of a subject that, unfortunately, gives too little scope to his abilities. His style is lively, and "less charged with witticism than that of <u>the Royal and Noble Authors</u>."

2   [KENRICK, WILLIAM.] Review of <u>Anecdotes of Painting in</u>

England. Monthly Review 26 (April):241–54.
Notes Walpole's ability to create "striking entertainment out of the dryest and most barren subjects" in both his Anecdotes of Painting and his Catalogue of Royal and Noble Authors. Describes the Anecdotes as an "ingenious and entertaining performance," marred by stylistic infelicities and by inadequate engravings.

3   Review of A Catalogue of the Royal and Noble Authors of England. Journal encyclopédique, no. 3 (May), p. 130.
Briefly compliments Walpole on the fairness of his criticism, which does justice to the royal and noble authors.

4   Review of A Catalogue of the Royal and Noble Authors of England. Mémoires pour l'histoire des sciences et beaux-arts 13 (June):1516.
A brief, favourable notice, contending that the authors' high rank has not influenced Walpole's critical judgments.

5   Review of Anecdotes of Painting in England. Critical Review 13 (March):233–43; (April):338–46.
A generally positive review, claiming that Walpole has "rendered the work as entertaining as the dryness of the subject would admit." Criticizes several details and finds Walpole "a little heterodox in some of his opinions," but admires his lively style and discerning judgment.

6   Review of Anecdotes of Painting in England. Journal encyclopédique, no. 4 (June), pp. 82–98.
A highly favourable review, with a brief account of the work's composition and lengthy excerpts in translation. Commends Walpole's preface and text but criticizes the engravings, of which only those of Grignion are satisfactory.

1763

1   Review of The Opposition to the Late Minister Vindicated. Monthly Review 28 (June):490.
Brief notice of a pamphlet listed by Hazen (1948.1) as probably by Walpole. Describes it, with some irony, as "a very sensible and masterly performance."

1764

1   [GUTHRIE, WILLIAM.] A Reply to the "Counter-Address"; Being a Vindication of a Pamphlet Entitled, "an Address to the Public, on the late Dismission of a General Officer." London: W. Nicoll, 46 pp.

A pamphlet responding to Walpole's <u>Counter-Address to the Public</u>, itself an answer to Guthrie's <u>Address to the Public</u> in which Guthrie defends the dismissal of General Conway. Accuses Walpole of numerous falsehoods and suggests that his support for Conway stems from a homosexual attachment.

2 [KENRICK, WILLIAM.] Review of <u>Anecdotes of Painting in England</u>, vol. 3. <u>Monthly Review</u> 30 (April):311-15.
   Regrets that the "singularity of style, and incorrectness of expression" found in the first two volumes are accentuated here. Criticizes several of Walpole's judgments, and again finds the engravings unsatisfactory.

3 Review of <u>A Catalogue of Engravers, who have been Born, or Resided, in England</u>. <u>Monthly Review</u> 30 (April):332.
   A brief notice, stating that the <u>Catalogue</u> has fewer personal anecdotes than the <u>Anecdotes of Painting</u> and is therefore "much dryer reading."

4 Review of <u>Anecdotes of Painting in England</u>, vol. 3. <u>Critical Review</u> 17 (February):113-29.
   A hostile review, much more critical than that of the first two volumes (1762.5). Walpole provides only "captious positive opinions, sometimes against the evidence of common sense." His work lacks organization, and the engravings are inadequate.

1765

1 [LANGHORNE, JOHN.] Review of <u>The Castle of Otranto</u>. <u>Monthly Review</u> 32 (February):97-99.
   Reviews <u>Otranto</u> as an anonymous work, quoting from the preface "on the supposition that the work really is a translation, as pretended." Admires the style, characterization, and insights into human nature, but not the "absurdities of Gothic fiction" or the "useless" and "insupportable" moral.

2 [LANGHORNE, JOHN.] Review of <u>The Castle of Otranto</u>, 2d ed. <u>Monthly Review</u> 32 (May):394.
   An indignant notice of <u>Otranto</u> as Walpole's novel, withdrawing "that indulgence we afforded to the foibles of a supposed antiquity." Objects both to the "preposterous phenomena" of the novel, and to the preface defending the worst parts of Shakespeare.

3 Review of <u>The Castle of Otranto</u>. <u>Critical Review</u> 19 (January):50-51.
   Reviews <u>Otranto</u> as an anonymous work. Quotes from the "translator's preface," declaring that "whether he speaks seriously or ironically, we neither know nor care." Is

surprised to find "such rotten materials" being published
and suspects that this is a "modern fabrick." Praises,
however, the characterization and the energetic narrative.

4   Review of The Castle of Otranto, 2d ed. Critical Review 19
     (June):469.
         Reviews Otranto as a work by Walpole. Questions his use
     of Shakespeare, in the preface, as an authority for mingling
     tragedy and comedy, but supports the criticism of Voltaire
     and wishes that it had been made more forcefully.

5   [WYNNE, WILLIAM.] "Letter to the Authors of the Critical
     Review." In A Miscellany, containing Several Law Tracts, by
     Edward Wynne. London: n.p., pp. 208-19.
         Reprint of 1759.7.

                                1766

1   A FRIEND TO ROUSSEAU. Letter to the Editor. St. James's
     Chronicle, 16-18 December.
         Defends the "distressed Rousseau" from Walpole, "that
     Butterfly Antiquarian." Walpole is a "Prince of Cockle
     Shells," who deserves to be thoroughly chastised by
     Rousseau. Attributed by Walpole, probably incorrectly, to
     Boswell. Reprinted: 1967.18.

2   AN ORTHODOX HOSPITABLE OLD ENGLISHMAN. Letter to the Editor.
     St. James's Chronicle, 27-29 November.
         A vigorous attack on Walpole's letter from the King of
     Prussia, an "indecent and barborous Piece." Attributed by
     Walpole, probably incorrectly, to Boswell. Reprinted:
     1967.18.

3   [GREEN, EDWARD BURNABY.] A Defense of Mr. Rousseau against the
     Aspersions of Mr. Hume, Mons. Voltaire, and their Associ-
     ates. London: S. Bladon, 44 pp.
         Criticizes Walpole for his impolite behaviour towards a
     foreigner, in satirizing Rousseau with his letter from the
     King of Prussia, and blames Hume for not defending Rousseau
     from Walpole's attack.

4   [HEATHCOTE, RALPH.] A Letter to the Honorable Mr. Horace
     Walpole, Concerning the Dispute between Mr. Hume and
     Mr. Rousseau. London: B. White, 23 pp.
         Examines the dispute between Hume and Rousseau, exonera-
     ting Walpole from all blame: "I do not believe, that you
     were even the innocent occasion of this fracas." Suggests
     that the quarrel would have arisen without Walpole's letter
     to Rousseau.

5 Review of A Letter to the Honorable Mr. Horace Walpole, Concerning the Dispute between Mr. Hume and Mr. Rousseau. Critical Review 22 (December):464-66.
   Takes a neutral attitude towards the dispute, quoting at length from the pamphlet and suggesting that it might be by Walpole himself.

6 Review of An Account of the Giants Lately Discovered. Journal encyclopédique, no. 8 (December), pp. 105-13.
   Notes the satire's success in London and praises its wit, elegance, and freedom from indecency. Provides lengthy extracts in translation.

7 Review of An Account of the Giants Lately Discovered. Monthly Review 35 (September):240-42.
   The satire is "a piece of pleasantry, not altogether unworthy the pen of a Voltaire or a Fielding" in careless mood. Its purpose is "to laugh at the credulity of the gaping public."

8 [ROSE, WILLIAM.] Review of A Letter to the Honorable Mr. Horace Walpole, Concerning the Dispute between Mr. Hume and Mr. Rousseau. Monthly Review 35 (December):469.
   Assuming that Walpole is the author of the pamphlet, deplores both his letter to Rousseau from the King of Prussia and its vindication. "We are not advocates for Mr. Rousseau; but there appears to be a degree of petulance and insolence in this, altogether unworthy the character of Mr. Walpole."

9 ROUSSEAU, J[EAN]-J[ACQUES]. "A l'auteur de Saint James's Chronicle à Londres." Année littéraire, no. 2, pp. 141-42.
   Reprints the French text of 1766.10, with a French translation of the editorial preface.

10 ROUSSEAU, J[EAN]-J[ACQUES]. "A l'Auteur du S. James's Chronicle, a Londres." St. James's Chronicle, 8-10 April.
   In French, with accompanying English translation. An indignant response to Walpole's spurious letter from the King of Prussia, which is "full of Extravagance and Malice." An editorial preface defends Walpole's letter as "a harmless Piece of Raillery, not calculated to injure the Philosopher in this Country." Reprinted: 1766.9, 1967.18, and in many editions of Rousseau's letters.

11 "Sentimens d'un Anglois impartial sur la querelle de Mrs Hume & Rousseau." Année littéraire, no. 7, pp. 314-19.
   Translation of 1766.2, with additional comments by the editor, E.C. Fréron.

12   X. Letter to the Editor. St. James's Chronicle, 3-6 May.
        Defends Rousseau from the attack in Walpole's letter from
        the King of Prussia, which "assumes the Name and affects the
        Stile of a great Prince, in order to throw a Ridicule on a
        very respectable Man."   Attributed by Walpole, probably
        incorrectly, to Boswell. Reprinted: 1967.18.

                              1767

1   [FRERON, E.C.]   "Précis pour M. J.J. Rousseau, &c." Année
        littéraire, no. 1, pp. 62-65.
        Explains that 1766.11 is merely a translation of a letter
        in the St. James's Chronicle, that its attacks on Walpole
        are excessive, and that no personal offence to Walpole was
        intended by the translation.

2   Review of Anecdotes of Painting in England, 2d ed. Critical
        Review 24 (July):56-58.
        An indignant response to Walpole's cavalier treatment of
        criticisms made in the review of the first edition
        (1764.4). Walpole has, however, provided "many curious
        anecdotes" to entertain the public.

3   Review of Anecdotes of Painting in England, 2d ed. Monthly
        Review 37 (November):390-91.
        Lists the additions made in the second edition of "this
        elegant and entertaining collection."

4   Review of Le Château d'Otrante. Mercure de France, April,
        p. 102.
        A brief notice of the first French translation of
        Otranto, treated as agreeable leisure reading.

                              1768

1   G[UIDICKINS], F[REDERICK] W[ILLIAM]. An Answer to Mr. Horace
        Walpole's late Work, Entitled, "Historic Doubts on the Reign
        and Life of King Richard the Third"; or, an Attempt to
        Confute Him from His Own Arguments. London: B. White, 99
        pp.
        A lengthy response to Historic Doubts. Admires Walpole's
        Catalogue of Royal and Noble Authors and his Anecdotes of
        Painting, but is unpersuaded by his defence of Richard III.
        The work does, however, display Walpole's "extensive
        learning and great ingenuity."

2   [GUTHRIE, WILLIAM.]   Review of An Answer to Mr. Horace
        Walpole's late Work. Critical Review 25 (March):213.

A brief notice, finding Guidickins's Answer as inane as Walpole's Historic Doubts.

3 [GUTHRIE, WILLIAM.] Review of Historic Doubts on the Life and Reign of King Richard the Third. Critical Review 25 (February):116–26.
A contemptuous review, refuting all of Walpole's major contentions and complaining of his lack of research. The work is "historic scribblism," although it does contain some entertaining anecdotes.

4 IMPARTIAL [IMPARTIALIS]. Letters to the Editor. London Chronicle, 10–12 March, p. 241; 24–26 March, p. 289; 12–14 April, p. 353; 23–26 April, p. 393; 10–12 May, p. 453; 28–31 May, p. 517.
A refutation of Historic Doubts in a series of letters signed both "Impartial" and "Impartialis." Finds numerous inconsistencies, inaccuracies, and improbabilities in "this very singular and affected performance," and presumes that Walpole is writing out of "zeal of party."

5 IMPARTIALIS. Letter to the Editor. London Chronicle, 29–31 March, p. 309.
Replies to the "angry Sceptic" of 1768.13, finding inconsistencies in his defence of Walpole.

6 [KIPPIS, ANDREW.] Review of An Answer to Mr. Horace Walpole's late Work. Monthly Review 38 (May):401–2.
The attempted refutation of Walpole's Historic Doubts is a "futile and insignificant performance, scarcely containing any thing that merits the least notice."

7 [KIPPIS, ANDREW.] Review of Historic Doubts on the Life and Reign of King Richard the Third. Monthly Review 38 (February):114–25.
A largely positive review, with copious extracts. Believes that "greater justice will now be done to Richard, since the ingenious Mr. Walpole hath undertaken his cause."

8 Review of Additional Lives to the First Edition of Anecdotes of Painting in England. Critical Review 25 (January):57–58.
Praises Walpole's industry in "rescuing the remains of former artists from oblivion," and is grateful for his "curious researches."

9 Review of Historic Doubts on the Life and Reign of King Richard the Third. Journal encyclopédique, no. 3 (April), pp. 78–86.
A favourable review, summarizing Walpole's arguments and observing that his wise reflections can only increase the renown that his talents have already gained.

10   Review of Historic Doubts on the Life and Reign of King Richard
      the Third. London Chronicle, 6-9 February, pp. 129-30; 9-11
      February, pp. 137-38.
          Summarizes Walpole's thesis, taking a neutral attitude
      towards its plausibility. Regards Walpole as an "ingenious-
      ly-speculative gentleman."

11   Review of Historic Doubts on the Life and Reign of King Richard
      the Third. Mercure de France, August, pp. 96-98.
          Walpole's history is well organized and interesting; he
      is perceptive, and does not overwhelm the reader with his
      erudition.

12   Review of Historic Doubts on the Life and Reign of King Richard
      the Third. Political Register 2 (March):185-86.
          A favourable review of Walpole's "very learned and inge-
      nious performance." He is not concerned with the support of
      party but with the investigation of truth, although his
      subject is "rather curious than important."

13   SCEPTIC. Letter to the Editor. London Chronicle, 17-19 March,
      p. 268.
          Replies to the first installment of 1768.4. The incon-
      sistencies found by Impartial in Historic Doubts are all due
      to his misrepresenting or mistaking Walpole's meaning.

                                    1769

1   [CHATTERTON, THOMAS?] "Histories of the Tête-à-Tête annexed.
      (No 34, 35.) Baron Otranto and Mrs. Heidelburgh." Town and
      Country Magazine 1 (December):617-20.
          A satire of Walpole and Kitty Clive, possibly by Chatter-
      ton. Belittles the "truly gothic" style of Strawberry Hill,
      and suggests that Walpole's Gothic taste was also responsi-
      ble for his admiration for Kitty Clive.

2   [GIBBON, EDWARD], and HUME, DAVID. Review of Historic Doubts
      on the Life and Reign of King Richard the Third. Mémoires
      littéraires de la Grande Bretagne 2:1-35.
          In French. An unsigned review by Gibbon, with notes
      (pp. 25-35) signed by Hume. Commends Walpole's Royal and
      Noble Authors and his Anecdotes of Painting, but observes
      that his over-fondness for epigrams and antitheses has been
      criticized in England. Finds several faults in Walpole's
      thesis in Historic Doubts. Hume's notes criticize Historic
      Doubts in more detail. Reprinted: 1815.1.

                                    10

1770

1 MILLES, DOCTOR [JEREMIAH]. "Observations on the Wardrobe
Account for the Year 1483; wherein are contained the
Deliveries made for the Coronation of King Richard the
Third, and some other Particulars relative to the History of
that Monarch." Archaeologia 1:361-83.

A detailed study of part of Historic Doubts. Rejects
Walpole's primary evidence for Richard's innocence of the
murder of the Princes by showing that what Walpole thought
was Richard's Coronation Roll was in fact his Wardrobe
Account. Contends that Richard is "not unjustly charged"
with the murders from which his apologists "have not been
able to clear him."

1771

1 MASTERS, ROBERT. "Some Remarks on Mr. Walpole's Historic
Doubts on the Life and Reign of King Richard the Third."
Archaeologia 2:198-215.

Designed as a supplement to Milles (1770.1), but more
acerbic in its refutation of Walpole's thesis. Historic
Doubts asserts facts "against the common current of almost
all the cotemporary historians, upon the slightest evidence." The new findings are merely "boasted discoveries."
Reprinted: 1772.1.

1772

1 MASTERS, ROBERT. Some Remarks on Mr. Walpole's "Historic
Doubts on the Life and Reign of King Richard the Third."
London: W. Bowyer & J. Nichols, 20 pp.
Reprint of 1771.1.

1774

1 Review of Le Château d'Otrante. Année littéraire, no. 3, pp.
82-89.

Criticizes the mixture of realism and romance in Otranto,
and is unimpressed by the prefatory criticisms of Voltaire
and the appeals to the example of Shakespeare. Finds
Otranto neither interesting nor amusing.

1778

1 REEVE, CLARA. Preface to The Old English Baron. A Gothic
Story. 2d ed. London: Edward & Charles Dilly, pp. iii-

viii.

 Otranto seeks to unite "the ancient Romance and the modern Novel" through its use of the marvellous, the manners of real life, and the pathetic. It is excellent in all respects, except for its excessive use of the marvellous; Walpole should have remained "within the utmost verge of probability."

1780

1 Review of Anecdotes of Painting in England. . . . To which is added the History of the Modern Taste in Gardening. Vols. 3-4. Annual Register 23:218-29.
 Extensive extracts, with complimentary running commentary. Commends Walpole's "humanity and benevolence" in delaying publication of the final volume of the Anecdotes, to protect surviving relatives of the artists. The work displays his "fine genius and lively talents."

2 Review of Anecdotes of Painting in England. . . . To which is added the History of the Modern Taste in Gardening. Vol. 4. Critical Review 50 (December):413-19.
 Regards Walpole as a "mannerist in his writings," remarkable for "a singlarity of sentiment, and a quaintness of expression peculiar to himself." Prefers the essay on gardening to the Anecdotes; it is written "in a clear and masterly style, without affectation or obscurity." The finest part of the Anecdotes is the essay on Hogarth. Reprinted in part: 1781.1.

1781

1 Review of Anecdotes of Painting in England. . . . To which is added the History of the Modern Taste in Gardening. Vol. 4. Edinburgh Magazine 51 (1 February):126-28.
 Reprinted from 1780.2.

2 Review of The Count of Narbonne, by Robert Jephson. Critical Review 52 (December):456-63.
 Commends Jephson for omitting the marvellous element of Otranto, which "would have made a ridiculous figure on the English stage." The play, however, suffers from the same defect as the novel: "the want of a proper moral lesson resulting from the whole."

3 [ROSE, WILLIAM.] Review of Anecdotes of Painting in England. . . . To which is added the History of the Modern Taste in Gardening. Vol. 4. Monthly Review 64 (February):129-37; (March):182-96.

Copious extracts from the <u>Anecdotes,</u> with scattered compliments to Walpole's abilities. The essay on gardening is
"the most entertaining part of a very entertaining work."
Wishes that living artists might find a critic of Walpole's
abilities.

1782

1   I., H.   "To Mr. Walpole."   <u>European Magazine</u> 1 (April):260-62.
Blames Walpole for the death of Chatterton, and contends
that Walpole's publication of <u>Otranto</u> first as a translation, then as an original work, was itself inexcusable.
Believes that <u>Otranto</u> was, in fact, "what it was first
announced for, a translation from the Italian."

2   [REED, ISAAC.]   "The Mysterious Mother."   In <u>Biographia
Dramatica, or, A Companion to the Playhouse,</u> by David
Erskine Baker.   Edited by Isaac Reed.   Vol. 2.   London:
Rivingtons, pp. 247-49.
A highly complimentary essay on Walpole's "admirable
play," which is "equal, if not superior, to any play of the
present century."   Regrets that the age is too delicate to
tolerate a stage performance and that Walpole is unwilling
to allow an extract to be printed.   Reprinted in part:
1791.3 and 1812.1.

3   Review of <u>Anecdotes of Painting in England.</u>   5 vols.   <u>New
Review</u> 1:355-64.
A highly favourable review, singling out the account of
Holbein for special praise.   Emphasizes the range of
subjects treated by Walpole, including Gothic architecture,
painted glass, medals, and coins, as well as painting.

4   Review of <u>The Count of Narbonne,</u> by Robert Jephson.   <u>European
Magazine</u> 1 (January):50-52.
<u>Narbonne</u> is "founded on a story extremely well told," and
"entirely calculated for the stage."   Jephson's adaptation
of <u>Otranto</u> is completely successful.

5   Review of <u>The Count of Narbonne,</u> by Robert Jephson.   <u>Monthly
Review</u> 66 (January):64-70.
<u>Otranto</u> is "a much more interesting and animated composi-
tion" than <u>Narbonne,</u> which does not do justice to the
novel.   Isabella and Matilda are drawn with "the most delicate address" by Walpole but not by Jephson, and Theodore,
likewise, is an interesting character in the novel but not
in the play.

1783

1   Letter to the Editor. Gentleman's Magazine 53 (February):121–
    22.
        Compliments the "learned and ingenious" Walpole on his
    Anecdotes of Painting. Suggests that a character in a
    painting by John Mabuse depicting the marriage of Henry VII,
    tentatively identified by Walpole as St. Thomas, is in fact
    St. Longius.

2   Review of Anecdotes of Painting in England. . . . To which is
    added the History of the Modern Taste in Gardening. Vol.
    4. Gentleman's Magazine 53 (January):52–54.
        Discusses the delayed publication of volume four of the
    Anecdotes and proposes some minor corrections and additions.

3   The Genuine Copy of a Letter Found Nov. 5, 1782, near
    Strawberry Hill, Twickenham. Addressed to the Hon. Mr.
    H---ce W----le. London: S. Bladon, 34 pp.
        A verbose, convoluted satire of Walpole for his treatment
    of Chatterton.

1784

1   ARISTARCHUS. Letter to the Editor. Gentleman's Magazine 54
    (July):509–10.
        Compares Walpole's Anecdotes of Painting favourably with
    Vasari's Lives of the Painters. Criticizes several
    passages, however, and blames Walpole for allowing his
    father's collection of paintings to be sold to the Empress
    Catherine. The editor points out that Walpole could not
    prevent "this unfortunate event."

* 2 [FENN, ELEANOR.] "Refined Morality" and "Heroic Sentiments."
    In The Female Guardian. Designed to Correct Some of the
    Foibles Incident to Girls, and Supply Them with Innocent
    Amusement for Their Hours of Leisure. London: J. Marshall.
        Source: Walpole, ed. Lewis and Wallace (1951.11), p.
    245. Two papers on Otranto contain brief extracts with a
    moralistic commentary. The novel, although unsuited "to the
    perusal of early youth," contains "beautiful passages,"
    "delicate morality" and "exalted characters." Walpole has
    "employed his pen in the service of virtue."

1787

1   Letter to the Editor. Public Advertiser, 5 September.
        Provides a list of books printed at Strawberry Hill, with
    the number of copies printed, "as their value, in a great

measure, depends upon their scarcity." The list is "copied
from a paper in the hand-writing of Mr. Walpole."

2   [STEEVENS, GEORGE.]   "The Mysterious Mother."   European
    Magazine 12 (September):191-93.
        The first printing of Steevens's essay on The Mysterious
    Mother, written for Biographia Dramatica (1782.2) but
    replaced by the essay by Reed. Admires the play but criti-
    cizes the narrowness and impropriety of its subject, the use
    of a "stage trick" in the fourth act, and the occasional
    employment of antiquated words. Introduced by a brief
    editorial preface, declaring the superiority of Steevens's
    essay to Reed's. Reprinted in part: 1809.1 and 1812.1.

                                1788

1   C., C.T. Letter to the Editor. Gentleman's Magazine 58
    (August):688-89.
        Prints an unpublished letter by Edward Bridgen responding
    to a review of Anecdotes of Painting (1783.2), with
    additional comments by "C.T.C." Expands the reviewer's
    remarks on Walpole's account of Roubilliac, and his monument
    for General Wolfe.

2   [MARSHALL.] "Walpole, Horace." In Catalogue of Five Hundred
    Celebrated Authors of Great Britain, Now Living. London:
    R. Faulder, under "Walpole."
        A brief survey of the life and works of Walpole, who "now
    resides in an advanced age at Twickenham." He is "a writer
    of considerable elegance, ingenuity and invention." He has
    been unfairly blamed for his treatment of Chatterton, but he
    does lack sensitivity.

                                1789

1   BELSHAM, WILLIAM. "Strictures on Walpole's Catalogue of Royal
    and Noble Authors." In Essays Philosophical, Historical,
    and Literary. Vol. 1. London: C. Dilly, pp. 338-62.
        A severe critique of Walpole's Catalogue, which is
    fanciful and has an "affected turn of thinking." Historic
    Doubts, similarly, displays "false refinement and affected
    singularity."

                                1791

1   CHRISTOPHER, ST. [pseud.]. Free and Candid Remarks on Mr.
    Walpole's "Historic Doubts on the Reign and Life of King
    Richard the Third." London: Edward L. Low, 64 pp.

Examines Historic Doubts in detail, quoting extensively
and rejecting all of Walpole's major contentions. Despite
his "great literary Reputation, and known Industry, in the
Researches of Antiquity," Historic Doubts is "mere sophisti-
cated casuistry."

2   Review of Essai sur l'art des jardins modernes. Critical
     Review, 2d ser. 2 (August):512–13.
          A review of the Duc de Nivernois' translation of Wal-
     pole's essay on gardening. Suggests that despite its well
     known merits, the essay is misleading in treating landscape
     gardening as a modern English invention: it was in fact
     developed by the ancient Persians.

3   WALPOLE, HORACE. The Mysterious Mother. Dublin: John Archer,
     William Jones, & Richard White, 102 pp.
          Contains an unsigned preface based on Reed (1782.2),
     using both paraphrase and direct quotation without acknowl-
     edgment.

1792

1   GLYNN, ROBERT [Scrutator]. Letter to the Editor. Cambridge
     Chronicle, June 16.
          Reprint of 1792.2.

2   GLYNN, ROBERT [Scrutator]. Letter to the Editor. European
     Magazine 21 (June):433–34.
          Replies to Seltzer (1792.3), affirming the authenticity
     of a letter from Walpole to Chatterton that Walpole denied
     having written. Why "this correspondence was to be dis-
     avowed on the part of Mr. W. is hard to conceive."

3   SELTZER, CHRIST. Letter to the Editor. Gentleman's Magazine
     62 (April):296.
          Denies that Henry [sic] Walpole ever wrote any letters to
     Chatterton, and demands "justice to the name of WALPOLE, to
     whom the learned world has long been so infinitely obliged."
     Is as ill informed about Walpole's correspondence with
     Chatterton as about his Christian name.

1795

1   LYSONS, DANIEL. "Strawberry-hill." In Environs of London.
     Vol. 3. London: A. Strachan, pp. 567–74.
          An account of Strawberry Hill at the end of Walpole's
     life, written by a friend and frequent visitor. Describes
     the building and part of Walpole's collections.

2   MASON, GEORGE. "Mr. Walpole's Treatise." In An Essay on Design in Gardening, rev. ed. London: C. Roworth, pp. 167–74.
    Criticizes Walpole's representation of ancient gardens in his essay on gardening, suggesting that he exaggerates the originality of modern English gardens. Also questions Walpole's disdain for scenes "intended to excite the pleasures of melancholy," but commends his observations on "modern improvements."

3   WALPOLE, HORACE. Il Castello di Otranto. Translated by Gio. Sivrac. London: J. Edwards, 254 pp.
    Contains a preface by the editor, probably Sivrac, commending Otranto as an extremely ingenious novel, dealing with the more bizarre aspects of human nature.

1796

1   B. Letter to the Editor. Monthly Magazine 2 (July):447.
    Contends that the source of The Mysterious Mother is "of an earlier date than the noble author imagined," and proposes some early-seventeenth-century sources.

1797

1   "Account of the Life and Writings of the Earl of Orford." Edinburgh Magazine 9 (April):265–71.
    Reprinted from 1797.6.

2   "Deaths in and near London." Monthly Magazine 3 (March):238.
    An obituary notice, surveying Walpole's life and works. Admires the Catalogue of Royal and Noble Authors, Walpole's "great work," more than his other writings. Otranto has given rise to many "strange compositions." All of Walpole's works possess "a playfulness of imagination, and a delicacy of wit."

3   IRONSIDE, EDWARD. "Strawberry Hill." In History and Antiquities of Twickenham. London: J. Nichols, pp. 87–105.
    A detailed account of the contents of Strawberry Hill, describing numerous paintings and drawings. Compiled at several different times; addenda dated 1793 and 1796 describe Walpole's acquisitions in his final years.

4   LEMOINE, HENRY. Typographical Antiquities. . . . Also a Particular and Complete History of the Walpolean Press, Established at Strawberry Hill; With an accurate List of every Publication issued therefrom, and the exact Number printed thereof. London: S. Fisher, pp. 91–94.

17

An annotated list of works printed at Strawberry Hill, based on Walpole's own catalogue in Description of the Villa (1774). The press is "a worthy example to the nobility" and its productions are in great demand.

5   "Memoirs of Horace Walpole, Earl of Orford." Universal Magazine 101 (September):145-48.
      An obituary notice based on 1797.6, reprinting some passages verbatim.

6   Obituary Notice. Gentleman's Magazine 67 (March):256-61; (August):707.
      An account of Walpole's life, writings, Strawberry Hill publications, and testament. Regards the Catalogue of Royal and Noble Authors and the Anecdotes of Painting as his major works. The Mysterious Mother is "worthy of perusal in the closet"; Otranto, regrettably, was "the archetype of all that miserable trash which now deluges the press." Reprinted in part: 1797.1, 5.

7   Obituary Notice. Times (London), 7 March, p. 3.
      Surveys Walpole's life and works, commending Royal and Noble Authors and Historic Doubts, which "prove his excellence as an English Antiquary." Compares his wit, elegance, and playfulness with those of Voltaire.

8   P., R. Letter to the Editor. Gentleman's Magazine 67 (February): 125-27.
      Challenges Walpole's assertion that no letters were exchanged between himself and Chatterton and hopes that the truth will soon be revealed, since those concerned, the author included, are "advancing fast in years." Walpole died within weeks of the letter's publication.

9   Review of The Mysterious Mother. Neue Bibliothek 60:349-55.
      A German review, describing the publishing history of The Mysterious Mother, summarizing the plot, and printing an extract. Praises the play highly, finding it well unified and powerfully written.

10 [TAYLOR, WILLIAM.] Review of The Mysterious Mother. Monthly Review, 2d ser. 23 (July):248-54.
      An enthusiastic review of Walpole's "far famed tragedy," which "may fitly be compared with the Oedipus Tyrannus of Sophocles." Summarizes the plot, prints a lengthy extract, and criticizes the characterization of Friar Benedict and the porter. Believes that the play "has attained an excellence nearly unimpeachable."

1798

1   [BURNEY, CHARLES.] Review of The Works of Horatio Walpole.
    Monthly Review, 2d ser. 26 (July):323-27; 27 (September):51-
    66; (October):171-89; (November):271-89.
        A lengthy, detailed review, more critical than 1798.3 but
    also concentrating on the lesser known writings. The Mys-
    terious Mother has "great force, and admirable writing,"
    although it "excites more disgust and horror than pathos."
    Many of Walpole's verses are "ingenious and pleasing." His
    views of Johnson display "contemptuous harshness," and his
    letter to Rousseau shows "bitterness and ingenious spite,"
    but his treatment of Chatterton is justifiable. Attempts
    some interpretation of the Hieroglyphic Tales, and in gen-
    eral emphasizes the wit, originality, and entertainment
    found in Walpole's works.

2   "Extracts from Horace Walpole's Works." Edinburgh Magazine 12
    (July):6-8; (August):106-8; (September):173-81; (October):
    276-82; (November):359-69; (December):427-32.
        Copious extracts from Walpole's Works, preceded by a
    brief, complimentary preface reprinted from 1798.3.

3   [PINKERTON, JOHN?] Review of The Works of Horatio Walpole.
    Critical Review, 2d ser. 23 (June):121-32; (July):248-56;
    24 (October):130-41.
        An extensive, highly favourable review, emphasizing the
    lesser known parts of Walpole's works. Finds his answers to
    the critics of Historic Doubts largely convincing, defends
    his dealings with Chatterton, and approves of his comments
    on Johnson. Is unimpressed by his "Detached Thoughts" or by
    his verses. Walpole's letters, first published here, are
    "exceedingly valuable," and the collected works make an
    "important addition to the stock of English literature."
    Reprinted in part: 1798.2.

4   [PINKERTON, JOHN.] "Walpoliana." Monthly Magazine 5 (March):
    197-99; (April):278-80; (May):356-59; (June):436-40; 6
    (July):36-38; (August):115-18; (October):276-79; (November):
    356-58; (December):442-44.
        A series of anecdotes and bons-mots spoken and written by
    Walpole, "communicated by a Literary Gentleman, for many
    years in habits of intimacy with Mr. Walpole." Continued:
    1799.1; revised: 1799.2.

5   Review of The Mysterious Mother. Intelligenzblatt der Allge-
    meinen Literatur-Zeitung, 24 February, p. 295.
        Calls for a German translation of The Mysterious Mother,
    omitting some cruel incidents and accusations against the
    Church. Although it has been overpraised by English crit-
    ics, The Mysterious Mother surpasses most dramatic works.

6   Review of The Works of Horatio Walpole. Lady's Monthly Museum
    1 (July):63-65.
        Criticizes Walpole's extravagant and purposeless way of
    life but admires his writings, singling out the Catalogue of
    Royal and Noble Authors and Anecdotes of Painting for
    special praise. His letters, however, are his principal
    achievement. Believes that for Walpole "every species of
    decency and morality are sacred things," and that he was "an
    honor to the British Peerage."

7   WALPOLE, HORACE. The Works of Horatio Walpole, Earl of Or-
    ford. [Edited by Mary Berry.] London: G.G. & J. Robinson,
    5 vols.
        Ostensibly edited by Robert Berry but in fact by his
    daughter, Mary Berry, who based the edition on Walpole's
    uncompleted Works of 1770. No subsequent collected edition
    has been published. A highly complimentary preface surveys
    Walpole's life and works, smoothing over difficulties
    wherever possible and stoutly defending his dealings with
    Chatterton.

                                1799

1   [PINKERTON, JOHN.] "Walpoliana." Monthly Magazine 7 (Janu-
    ary):39-41; (April):216-18; (May):300-301.
        Continuation of 1798.4

2   [PINKERTON, JOHN.] Walpoliana. London: R. Phillips, 2 vols.
        Miscellaneous letters and anecdotes by Walpole in a high-
    ly unreliable text, reprinted from 1798.4 and 1799.1 with
    extensive additions. A preface, describing the work as a
    "little lounging miscellany," is followed by a "biographical
    sketch," with several criticisms of Walpole's works and
    conduct, and the most detailed description of his person and
    mannerisms by a contemporary. Regards Walpole's letters,
    The Mysterious Mother, and Anecdotes of Painting as his
    principal works.

3   W., J. Letter to the Editor. Monthly Magazine 7 (February):
    112.
        Points out an "egregious blunder" by Walpole in Walpoli-
    ana (1798.4).

                                1800

* 1 BLAKEWAY, J.B., and MALONE, EDMOND. "Upon the Anti-Christian
     Doctrines of the Monthly Magazine." Porcupine, 25 December.
        Source: Osborn (1967.17), pp. 322-23. Responds to
     Pinkerton (1799.2), indignantly denying the authenticity of

criticisms of Christianity attributed to Walpole in
Walpoliana: "it is a base injustice to his memory" to
publish such remarks after his death.

2   [BURNEY, CHARLES.] Review of *Walpoliana*. *Monthly Review*, 2d
     ser. 32 (June):178-84.
        A severe review of Walpole's anecdotes, which are "flat
     and insipid when read," although "supremely comic and amus-
     ing" when spoken by Walpole. Emphasizes Walpole's fondness
     for the "quaint and the queer," and criticizes several
     "inelegant colloquial barbarisms" in his style.

3   G. Letter to the Editor. *Gentleman's Magazine* 70 (January):
     30-31.
        Points out a blunder in *Walpoliana* (1799.2), blaming
     Pinkerton rather than Walpole. Believes that Walpole's
     character is "most insidiously and unmercifully traduced" in
     Pinkerton's introduction.

4   WALPOLE, HORACE. *Historische, litterarische und unterhaltende*
     Schriften von Horatio Walpole. Translated and edited by
     A[ugust] W[ilhelm von] Schlegel. Leipzig: Johann Friedrich
     Hartknoch, 446 pp.
        A translation of part of volume four of Walpole's *Works*
     (1798.7). A preface by Schlegel contains critical comments:
     Walpole's "Reminiscences" are loquacious and stylistically
     careless at times, his letter to Rousseau reveals his con-
     tempt for scholars, his views of Chesterfield and Johnson
     show his independence, "Detached Thoughts" is brief but
     significant, and *Hieroglyphic Tales* displays a lack of
     imagination.

5   WALPOLE, HORACE. *Règne de Richard III, ou Doutes historiques*
     sur les crimes qui lui sont imputés. Translated by Louis
     XVI, [edited by Pierre Roussel d'Epinal]. Paris: Debray,
     263 pp.
        A translation of *Historic Doubts*, made by Louis XVI in
     his final years. A preface by Roussel d'Epinal (see Duck-
     worth, 1979.6) considers the merits of the translation and
     discusses Louis XVI's interest in Walpole's work. *Historic*
     Doubts is best judged by its favourable reception in
     England.

                              1801

1   WHYTE, S. "On the Plot of Lord Orford's *Mysterious Mother*."
     Monthly Mirror 11 (March):187-91.
        Contrasts Walpole's account of his source for *The Myste-*
     rious Mother with alternative sources, to "afford a gratifi-
     cation to curiosity." Avoids discussion of the play itself.

1804

1   Review of The Castle of Otranto. Monthly Mirror 18 (October):
    246.
        A brief notice. Otranto is an "admirable production, the
    foundation of all the subsequent romances of any merit pub-
    lished in England."

1806

1   WALPOLE, HORACE. A Catalogue of the Royal and Noble Authors of
    England, Scotland, and Ireland. Enlarged and Continued by
    Thomas Park. London: John Scott, 5 vols.
        A gushing introduction describes the method of expanding
    Walpole's work: "annexing an irregular colonade, in a
    plainer style of architecture, to lord Orford's gorgeous
    temple of patrician fame."

1807

1   [MOODY, CHRISTOPHER LAKE.] Review of A Catalogue of the Royal
    and Noble Authors of England, Scotland, and Ireland. Month-
    ly Review, 2d ser. 53 (August):421-32.
        Finds Thomas Park's continuation inferior to Walpole's
    original work, which "contains bold and spirited sketches of
    character, executed in a peculiar style." Compares the
    Catalogue with Strawberry Hill; both are "rather curious
    than magnificent," and "furnish much amusement for the
    virtuoso and antiquary, within a narrow compass."

1808

1   EDWARDS, EDWARD. Anecdotes of Painters who have Resided or
    been Born in England. . . . Intended as a Continuation to
    the Anecdotes of Painting by the Late Horace Earl of
    Orford. London: Leigh & Sotheby, 327 pp.
        A preface by Edwards contains a brief biographical sketch
    of Walpole and contends that while he was well able to
    organize and polish Vertue's rough materials, he did not
    undertake original research. The weakest part of Walpole's
    work is the fourth volume, dealing with the most recent
    artists.

1809

1   H[ASLEWOOD], J[OSEPH]. "The Mysterious Mother." In Censura
    Literaria. Edited by Sir Egerton Brydges. Vol. 9. London:

Longman, pp. 184-94.

Discusses Walpole's sources for The Mysterious Mother, reprints part of Steevens's essay (1787.2), and declares that the play is "replete with wretchedness, disgust, and horror." Condemns Walpole for his guile in increasing interest in the play by suppressing it, and for his "cold frigid conduct" towards Chatterton.

1810

1   B[AKER], G[EORGE]. A Catalogue of Books, Poems, Tracts, and Small Detached Pieces, Printed at the Press at Strawberry-Hill, Belonging to the late Horace Walpole, Earl of Orford. London: J. Barker, 16 pp.
    The first formal bibliography of the Strawberry Hill Press. Attempts to list all of its productions and to record some of the numbers printed.

2   du DEFFAND, MARQUISE. Letters of the Marquise du Deffand to the Hon. Horace Walpole, Afterwards Earl of Orford, from the Year 1766 to the Year 1780. [Edited by Mary Berry.] London: Longman, 4 vols.
    A highly inaccurate selection of Mme du Deffand's letters to Walpole, with light annotations. A preface by Mary Berry considers the difficulties of Walpole's friendship with the Marquise, noting the lively expressions in her letters and his fear of ridicule, which accounts for the "ungracious language" of his replies. Regrets the absence of "public events and public characters" in the letters of two writers well known for their "knowledge of the world."

3   GREEN, THOMAS. Diary entries. In Extracts from the Diary of a Lover of Literature. Ipswich: John Raw, pp. 23, 43, 124-26.
    Diary entries on Walpole, written in 1797. Otranto is "insipid" and the prefatory remarks on Voltaire "just, but feeble." The Mysterious Mother is outstanding, Historic Doubts persuasive, the "Fugitive Pieces" elegant, the Hieroglyphic Tales wild and whimsical. The letters are gracefully written, but display "a sickly fastidious delicacy."

4   WALPOLE, HORACE. The Castle of Otranto. In The British Novelists. Edited by Mrs. [Anna Laetitia] Barbauld. Vol. 22. London: F.C. and J. Rivington, pp. 193-303.
    A brief preface describes Otranto as a "slight performance," displaying a rich imagination. The Mysterious Mother has some fine lines but a "disgustingly repulsive" subject. Notes Walpole's interest in French literature.

1811

1   DIBDIN, THOMAS FROGNALL. "The Alcove." In <u>Bibliomania; or</u> <u>Book Madness: A Bibliographical Romance</u>. Rev. ed. London: Longman, pp. 715-25.
    A list, in the form of an extended footnote, of Strawberry Hill publications. Less comprehensive than Baker (1810.1), but contains intriguing and sometimes misleading annotations.

2   du DEFFAND, MARQUISE. <u>Lettres de la Marquise du Deffand à</u> <u>Horace Walpole, depuis Comte d'Orford, écrites dans les</u> <u>années 1766 à 1780</u>. [Edited by Artaud de Montor.] Paris: Treuttel & Würtz, 4 vols.
    The first French edition of Mme du Deffand's letters to Walpole. Based on Mary Berry's edition (1810.2), with translations of her preface, introduction, and notes, and a bowdlerized version of her already bowdlerized text. A brief preface by de Montor expresses satisfaction with Berry's editing and critical material. Revised: 1812.3.

3   [GRANT, CHARLES, and CROKER, JOHN WILSON.] Review of <u>Letters</u> <u>of the Marquise du Deffand to the Hon. Horace Walpole</u>. <u>Quarterly Review</u> 5 (May):498-528.
    The last part of this extensive review gives a favourable account of Walpole. The extracts from his letters to Mme du Deffand reveal his lively French style and his fine moral feelings. He is always sincere, but at times his sincerity becomes excessive harshness.

4   [PLAYFAIR, JOHN.] Review of <u>Letters of the Marquise du Deffand</u> <u>to the Hon. Horace Walpole</u>. <u>Edinburgh Review</u> 17 (February): 290-311.
    Discusses Walpole's friendship with Mme du Deffand, criticizing his excessive fear of her expressions of emotion. Also considers Walpole's views on <u>Otranto,</u> which he overestimated, and on Voltaire, to whom he was unjust.

5   WALPOLE, HORACE. <u>The Castle of Otranto</u>. [Introduction by Walter Scott.] Edinburgh: James Ballantyne, 152 pp.
    The best known essay on <u>Otranto,</u> reprinted in numerous subsequent editions of the novel. Discusses the circumstances of its composition, publication, and reception and commends the mixture of natural and supernatural, although some of the supernatural occurrences "are brought forward into too strong daylight." <u>Otranto</u> displays the same powerful dramatic talent found in <u>The Mysterious Mother</u>, and Walpole's style is "pure and correct English."

6   WALPOLE, HORACE.   The Mysterious Mother.   In The British
    Drama.   [Introduction by Walter Scott?] 5 vols. London:
    William Miller, 1:i–vii; 2:549–79.
        An introduction to volume one, "Remarks on the English
    Tragedy," contends that The Mysterious Mother is "executed
    with great ability, and, in many scenes, similar to the
    powerful and gloomy style of Massinger."   The subject of
    incest, however, is a "radical defect," and makes the play
    "more   unnaturally   horrid   than   even   the   Oedipus   of
    Sophocles."

1812

1   BAKER,   DAVID   ERSKINE;   JONES,   STEPHEN;   REED,   ISAAC;   [and
    STEEVENS, GEORGE].   "Walpole" and "The Mysterious Mother."
    In Biographia Dramatica, or, A Companion to the Playhouse,
    by David Erskine Baker.   Edited by Isaac Reed and revised by
    Stephen Jones. 3 vols. London: Longman, 1:735; 3:65–69.
        Contains a biographical note on Walpole and an essay on
    The Mysterious Mother, which combines material by Reed
    (1782.2)   and   Steevens   (1787.2),   edited   by   Jones.   This
    curious hybrid is discussed by Perkinson (1939.17).

2   [D'ISRAELI,   ISAAC.]   "The   Pains   of   Fastidious   Egotism."   In
    Calamities of Authors; Including Some Inquiries Respecting
    Their Moral and Literary Characters.   Vol. 1. London: John
    Murray, pp. 101–27.
        An elegant, influential essay, analyzing Walpole's liter-
    ary and personal shortcomings.   In letter-writing he was
    "without a rival," but the shallowness of his thoughts and
    feelings incapacitated him in other literary endeavours.
    Otranto and The Mysterious Mother are "productions of
    ingenuity,   rather   than   genius,"   Royal   and   Noble   Authors
    creates   an   artificial   category,   and   Anecdotes   of   Painting
    lacks original research.

3   du DEFFAND, MARQUISE.   Lettres de la Marquise du Deffand à
    Horace Walpole, depuis Comte d'Orford, écrites dans les
    années 1766 à 1780.   [Edited by Artaud de Montor.]   2d ed.
    Paris: Treuttel & Würtz, 4 vols.
        A revised edition of 1811.2, with a table of contents and
    a new preface claiming that many errors in both the English
    and first French editions have been corrected.

4   MAJOR, JOHN.   A Catalogue of Rare Books and Tracts; Printed at
    the Private Press of the Hon. Horace Walpole (Afterwards
    Earl of Orford) at Strawberry Hill.   London: Harding &
    Wright, 3 pp.
        A bookseller's catalogue, with annotations.   Notes the
    "increasing scarcity" of Strawberry Hill productions, and

25

the "irresistible interest" of all subjects connected with
Walpole.

5   Notice biographique sur Horace Walpole, comte d'Orfort [sic].
    Traduit de l'anglais. Paris: Galignani, 23 pp.
         A translation of an unlocated article in the Monthly
    Repertory. Provides an outline of Walpole's life, some
    notes on his manners and taste, and a brief discussion of
    his writings. Regards Anecdotes of Painting as the founda-
    tion of his works, the letters as the centrepiece, and The
    Mysterious Mother as the crown.

6   R., H. Letter to the Editor. Gentleman's Magazine 82 (Septem-
    ber): 206-7.
         Replies to D'Israeli (1812.2), claiming that he has drawn
    only Walpole's worst features. Defends Otranto, in particu-
    lar, for its "picturesque fancy, invention," and pathos.

1813

1   [McCREERY, JOHN.] A Catalogue of Books and Tracts Printed at
    the Private Press of the Hon. Horace Walpole. London: J.
    McCreery, 12 pp.
         A bookseller's catalogue, listing books and miscellaneous
    items published at the Strawberry Hill Press, as well as
    works by Walpole published elsewhere. Each item is briefly
    annotated. These publications, with Strawberry Hill itself
    and its contents, will create "a lasting monument" to
    Walpole's judgment and taste.

1814

1   HARDINGE, GEORGE. "Horace Walpole." In Literary Anecdotes of
    the Eighteenth Century: Comprizing Biographical Memoirs of
    William Bowyer, by John Nichols. Vol. 7. London: Printed
    for the Author, pp. 525-27.
         A portrait of Walpole, emphasizing his effeminacy and
    excessive wit, and regretting his lack of humour. Admires
    Otranto, The Mysterious Mother, and Historic Doubts, but not
    Walpole's verse, in which he "terribly failed." His letters
    are the finest of his age. Reprinted: 1973.21

1815

1   GIBBON, EDWARD, and HUME, DAVID. "Doutes historiques sur la
    vie et le règne du roi Richard III. par M. Horace Walpole."
    In Miscellaneous Works of Edward Gibbon, Esq. Edited by
    John, Lord Sheffield. Vol. 3. London: John Murray, pp.

156-67.
Reprint of 1769.2

1816

1   BREWER, J[AMES] NORRIS. "Strawberry Hill." In <u>London and</u>
     <u>Middlesex; or, an Historical, Commercial, & Descriptive</u>
     <u>Survey of the Metropolis of Great-Britain</u>, by Edward
     W[edlake] Brayley, J. Nightingale, and J[ames] Norris
     Brewer. Vol. 4. London: J. Harris, pp. 397-422.
          An account of Walpole's collection at Strawberry Hill,
     based on his <u>Description of the Villa</u>. Criticizes Walpole's
     frigid character, his treatment of Chatterton, and his
     writings, of which <u>Otranto</u> is the most successful.

1817

1   BELOE, WILLIAM. "H..... W......" In <u>The Sexagenarian; or, the</u>
     <u>Recollections of a Literary Life</u>. Edited by Thomas
     Rennell. Vol. 1. London: F.C. & J. Rivington, pp. 266-95.
          Anecdotes of Beloe's dealings with Walpole in the 1790s.
     Walpole is portrayed as parsimonious, hypocritical, and
     highly affected. He was, however, an "entertaining compan-
     ion," and "a very polished and accomplished gentleman."

2   CHALMERS, ALEXANDER. "Walpole (Horace)." In <u>The General</u>
     <u>Biographical Dictionary</u>. Vol. 31. London: J. Nichols,
     pp. 56-66.
          A survey of Walpole's life and works, with some severe
     criticisms of his deceitfulness and insincerity. Admires
     <u>The Mysterious Mother</u>, despite its unsuitable subject, and
     <u>Otranto</u>, which "displays great powers." Walpole's letters
     have been praised for their wit, but they reveal the defects
     of his character.

3   EVANS, JOHN. "Letter VI" and "Letter VII." In <u>An Excursion to</u>
     <u>Windsor, in July, 1810</u>. London: Sherwood, Neely & Jones,
     pp. 157-205.
          An account of Walpole's collection at Strawberry Hill,
     taken from his <u>Description of the Villa</u> with some additional
     comments. Also provides an inaccurate survey of Walpole's
     life and works, dwelling on his dealings with Chatterton.

4   WALPOLE, HORACE. The Castle of Otranto. In "The Old English
     Baron: A Gothic Story." By Clara Reeve. And "The Castle
     of Otranto." By Horace Walpole. London: J. Walker, pp.
     1-116.
          Contains an unsigned "Biographical Preface," surveying
     Walpole's life and discussing his novel. <u>Otranto</u> has

influenced subsequent writers, such as Mrs. Radcliffe, but
it displays a genius not often found in Walpole's imitators.

1818

1   HARDINGE, GEORGE. "Vindication of Lady Mary Wortley Montagu"
    and "Expostulatory Remarks on 'Letters by Madame du Deffand
    to the late Earl of Orford.'"   In Miscellaneous Works, in
    Prose and Verse, of George Hardinge. Vol. 3. London: J.
    Nichols, pp. 145-310.
       Two highly critical essays. The first defends Lady Mary
    from satirical comments made in Walpole's letters, and
    deplores his "effeminate style." The second, a garrulous
    piece signed "The Old Grandmother," condemns Mme du
    Deffand's loose morals and wonders why Walpole was
    interested in such a dissolute woman.

2   [HAZLITT, WILLIAM.] Review of Letters from the Hon. Horace
    Walpole, to George Montagu. Edinburgh Review 31 (Decem-
    ber):80-93.
       Depicts Walpole as "the very prince of Gossips," noting
    his frivolity and love of trifles. He "envied all great
    minds," quarrelled with most of his friends, and abused them
    behind their backs. His letters are lively and witty but
    trivial. Reprinted: 1904.5 and 1933.3.

3   [MARTIN, JOHN.] Names of Persons Mentioned in the Foregoing
    Letters. London: Rodwell & Martin, 8 pp.
       A pamphlet, identifying many of the names deleted in
    1818.10.

4   [MURRAY, JOHN.] "Nine Unpublished Letters of Horace Walpole."
    Blackwood's Magazine 4 (November):148-55.
       Introduces some letters from Walpole to Cole with a trib-
    ute to Walpole as a letter-writer and a condemnation of the
    man, who lacked "all sympathy for every human being." The
    text of the letters is highly inaccurate, conflating pas-
    sages from several sources.

5   Review of Letters from the Hon. Horace Walpole, to George
    Montagu. American Monthly Magazine 3 (June):110-19.
       Reprint of 1818.7.

6   Review of Letters from the Hon. Horace Walpole, to George
    Montagu. British Critic, n.s. 9 (June):586-90.
       A highly critical account of Walpole's life, writings,
    and his "Baby-house at Strawberry Hill." His only remark-
    able work is The Mysterious Mother, and this contains "dark
    abominations." He was a "heartless trifler," whose letters
    are malicious and tasteless.

7   Review of <u>Letters from the Hon. Horace Walpole, to George Montagu</u>. <u>Literary Gazette</u>, 7 February, pp. 85–86; 14 February, pp. 99–101; 21 February, pp. 118–19; 28 February, pp. 134–35.
     Copious extracts from Walpole's letters, which are often "exceedingly scandalous" but always amusing. Emphasizes Walpole's wit and fondness for satire. Reprinted: 1818.5.

8   [SCOTT, WALTER.] Review of <u>Letters from the Hon. Horace Walpole, to George Montagu</u>. <u>Quarterly Review</u> 19 (April): 118–31.
     A balanced review, commending the elegance and liveliness of Walpole's letters but regretting their superficiality. Admires Walpole's "Reminiscences," and prefers <u>The Mysterious Mother</u> to <u>Otranto</u>. His character is marred by selfishness and vanity.

9   "Strawberry Hill." In <u>Descriptions to the Plates of Thames Scenery</u>. Engraved by W.B. Cooke & G. Cooke. London: John Murray, no pagination.
     A brief description of Strawberry Hill, "a picture of the master's mind who formed it, in which there was nothing great." Walpole's works are largely undistinguished; the most significant is <u>Anecdotes of Painting</u>.

10   WALPOLE, HORACE. <u>Letters from the Hon. Horace Walpole, to George Montagu, Esq. From the Year 1736, to the Year 1770</u>. [Edited by John Martin.] London: Rodwell & Martin, 446 pp.
     Prints Walpole's letters to Montagu, with light annotations, deleting numerous personal names. A prefatory note identifies Montagu as Walpole's "intimate friend." Revised: 1819.5.

11   WALPOLE, HORACE. <u>Letters from the Hon. Horace Walpole, to the Rev. William Cole, and Others; from the Year 1745, to the Year 1782</u>. [Edited by John Martin.] London: Rodwell & Martin, 259 pp.
     Prints Walpole's letters to Cole and to Thomas Birch. Includes very brief annotations and a prefatory note on Cole.

12   WALPOLE, HORACE. <u>Lettres d'Horace Walpole, depuis Comte d'Orford, à Georges Montagu, membre du parlement d'Angleterre et sécretaire particulier de Lord North, depuis l'année 1736 jusqu'en 1770</u>. [Edited by M. Charles-Malo.] Paris: Louis Janet, 448 pp.
     A translation of 1818.10, with a highly corrupt, bowdlerized, and abridged text. A preface claims that the deletions have improved the French edition. An introduction surveys Walpole's life and works, emphasizing the significance of <u>Anecdotes of Painting,</u> and a collection of "Walpol-

iana," not taken from Pinkerton (1799.2), is appended.

13 [WILSON, JOHN.] "Horace Walpole's Letters to Mr. Montagu."
    Blackwood's Magazine 3 (May):162-68.
        Review of 1818.10, consisting largely of extracts. The
    letters present "a complete and unflattering portrait" of
    Walpole, but provide fascinating information on his age.

                                1819

1   C. Review of Letters from the Hon. Horace Walpole, to George
    Montagu. Analectic Magazine 13 (January):1-8.
        Extracts from the letters, with a brief biographical
    sketch. Finds the letters more amusing than instructive.

2   Review of Letters from the Hon. Horace Walpole, to George
    Montagu, and Letters from the Hon. Horace Walpole, to the
    Rev. William Cole. Monthly Review, 2d ser. 90 (September):
    1-14.
        Regards Walpole's letters as a kaleidoscope, in which
    worthless subjects "fall into endless and beautiful vari-
    eties of shape and colour." Concerned with Walpole's
    lively, graceful style, rather than his subject matter.

3   Review of Letters from the Hon. Horace Walpole, to the Rev.
    William Cole. British Critic, n.s. 11 (April):402-8.
        Regards Walpole as frivolous, unoriginal, and superfi-
    cial, but a "delightful correspondent" who faithfully
    recorded "all the literary fashionable and political gossip
    of the day."

4   Review of Letters from the Hon. Horace Walpole, to the Rev.
    William Cole. Literary Gazette, 9 January, pp. 17-18; 16
    January, pp. 34-35.
        A series of extracts, with enthusiastic running commen-
    tary. Emphasizes the entertainment that Walpole's letters
    afford.

5   WALPOLE, HORACE. Letters from the Hon. Horace Walpole, to
    George Montagu, Esq. From the Year 1736, to the Year 1770.
    2d ed. [Edited by John Martin.] London: Rodwell & Martin,
    446 pp.
        Revised edition of 1818.10, identifying most of the
    omitted personal names by filling in the blanks.

6   "Walpole's Letters." British Review 13 (May):257-80.
        Review of 1818.10-11. Censures Walpole's immorality and
    lack of Christian principles. He lacks any concern for his
    fellow man, and is superficial, artificial, and affected.

1820

1   "Horatio Walpole, Fourth Earl of Orford." In The Lives of
Eminent & Remarkable Characters, Born or Long Resident in
the Counties of Essex, Suffolk, & Norfolk. London:
Longman, under "Walpole."
    A brief survey of Walpole's life and works. He "particu-
larly excelled as a letter-writer"; his "failings were vani-
ty and insincerity."

2   WALPOLE, HORACE. Private Correspondence of Horace Walpole,
Earl of Orford. London: Rodwell & Martin, 4 vols.
    The first collected edition of Walpole's letters. A
brief preface declares that Walpole's "distinguished talent
as a letter-writer has not been questioned," and points out
his detailed knowledge of his age. Revised: 1837.2.

1822

1   [ALLEN, JOHN, and JEFFREY, FRANCIS.] Review of Memoires of the
Last Ten Years of the Reign of George the Second. Edinburgh
Review 37 (June):1, 19-46.
    An extensive account of the political background of the
Memoires. The work contains "acrimonious strictures" but is
highly entertaining and provides "minute and circumstantial
details" about Walpole's age.

2   [CROKER, JOHN WILSON.] Review of Memoires of the Last Ten
Years of the Reign of George the Second. Quarterly Review
27 (April):178-215.
    A lengthy, hostile analysis of the Memoires from a Tory
standpoint. Walpole "had the feelings of a tiger cat, sometimes sportive, sometimes ferocious, always cruel." His
work is full of slander, malice and falsehood, and should be
read with "extreme caution and doubt."

3   HAWKINS, LAETITIA-MATILDA. Anecdotes, Biographical Sketches
and Memoirs. Vol. 1. London: F.C. & J. Rivington, 351 pp.
    Contains affectionate personal anecdotes of Walpole
throughout, with occasional, tentative comments on his
works. Notes the originality of Otranto and the "enormous
indecency" of The Mysterious Mother. Includes a favourable
review of Walpole's Memoires of George II by Henry Hawkins,
Laetitia-Matilda's brother.

4   Q. Review of Memoires of the Last Ten Years of the Reign of
George the Second. Examiner, March 10, pp. 153-54.
    Deplores Walpole's "puerile personality, fiddle-faddle,
and fondness for little wit," and his corrupt, typically

French manner of writing. His <u>Memoires</u> are neither entertaining nor serious history.

5   Review of <u>Memoires of the Last Ten Years of the Reign of George the Second</u>. <u>Album</u> 1 (April):164–81.
    Recognizes Walpole's gift for creating vivid portraits of his contemporaries, but finds the <u>Memoires</u> less interesting and more artificial than his "Reminiscences" or his letters. His style is also less pleasing here: "harsh, involved, and frequently ungrammatical."

6   Review of <u>Memoires of the Last Ten Years of the Reign of George the Second</u>. <u>Gentleman's Magazine</u> 92 (March):233–38; (April):341–43.
    Criticizes the "injustice and gross venality" of Walpole's strictures of his contemporaries, and the levity of his style. Finds his wish for posthumous publication cowardly.

7   Review of <u>Memoires of the Last Ten Years of the Reign of George the Second</u>. <u>Literary Gazette</u>, 9 March, pp. 143–46; 16 March, pp. 161–63; 23 March, pp. 178–79; 30 March, pp. 194–95; 6 April, pp. 212–13; 13 April, pp. 230–32; 20 April, pp. 244–47.
    Deplores the publication of Walpole's <u>Memoires</u>, with their "system of posthumous assassination." Blames Walpole for his "premeditated cruelty," illustrated by copious extracts. The work is "cowardly, malicious, and unjust." Reprinted in part: 1822.10.

8   Review of <u>Memoires of the Last Ten Years of the Reign of George the Second</u>. <u>Monthly Review</u>, 2d ser. 98 (May):1–13.
    A favourable review. The <u>Memoires</u> are well written, "illustrate the manners of the age," and contain valuable material for the historian. Walpole's portraits of his contemporaries are particularly successful.

9   WALPOLE, HORACE. <u>Memoires of the Last Ten Years of the Reign of George the Second</u>. [Edited by Lord Holland, introduction by James Mackintosh.] London: John Murray, 2 vols.
    A highly corrupt, heavily censored text, with inaccurate, misleading annotations by Lord Holland. Mackintosh's preface describes the composition of the memoirs and discusses Walpole's involvement in the politics of his age. His memoirs contain "much curious and original information," founded on either his personal knowledge or identified sources. His judgments were constantly changing: he was a "bitter but placable enemy," and, with the exception of Conway, "an inconstant friend." Revised: 1846.12.

10 "Walpole's Secret Memoirs." <u>Atheneum</u> 11 (15 June):223–25;

(1 July):278-80.
Reprinted from 1822.7.

1823

1   STEWART, JOHN. "Horace Walpole." In <u>Collections and Recollec-</u>
<u>tions; or, Historical, Biographical, and Miscellaneous Anec-</u>
<u>dotes, Notices, and Sketches.</u> Edinburgh: Oliver & Boyd,
pp. 124-25.
A brief, vituperative portrait. Walpole was, "like many
<u>other persons of imbecile mind,</u> a strange compound of incon-
sistency."

1824

1   du DEFFAND, MARQUISE. <u>Lettres de la Marquise du Deffand à</u>
<u>Horace Walpole. . . . Nouvelle édition augmentée des</u>
<u>extraits des lettres d'Horace Walpole.</u> Introduction by
A[dolphe] T[hiers]. Paris: Ponthieu, 4 vols.
An introduction studies Walpole's relationship with Mme
du Deffand, harshly criticizing both for their idleness but
recognizing their abilities. They were well matched, since
each had a talent for seeing the worst in others. Mme du
Deffand was overwhelmed by love for Walpole, who had no real
affection for her.

2   WATT, ROBERT. "Walpole, The Right Hon. Horace, Earl of
Orford." In <u>Bibliotheca Britannica or A General Index to</u>
<u>British and Foreign Literature.</u> Vol. 2. Edinburgh: A.
Constable, p. 946.
A short bibliography of works by Walpole published during
and after his lifetime.

1825

1   B[EDFORD, DUKE OF]. <u>A Catalogue of Miniature Portraits in</u>
<u>Enamel by Henry Bone, Esq. R.A. in the Collection of the</u>
<u>Duke of Bedford at Woburn Abbey.</u> London: Shakespeare
Press, 63 pp.
Quotes Walpole's catalogue of Bedford's portraits by Bone
throughout, commending his "brief but pointed remarks."
Also discusses Walpole's reluctance to assume the title of
Earl of Orford.

2   Review of <u>Letters from the Honble. Horace Walpole, to the Earl</u>
<u>of Hertford.</u> <u>Literary Gazette,</u> June 18, pp. 388-90.
Extracts from Walpole's letters, with approving commentary on their wit and detail.

3   Review of Letters from the Honble. Horace Walpole, to the Earl
     of Hertford. Monthly Review, 2d ser. 108 (September):32-37.
     Walpole's letters to Hertford are "of considerable
     value," but marred by his prejudices and love of ridicule.

4   SCOTT, SIR WALTER. "Life and Character of Walpole." Museum 6,
     no. 34:289-302.
     Reprinted from 1811.5.

5   WALPOLE, HORACE. Letters from the Honble. Horace Walpole, to
     the Earl of Hertford, during His Lordship's Embassy in
     Paris. To Which are Added Mr. Walpole's Letters to the
     Rev. Henry Zouch. [Edited by John Wilson Croker.] London:
     Charles Knight, 285 pp.
     Contains extensive notes by Croker, constantly correcting
     inaccuracies and "malicious" statements in Walpole's
     letters. The preface, however, takes a more favourable
     attitude, declaring that Walpole's letters have "already
     attained the highest rank in the department of English
     literature."

1826

1   MORGAN, LADY. "Strawberry Hill." New Monthly Magazine 17
     (August):121-28; (September):256-67.
     A highly complimentary essay, defending Walpole from his
     critics. Otranto founded a "delightful school of literary
     fiction," and Walpole's letters are always interesting. His
     leading trait was "a quick and delicate perception of the
     truth of things." Also describes and admires Walpole's
     collection at Strawberry Hill.

2   WALPOLE, HORACE. Anecdotes of Painting in England. Edited by
     James Dallaway. London: John Major, vols. 1-2.
     An edition of Walpole's Anecdotes, with considerable
     additions by Dallaway. An introduction criticizes Walpole's
     choice of portraits and engravers in the original edition,
     but commends his interest in English painting and the indus-
     try with which he compiled his work. Continued: 1827.3 and
     1828.2.

3   WALPOLE, HORACE, Réminiscences d'Horace Walpole. [Translated
     by Delattre.] Paris: Librairie universelle de Mongie Aîné,
     208 pp.
     A translation of Walpole's "Reminiscences," first pub-
     lished in 1798.7. Contains an unsigned foreword, historical
     notes, and an introduction contending that the "Reminis-
     cences" give a closer insight into the manners and customs
     of upper-class society in Walpole's age than any other
     work. Discusses Walpole's principal writings and his

relations with Gray, Mme du Deffand, Chatterton, and others.

1827

1   Review of Anecdotes of Painting in England, vols. 1-3. Literary Gazette, 30 June, pp. 407-8.
    Admires the "intrinsic excellence" of Walpole's work, which Dallaway has brought to perfection.

2   Review of Anecdotes of Painting in England, vols. 1-4. Retrospective Review, n.s. 1, pt. 3:415-19.
    Believes that "the world has not done justice" to Walpole, and that his Anecdotes is a serious historical work. His reputation as a dilettante is undeserved.

3   WALPOLE, HORACE. Anecdotes of Painting in England. Edited by James Dallaway. London: John Major, vols. 3-4.
    Continuation of 1826.2. Reprinted: 1982.8.

1828

1   Review of Anecdotes of Painting in England, vol. 5. Gentleman's Magazine 98 (May):431-32.
    Walpole's Anecdotes "leaves competition at a distance." He has been ungenerously criticized, and was "the first man of taste in his day."

2   WALPOLE, HORACE. Anecdotes of Painting in England. Edited by James Dallaway. London: John Major, vol. 5.
    Completion of 1827.3.

1829

1   JOHNSON, GEORGE W. "Horace Walpole, Earl of Orford." In A History of English Gardening, Chronological, Biographical, Literary, and Critical. London: Baldwin & Cradock, pp. 240-41.
    Criticizes the superficiality of Walpole's research and his religious scepticism. In his essay "On Modern Gardening," historians who differ from his views "are passed over with indifference and contempt."

1830

1   WALPOLE, HORACE. The Castle of Otranto: A Gothic Story. . . . And The Old English Baron: A Gothic Story. Preface by Ω. London: J. Smith, 291 pp.

A pseudonymous preface outlines Walpole's life and commends Otranto, which combines "all the interest and unities
of the ancient dramatic romance, with the elegance and
refinement of the modern."

1833

1   [BISSET, ANDREW?] Review of Letters of Horace Walpole, Earl of
    Orford, to Sir Horace Mann. Westminster Review 19
    (October):361-66.
        Walpole's letters expose the real nature of the public
    figures of his age, and provide valuable material for
    historians.

2   "Character and Writings of Horace Walpole." New Monthly
    Magazine 38 (August):422-32.
        A garrulous survey of Walpole's writings with special
    praise for The Mysterious Mother, which expresses "the dark
    secrets of humanity."

3   "Horace Walpole's Letters to Sir Horace Mann." Museum 23, no.
    136:457-68.
        Reprinted from 1833.4, 7.

4   [JOHNSTONE, CHRISTIAN.] Review of Letters of Horace Walpole,
    Earl of Orford, to Sir Horace Mann. Tait's Edinburgh Maga-
    zine 3 (July):421-36.
        Contends that Walpole's reputation is now lower than
    during his lifetime but higher than immediately after his
    death. His published works are mediocre, but his memoirs
    and letters are invaluable for their detailed commentary on
    eighteenth-century England. Reprinted in part: 1833.3.

5   [MACAULAY, THOMAS BABINGTON.] Review of Letters of Horace
    Walpole, Earl of Orford, to Sir Horace Mann. Edinburgh
    Review 58 (October):227-58.
        By far the best known and most influential essay on
    Walpole, epitomizing early-nineteenth-century attitudes and
    establishing a stereotype still widely accepted today. Many
    phrases have been quoted ad nauseam: Walpole's mind was
    "unhealthy and disorganized," "a bundle of inconsistent
    whims and affectations. His features were covered by mask
    within mask." Relying primarily on a series of paradoxes
    and antitheses, Macaulay savages Walpole's character and
    most of his writings, reserving guarded praise for Otranto
    and the letters. The second part of the essay, primarily an
    analysis of mid-eighteenth-century politics, is less daz-
    zling but more substantial. Reprinted: 1834.2 (in part),
    1843.4, and in numerous collections of Macaulay's essays.

6 Review of <u>Letters of Horace Walpole, Earl of Orford, to Sir Horace Mann</u>. <u>Athenaeum</u>, 8 June, pp. 354–57; 15 June, pp. 382–84; 22 June, pp. 397–98.
   A highly favourable review of "incomparably the best English letter writer," with copious extracts from the letters.

7 Review of <u>Letters of Horace Walpole, Earl of Orford, to Sir Horace Mann</u>. <u>Literary Gazette</u>, 1 June, pp. 337–39; 8 June, pp. 356–59; 15 June, pp. 374–76; 20 July, p. 458.
   Extensive extracts from the letters with a highly enthusiastic commentary. The letters to Mann are "superior to any even of Walpole's preceding volumes." Reprinted in part: 1833.3.

8 Review of <u>Letters of Horace Walpole, Earl of Orford, to Sir Horace Mann</u>. <u>Monthly Review</u>, n.s. 4 (October):221–39.
   Marvels at Walpole's successive posthumous publications and greatly admires his letters, which unite "ease, flexibility, and happiness of expression."

9 WALPOLE, HORACE. <u>Letters of Horace Walpole, Earl of Orford, to Sir Horace Mann, British Envoy at the Court of Tuscany</u>. Edited by Lord Dover. London: Richard Bentley, 3 vols.
   Contains a preface and an extensive introduction by Lord Dover. The preface regards Walpole's letters to Mann as his most interesting, because of the intimacy of the correspondents and because of Walpole's desire to inform Mann about English affairs. The frequently reprinted introduction comments favourably on most of Walpole's works, with high praise for <u>Otranto</u> and <u>The Mysterious Mother</u>, but regards his correspondence as his greatest achievement.

1834

1 BRAYLEY, EDW[ARD] W[EDLAKE]. "Original Letter of Lord Orford." In <u>Graphic and Historical Illustrator: An Original Miscellany of Literary, Antiquarian, and Topographical Information</u>. London: J. Chidley, pp. 234–35.
   Prints a letter from Walpole to William Beloe of 2 November 1792, with a brief preface and notes. Contends that Beloe (1817.1) "studiously attempts to depreciate" Walpole's character, although he had flattered Walpole to gain his friendship.

2 [MACAULAY, THOMAS BABINGTON.] Review of <u>Letters of Horace Walpole, Earl of Orford, to Sir Horace Mann</u>. <u>Select Journal</u> 3 (April):166–85.
   Reprints the second part of 1833.5. An editorial preface claims that Macaulay's portrait of Walpole in the first part

of his essay is unjust "to that witty, brilliant man." Of
all Walpole's writings only his Memoires are indefensible.

3   MARTIN, JOHN. "Strawberry Hill." In A Bibliographical Cata-
    logue of Books Privately Printed. London: J. & A. Arch,
    pp. 487-513.
       A careful bibliography of Strawberry Hill productions,
    with a brief history of Walpole's press. The recent
    publication of Walpole's letters to Mann and Montagu should
    "establish the literary claims as well as the private
    character of this distinguished writer."

4   [MITFORD, JOHN.] "Letters of Horace Walpole to Sir Horace
    Mann." Gentleman's Magazine, n.s. 1 (January):22-28;
    (February):130-37; (April):364-71.
       Extracts from the letters with a brief life of Walpole,
    an account of his activities at Strawberry Hill, and a
    discussion of his writings. None of his published works
    compare with his "unrivalled Correspondence."

5   NICHOLS, JOHN GOUGH. "The 'Authoresses' of Horace Walpole."
    In Life of Henry Earl of Arundel. . . . Illustrated with
    Historical Notes, and Critical Remarks on Several Articles
    of Walpole's "Royal and Noble Authors." London: John
    Bowyer Nichols, pp. 29-31.
       Exposes an "extraordinary chain of errors" in Walpole's
    account of several noble ladies in his Royal and Noble
    Authors, and notes several other errors in Walpole's work.

6   WALPOLE, HORACE. The Castle of Otranto: A Gothic Story. In
    Standard Novels. No. XLI. "Vathek" . . . "The Castle of
    Otranto" . . . "The Bravo of Venice." London: Richard
    Bentley, pp. 119-250.
       Contains an abridgment of Dover's introduction to 1833.9,
    and an anonymous critical preface drawing heavily on Scott's
    (1811.5). Applauds Otranto throughout and disagrees with
    Scott's occasional criticisms.

                              1835

1   LODGE, EDMUND. "Horatio Walpole, Fourth Earl of Orford." In
    Portraits of Illustrious Personages of Great Britain. Vol.
    12. London: Harding & Lepard, pp. 1-7.
       Surveys Walpole's life, works, and critical reputation.
    Commends The Mysterious Mother, despite its "revolting" sub-
    ject, and regards the letters as among the best in English,
    but dislikes the memoirs. Notes that Walpole has recently
    been severely criticized and that his reputation is now
    lower than during his lifetime.

1836

1 CUNNINGHAM, GEORGE GODFREY. "Horace Walpole, Earl of Orford." In Lives of Eminent and Illustrious Englishmen, from Alfred the Great to the Latest Times. Vol. 6, pt. 1. Glasgow: A. Fullarton, pp. 207-13.
Singles out The Mysterious Mother as Walpole's only major work, despite its "disgusting and revolting" subject. Walpole's other writings are less significant; even the admired letters "contain little feeling," and confuse events of small and great importance.

1837

1 "Horace Walpole's Correspondence with George Montagu." New Monthly Magazine 49 (January):132-36.
Regards Walpole as a "bewitching" correspondent, whose letters are for all time. They abound in "heartiness" and "earnestness" and vividly convey the spirit of Walpole's age.

2 WALPOLE, HORACE. Correspondence of Horace Walpole with George Montagu . . . &c. Rev. ed. London: Henry Colburn, 3 vols.
A bowdlerized edition of the Private Correspondence (1820.2), with a new preface and additional notes. The anonymous editor has deleted "several passages, unsuited to the taste of the present period, more particularly to that of Female Readers."

1839

1 BRUNET, J[ACQUES]-C[HARLES]. "Walpole, earl of Orford (Horace)." In Manuel du libraire et de l'amateur de livres, 4th ed. Vol. 4. Brussels: Société Belge de libraire, pp. 523-24.
A brief, annotated bibliography, listing Walpole's major works. Useful for its descriptions of French translations. Revised: 1864.2.

1840

1 B[ERRY], M[ARY]. "Advertisement to the Letters Addressed to the Miss Berrys." In 1840.7, vol. 6:vii-xx.
A response to Macaulay by a close friend of Walpole, who contends that his editors and critics have failed in "their account of his private life, and their appreciation of his individual character." Emphasizes the warmth of Walpole's feelings, his generosity, sincerity, directness, and "super-

eminent abilities." Reprinted: 1844.1.

2   GREY, CHARLES EDWARD.   "To the Editor of the Letters of Horace
     Walpole, Earl of Orford." In 1840.7, vol. 6:xxi-xxviii.
          Claims that Walpole was Junius, providing several paral-
     lel passages from Walpole's memoirs and Junius's letters.
     Believes that the style of both writers is characterized by
     "equivocal compliment," that both use legalisms, and that a
     "host of small facts" supports the identification.

3   Review of The Letters of Horace Walpole.   Athenaeum, 25
     January, pp. 68-69; 14 March, pp. 206-7; 9 May, pp. 365-67;
     11 July, pp. 548-50; 12 September, pp. 709-11; 28 November,
     pp. 942-44; 5 December, pp. 962-64.
          Copious extracts from the letters, which are "unequalled
     in the language," providing "a most amusing and instructive
     commentary" on political and social affairs.   Criticizes,
     however, Walpole's indifference to political reform and his
     remarks on literature, "a mass of contradictory absurdity."

4   Review of The Letters of Horace Walpole. Literary Gazette, 25
     January, pp. 50-51; 14 March, pp. 163-64; 16 May, pp. 307-8;
     11 July, pp. 445-47; 28 November, pp. 766-67; 26 December,
     pp. 827-29.
          Lengthy extracts from Walpole's letters, with enthusias-
     tic commentary: they are "the best brief chronicles of the
     stirring period to which they relate."

5   Review of The Letters of Horace Walpole, vols. 1, 5. Monthly
     Review, n.s. 1 (March):314-22; n.s. 3 (October):291-92.
          Admires Walpole's lively style and his knowledge of the
     world, but finds him cold, superficial, sarcastic, and an
     unsubtle critic.   Believes that in his later letters he is
     approaching second childhood.

6   WALPOLE, HORACE.   The Castle of Otranto: A Gothic Story.
     Introduction by G.M.B. London: Joseph Thomas, 142 pp.
          Contains a publisher's advertisement, stating that the
     edition is based on that of 1765, collated with that of
     1798. A memoir of Walpole by "G.M.B." surveys Walpole's
     life and works, declaring that Otranto is his only outstand-
     ing performance. Admires his letters, but finds the man
     vain, insincere, and selfish.

7   WALPOLE, HORACE.   The Letters of Horace Walpole, Earl of
     Orford. [Edited by John Wright.] London: Richard Bentley,
     6 vols.
          Claims, falsely, to present all of Walpole's letters in
     accurate texts. A preface commends the letters' interest
     and utility, and reprints most of Lord Dover's introduction
     (1833.9). The letters, in chronological order, are anno-

tated with notes by Walpole, Dover, and Wright. Volume six includes 1840.1-2.

1841

1 [MITFORD, JOHN.] "Junius." Gentleman's Magazine, n.s. 15 (March):227-41.
Studies Grey's claim (1840.2) that Walpole was Junius, finding it "worthy of attention and investigation," but not persuasive. Walpole, the polished master of Strawberry Hill, did not resemble Junius, the "political assassin."

2 Review of The Letters of Horace Walpole, vol. 6. Monthly Review, n.s. 1 (January):17-23.
Responds to Berry (1840.1), mediating between her flattering portrait of Walpole and Macaulay's diatribe. Regrets the lack of seriousness in Walpole's letters, "however pleasant may be their style."

3 "Walpoliana." Christian Reformer 8 (June):343; (July):400-1; (August):482-85; (September):547-52; (October):623-27; (December):742-47.
Copious extracts from Walpole's letters (1840.7), with a sternly moralistic commentary. Continued: 1842.27.

1842

1 [ADAMS, CHARLES FRANCIS.] Review of The Letters of Horace Walpole. North American Review 55 (July):1-44.
A lengthy essay on Walpole's letters, which are part of "the first rank in British literature." Concerned largely with Walpole's commentary on contemporary politics, with some consideration of his personal friendships. Considers Grey's suggestion (1840.2) that Walpole was Junius plausible, but not quite convincing.

2 "A Note of Interrogation." Times (London), 11 April, p. 5.
Deplores the inaccurate catalogue of the Strawberry Hill Sale (1842.18), and wonders how Walpole could legally have come to own a piece of stained glass from the church of Bexhill.

3 [BURN, J.H.] Aedes Strawberrianae. Names of Purchasers and the Prices to the Detailed Sale Catalogue of the Collection of early Drawings, Etchings, and Prints, Engraved Portraits of eminent British Characters, Drawings and rare Reproductions of Hogarth, Manuscripts and Works relative to the Fine Arts; withdrawn from Strawberry-Hill for sale in London. London: J.H. Burn, 20 pp.

Lists the items at the ten day London sale, with names of
purchasers and prices paid.

4   [BURN, J.H.]   Aedes Strawberrianae. Names of Purchasers and
     the Prices to the Sale Catalogue of the choice Collections
     of Art and Virtu, at Strawberry-Hill Villa, formed by Horace
     Walpole, Earl of Orford. London: J.H. Burn, 58 pp.
          Lists all the items at the Strawberry Hill Sale, with
     names of purchasers and prices paid. A prefatory "Apology
     for Strawberry Hill" is taken from Walpole's Description of
     the Villa.

5   [COSTELLO, DUDLEY?]   "A Gossip about Horace Walpole."   Ains-
     worth's Magazine 1 (May):239-45.
          Contends that Walpole's affection for Strawberry Hill
     replaced emotional attachments: "love was not in Walpole's
     line."   Strawberry Hill was ideally suited to his taste,
     because of its size, location, and "improvable capabili-
     ties."   Reprinted in part: 1842.6.

6   [COSTELLO, DUDLEY?]   "A Gossip about Horace Walpole."   Mirror,
     n.s. 1 (7 May):297-99.
          Reprinted from 1842.5, with an editorial comment that
     Walpole's name is "being suddenly revived by the sale of his
     large collection of paintings &c."

7   [COSTELLO, DUDLEY.]   "Strawberry Hill."   Ainsworth's Magazine
     1 (March):100-107.
          An illustrated account of Walpole's collection at Straw-
     berry Hill, written just before the 1842 sale. Regrets the
     imminent dispersal of objects "on whose acquirement a whole
     life has been spent."   Reprinted: 1842.18; translated:
     1842.9.

8   COSTELLO, DUDLEY.   "Strawberry Hill Re-Visited."   Ainsworth's
     Magazine 1 (March):168-76.
          Signed continuation of 1842.7, providing further informa-
     tion on many of the objects previously discussed.

9   COSTELLO, DUDLEY [W. HARRISON AINSWORTH].   "Description des
     trésors de Strawberry-Hill."   Cabinet de l'amateur et de
     l'antiquaire 1:444-54.
          A translation of 1842.7, attributed here to Ainsworth but
     in fact by Costello.

10   G., E.   "Strawberry-Hill."   Cabinet de l'amateur et de l'anti-
     quaire 1:433-41.
          A survey, in French, of Walpole's life at Strawberry
     Hill, inspired by the sale of 1842.

11   "Horace Walpole and Strawberry Hill."   Bentley's Miscellany 11

(June):552-64.
Reprints most of Lord Dover's introduction to 1833.9, adding a discussion of Walpole's letters and an account of Strawberry Hill.

12   L[ONG], C[HARLES] E[DWARD]. Letter to the Editor. <u>Gentleman's Magazine</u>, n.s. 18 (July):24.
Provides information on four portraits on panel owned by Walpole, sold at the twenty-first day's sale at Strawberry Hill.

13   L[ONG, CHARLES EDWARD]. Letter to the Editor. <u>Gentleman's Magazine</u>, n.s. 18 (August):156-58.
More information on the portraits discussed in 1842.12, and on another portrait owned by Walpole. Disagrees with several remarks by Nichols (1842.15).

14   [MITFORD, JOHN.] "Strawberry Hill." <u>Gentleman's Magazine</u>, n.s. 17 (June):571-91.
Review article on 1840.7. Discusses letters by Walpole illustrating his improvements at Strawberry Hill, which has now, after the 1842 sale, been "despoiled and rifled of all its charms."

15   N[ICHOLS], J[OHN] G[OUGH]. "The Pictures at Strawberry Hill." <u>Gentleman's Magazine</u>, n.s. 18 (July):16-24; (August):147-56; (September):257-65; (October):377-81; (November):474-80; (December):599-610.
Beginning as an account of paintings owned by Walpole, continues as a discussion of his "treasures," including miscellaneous antiquities, china, glass, and books. Criticizes the "rambling and ill-arranged Catalogue" of the 1842 sale.

16   "Pilgrimages in London, &c." <u>Britannia</u>, 2 April, 9 April, 23 April.
A discursive account of Strawberry Hill and Walpole. Finds Walpole "the pleasantest of letter-writers," but narrow-minded and trivial.

17   ROBINS, GEORGE, [and DODD, THOMAS]. <u>A Catalogue of the Collection of Scarce Prints, Removed from Strawberry Hill.</u> London: Smith & Robins, 131 pp.
Signed by Robins but compiled by Dodd as a catalogue to the sale of Walpole's prints and illustrated works held at Robins's London auction rooms in June 1842. Contains an opening "address" by Dodd, advertising the "innumerable gems" in Walpole's collection.

18   ROBINS, GEORGE, [and WOODBURNE, SAMUEL]. <u>A Catalogue of the Classic Contents of Strawberry Hill Collected by Horace</u>

<u>Walpole</u>. London: Smith & Robins, 250 pp.
    Signed by Robins but compiled by Woodburne (see Merritt,
1915.4, p. 41). The seven editions of this catalogue, all
published in 1842, are described by Merritt and by Hazen
(1947.9). Despite its numerous inaccuracies and frequent
absurdities, it remains an indispensable guide to Walpole's
collections. Merritt recommends the fifth edition for its
coverage of the entire twenty-four day sale, and the sixth
edition, together with 1842.17, for the most detailed and
reliable descriptions of particular items. Contains laudatory prefatory remarks by Robins, a reprint of 1842.7, and
further "preliminary remarks" by Woodburne on Walpole's
collection of prints.

19   "Strawberry Hill." <u>Court Journal</u>, 2 April, pp. 245-46.
         Depicts Walpole as a spoiled dilettante, "the last of the
    maccaronis," and a "high-bred old maid." His works are also
    trivial, and <u>The Mysterious Mother</u> is "hateful."

20   "Strawberry Hill." <u>Penny Magazine</u> 11 (7 May):181-84.
         Discusses Walpole's letters, as well as Strawberry Hill,
    contending that they deal with the aristocracy and the mob
    but ignore the middle class. Believes that the letters will
    survive long after Strawberry Hill is forgotten. Abridged
    from "London," an unidentified source.

21   "Strawberry Hill." <u>Times</u> (London), 28 March, p. 5; 29 March,
    p. 5; 2 April, p. 5; 4 April, p. 4; 7 April, p. 5; 11 April,
    p. 5; 14 April, p. 7; 25 April, p. 7; 26 April, p. 6; 27
    April, p. 7; 29 April, p. 7; 2 May, p. 7; 5 May, p. 3; 6
    May, p. 7; 7 May, p. 7; 10 May, p. 6; 13 May, p. 10; 18 May,
    p. 5; 24 May, p. 9.
         A series of articles, describing Strawberry Hill and its
    contents before and during the sale. Takes a condescending,
    hostile attitude towards Walpole: his taste as a collector
    is corrupt and uninformed, and his writings, such as <u>Otran-
    to</u>, are obsolete. Strongly criticizes Robins for his extra-
    vagant presentation of Walpole's collection and repeatedly
    warns the public against purchasing it.

22   "Strawberry Hill & Horace Walpole." <u>Illustrated London News</u>,
    21 May, pp. 24-26.
         Traces the history of Strawberry Hill and describes part
    of Walpole's collection, with illustrations. Emphasizes
    Walpole's effeminacy and love of gossip.

23   "Strawberry-Hill Collection." <u>Athenaeum</u>, 9 April, pp. 317-19;
    16 April, pp. 340-42; 23 April, pp. 363-64.
         An enthusiastic account of Walpole's collection of
    paintings, sculptures, enamels, painted glass and pottery.

24   "Strawberry Hill - Horace Walpole."   Athenaeum, 2 April, pp.
      293-94.
           A general survey of Walpole's achievement, taking a
      moderate position: he was neither one of the "Nine British
      Worthies," nor merely a "tasteful superficialist."   Con-
      siders the influence of Strawberry Hill and admires The
      Mysterious Mother.

25   STRONG, W[ILLIAM].   A Catalogue . . . principally from the
      Collection of Horace Walpole.   Bristol: W. Strong, 188 pp.
           A bookseller's catalogue, listing books and portraits
      from Walpole's collection at Strawberry Hill.

26   "The Strawberry-Hill Collection."   Art-Union 4 (May):108.
           A critical view of Walpole's art collection, which
      contains "not one first-class picture."   Admires Walpole's
      miniatures, however, which he justly claimed were the
      "finest in the country."

27   "Walpoliana."   Christian Reformer 9 (January):22-25; (March):
      142-45; (April):219-22; (May):270-76; (July):399-402; (Au-
      gust):478-81.
           Conclusion of 1841.3.

                                   1843

1   AN OLD MAN. "Walpole and his Friends."   Fraser's Magazine 27
      (June):629-42; 28 (July):15-30.
           A discussion of Walpole's life and times, primarily
      concerned with eighteenth-century politics. Admires Otranto
      and The Mysterious Mother, but believes that Walpole's
      letters are his primary achievement.

2   [CROKER, JOHN WILSON.]   Review of Letters of Horace Walpole,
      Earl of Orford, to Sir Horace Mann.   Quarterly Review 72
      (September):516-52.
           Contrasts the importance of Walpole's letters with the
      insignificance of his formal works.   The letters are not
      merely a fund of amusing gossip but an invaluable chronicle
      of Walpole's age, of greater significance than any other
      source.   Warns, however, against accepting Walpole's judg-
      ments too readily, and dislikes the man while admiring the
      writer.   Deplores the incompetent editing.

3   JESSE, JOHN HENEAGE.   "The Hon. Horace Walpole."   In George
      Selwyn and his Contemporaries.   Vol. 2.   London: Richard
      Bentley, pp. 1-11.
           Summarizes Walpole's life, drawing on Dover (1833.9) and
      Berry (1840.1), and prints a letter from Walpole to Selwyn.

4   MACAULAY, THOMAS BABINGTON. "Horace Walpole." In Critical and
    Historical Essays, Contributed to the Edinburgh Review.
    Vol. 2. London: Longman, pp. 98-145.
        Reprint of 1833.5, in the first collected edition of
    Macaulay's essays.

5   [MITFORD, JOHN.] Review of Letters of Horace Walpole, Earl of
    Orford, to Sir Horace Mann. Gentleman's Magazine, n.s. 20
    (September):227-47.
        Copious extracts from the letters, with running commen-
    tary. Admires Walpole's correspondence, but believes that
    his age is still too recent for his abilities to be fairly
    judged.

6   Review of Letters of Horace Walpole, Earl of Orford, to Sir
    Horace Mann. Athenaeum, 8 July, pp. 624-26.
        Extracts from the letters, with an approving commentary.
    Finds them gossipy and entertaining, and believes that
    Walpole is "better appreciated now than in his own day."

7   Review of Letters of Horace Walpole, Earl of Orford, to Sir
    Horace Mann. Monthly Review, n.s. 2 (August):507-14.
        Walpole's letters to Mann are trivial and not worth
    publishing; Walpole was "at best a piece of brilliancy, and
    only the idol for the worship of Strawberry Hill devotees."
    Deplores his lack of gravity and piety.

8   WALPOLE, HORACE. Letters of Horace Walpole, Earl of Orford, to
    Sir Horace Mann. Concluding Series. London: Richard
    Bentley, vols. 1-2.
        Sequel to 1833.9, with letters containing "racy anec-
    dotes" that might earlier have caused offence. Includes a
    brief advertisement and sketchy notes. Completed: 1844.9.

                                1844

1   [BERRY, MARY.] "Advertisement to the Letters Addressed by Lord
    Orford to the Miss Berrys." In A Comparative View of Social
    Life in England and France, From the Restoration of Charles
    the Second to the Present Time. Rev. ed. Vol. 2. London:
    Richard Bentley, pp. 144-57.
        Reprint of 1840.1.

2   [CROKER, JOHN WILSON.] Review of Letters of Horace Walpole,
    Earl of Orford, to Sir Horace Mann, vols. 3-4. Quarterly
    Review 74 (October):395-416.
        Replies indignantly to the advertisement in 1844.9,
    attributing it to Mary Berry, and continues to criticize the
    incompetent editing of Walpole's letters.

3 [DEACON, WILLIAM F.]   "Selwyn, Walpole, and Brummell."
   Bentley's Miscellany 16 (September):288-99.
           Walpole, like Selwyn and Beau Brummell, was "a man of
   peculiarly artificial character." His letters and memoirs
   are of great significance, and he alone, of the trio, has
   done "full justice to his powers."

4 "Horace Walpole and Mr. Macaulay." Democratic Review 14
   (April):353-64.
           Review article on Walpole's letters (1840.7) and Mac-
   aulay's essay (1843.4). Commends the letters and considers
   Macaulay's attack merely a vulgar curiosity, refuting each
   of its principal charges.

5 "Letters of Horace Walpole, Earl of Orford." Southern Literary
   Messenger 10 (December):758-63.
           Review of 1843.8. Concentrates on Walpole's sympathy for
   the American colonists and finds his attitudes congenial to
   the "patriotism of our people."

6 Review of Letters of Horace Walpole, Earl of Orford, to Sir
   Horace Mann, vols. 3-4. Athenaeum, 11 May, pp. 423-24.
           Expresses disappointment with the dullness of this
   collection. The letters are merely "sweepings"; Walpole's
   long separation from Mann spoiled the intimacy of their
   correspondence.

7 Review of Memoirs of the Reign of King George the Third, vols.
   1-2. Athenaeum, 28 December, pp. 1189-91.
           Uses Walpole's Memoirs to discuss mid-eighteenth-century
   history, noting the harshness of his judgments.

8 Review of Memoirs of the Reign of King George the Third, vol.
   1. Literary Gazette, 28 December, pp. 841-44.
           A largely positive review, admitting Walpole's prejudices
   but praising his matchless knowledge of his age.

9 WALPOLE, HORACE. Letters of Horace Walpole, Earl of Orford, to
   Sir Horace Mann. Concluding Series. London: Richard
   Bentley, vols. 3-4.
           Completion of 1843.8. Includes an unsigned advertisement
   responding to Croker (1843.2), strongly refuting his claims
   that Walpole was profligate and that his letters are unreliable. In 1844.2 Croker attributes this piece to Mary Berry.

                              1845

1 [ADAMS, CHARLES FRANCIS.]   "Horace Walpole's Letters and
   Memoirs." North American Review 61 (October):422-55.
           Review article on 1844.9 and 1845.14. Suggests that as

                                47

Walpole's letters and memoirs grow in bulk they diminish in interest: satiety "is peculiarly likely to happen in epistolary composition." Studies Walpole's view of the politics of his age, concluding that he "makes the estimate of a contemporary, and not of a moralist, or a historian."

2   [ALISON, ARCHIBALD.] "British History during the Eighteenth Century." Blackwood's Magazine 57 (March):353-68.
    Review article on 1845.14. Adopts a moderate attitude towards Walpole's Memoirs, finding them an invaluable source of information but marred by Walpole's prejudices and levity. Reprinted: 1850.1.

3   CHASLES, PHILARETE. "Les deux Walpole." Revue des deux mondes, n.s. 10 (April):59-95.
    Review article on 1845.14. Analyzes Walpole's Memoirs, noting the imbalances caused by his excessive admiration for his father. The memoirs are an invaluable source of information, but Walpole's contempt for his father's adversaries must be discounted. Reprinted: 1846.2.

4   [CROKER, JOHN WILSON.] Review of Memoirs of the Reign of King George the Third. Quarterly Review 77 (December):253-98.
    A detailed, highly critical analysis of Walpole's Memoirs, which are malicious, unreliable, and filled with personal prejudice. Believes that they can only damage Walpole's reputation, arousing "disgust or indignation."

5   "Horace Walpole's Memoirs of the Reign of George III." Dublin University Magazine 26 (September):327-45.
    Continuation of 1845.7 by a different, unknown author. Takes a more critical attitude to Walpole, contending that although he was well placed to observe society, neither his fictional nor historical works have much merit.

6   [JOHNSTONE, CHRISTIAN.] "Walpole's Memoirs of the Reign of George III." Tait's Edinburgh Magazine 12 (February):117-24.
    Walpole's Memoirs, like his letters, are caustic and treacherous: he "acted on the principle of telling posterity, and keeping what he said secret from his own age." His career was one of disappointment, and Strawberry Hill is a "baby castle." The Memoirs do, however, provide a valuable record of their time.

7   [LEVER, CHARLES JAMES.] Review of Memoirs of the Reign of King George the Third. Dublin University Magazine 25 (February):227-41.
    Consists largely of quotations. Believes that although Walpole is a biased historian, his Memoirs are important and often accurate.

8   [MITFORD, JOHN.] Review of <u>Memoirs of the Reign of King George</u>
     <u>the Third</u>. <u>Gentleman's Magazine</u>, n.s. 24 (October):377-80.
          Defends Walpole from Macaulay's criticisms, emphasizing
     the warmth of his friendships but admitting the charge of
     affectation. His <u>Memoirs</u> are occasionally biased, but they
     display a "steadfast observation and a keen sagacity."

9   Review of <u>Memoirs of the Reign of King George the Third</u>, vols.
     3-4. <u>Athenaeum</u>, 23 August, pp. 831-33; 30 August, pp. 855-
     57.
          Continuation of 1844.7, using Walpole as the primary
     source for an essay on the age of George III but questioning
     his reliability.

10   Review of <u>Memoirs of the Reign of King George the Third</u>.
     <u>Examiner</u>, 1 February, pp. 67-69; 23 August, pp. 532-34.
          Considers Walpole's <u>Memoirs of George III</u> inferior to his
     <u>Memoirs of George II</u>, although "most cleverly written."
     Emphasizes the bitterness and fault-finding in the <u>Memoirs</u>,
     and illustrates these qualities with substantial quota-
     tions. The <u>Memoirs</u> are the least interesting or edifying of
     Walpole's works.

11   Review of <u>Memoirs of the Reign of King George the Third</u>, vols.
     2-4. <u>Literary Gazette</u>, 6 January, pp. 6-8; 23 August, pp.
     559-61.
          Continuation of 1844.8. Contends that Walpole's <u>Memoirs</u>
     are well informed, and that he was no more biased than other
     historians.

12   STONE, MRS. [ELIZABETH]. "Stars of Fashion. - Horace Wal-
     pole." In <u>Chronicles of Fashion, from the Time of Elizabeth</u>
     <u>to the Early Part of the Nineteenth Century</u>. Vol. 2. Lon-
     don: Richard Bentley, pp. 134-58.
          A gushing account of Walpole's life, dwelling primarily
     on Strawberry Hill and on Walpole's place in fashionable
     society. Admires <u>Otranto</u> and the letters.

13   "Strawberry Hill and its Owners." In <u>Pen and Ink Sketches: By</u>
     <u>a Cosmopolitan</u>. To which is Added Chatterton: A Romance of
     <u>Literary Life</u>. Boston: William Hayden, pp. 179-83.
          Imagines Walpole, Gray and Mason at Strawberry Hill, dis-
     cussing Chatterton. Sympathizes with Chatterton and con-
     demns Walpole for hypocrisy and cruelty.

14   WALPOLE, HORACE. <u>Memoirs of the Reign of King George the</u>
     <u>Third</u>. Edited by Sir Denis le Marchant. London: Richard
     Bentley, 4 vols.
          An inaccurate and bowdlerized edition, suppressing pas-
     sages "of an indecent tendency." Contains a brief, apolo-
     getic preface and unreliable notes. Revised: 1894.8.

1846

1   [ADAMS, CHARLES FRANCIS.]   Review of Memoirs of the Reign of
    King George the Third, vols. 3-4.   North American Review 62
    (April):269-94.
        Regrets that Walpole's Memoirs stop at a time when, to
    Americans, "the history becomes most interesting."   Warns
    that readers of Walpole's history must make great allowances
    for his acrimony and personal enmities.

2   CHASLES, PHILARETE.   "Robert Walpole peint d'après son fils."
    In Le dix-huitième siècle en Angleterre.   Vol. 1.   Paris:
    d'Amyot, pp. 157-210.
        Reprint of 1845.3, with a new title.

3   "Critics, Authors, Editors, and Publishers: Their Duties."
    Literary Gazette, 31 October, pp. 921-23.
        Review article on 1846.12.   Evaluates, with heavy irony,
    Lord Holland's editing of Walpole's Memoirs, the Athenaeum's
    review (1846.8), and Fox's reply (1846.6).

4   [FOX, CHARLES R.]   "Lord Holland's Edition of Walpole's 'George
    the Second.'"   Athenaeum, 10 October, pp. 1043-44.
        A letter by Fox, Lord Holland's son, defending his
    father's edition of Walpole's Memoirs, is accompanied by a
    renewal of the criticisms made in 1846.8.

5   [FOX, CHARLES R.]   "Lord Holland's Edition of Walpole's 'George
    the Second.'"   Athenaeum, 17 October, p. 1069.
        A second letter from Fox, modifying his criticism of
    1846.8, with an editorial rebuttal.

6   FOX, CHARLES R.   "The Late Lord Holland and the Athenaeum."
    Examiner, 10 October, p. 643.
        A highly indignant letter, also sent to several London
    newspapers, complaining of the Athenaeum's review of his
    father's edition of Walpole's Memoirs (1846.8).   Regards
    Walpole as a "very malicious as well as capricious writer,"
    who well deserved to be bowdlerized by Lord Holland.

7   JAMES, L.   "Walpole's 'George the Second.'"   Athenaeum, 7
    November, p. 1149.
        Points out that the change of title of Walpole's Memoirs
    (1846.12) might make readers assume that the work was an
    extension of 1822.9, rather than a second edition.

8   Review of Memoirs of the Reign of King George the Second.
    Athenaeum, 3 October, pp. 1013-14.
        Deplores both Lord Holland's original edition of the
    Memoirs (1822.9) and its republication.   Believes that it is
    a valuable historical work, awaiting a reliable edition.

9   Review of <u>Memoirs of the Reign of King George the Second</u>.
     <u>Examiner</u>, 10 October, pp. 643-45.
     Finds Walpole's <u>Memoirs</u> "stiff and unconventional" com-
     pared to his delightful correspondence.   Welcomes the new
     edition, however, and provides extensive extracts.

10   Review of <u>Memoirs of the Reign of King George the Third</u>.
     <u>Oxford and Cambridge Review</u> 2 (April):201-25.
     Walpole's memoirs are merely "gossipy sketches" that
     detract from his reputation as a letter writer.   He lacks
     "any idea" of proportion, freely intermingling the essential
     and the banal, and is thus a failure as a historian.

11   WALPOLE, HORACE.   <u>Horaz Walpole's, Grafen von Orford, Denk-</u>
     <u>würdigkeiten aus der Regierungszeit Georgs II. und Georgs</u>
     <u>III</u>.   Edited by F[rank] E[rnst] Pipitz, translated by
     G[eorg] Fink.   Bibliothek ausgewählter Memoiren des XVIII.
     und XIX.   Jahrhunderts.   Constanz: Verlags-Buchhandlung
     Belle-Vue, vol. 1.
     A translation of Walpole's memoirs of George II and
     George III with an extensive introduction, dealing more with
     eighteenth-century politics than with Walpole.   Continued:
     1847.2 and 1848.9.

12   WALPOLE, HORACE.   <u>Memoirs of the Reign of King George the</u>
     <u>Second</u>.   Edited by Lord Holland, [introduction by James
     Mackintosh].   London: Colburn, 3 vols.
     Slightly revised edition of 1822.9, with a new title, a
     few omissions, and some additional misprints.

                                  1847

1   [CROLY, GEORGE.]   "The Reign of George the Second."   <u>Black-</u>
     <u>wood's Magazine</u> 61 (February):194-212.
     A eulogistic review article on 1846.12.   Questions Wal-
     pole's claim not to be a historian, preferring his <u>Memoirs</u>
     to formal history such as Gibbon's.   Walpole is "now an
     English classic," and the greatest of all letter writers.

2   WALPOLE, HORACE.   <u>Horaz Walpole's, Grafen von Orford</u>. . . .
     Vol. 2.
     Continuation of 1846.11.

                                  1848

1   [CROKER, JOHN WILSON.]   "Horace Walpole's Letters to the
     Countess of Ossory."   <u>Eclectic Magazine</u> 15 (October):186-95.
     Reprint of 1848.2.

                                   51

2   [CROKER, JOHN WILSON.]   Review of <u>Letters Addressed to the</u>
     <u>Countess of Ossory</u>. <u>Quarterly Review</u> 83 (June):110-27.
          Praises the wit and sagacity of Walpole's letters, but
     deplores his insincerity and dishonesty.   Strongly criti-
     cizes the defective editing of his letters and calls for a
     new, properly annotated edition. Reprinted: 1848.1.

3   "Early Times of George III."   <u>Literary Gazette</u>, 6 May, pp.
     306-7; 13 May, pp. 325-26; 27 May, pp. 357-59.
          Review of 1848.10, consisting largely of excerpts.
     Admires Walpole's letters and finds Walpole much more reli-
     able than his "cavillers" have allowed.

4   [HAYWARD, ABRAHAM.]   Review of <u>Letters Addressed to the</u>
     <u>Countess of Ossory</u>. <u>Edinburgh Review</u> 88 (October):339-60.
          Supports Macaulay's view of Walpole, comparing his mind
     with Strawberry Hill: both were affected and pretentious.
     Walpole's taste was corrupt, and his criticism of other
     authors was usually petulant and unsound.   Reprinted:
     1849.2.

5   [MITFORD, JOHN.] Review of <u>Letters Addressed to the Countess</u>
     <u>of Ossory</u>. <u>Gentleman's Magazine</u>, n.s. 30 (September):227-
     43.
          Admires Walpole's "very agreeable and even instructive"
     letters, but deplores their careless editing.   Supplies
     extensive extracts, with commentary, illustrating Walpole's
     views on politics, literature, and drama.

6   NICHOLS, JOHN BOWYER.   "Dr Lort's Vindication of Mr. Walpole
     with Regard to Chatterton."   In <u>Illustrations of the Liter-</u>
     <u>ary History of the Eighteenth Century</u>.   Vol. 7.   London:
     J.B. Nichols, pp. 556-65.
          Reprints a passage vigorously defending Walpole's deal-
     ings with Chatterton, taken from the entry on Chatterton in
     Andrew Kippis's <u>Biographia Britannica</u>, vol. 4 (1789).
     Nichols himself remains neutral on the subject.

7   Review of <u>Letters Addressed to the Countess of Ossory</u>.
     <u>Athenaeum</u>, 6 May, pp. 453-55; 13 May, pp. 483-85; 20 May,
     pp. 506-8.
          Extracts from the letters, with a commentary. Notes that
     they show Walpole primarily in his old age, and as a
     gossip. Criticizes the carelessness of the editing.

8   Review of <u>Letters Addressed to the Countess of Ossory</u>.
     <u>Examiner</u>, 6 May, pp. 291-92.
          Each new edition of Walpole's letters is delightful: he
     "makes readable everything he touches."   He has raised the
     art of letter writing into an "independent literature."   His
     letters reveal the excellence of his character; he has been

unjustly maligned.

9 WALPOLE, HORACE. Horaz Walpole's, Grafen von Orford. . . .
   Vol. 3.
       Completion of 1846.11.

10 WALPOLE, HORACE. Letters Addressed to the Countess of Ossory,
    From the Year 1769 to 1797. Edited by R. Vernon Smith.
    London: Richard Bentley, 2 vols.
        An inaccurate, incomplete, and sketchily annotated edi-
    tion. A brief preface contends that the letters show
    Walpole "in a more amiable attitude, as to feelings and
    friendships, than he has hitherto stood," and an advertise-
    ment lists previous editions of his letters. Revised:
    1848.11.

11 WALPOLE, HORACE. Letters Addressed to the Countess of Ossory,
    From the Year 1769 to 1797. Edited by R. Vernon Smith. 2d
    ed. London: Richard Bentley, 2 vols.
        Revision of 1848.10, with a preface lamely responding to
    Croker (1848.2). Defends the decision not to bowdlerize the
    text, but admits that the annotation is sketchy.

                              1849

1 C[ROKER, JOHN WILSON]. "Anecdotes of the Civil Wars." Notes
   and Queries, 1st ser. 1 (8 December):93.
       Asks for the source of an anecdote in an unnamed work by
   Walpole.

2 [HAYWARD, ABRAHAM.] Review of Letters Addressed to the
   Countess of Ossory. Living Age 20 (January):29-38.
       Reprint of 1848.4

3 P., G.F. "Ten Minutes Gossip about Strawberry Hill." People's
   and Howitt's Journal 8:341-43.
       Chiefly concerned with the sale of 1842. Walpole was
   "trifling," and Strawberry Hill suited his "somewhat puerile
   tastes." He lacked both political aptitude and literary
   talent; his house was a mere plaything.

4 Review of Letters Addressed to the Countess of Ossory. Sovre-
   mennik [Contemporary] 14, pt. 4:55-64.
       In Russian. Prefers Walpole's memoirs and letters to
   Otranto and the deplorable Mysterious Mother. His correspondence contains highly prejudiced views of his contemporaries, but is interesting for its descriptions of English
   and French society. He had little political influence, but
   was admired by his age for his writings.

5   WALPOLE, HORACE. <u>Anecdotes of Painting in England</u>. Edited by
     Ralph N. Wornum. London: Bohn, 3 vols.
          A revision of Dalloway's edition (1826.2), with addition-
     al notes.

                                    1850

1   ALISON, ARCHIBALD. "British History During the Eighteenth
     Century." In <u>Essays Political, Historical and Miscellane-</u>
     <u>ous</u>. Vol. 3. Edinburgh: William Blackwood, pp. 311-39.
          Reprint of 1845.2.

2   B., C.W. "Anecdotes of the Civil Wars." <u>Notes and Queries</u>,
     1st ser. 1 (23 March):338-39.
          Replies to Croker (1849.1), with further comments by the
     editor.

3   [BELL, ROBERT.] "Inedited Letters of Celebrated Persons -
     Horace Walpole." <u>Bentley's Miscellany</u> 27 (May):521-26;
     (June):619-23.
          Prints some unpublished letters, with introductory
     remarks. The letters display Walpole's "better and more
     earnest qualities," but the literary judgments they contain
     are uncertain: "he cannot read any production antecedent to
     Dryden and Pope."

4   HALL, SPENCER. "Unpublished Letter of Horace Walpole." <u>Notes</u>
     <u>and Queries</u>, 1st ser. 1 (2 March):273-74.
          Transcribes a letter by Walpole of 28 July 1771, and
     enquires about the recipient.

5   KEANE, WILLIAM. "Strawberry Hill House, Twickenham." In <u>The</u>
     <u>Beauties of Middlesex</u>. Chelsea: T. Wilsher, pp. 189-90.
          A brief account of Strawberry Hill, emphasizing its fra-
     gility. <u>Otranto</u> is "a whimsical description of Strawberry
     Hill."

6   SAINTE-BEUVE, C[HARLES] A[UGUSTIN]. "Lettres de la Marquise du
     Deffand." <u>Constitutionnel</u>, 11 March.
          Walpole brought out Mme du Deffand's true character by
     awakening her emotions. She had previously been seen as a
     hard, insensitive woman, but her feelings for Walpole
     revealed her passionate nature. Walpole compensated for his
     occasionally harsh treatment of her by depicting her favour-
     ably to his friends. Reprinted: 1850.7.

7   SAINTE-BEUVE, C[HARLES] A[UGUSTIN]. "Lettres de la Marquise du
     Deffand." In <u>Causeries du lundi</u>. Vol. 1. Paris: Garnier,
     pp. 412-31.
          Reprint of 1850.6.

1851

1 BRAYBROOKE. "Horace Walpole at Eton." Notes and Queries, 1st
   ser. 4 (20 September):206.
   Quotes an anecdote of Walpole at Eton by his school-
   fellow, Jacob Bryant.

2 C. "Horace Walpole." Christian Reformer 7 (July):385–97.
   Review of 1851.20. "Another series of Walpole's Correspondence! quoth the wondering public. When will it end?"
   Yet Walpole's letters are always engaging, and Walpole has
   been unjustly censured. The Mysterious Mother, Otranto, and
   Historic Doubts are, admittedly, inferior, but the letters
   are unsurpassed. A cheap, collected edition in chronological order is called for.

3 [CROKER, JOHN WILSON.] Review of The Correspondence of Horace
   Walpole, Earl of Orford, and the Rev. William Mason. Living
   Age 30 (27 September):577–90.
   Reprint of 1851.4.

4 [CROKER, JOHN WILSON.] Review of The Correspondence of Horace
   Walpole, Earl of Orford, and the Rev. William Mason. Quarterly Review 89 (June):135–69.
   Emphasizes both the great importance of Walpole's
   letters, which make him the "historian of his time," and his
   "congenial defects." Regards Mitford as the worst of all
   Walpole's editors. Reprinted: 1851.3.

5 [DILKE, CHARLES WENTWORTH.] Review of The Correspondence of
   Horace Walpole, Earl of Orford, and the Rev. William Mason.
   Athenaeum, 10 May, pp. 493–95; 17 May, pp. 520–23; 24 May,
   pp. 548–50.
   Considers the suggestion that Walpole might have been
   Junius, assisted by Mason or another friend, and concludes
   by finding Mason himself a more probable candidate.
   Reprinted: 1875.3.

6 "Horace Walpole." Gentleman's Magazine, n.s. 36 (July):45–49.
   Review article on 1851.20, 22. Finds Williams's anonymous biography of Walpole worthless, and deplores Warburton's part in its publication. Admires Walpole as a letter
   writer, but considers Strawberry Hill, now a "tottering
   ruin," absurd. Criticizes Walpole's poor taste in contemporary literature and assumes that his relationship with
   Mason was one of convenience, rather than a real friendship.

7 "Horace Walpole and his Contemporaries." Dublin University
   Magazine 37 (June):683–703.
   Review article on 1851.22. As a letter-writer Walpole is
   unrivalled. Of his formal works both Otranto and The

Mysterious Mother are impressive and original achievements,
but Historic Doubts is his most significant publication.
The anonymous biography, in general, devalues Walpole's
accomplishments. Reprinted: 1851.8.

8   "Horace Walpole and his Contemporaries." Eclectic Magazine 23
     (July):368-85.
            Reprint of 1851.7.

9   "Horace Walpole's Opinions of his Contemporaries." Inter-
     national Monthly Magazine 3:488-89.
            Condemns Walpole's "monstrous persistence" in belittling
     the great writers of his age, and finds his preference for
     his own circle "mighty ridiculous."

10   HUNT, LEIGH. "Horace Walpole and Pinkerton." In Table-Talk.
     To which are added Imaginary Conversations of Pope and
     Swift. London: Smith, Elder, pp. 39-41.
            A brief account of Walpole's dealings with Pinkerton.
     Sees Pinkerton as an "overweening mediocrity," and Walpole
     as a mixture of sense, foppery, and insincerity.

11   J., W. "Walpole and Junius." Notes and Queries, 1st ser. 4
     (15 November):395.
            Replies to an unlocated item in Notes and Queries by
     "Clericus." Denies that Walpole was Junius.

12   MILLS, ABRAHAM. "Horace Walpole." In The Literature and the
     Literary Men of Great Britain and Ireland. Vol. 2. New
     York: Harper, pp. 522-24.
            A biographical sketch, with a brief survey of Walpole's
     works. Commends the dialogue and style of Otranto, but
     regards Walpole's letters as his principal achievement.

13   [MITFORD, JOHN.] "Horace Walpole and the Literary World of the
     Eighteenth Century." Bentley's Miscellany 29 (June):567-84.
            Review article on 1851.20: the editor reviews his own
     edition. Commends Otranto and The Mysterious Mother, but
     regards Walpole's letters as his principal achievement. His
     fame rests "more upon the general impression produced by his
     writings, than by any particular example."

14   Review of Memoirs of Horace Walpole and his Contemporaries.
     Athenaeum, 19 April, pp. 425-26.
            Censures the dishonest way in which the biography of
     Walpole has been published, and hopes that the correspon-
     dence with Mason (1851.20) will be "a more lively affair."

15   Review of Memoirs of Horace Walpole and his Contemporaries.
     Eclectic Review, 5th ser. 2 (December):683-96.
            Regards Walpole's indolence, effeminacy, frivolity, and

cynicism as representative of his age. His treatment of Rousseau was "as unfeeling as it was unprovoked"; that of Chatterton was "heartless cruelty." His letters are lively and amusing, but deficient in moral seriousness; his other writings are read chiefly by "political gossip-hunters" and "semi-antiquarians." Reprinted: 1852.5.

16 Review of Memoirs of Horace Walpole and his Contemporaries. Literary Gazette, 5 April, pp. 251-52; 7 June, pp. 403-5.

Deplores the manner in which Warburton has lent his name as "editor" to an anonymous biography of Walpole, and believes that Walpole would have "stood aghast" at its style.

17 Review of The Correspondence of Horace Walpole, Earl of Orford, and the Rev. William Mason. Examiner, 10 May, pp. 291-93.

.Walpole's letters are always enjoyable, and make a "really important contribution to the history of his time." Those to Mason, however, reveal his surprising misjudgments of his contemporaries, as well as his "studied injustice to Chatterton." Reprinted: 1851.19.

18 Review of The Correspondence of Horace Walpole, Earl of Orford, and the Rev. William Mason. Literary Gazette, 10 May, pp. 339-40; 7 June, pp. 403-5.

Supports Macaulay's view of Walpole, which is now the "general opinion." Appreciates Walpole's wit and lively style, but deplores his shallowness and poor critical judgment.

19 Review of The Correspondence of Horace Walpole, Earl of Orford, and the Rev. William Mason. Living Age 29 (21 June):563-67. Reprint of 1851.17.

20 WALPOLE, HORACE. The Correspondence of Horace Walpole, Earl of Orford, and the Rev. William Mason. Edited by Rev. J[ohn] Mitford. London: Richard Bentley, 2 vols.

An inaccurate, bowdlerized text of Walpole's and Mason's correspondence, with a preface discussing their relationship and uninformative notes. Responds to Grey (1840.2), denying that Walpole was Junius.

21 WARBURTON, ELIOT. "Personal Habits and Character of the Walpoles." Harper's New Monthly Magazine 3 (June):79-80.

An account of the two Horace Walpoles, uncle and nephew, based on material by Williams in 1851.22.

22 [WILLIAMS, ROBERT FOLKESTONE.] Memoirs of Horace Walpole and his Contemporaries; including Numerous Original Letters Chiefly from Strawberry Hill. Edited by Eliot Warburton. London: Henry Colburn, 2 vols.

The first full-length biography of Walpole, written anonymously by Williams. Contains an introduction by Warburton, contending that little is known of Walpole's private life and criticizing Mary Berry's panegyric (1840.1). The biography studies Walpole's career chronologically, relying heavily on his letters. A section on his works declares that The Mysterious Mother is his greatest achievement. Inflated, unreliable, clumsily written, and condemned by contemporary reviewers.

1852

1   [CROKER, JOHN WILSON.]   "The Garland."   Quarterly Review 90 (March):311-13.
    Transcribes Walpole's poetic eulogy on George III, written in 1761, deploring the disparity between it and Walpole's attitude to George III in his memoirs. Believes that the poem shows Walpole as a contemptible sycophant.

2   REMUSAT, CHARLES de.   "Goratsii Val'pol'"   [Horace Walpole]. Biblioteka dlya chteniia [Library for Reading] 115, pt. 3: 96-110; 116:1-28.
    Abridged Russian translation of 1852.3.

3   REMUSAT, CHARLES de.   "Horace Walpole."   Revue des deux mondes, 6th ser. 15 (1 July):44-71; (15 July):201-40.
    An extensive biographical and critical study. Regards Walpole as an amateur in everything except letter writing. He was artificial but displayed good judgment when not blinded by his prejudices. He had a strong character, which was partly responsible for the cooling of his friendships with several important contemporaries. Reprinted: 1856.3.

4   [REMUSAT, CHARLES de.]   "Ores Val'pol'"   [Horace Walpole]. Otechestvennye zapiski [Fatherland Notes] 84, pt. 7, no. 10:63-75.
    Abridged Russian translation of 1852.3.

5   Review of Memoirs of Horace Walpole and his Contemporaries. Living Age 32 (7 February):241-46.
    Reprint of 1851.15.

1853

1   [HORE, HERBERT FRANCIS.]   "The Old Countess of Desmond." Quarterly Review 92 (March):329-54.
    Discusses an Irish Countess about whom Walpole wrote an essay, "An Inquiry into the Person and Age of the Long-lived Countess of Desmond," and whom he cites in Historic Doubts.

Finds Walpole's historical research superficial and highly inaccurate.

1854

1   CORNEY, BOLTON. "A Strawberry-Hill Gem." Notes and Queries, 1st ser. 9 (7 January):3-5.
    Criticizes Walpole's Strawberry Hill edition of Hamilton's Mémoires. Its text is inaccurate and its prefaces and notes are taken from other editions, without acknowledgment.

2   de la ROQUETTE, DEZOS. "Walpole (Horace)." In Biographie universelle (Michaud) ancienne et moderne. Nouvelle édition. Vol. 44. Paris: C. Desplaces, pp. 294-98.
    A survey of Walpole's life and works, useful for its information on French translations and criticism of his writings. Prefers Otranto to his other works. Admires the letters, but criticizes Walpole's literary judgments.

3   SAGE, E.J. "London Topographical Queries. 3." Notes and Queries, 1st ser. 10 (19 August):147.
    Enquires about the address of Walpole's house in Berkeley Square. The editor replies that it was number ten.

4   "Walpole and Macaulay." Notes and Queries, 1st ser. 9 (28 January):74.
    Suggests that the source for an image of Macaulay's, a New Zealander surveying London from the ruins of Westminster Bridge, might have been Walpole's image of a "curious native of Lima" in a letter to Horace Mann.

1855

1   DANIEL, GEORGE. "An Inedited Letter of Horace Walpole." Illustrated London News, 22 December, p. 723.
    Prints a letter from Walpole to Sylvester Douglas of 15 February 1792 on The Mysterious Mother. A prefatory note observes that Walpole has rendered interesting "a revolting and improbable plot by his consummate art and graceful poetry."

2   "Horace Walpole. With an Engraving." Eclectic Magazine 36 (December):1141.
    An engraving of Walpole is accompanied by a respectful biographical sketch, emphasizing his good manners and affability.

1856

1   BENTLEY, RICHARD. "Letters of Horace Walpole." <u>Notes and</u>
    <u>Queries</u>, 2d ser. 2 (26 July):66-67.
            Announces the forthcoming publication of Walpole's
    <u>Letters</u> (1857.7), claiming that "the edition will be
    carefully edited."

2   "Notes on Books, Etc." <u>Notes and Queries</u>, 2d ser. 2 (27 Decem-
    ber):518-19.
            An editorial, commending the new edition of Walpole's
    letters (1857.7). Walpole is "pre-eminent as a letter-
    writer," and he has been well edited by Cunningham.

3   REMUSAT, CHARLES de.   "Horace Walpole (1717-1797)."   In
    <u>L'Angleterre au dix-huitième siècle</u>. Vol. 2.   Paris:
    Didier, pp. 1-117.
            Reprint of 1852.3.

4   W., W. "Walpole, and Whittington and his Cat." <u>Notes and</u>
    <u>Queries</u>, 2d ser. 2 (2 August):88.
            Enquires about an essay on Whittington to which Walpole
    alludes in a letter to Cole of 8 January 1773.

5   WALLACE, HORACE BINNEY. "Memoirs of the Reign of King George
    the Third. By Horace Walpole." In <u>Literary Criticisms and</u>
    <u>Other Papers</u>. Philadelphia: Parry & McMillan, pp. 124-28.
            Highly critical of Walpole and of all his writings, which
    are treated as amusing trifles but grossly inaccurate and
    irresponsible. Reprinted from an unlocated source.

6   Y., J. "Walpole and Whittington." <u>Notes and Queries</u>, 2d ser.
    2 (9 August):117.
            Replies to W.W. (1856.4), stating that the essay on
    Whittington is by Samuel Pegge.

1857

1   [DILKE, CHARLES WENTWORTH.] Review of <u>The Letters of Horace</u>
    <u>Walpole</u>, vols. 1-2. <u>Athenaeum</u>, 13 June, pp. 752-53.
            Concerned with the shortcomings of Cunningham's editing,
    rather than with Walpole's letters.

2   [JACOX, FRANCIS.] "Mingle-Mangle by Monkshood. Retrospective
    Reviewals: VI - Horace Walpole's Letters." <u>Bentley's Mis-</u>
    <u>cellany</u> 42 (November):491-504.
            Review article on 1857.7. Uses Walpole's letters as
    sources of information on the Duke of Cumberland and Lord
    Carteret. Finds the letters an invaluable guide to Wal-
    pole's age, "wonderfully minute as well as comprehensive."

3   L. "Passage of Horace Walpole." <u>Notes and Queries</u> 2d ser. 3 (17 January):42–43.
    Explains a passage in a letter from Walpole to the Countess of Upper Ossory of 4 August 1783.

4   Review of <u>The Letters of Horace Walpole</u>, vol. 1. <u>Examiner</u>, 17 January, p. 37.
    Commends the new edition of Walpole's letters, and expects the forthcoming volumes to contain letters "distinctly illustrative of good points in the writer's character." Reprinted: 1857.6.

5   Review of <u>The Letters of Horace Walpole</u>, vols. 1–6. <u>Literary Gazette</u>, 10 January, pp. 29–30; 11 July, pp. 661–62; 12 September, pp. 875–86; 31 October, pp. 1046–47; 26 December, p. 1237.
    Regards Walpole's letters as his most significant work, but dislikes and pities the writer. Traces the history of the letters' publication and provides extensive extracts.

6   Review of <u>The Letters of Horace Walpole</u>, vol. 1. <u>Living Age</u> 52 (7 March):621–23.
    Reprint of 1857.4.

7   WALPOLE, HORACE. <u>The Letters of Horace Walpole, Earl of Orford</u>. Edited by Peter Cunningham. London: Richard Bentley, vols. 1–6.
    The standard edition of Walpole's letters until Mrs. Toynbee's (1903.4), although the text is bowdlerized and inaccurate and the annotations inadequate. Arranges the letters chronologically, with notes by Cunningham and by several previous editors. Contains a brief advertisement and the prefaces to all the previous editions of the letters. Continued: 1858.13 and 1859.11.

8   "Walpole's Letters." <u>Saturday Review</u> 3 (30 May):506–8.
    Review of 1857.7. Admires Walpole's anecdotal letters, which provide a faithful record of his petty, gossipy age. Refutes Macaulay's criticisms of Walpole's character: his "loves, hates, and tastes were all sincere."

1858

1   A., M. "Arthur Moore." <u>Notes and Queries</u>, 2d ser. 5 (2 January):8–9.
    Enquires about the burial place of Arthur Moore, named in a letter from Walpole to Mann of 1 September 1756.

2   [DILKE, CHARLES WENTWORTH.] Review of <u>The Letters of Horace Walpole</u>, vols. 3–8. <u>Athenaeum</u>, 21 August, pp. 223–25.

Extracts from Walpole's letters, with an admiring
commentary. The whole series is "incomparable."

3   E., M. "Horace Walpole and Madame du Deffand." Notes and
    Queries, 2d ser. 6 (16 October):310.
        Enquires whether Walpole's letters to Mme du Deffand have
    been published, and whether the manuscripts are still
    extant.

4   H., S.H. "Foote and the Duchess of Kingston." Notes and
    Queries, 2d. ser. 5 (30 January):85-87.
        Responds to 1858.10, providing further information.

5   "Horace Walpole in his Old Age." Dublin University Magazine
    52 (November):525-37.
        A sentimental discussion of Walpole's later years, con-
    centrating on his friendships with Mme du Deffand, Kitty
    Clive, Anne Conway, and George Selwyn. Reprinted: 1858.6.

6   "Horace Walpole in his Old Age." Living Age 59 (25 December):
    915-24.
        Reprint of 1858.5.

7   [JACOX, FRANCIS.] "Mingle-Mangle by Monkshood. Retrospective
    Reviewals: VIII - Horace Walpole Again." Bentley's Miscel-
    lany 43 (April):352-62.
        Refutes Macaulay's criticisms of Walpole, drawing atten-
    tion to Mary Berry's flattering portrait (1840.1). When
    complete, the new edition of Walpole's letters (1857.7) will
    "form an incomparable record of the eighteenth century"; it
    is "the fullest, richest, minutest account we possess." The
    letters constitute an eighteenth-century encyclopaedia.

8   [LAWRANCE, HANNAH.] "Horace Walpole." British Quarterly
    Review 27 (April):462-500.
        Review article on 1798.7, 1857.7, and 1858.13. Surveys
    Walpole's life and writings, placing his letters far above
    his other works. Takes a Victorian view of Walpole's age,
    holding it responsible for his vices.

9   N., Q. "Who was Mrs. Quon?" Notes and Queries, 2d ser. 5 (2
    January):8.
        Enquires about a Mrs. Quon, named in a letter from Wal-
    pole to George Montagu of 19 May 1756.

10 PHILO WALPOLE. "Foote and the Duchess of Kingston." Notes and
    Queries, 2d ser. 5 (9 January):22-24.
        Transcribes some angry letters exchanged by Samuel Foote
    and the Duchess of Kingston. Walpole discusses their dis-
    pute in a letter to Mann of 7 September 1775.

11   UNEDA. "Horace Walpole's 'Letters.'"   <u>Notes and Queries</u>, 2d
     ser. 6 (16 October):308.
         Notes two misplaced letters and a misprint in Cunning-
     ham's edition (1858.13).

12   W., S.D. "Dr. Dodd's Simony and Marriage." <u>Notes and Queries</u>,
     2d ser. 5 (2 January):8.
         Explains a passage in a letter from Walpole to the Count-
     ess of Upper Ossory of 29 January 1774.

13   WALPOLE, HORACE. <u>The Letters of Horace Walpole, Earl of Or-
     ford</u>. Edited by Peter Cunningham. London: Richard Bent-
     ley, vols. 7–8.
         Continuation of 1857.7.

                                1859

1   [DILKE, CHARLES WENTWORTH.] Review of <u>The Letters of Horace
     Walpole</u>, vol. 9. <u>Athenaeum</u>, 22 January, pp. 112–13.
         Enjoys the vivacity of Walpole's letters to the Berrys
     and finds his collected letters "one of the most fascinating
     books of light literature" in any language.

2   [DONNE, WILLIAM BODHAM.] "Horace Walpole." <u>Bentley's Quarter-
     ly Review</u> 1 (March):227–58.
         Review article on the <u>Letters</u> (1857.7, 1858.13, 1859.
     11). Studies Walpole's life and works, treating his letters
     as his major achievement but also commending <u>Otranto</u> and
     noting the influence of Strawberry Hill.   Reprinted:
     1859.3.

3   [DONNE, WILLIAM BODHAM.] "Horace Walpole." <u>Living Age</u> 61 (7
     May):326–44.
         Reprint of 1859.2.

4   [DORAN, JOHN?] "Last Journals of Horace Walpole."   <u>Tait's
     Edinburgh Magazine</u> 26 (April):192–98.
         An account of English politics from 1771 to 1783, drawing
     heavily on Walpole's <u>Journal</u>. Finds his commentary full of
     interest and a "valuable book of reference," although parti-
     san.

5   [JACOX, FRANCIS.]   "The Last Journals of Horace Walpole."
     <u>Bentley's Miscellany</u> 45 (March):304–11.
         Finds Walpole unreliable as a historian, but replete with
     "ridiculous stories and amusing ana."   The journals are
     astonishingly varied, and Doran's gossipy annotations
     further enliven an already lively text.

6   [JACOX, FRANCIS.]   "Walpole's Letters, Complete."   <u>Bentley's</u>

                                63

Miscellany 45 (February):186-88.
Review of 1859.11. A continuation of 1857.2 and 1858.7, taking the same highly complimentary attitude to Walpole's letters.

7   Review of Journal of the Reign of King George the Third. Athenaeum, 1 January, pp. 9-11; 29 January, pp. 147-48.
Extracts from Walpole's Journal, with commentary. Believes that it has a "strange, stinging interest," although "prejudiced, incomplete, angry."

8   "The Last Journals of Horace Walpole." Dublin University Magazine 53 (April):449-55.
Although highly critical of Walpole's personality, emphasizing his pettiness and selfishness, regards his letters and memoirs as invaluable. He has "ridiculous prejudices and self-conceit," yet he was a perceptive and industrious historian.

9   "The Last Journals of Horace Walpole." Saturday Review 7 (19 February):216-17.
Walpole was an acute observer of his age, but his journals are largely gossip: "nothing is exactly false or true." They are malicious but amusing; Walpole expressed his universal antipathies in an elegant style. The journals throw some new light on the eighteenth century, but more on Walpole himself.

10 WALPOLE, HORACE. Journal of the Reign of King George the Third, from the Year 1771 to 1783. Edited by Dr. [John] Doran. London: Richard Bentley, 2 vols.
An extremely unreliable edition, presenting several newspaper clippings pasted by Walpole into his journal as Walpole's own writings. Includes brief annotations and a short introduction, recommending Walpole as the chronicler of his age.

11 WALPOLE, HORACE. The Letters of Horace Walpole, Earl of Orford. Edited by Peter Cunningham. London: Richard Bentley, vol. 9.
Completion of 1858.13. Includes a preface, surveying Walpole's epistolary friendships, an alphabetical list of Walpole's correspondents, an appendix, with additions and corrections, and an index.

1860

1   JAYDEE. "Anecdote in Walpole's Letters." Notes and Queries, 2d ser. 10 (8 September):191.
Enquires about the same anecdote discussed by Croker

(1849.1) and C.W.B. (1850.2). An editorial note provides a source for the anecdote.

2   REESE, W.B. "Horace Walpole and Junius Identified." Southern Literary Messenger 31 (September):161-79; (October):296-314.
    Confidently identifies Walpole as Junius, and Kitty Clive as Walpole-Junius's amanuensis. The case is made at length and in detail, but it has not been accepted.

3   "The Literary Suburb of the Eighteenth Century. Chapter VII. Strawberry Hill." Fraser's Magazine 62 (July):94-100.
    A gossipy account of Walpole at Strawberry Hill. Suggests that his interest in the Countess of Suffolk stemmed from his liking for "antiquarian remains."

4   WALL, JAMES W. "Strawberry Hill." Knickerbocker Magazine 16 (October):397-404.
    Contrasts Strawberry Hill in its prime with its present dilapidated condition, and attempts an imaginative reconstruction. Believes that Walpole "embodied the peculiarities, graces, and defects" of his age. Reprinted: 1866.7.

5   WALPOLE, HORACE. A Supplement to the Historic Doubts on the Life and Reign of King Richard the Third. Edited by E[dward] C[raven] H[awtrey]. Philobiblon Society Miscellanies 6, no. 3. 115 pp.
    Reprints Walpole's supplement to his Historic Doubts, first published in 1798.7, with a preface contending that the supplement will "rather be considered an ingenious piece of special pleading, than a valuable contribution to English history." Contains four pages of text omitted in the Works.

1861

1   DORAN, J[OHN]. "The Father of Catherine Shorter, Lady Walpole." Notes and Queries, 2d ser. 12 (6 July):14.
    Responds to Phillips (1861.3), with more information on the ancestry of Walpole's mother. Walpole "was quite justified in not being ashamed of his descent."

2   PHILLIPS, JOHN PAVIN. "Present to Horace Walpole." Notes and Queries, 2d ser. 12 (30 November):432.
    Prints an extract from a diary by Sir Erasmus Philipps, mentioning a "Pacing Mare" given as a present to Walpole in 1724.

3   PHILLIPS, JOHN PAVIN. "The Mother of Horace Walpole." Notes and Queries, 2d ser. 11 (18 May):385-86.
    Defends the pedigree of Walpole's mother, Catherine Shorter.

4   WALPOLE, HORACE.   "Horace Walpole's MS Notes on Bayle's Dic-
     tionary."   Philobiblon 1 (December):5-8.
         Transcribes Walpole's marginalia on Bayle's Dictionary.
     An unsigned preface declares that Walpole's notes contain
     "some curious facts and opinions, evincing his knowledge,
     acuteness and ill nature."   Completed: 1862.2.

                                  1862

1   R., R.J.   "Horace Walpole."   Notes and Queries, 3d ser. 2 (1
     November):350, 352.
         Enquires about an edition of Walpole's Catalogue of
     Engravers of 1794 and about a manuscript copy of his Royal
     and Noble Authors, with a letter from Walpole to Dr. Birch.
     The editor replies with information on their location.

2   WALPOLE, HORACE.   "Horace Walpole's MS Notes on Bayle's Dic-
     tionary."   Philobiblon 1 (January):27-32, 46.
         Completion of 1861.4.

3   WALPOLE, HORACE.   "Walpole's Ovid."   Philobiblon 1 (January):
     44.
         Transcribes some annotations by Walpole on his copy of
     Ovid's works, dated 1733, when he was at Eton.

                                  1863

1   H., S.   "Letter from Horace Walpole."   Notes and Queries, 3d
     ser. 4 (10 October):284.
         Quotes a letter from Walpole to William Parsons, criti-
     cizing The Mysterious Mother, and defends Walpole from his
     own criticisms.   Finds the subject of the play admissible,
     but much of the poetry merely "flatulent declamation."

2   "Horace Walpole" and "Horace Walpole on Balloons." In The Book
     of Days. Edited by R. Chambers. Edinburgh: W.R. Chambers,
     pp. 323-26.
         Regards Walpole as effeminate, frivolous, and heartless,
     but admires his historical works, his correspondence, and
     his collections at Strawberry Hill.   Also considers his
     interest in ballooning in 1784, with quotations from his
     letters.

                                  1864

1   BOHN, HENRY G.   "Strawberry Hill Press."   In 1864.5, vol. 4,
     Appendix, pp. 237-45.
         A list of books, detached pieces, labels for books, and

cards of address, printed by Walpole at Strawberry Hill. Most of the items are briefly annotated.

2   BRUNET, JACQUES-CHARLES. "Walpole (Horatio)." In Manuel du librairie et de l'amateur de livres, 5th ed. Vol. 5. Paris: Firmin Didot, pp. 1406-9.
     Revision of 1839.1.

3   CHITTELDROOG. "Walpole's 'Royal and Noble Authors.'" Notes and Queries, 3d ser. 6 (8 October):283.
     Enquires about the number of impressions of Park's edition of Royal and Noble Authors (1806.1). The editor replies that there was only one edition, with emendations in subsequent impressions.

4   du DEFFAND, MARQUISE. Lettres de la Marquise du Deffand à Horace Walpole, écrites dans les années 1766 à 1780. . . . Introduction by M. A[dolphe] Thiers. Edited by A. Firmin Didot. Bibliothèque des mémoires pendant le 18e. siècle. Paris: Firmin Didot, 2 vols.
     Contains a preface by Firmin Didot, an account of previous French and English editions of Mme du Deffand's letters to Walpole by A. Taillandier, a portrait of Mary Berry, also by Taillandier, and a reprint of Thiers's essay on Mme du Deffand (1824.1).

5   LOWNDES, WILLIAM THOMAS, and BOHN, HENRY G. "Strawberry-Hill" and "Walpole, Horace." In The Bibliographer's Manual of English Literature. By William Thomas Lowndes, edited by Henry G. Bohn. 4 vols. London: George Bell, 3:2530-31; 4:2818-23.
     The section on Strawberry Hill contains a brief, annotated list of catalogues of Walpole's collections. The section on Walpole provides the fullest bibliography of his works until Hazen's (1942.5 and 1948.1). Also contains 1864.1.

1865

1   BERRY, MISS [MARY]. Extracts of the Journals and Correspondence of Miss Berry from the Year 1783 to 1852. Edited by Lady Theresa Lewis. London: Longmans, Green, 3 vols.
     The first two volumes contain letters and journal entries to and about Walpole throughout. Also prints many letters from Walpole to Mary Berry for the first time, with editorial comments.

2   de LESCURE, M[ATHURIN], ed. "Madame du Deffand, sa vie, ses amis, son salon, ses lettres." Introduction to Correspondance complète de la Marquise du Deffand avec ses amis le

Président Hénault, Montesquieu, d'Alembert, Voltaire, Horace
Walpole. Vol. 1. Paris: Henri Plon, pp. i-ccxvii.
  An extensive account of Mme du Deffand's life, writings,
and relationship with Walpole. Regards Walpole as the
wittiest man ·in eighteenth-century England and admires his
taste. Believes that both Walpole and Mme du Deffand were
responsible for the difficulties of their friendship; Walpole was, indeed, tyrannical, but only in response to Mme du
Deffand's unreasonable demands.

3 [HAYWARD, ABRAHAM.] Review of Extracts of the Journals and
  Correspondence of Miss Berry. Edinburgh Review 122 (October):297-336.
    Considers Walpole's friendship with the Miss Berrys and
Mary Berry's reply to Macaulay (1840.1), an undertaking
"beyond anyone's strength." Depicts Mary Berry as the owner
of a favourite dog, denying "his snappishness on the plea
that 'he never bites me.'"

4 "Witty Women and Pretty Women of the Time of Horace Walpole."
  London Society 8 (October):319-28; (November):451-59.
    Review article on 1865.1. Walpole is the "brilliant
writer" whose correspondence and journals furnish Mary
Berry's accounts of "female celebrities." His skill in
description is unsurpassed: "What a magazine writer he
would have been in these days!" Reprinted: 1866.8.

1866

1 "Horace Walpole." Athenaeum, June 16, p. 820.
    Discusses the signification of "Onuphrio Muralto," the
supposed author of Otranto, showing how "Walpole" can be
turned into "Muralto" but not how "Horace" can become
"Onuphrio."

2 "Horace Walpole and Adam the Architect." Builder 24 (6 January):6.
    Prints a letter from Walpole to Robert Adam on the re-
modelling of Strawberry Hill, with a prefatory note.

3 "Junius." Sharpe's London Magazine, n.s. 28 (April):180-87;
  (May):234-38.
    Identifies Walpole as Junius and Kitty Clive as his aman-
uensis, ignoring Grey (1840.2) and Reese (1860.2) who both
make the same "discovery."

4 "Miss Berry's Journals and Correspondence." Christian Reformer
  33 (January):128-55.
    Review of 1865.1. Many of Walpole's letters to Mary
Berry are "utterly frivolous," denoting "a mind unstrung and

disorganized previous to its final decay." The letters show
Walpole in his old age, more pathetic but also more amiable
than in his youth or maturity. Believes that Walpole called
Mary and Agnes Berry his "twin wives" to disguise his "hope-
less devotion" to Mary.

5 NICHOLS, JOHN GOUGH.   "The Pictures Once at Strawberry Hill
   Attributed to English History." Notes and Queries, 3d ser.
   10 (28 July):61-62.
      Discusses three pictures owned by Walpole, correcting his
   "fantastic theories" about their subjects.

6 RATHERY, E.-J.-B. "Walpole (Horace)." In Nouvelle biographie
   générale.   Edited by [Jean Chrétien Ferdinand] Hoefer.
   Vol. 46. Paris: Firmin Didot. pp. 535-36.
      A survey of Walpole's life and works, emphasizing his
   French interests and relationships.   Regards his correspondence as his greatest achievement.

7 WALL, JAMES W. "Strawberry Hill." Galaxy 1 (15 July):553-58.
   Reprint of 1860.4.

8 "Witty Women and Pretty Women of the Time of Horace Walpole."
   Eclectic Magazine 66 (January):43-52.
      Reprint of 1865.4.

                                1867

1 H. "Horace Walpole." Notes and Queries, 3d ser. 12 (19 October):305.
      Replies to 1866.1, with a highly implausible proposal for
   turning "Horace" into "Onuphrio."

2 KNIGHT, CHARLES.   "Gray, West, and Walpole," and "Horace
   Walpole and the Miss Berrys." In Half-Hours with the Best
   Letter-Writers and Autobiographers.   London: George Routledge, pp. 61-86, 261-74.
      Discusses Walpole's friendships with West and Gray and
   with Mary and Agnes Berry, with copious extracts from his
   correspondence.   Finds Macaulay's strictures on Walpole more
   persuasive than Mary Berry's rebuttal (1840.1), and sees
   Walpole's feelings for Mary Berry as "an exhibition of
   dotage."

3 WALPOLE, HORACE. Horace Walpole's Marginal Notes, Written in
   Dr. Maty's Miscellaneous Works and Memoirs of the Earl of
   Chesterfield.   2 vols. 4to. 1777.   Philobiblon Society
   Miscellanies 10 (1866-67). 59 pp.
      An inaccurate transcript, without introduction, of margi-
   nalia by Walpole. Revised: 1868.1.

1868

1   WALPOLE, HORACE. Horace Walpole's Marginal Notes, Written in
     Dr. Maty's Miscellaneous Works and Memoirs of the Earl of
     Chesterfield. 2 vols. 4to. 1777. Edited by R.S. Turner.
     Philobiblon Society Miscellanies 11 (1867-68). 80 pp.
        Corrected edition of 1867.3. A prefatory note states
     that Turner did not edit the previous version.

1869

1   HARLOWE, S.H. "Unpublished Letter from Horace Walpole to T.
     Astle, Esq., F.R.S." Notes and Queries, 4th ser. 3 (6
     March):216.
        Prints a letter from Walpole to Thomas Astle, thanking
     him for "the most superb of all Royal Locks." The lock is
     illustrated and discussed by Ross (1942.8) and Blair
     (1966.2).

2   "Unpublished Letters of Horace Walpole." Notes and Queries,
     4th ser. 3 (2 January):2-4.
        Prints a series of letters from Walpole to the Bishop of
     Carlisle, with a brief introduction. The letters are "very
     characteristic" and show Walpole as a "steadfast friend."

3   YEOWELL, J. "Horace Walpole." Notes and Queries, 4th ser. 4
     (28 August):175.
        Enquires about the whereabouts of Walpole's manuscript
     notes on Pennant's London.

1870

1   AN OLD IRISH LADY. "Inedited Letter of Horace Walpole." Notes
     and Queries, 4th ser. 6 (6 August):107-8.
        Prints a letter from Walpole to Robert Jephson of 8
     November 1777, with a brief introductory comment.

2   "Horace Walpole, Earl of Orford." In Episodes of Fiction; or,
     Choice Stories from the Great Novelists. Edinburgh:
     William P. Nimmo, pp. 113-21.
        Includes a passage from Otranto, "The Mysterious Helmet,"
     a biographical sketch of Walpole, and a commentary on
     Otranto, which is depicted as a slight but influential
     work. Prefers Walpole's letters and Memoirs. As a man, he
     "neither commands our respect nor wins our esteem."

1871

1 ALLIBONE, S[AMUEL] AUSTIN. "Walpole, Rt. Hon. Horace (Horatio,) Earl of Orford." In <u>A Critical Dictionary of English
   Literature and British and American Authors Living and
   Deceased. From the Earliest Accounts to the Latter Half of
   the Nineteenth Century.</u> Vol. 3. Philadelphia: J.B.
   Lippincott, pp. 2554-59.
       An invaluable guide to eighteenth and nineteenth-century
   criticism of Walpole in books and periodicals. Difficult to
   use and often inaccurate, but the fullest list of early
   criticism to date. Includes many critical extracts and
   comments by Walpole on the reception of his works, with a
   few original remarks by Allibone and a biographical sketch.

2 "Horace Walpole and Strawberry Hill." <u>St James's Magazine</u> 27
   (October-March):567-72.
       A brief biographical sketch of Walpole and a history of
   Strawberry Hill, with an account of the sale of 1842.
   <u>Otranto</u> was a brilliant success in its day, but "is now
   comparatively forgotten." Walpole's other writings are all
   ephemeral, and his treatment of Chatterton was reprehensible.

3 WALPOLE, HORACE. <u>Notes on the Poems of Alexander Pope.</u> Edited
   by Sir William Augustus Fraser. London: Chiswick Press, 54
   pp.
       Transcribes Walpole's marginalia on his set of Pope's
   <u>Works,</u> without an introduction. Revised: 1876.6.

1872

1 COBBETT, R[ICHARD] S[TUTELY]. "Strawberry Hill." In <u>Memorials
   of Twickenham: Parochial and Topographical.</u> London: Smith,
   Elder, pp. 294-334.
       Studies the history and contents of Strawberry Hill,
   drawing heavily on Walpole's <u>Description of the Villa</u> and on
   Robins's catalogue (1842.18). Includes a biographical
   sketch of Walpole and a brief account of his works, in which
   only his letters find favour.

2 EASTLAKE, CHARLES L[OCK]. "Horace Walpole." In <u>A History of
   the Gothic Revival.</u> London: Longmans, pp. 42-49.
       Studies Walpole's Gothic remodelling of Strawberry Hill,
   and compares the influence of Strawberry Hill with that of
   <u>Otranto.</u> Regards Walpole as a superficial but influential
   amateur in the fields of architecture and literature.
   Reprinted: 1970.7.

3 [STEPHEN, LESLIE.] "Horace Walpole." <u>Cornhill Magazine</u> 25

(June):718-35.
A highly influential essay with a famous opening sen-
tence: "The History of England, throughout a very large
segment of the eighteenth century, is simply a synonym for
the works of Horace Walpole." Responds to Macaulay's criticisms by treating Walpole as a historian, and as a major
influence on literature and architecture through Otranto and
Strawberry Hill.   Dislikes the man but admires his writings. Reprinted: 1872.4-5, 1876.4, and in numerous subsequent editions of Stephen's essays.

4   [STEPHEN, LESLIE.]   "Horace Walpole."   Every Saturday 13 (29
June):113-19.
Reprint of 1872.3.

5   [STEPHEN, LESLIE.]   "Horace Walpole."   Living Age 114 (6 July):
3-14.
Reprint of 1872.3.

6   WALPOLE, HORACE.   Lettres de Horace Walpole écrites à ses amis
pendant ses voyages en France (1737-1775).   Edited by Comte
de Baillon. Paris: Didier, 324 pp.
A translation of Walpole's letters from France.   An
introduction notes Walpole's wit and epistolary talents and
discusses some of his friendships. Claims that although he
proposed to Mary Berry he was never in love, and that
passion played no part in his life.

1873

1   WARREN, CHARLES F.S. "Bexhill Church and Horace Walpole."
Notes and Queries, 4th. ser. 12 (13 December):474.
Enquires about the location of a window from Bexhill
Church owned by Walpole and sold at the Strawberry Hill Sale
of 1842. Answered by Milner-Gibson-Cullum (1890.11).

1874

1   BARBEY d'AUREVILLY, J[ULES]-A[MEDEE].   Review of Lettres de
Horace Walpole écrites à ses amis pendant ses voyages en
France.   Constitutionnel, 21 September.
Ranks Walpole high, but not first, among letter writers
of the eighteenth century. Criticizes his typically English
frigidity, and depicts him as a precursor of Beau Brummell
and the dandies. Reprinted: 1892.1.

2   LINDIS.   "Horace Walpole's Charade."   Notes and Queries, 5th
ser. 1 (13 June):475.
Replies to N.H.R. (1874.3); the solution is vapeur.

3   R., N.H.   "A French Charade."   <u>Notes and Queries</u>, 5th ser. 1 (16 May):385.
    Asks for assistance in solving a French charade sent by Walpole to the Countess of Upper Ossory.

4   SUMNER, CHARLES.   "Horace Walpole."   In <u>Prophetic Voices Concerning America</u>.   Boston: Lee & Shepherd, pp. 46-51.
    Considers Walpole's increasing sympathy for the American colonists and his predictions of American liberty.   Outlines his life and commends his letters and memoirs.   Revised from an unlocated article in <u>Atlantic Monthly</u>.

1875

1   CHARNOCK, R.S.   "Princess of Serendip."   <u>Notes and Queries</u>, 5th ser. 3 (22 May):417.
    Replies to M.N.S. (1875.5), connecting "Serendip" with "Ceylon."

2   CHILDERS, R.C.   "Princess of Serendip."   <u>Notes and Queries</u>, 5th ser. 3 (26 June):517.
    Replies to Charnock (1875.1), denying the connection between "Serendip" and "Ceylon."

3   DILKE, CHARLES WENTWORTH.   Review of <u>The Correspondence of Horace Walpole, Earl of Orford, and the Rev. William Mason</u>.   In <u>The Papers of a Critic</u>.   Edited by Sir Charles Wentworth Dilke.   Vol. 2.   London: John Murray, pp. 154-70.
    Reprint of 1851.5.

4   JESSE, J[OHN] HENEAGE.   "Horace Walpole, Earl of Orford."   In <u>Memoirs of Celebrated Etonians</u>.   Vol. 2.   London: Richard Bentley, pp. 17-48.
    A biographical sketch, concentrating on Walpole's friendships with other Etonians.   Largely avoids commentary on his works, but pronounces his letters "incomparable."

5   S., M.N.   "Princess of Serendip."   <u>Notes and Queries</u>, 5th ser. 3 (27 February):169.
    Enquires about Walpole's source for his term "serendipity."

6   SOLLY, EDWARD.   "Princess of Serendip."   <u>Notes and Queries</u>, 5th ser. 3 (17 April):316.
    Replies to M.N.S. (1875.5), quoting Walpole's letter to Mann of 28 January 1754 on <u>The Three Princes of Serendip</u>.

1876

1   DORAN, JOHN.   "Mann" and Manners at the Court of Florence,
    1740-1786. London: Richard Bentley, 2 vols.
        Contains garbled extracts from Walpole's correspondence
    with Mann throughout, with a vapid commentary on their
    friendship.

2   [HAYWARD, ABRAHAM.]   "Strawberry Hill."   Living Age 131 (25
    November):477-99.
        Reprint of 1876.3.

3   [HAYWARD, ABRAHAM.]   "Strawberry Hill."   Quarterly Review 142
    (October):303-45.
        A discursive survey of Walpole's life and writings, con-
    cluding with a study of the Strawberry Hill Sale of 1842.
    Believes that Walpole's collection was unjustly criticized
    by the Times (1842.21), and defends Robins's oratund des-
    criptions (1842.18). Reprinted: 1876.2, 1880.1.

4   STEPHEN, LESLIE.   "Horace Walpole."   In Hours in a Library, 2d
    ser. London: Smith, Elder, pp. 154-97.
        Reprint of 1872.3.

5   THORNE, JAMES.   "Strawberry Hill."   In Handbook to the Environs
    of London. Vol. 2. London: John Murray, pp. 580-88.
        An admiring survey of Walpole's remodelling of Strawberry
    Hill and of his collections, which were "even more remark-
    able than the house."

6   WALPOLE, HORACE.   Notes on the Poems of Alexander Pope.   2d
    ed.   Edited by Sir William Augustus Fraser. London: F.
    Harvey, 108 pp.
        An expanded, corrected edition of 1871.3, with a brief
    preface stating that Walpole's marginalia have been trans-
    cribed verbatim.

1877

1   PAPINI, ALESSANDRO.   Società e corte di Firenze sotto il regno
    di Francesco II e Leopoldo I di Lorena-Absburgo.   Florence:
    G. Barbèra, 220 pp.
        Draws on Walpole's correspondence with Mann throughout
    for an account of Florentine society.

1878

1   C.   "Serendipity."   Notes and Queries, 5th ser. 10 (27 July):
    68.

Another enquiry about the etymology of Walpole's term.

2 [HAYWARD, ABRAHAM.] "Madame du Deffand." Quarterly Review 146
(July):141-81.
Review article on 1864.4 and 1865.2. Studies Walpole's
correspondence with Mme du Deffand, emphasizing his sensi-
tivity to ridicule and blaming both for the difficulties in
their relationship. Reprinted: 1880.1.

3 MARSH, J.F. "'Serindip': 'Serendipity.'" Notes and Queries,
5th ser. 10 (3 August):98-99.
Replies to C. (1878.1), mentioning a "Serendib" in the
Arabian Nights.

4 SOLLY, EDWARD. "'Serindip': 'Serendipity.'" Notes and Queries, 5th ser. 10 (3 August):98.
Replies to C. (1878.1), citing Walpole's source for
"serendipity" as Travels and Adventures of Three Princes of
Sarendip.

1880

1 HAYWARD, A[BRAHAM]. "Madame du Deffand and her Correspondents"
and "Strawberry Hill." In Sketches of Eminent Statesmen and
Writers, with Other Essays. Vol. 2. London: John Murray,
pp. 129-85, 243-304.
Reprints of 1878.2 and 1876.3, with slight additions.

2 M., A. "Walpoliana." Notes and Queries, 6th ser. 1 (29 May):
433.
Calls for the clarification of obscurities in Walpole's
letters, "our most amusing and instructive history of English social life in the last century."

3 SCOONES, W[ILLIAM] BAPTISTE, ed. "Walpole, the Hon. Horace."
In Four Centuries of English Letters. Selections from the
Correspondence of One Hundred and Fifty Writers from the
Period of the Paston Letters to the Present Day. New York:
Harper, pp. 258-73.
Includes five letters by Walpole, with brief critical
comments. Regards Walpole's as "the best and most enter-
taining collection of letters in our language."

1881

1 "Strawberry Hill." American Architect and Building News 10
(29 October):210.
Discusses Walpole's collecting and building at Strawberry
Hill, and traces the history of the house from his death to

1881, before its impending sale in 1888.

2   "Strawberry Hill." Builder 41 (13 August):199-200.
     Walpole resolved to turn a simple cottage into an
     "enchanted castle," defying the "rigid and stately rules of
     architecture" and achieving a "natural simplicity" in his
     garden. He successfully paved the way for neo-Gothic
     architecture and for a new form of landscape gardening. His
     correspondence is his only important literary work.

                              1882

1   BATES, WILLIAM. "The 'Strawberry Hill' Catalogue." Notes and
     Queries, 6th ser. 5 (10 June):441-42.
     Attempts to unravel the complex publishing history of the
     Strawberry Hill Sale Catalogues and the Aedes Strawberrianae
     of 1842.

2   GOSSE, EDMUND. "The Grand Tour." In Gray. English Men of
     Letters. London: Harper, pp. 23-45.
     An account of Gray and Walpole's Grand Tour and of their
     quarrel, asserting that "Walpole was the offender."

3   TUCKERMAN, BAYARD. "The Castle of Otranto." In A History of
     English Prose Fiction from Sir Thomas Malory to George
     Eliot. London: Sampson Low, pp. 259-64.
     Contends that Otranto can only be appreciated when read
     in suitably eerie surroundings, and that the combination of
     realism and the supernatural is unsuccessful. Regrets that
     Walpole did not attempt any realistic fiction.

                              1883

1   FILON, AUGUSTIN. "Correspondance d'H. Walpole," and "Romans
     fantastiques." In Histoire de la littérature anglaise
     depuis ses origines jusqu'à nos jours. Paris: Hachette,
     pp. 461-63.
     Emphasizes Walpole's effeminacy and regards his letters
     as trivial gossip, rather than history. Otranto, similarly,
     is a mediocre novel, but influential and amusing.

2   PERRY, THOMAS SERGEANT. "Appearance of Romanticism: Walpole's
     Castle of Otranto." In English Literature in the Eighteenth
     Century. New York: Harper, pp. 362-70.
     Compares the "sham Gothic" of Otranto with that of Straw-
     berry Hill, acknowledging that both were influential. Finds
     Otranto silly, obsolete, and "nearly unreadable."

3   SOLLY, EDWARD. "Strawberry Hill." Notes and Queries, 6th

ser. 7 (2 June):427.
Prints a couplet by Pope, a parody by Walpole, and a recent parody of Walpole's parody.

4 "Strawberry Hill." American Architect and Building News 13 (23 June):295-96.
A description of Strawberry Hill and its contents, primarily in the nineteenth century, taken from the London Daily News.

5 Strawberry Hill. A Catalogue of the Contents of the Mansion . . . . London: n.p., 112 pp.
The catalogue of a sale of items at Strawberry Hill. Includes parts of Walpole's collection not sold in 1842.

1884

1 "Horace Walpole." Spectator 57 (2 February):156-67.
Review of 1884.3. Regards Walpole as "one of the best" as well as "the most voluminous of letter-writers," although his other works are now "almost forgotten."

2 "Horace Walpole and his World." Saturday Review 57 (22 March): 385-86.
Review of 1884.3. Contends that Walpole's letters do not provide a comprehensive guide to his age: he saw "but one small part of the whole of English life." Walpole's judgments of contemporary writers are equally misleading, and he was ill-informed about changes in religion and economics.

3 SEELEY, L[EONARD] B[ENTON], ed. Horace Walpole and his World. Select Passages from his Letters. London: Jackson & Halliday, 296 pp.
An awkward combination of biography and selected letters. The first chapter is a biographical sketch, examining Walpole's place in society and his taste in literature and the arts, but largely avoiding commentary on his works. The remainder is a series of extracts from Walpole's letters, with a critical commentary. Walpole is depicted as the greatest of English letter writers.

1885

1 BABEAU, ALBERT. "Horace Walpole." In Les voyageurs en France, depuis la Renaissance jusqu'à la Revolution. Paris: Firmin-Didot, pp. 244-47.
Walpole did not share the prejudices of other British travellers to France, such as Smollett, although his observations are often superficial. The comments in his letters

on the society and manners of Paris are of particular
interest.

2   GALTON, ARTHUR. "Horace Walpole." In Urbana Scripta: Studies
    of Five Living Poets. London: Elliot Stock, pp. 211-37.
        A survey of Walpole's life and writings, focusing on his
    letters and his relationship with Gray. Ascribes Sainte-
    Beuve's approval of Walpole (1850.7) to Walpole's having "so
    much about him that was French." Walpole's tastes looked
    towards the nineteenth century.

                                1886

1   BUCKLEY, W.E. "Passage in Walpole's 'Anecdotes of Painting.'"
    Notes and Queries, 7th ser. 1 (3 April):266-67.
        Enquires about a puzzling passage in Anecdotes of Paint-
    ing on a painting of the marriage of Henry VI.

2   WALPOLE, HORACE. The Castle of Otranto. Introduction by
    H[enry] M[orley]. London: Cassell, 197 pp.
        An introduction offers a biographical sketch of Walpole
    and discusses Otranto, which was "an early sign of the
    reaction towards romance in the late eighteenth century."

                                1887

1   HAZLITT, W[ILLIAM] CAREW. "Walpole and the Gardeners of the
    Eighteenth Century." In Gleanings in Old Garden Litera-
    ture. London: Elliot Stock, pp. 186-202.
        Supports Walpole's condemnation of the "geometrical
    style" of gardening, and considers his attitude to William
    Temple, Kent, and Capability Brown. Finds Walpole's essay
    on gardening intelligent and instructive, yet also "dis-
    agreeably affected and artificial."

2   WOTTON, MABEL E., ed. "Horace Walpole." In Word Portraits of
    Famous Writers. London: Richard Bentley, pp. 319-23.
        A useful collection of descriptions of Walpole's appear-
    ance, taken from contemporary sources.

                                1888

1   DAWSON, GEORGE. "Horace Walpole." In Shakespeare and Other
    Lectures. Edited by George St. Clair. London: Kegan Paul,
    pp. 223-33.
        Provides extracts from Walpole's letters and a discussion
    of his friendships. Despite his affectations and eccentric-
    ities, Walpole was the greatest English letter writer and

the founder of Gothic architecture and fiction.

2 FREY, ALBERT R. "Walpole, Horace." In Sobriquets and Nick-
    names. Boston: Ticknor, p. 476.
        A list of eight sobriquets and nicknames for Walpole,
    each of which is discussed in the body of the work.

3 KEENE, H.G. "Collection of H. Walpole." Notes and Queries,
    7th ser. 6 (27 October):330.
        Replies to Way (1888.6), noting that there are catalogues
    of both the Strawberry Hill Sale of 1842 and the smaller
    sale of 1883.

4 [NELSON, WILLIAM FRANCIS.] "Horace Walpole and Madame du
    Deffand." Living Age 176 (24 March):741–46.
        Reprint of 1888.5.

5 [NELSON, WILLIAM FRANCIS.] "Horace Walpole and Madame du
    Deffand." Temple Bar 82 (March):340–50.
        A gossipy account of Walpole and Parisian society.
    Glosses over the tensions in his relationship with Mme du
    Deffand. Reprinted: 1888.4.

6 WAY, R.E. "Collection of Horace Walpole." Notes and Queries,
    7th ser. 6 (22 September):228.
        Enquires about the catalogue of the Strawberry Hill Sale.

                                  1889

1 BERESFORD, S.B. "'Heiress of Pinner.'" Notes and Queries, 7th
    ser. 8 (14 December):467.
        Enquires in which of his letters Walpole refers to the
    "Heiress of Pinner."

2 COKE, LADY MARY. The Letters and Journals of Lady Mary Coke.
    Edited by James A. Home. Introduction by Lady Louisa
    Stuart. Edinburgh: David Douglas, vols. 1–2.
        Numerous references to Walpole in both Stuart's introduc-
    tion and in Coke's letters and journals. Continued: 1892.2
    and 1896.1.

3 DOBSON, AUSTIN. "Horace Walpole's Printing-Press." Library
    1:313–19.
        A brief account of the productions of the Strawberry Hill
    Press, of which Walpole's own Anecdotes of Painting was "the
    most considerable effort." Revised: 1896.2.

4 "Horace Walpole's Letters." Saturday Review 68 (23 November):
    597–98.
        Review of 1890.18, deploring the botched annotations and

calling for a "skilful and discriminating selection from Walpole's letters."

5   "Letters of Horace Walpole." Literary World 40 (29 November): 443-44.
    Review of 1890.18. Finds Walpole's letters charming and amusing, but believes that he has been overpraised as much as underrated. Regrets that his memoirs are not being reprinted.

6   MARSHALL, ED. "Collection of H. Walpole." Notes and Queries, 7th ser. 7 (12 January):34.
    Replies to Way (1888.6) by recording, inaccurately, the titles of the Strawberry Hill Sale Catalogues and Aedes Strawberrianae of 1842.

7   MARSHALL, JULIAN. "Collection of H. Walpole." Notes and Queries, 7th ser. 7 (26 January):76.
    Corrects Ed. Marshall (1889.6) by noting the titles of the two principal Strawberry Hill Sale Catalogues of 1842, and of the two versions of Aedes Strawberrianae.

1890

1   "A Forgotten Immortal." Atlantic Monthly 65 (January):139-41.
    A portrait of Margaret, Lady Bingham, as seen in Walpole's letters. Walpole admired her paintings and wrote verses for her daughter.

2   B., G. "The Letters of and to Horace Walpole." Notes and Queries, 7th ser. 9 (26 April):335.
    Notes that an edition of Walpole's letters published by Bohn in 1861 is that first published by Bentley (1857.7).

3   B., G.F.R. "The Letters of and to Horace Walpole." Notes and Queries, 7th ser. 9 (5 April):276.
    Replies to Mason (1890.10), referring him to Cunningham's preface to his collected edition of Walpole's letters (1859.11).

4   DOBSON, AUSTIN. Horace Walpole: A Memoir. With an Appendix of Books Printed at the Strawberry Hill Press. London: James R. Osgood, 370 pp.
    An accurate and straightforward biography, dressed up in an elaborately printed, copiously illustrated edition. Proceeds chronologically, with a final chapter studying Walpole's reputation from Macaulay's essay (1833.5) to the present. Stronger on Walpole's literary works, his letters and Strawberry Hill than on his politics or memoirs. Much improved in three subsequent editions: 1893.1, 1910.1, and

1927.3.

5 HOPE, HENRY GERALD. "The Letters of and to Horace Walpole." <u>Notes and Queries</u>, 7th ser. 9 (5 April):275-76.
Replies to Mason (1890.10), citing Cunningham's claim (1859.11) to have included all of Walpole's letters in his edition.

6 "Horace Walpole's Letters." <u>Literary Opinion & Reader's Miscellany</u> 5 (1 March):9-11.
Reprint of 1890.9.

7 "Horace Walpole's Letters." <u>Spectator</u> 64 (15 February):242-43.
Review of 1890.18. Regards Walpole as "the most readable of letter writers" and as an astute observer of his age. He is at his best as "a collector of good sayings."

8 HOUSDEN, J.A.J. "'Heiress of Pinner.'" <u>Notes and Queries</u>, 7th ser. 9 (1 February):95-96.
Replies to Beresford (1889.1), citing a passage in Walpole's letter to the Countess of Upper Ossory of 3 November 1782 on the "heiress of Pinner."

9 "Letters of Horace Walpole." <u>Times</u> (London), 7 February, p. 3.
Review of 1890.18. Agrees with Macaulay's view of Walpole as artificial and affected, but enjoys his letters for their fascinating style and intrinsic interest. Reprinted: 1890.6.

10 MASON, C. "The Letters of and to Horace Walpole." <u>Notes and Queries</u>, 7th ser. 9 (8 March):189.
Enquires whether all of Walpole's letters have been published.

11 MILNER-GIBSON-CULLUM, G. "Bexhill Church and Horace Walpole." <u>Notes and Queries</u>, 7th ser. 9 (5 April):276.
Replies to Warren (1873.1), stating that he himself owns the window from Bexhill Church sold at the Strawberry Hill Sale of 1842.

12 PRIDEAUX, W[ILLIAM] F[RANCIS]. "The Letters of and to Horace Walpole." <u>Notes and Queries</u>, 7th ser. 9 (31 May):437-38.
Replies to Mason (1890.10), stating that "many valuable additions might be made to Walpole's collected letters." Also compares Walpole with Johnson, pointing out the attractions of Johnson's conversation and of Walpole's letters.

13 PRIDEAUX, W[ILLIAM] F[RANCIS]. "Walpole's Letters." <u>Notes and Queries</u>, 7th ser. 10 (25 October):322-23.
Notes that Walpole kept a diary or journal, and criticizes the index to Cunningham's edition of the letters

(1859.11).

14   RAE, W. FRASER. "Horace Walpole's Letters." <u>Living Age</u> 184 (1
      March):544-52.
          Reprint of 1890.15.

15   RAE, W. FRASER. "Horace Walpole's Letters." <u>Temple Bar</u> 88
      (February):188-201.
          Refutes Macaulay's view of Walpole, and believes that his
      "popularity increases as the years pass away." Admires the
      letters but not the man, who was "the most affected and con-
      ceited Englishman" of his day. Reprinted: 1890.14.

16   THANET, OCTAVE. "The Letters of Horace Walpole." <u>Dial</u> 11
      (July):66-67.
          Review of 1890.18. Contrasts Walpole's letters favour-
      ably with <u>Otranto</u>: they "delight each successive genera-
      tion." Commends his dislike of the American war and of
      Samuel Richardson, and believes that he surpasses Sir
      Charles Grandison in embodying "the eighteenth century ideal
      of a fine gentleman."

17   TOVEY, DUNCAN C., ed. <u>Gray and his Friends. Letters and
      Relics in Great Part Hitherto Unpublished</u>. Cambridge:
      Cambridge University Press, 312 pp.
          Contains unpublished correspondence among Walpole, Gray,
      West, and Ashton, with annotations. An introduction dis-
      cusses Walpole's quarrel with Gray, without apportioning
      blame.

18   WALPOLE, HORACE. <u>Letters of Horace Walpole</u>. Edited by Charles
      Duke Yonge. London: T. Fisher Unwin, 2 vols.
          A selection of Walpole's letters, with highly inaccurate
      notes and introduction: believes that Walpole printed his
      own memoirs at Strawberry Hill. Admires the correspondence,
      but finds Walpole's other works of little interest.

19   WALPOLE, HORACE. <u>The Best Letters of Horace Walpole</u>. Edited
      by Anna B. McMahan. Chicago: A.C. McClurg, 305 pp.
          An introduction summarizes Walpole's life and evaluates
      his letters. Believes that he was "as much overrated in his
      life as he was underrated after his death." The text is
      unreliable.

                                    1891

1   "Horace Walpole." <u>Saturday Review</u> 71 (7 February):177.
          Review of 1890.4. Contrasts Dobson's biography of
      Walpole favourably with Macaulay's essay, but acknowledges
      Walpole's affectation and eccentricity.

2   "Horace Walpole." <u>Spectator</u> 66 (2 May):626-27.
      Review of 1890.4. Believes that Macaulay's delight in
    antitheses was responsible for his extravagant attack on
    Walpole, and takes a more balanced view. Walpole is not
    "one of the heroes of letters," but he has several "amiable
    traits."

3   [MAYER, GERTRUDE TOWNSHEND.] "Horace Walpole's Twin Wives."
    <u>Living Age</u> 189 (18 April):131-44.
      Reprint of 1891.4.

4   [MAYER, GERTRUDE TOWNSHEND.] "Horace Walpole's Twin Wives."
    <u>Temple Bar</u> 91 (March):343-67.
      Discusses Walpole's relationship with Mary and Agnes
    Berry, commending his chivalry and kindness towards them.
    Reprinted: 1891.3 and 1894.3.

5   PRIDEAUX, W[ILLIAM] F[RANCIS]. "Walpole's 'Letters.'" <u>Notes
    and Queries</u>, 7th ser. 12 (17 October):303-4.
      Complains that a reissue of Cunningham's edition (1891.9)
    has failed to incorporate any of the unpublished letters, or
    to improve the index.

6   RAE, W. FRASER. "Walpole's Hints for Discovering Junius."
    <u>Athenaeum</u>, 24 January, pp. 121-23.
      Discusses a manuscript by Walpole, "Hints for Discovering
    Junius," and provides a facsimile. Neither supports nor re-
    futes Walpole's assumption that Junius was Wolfran Cornwall.

7   RUSSELL, CONSTANCE. "Meaning of Quotation Wanted." <u>Notes and
    Queries</u>, 7th ser. 12 (19 December):494.
      Replies to Vernon (1891.8), with information on the fran-
    tic Washingtons.

8   VERNON. "Meaning of Quotation Wanted." <u>Notes and Queries</u>, 7th
    ser. 12 (28 November):428.
      Enquires what Walpole meant when he wrote that "The Wash-
    ingtons were certainly a very frantic race."

9   WALPOLE, HORACE. <u>The Letters of Horace Walpole, Fourth Earl of
    Orford</u>. Edited by Peter Cunningham. London: Richard
    Bentley, 9 vols.
      A revised edition of 1857.7, with a corrected text and
    rearranged prefatory material.

                              1892

1   BARBEY d'AUREVILLY, J[ULES]-A[MEDEE]. "Horace Walpole." In
    <u>Les oeuvres et les hommes. Littérature épistolaire</u>. Paris:
    A. Lemerre, pp. 241-56.

Reprint of 1874.1.

2   COKE, LADY MARY. The Letters and Journals of Lady Mary Coke.
     Edited by James A. Home. Introduction by Lady Louisa
     Stuart. Vol. 3. Edinburgh: David Douglas: 496 pp.
     Continuation of 1889.2.

3   DIDIER, EUGENE L. "Strawberry Hill. A Picture of English
     Social Life in the Eighteenth Century." Chatauquan 14 (Feb-
     ruary):577–87.
          A gossipy account of Walpole and his contemporaries with
     frequent quotations from his letters, which are "his best
     passport to posterity."

4   DOBSON, AUSTIN. "A Day at Strawberry Hill." In Eighteenth
     Century Vignettes. 1st Ser. London: Chatto, pp. 158–66.
          Uses Walpole's letters, his Description of the Villa, and
     Pinkerton's Walpoliana (1799.2) to reconstruct a typical day
     at Strawberry Hill. Revised version of an unlocated
     article.

5   VERNON. "Meaning of Quotation Wanted." Notes and Queries, 8th
     ser. 1 (30 January):96–97.
          Replies to Russell (1891.7), seeking further information
     on the frantic Washingtons.

                              1893

1   DOBSON, AUSTIN. Horace Walpole: A Memoir. With an Appendix
     of Books Printed at the Strawberry Hill Press. 2d ed. Lon-
     don: J.R. Osgood, 328 pp.
          Revision of 1890.4, with fewer illustrations but many
     more annotations and a corrected text.

2   HERPIN, CLARA [Lucien Perey]. Le Président Hénault et Madame
     du Deffand. Paris: Calmann Lévy, 548 pp.
          Discusses Walpole throughout. States that he bitterly
     criticized French society until it started flattering him by
     praising his wit and discretion. He grew tired of Mme du
     Deffand's warm affection for him; what he wanted to read in
     her letters was not descriptions of the state of her soul
     but a chronicle of Parisian life.

                              1894

1   HIGHT, JAMES. "Horace Walpole 1717–1797." In Manual of Eng-
     lish Literature. Era of Expansion, 1750–1850. By J. Mac-
     millan Brown. Christchurch: Whitcombe & Tombs, pp. 375–76.
          A list of Walpole's principal works, with a very sketchy

parallel list of the major events in his life.

2 KER, W[ILLIAM] P. "Horace Walpole." In English Prose Selections. Edited by Sir Henry Craik. Vol. 4. London: Macmillan, pp. 223-40.
    Excerpts from Walpole's works and letters, with an introduction emphasizing the importance of the letters and memoirs. Otranto, in contrast, "has lost its former reputation."

3 MAYER, GERTRUDE TOWNSHEND. "Mary and Agnes Berry: Horace Walpole's Twin Wives." In Women of Letters. Vol. 1. London: Richard Bentley, pp. 305-54.
    Revised, expanded version of 1891.4.

4 [NELSON, WILLIAM FRANCIS.] "Horace Walpole." Eclectic Magazine 123 (July):114-21.
    Reprint of 1894.6.

5 [NELSON, WILLIAM FRANCIS.] "Horace Walpole." Living Age 201 (23 June):740-48.
    Reprint of 1894.6.

6 [NELSON, WILLIAM FRANCIS.] "Horace Walpole." Temple Bar 102 (May):79-90.
    A survey of Walpole's life and letters, ignoring his other works. Reprinted: 1894.4-5.

7 RALEIGH, WALTER. "Castle of Otranto." In The English Novel: A Short Sketch of its History. London: John Murray, pp. 221-26.
    Ranks Walpole among the "founders of modern Romanticism," although Otranto was written in "blundering dilettante fashion." It was, however, more serious in intention than Strawberry Hill, and Walpole's remarks in his preface to the second edition are of considerable interest.

8 WALPOLE, HORACE. Memoirs of the Reign of King George the Third. Edited by G.F. Russell Barker. London: Lawrence & Bullen, 4 vols.
    An edition based on le Marchant's (1845.14), retaining its bowdlerized, inaccurate text and adding further errors. Provides some new annotations and omits some of le Marchant's. A preface surveys Walpole's life and gives the publishing history of his memoirs, which are "a valuable addition to the history of the time."

1895

1 MITCHELL, DONALD G. "A Courtier." In English Lands, Letters,

and Kings. Queen Anne and the Georges. New York: Charles
Scribner's, pp. 83–88.
   An impressionistic portrait of Walpole. Advocates reading Otranto in a lonely country house, and envisions Walpole
as a "fastidious old man" at Strawberry Hill.

2   Review of Memoirs of the Reign of King George the Third.
    Athenaeum, 5 October, pp. 445–46.
       Considers the value of the Memoirs to historians, and
    notes the "general accuracy of the facts." Regards Walpole
    as well qualified for his task, despite his occasional prej-
    udices and lack of a sense of proportion.

3   ROSSMAN, VINCENT D. "A Prince of Scribblers." Catholic World
    60 (March):806–15.
       Sharply criticizes Walpole under such headings as "Wal-
    pole as a Rococo Crank," "Dearly Loved a Lord in Letters,"
    "Gingerbread Criticism," "A Sham Philanthropist," and "An
    Unreverend Old Age." Approves, however, of Walpole's judg-
    ments about French society and of his opposition to slavery.

4   TOYNBEE, HELEN. "A Misplaced Letter of Horace Walpole."
    Academy 48 (28 December):567–68.
       The first of a series of articles, from 1895 to 1901,
    correcting numerous errors in Cunningham's edition of
    Walpole's letters (1857.7).

5   WHEATLEY, H[ENRY] B. "Horace Walpole and his Book-Plates."
    Journal of the Ex Libris Society 5 (July):125–29.
       After a general survey of Walpole's life, works, and
    activities at Strawberry Hill, describes and illustrates his
    book-plates. Two are undisputed; a third, with a view of
    Strawberry Hill, is a vignette used in title-pages of Straw-
    berry Hill books, but was probably never used by Walpole as
    a book-plate.

1896

1   COKE, LADY MARY. The Letters and Journals of Lady Mary Coke.
    Edited by James A. Home. Introduction by Lady Louisa
    Stuart. Vol. 4. Edinburgh: David Douglas, 544 pp.
       Completion of 1892.2, with an index to the four volumes.

2   DOBSON, AUSTIN. "The Officina Arbuteana." In Eighteenth Cen-
    tury Vignettes. 3rd ser. London: Chatto, pp. 206–22.
       Revision of 1889.3.

3   FIRTH, C.H. "Horace Walpole's Memoirs of the Reign of King
    George III." English Historical Review 11 (January):170–71.
       Review of 1894.8. Walpole's memoirs contain "valuable

material for historians," and deserve a more fully annotated edition.

4 TOYNBEE, HELEN. "Horace Walpole and his Editors." Academy 49 (9 May):385; 50 (8 August):99.
   Continuation of 1895.4. From 1897 to 1901 the series continues in Notes and Queries.

5 "Walpole's Memoirs of George III." Critic 28 (4 January):3.
   Review of 1894.8. Prefers Walpole as political historian to Walpole as literary critic. His memoirs provide "a brilliant, if not wholly accurate, picture of the political world of his time."

1897

1 ROBINSON, FREDERICK S. "Pliny the Elder and Horace Walpole." In The Connoisseur: Essays on the Romantic and Picturesque Associations of Art and Artists. London: George Redway, pp. 175-84.
   Believes that Walpole was "too humble" in his attitude to Anecdotes of Painting: he was not Macaulay's fribble but rather the English Vasari. He had the gifts of common sense, good taste, and terse expression.

2 TOYNBEE, HELEN. "Horace Walpole and his Editors." Notes and Queries, 8th ser. 11 (1 May):346; (19 June):492-93; 8th ser. 12 (7 August):104; (9 October):290-91; (20 November): 414; (18 December):493-94.
   Continuation of 1896.4.

3 TOYNBEE, HELEN. "Walpole and 'St. Hannah.'" Temple Bar 110 (March):371-83.
   Discusses Walpole's friendship with Hannah More, showing that despite their considerable differences Walpole admired More's writings and enjoyed her company. Emphasizes her "moral excellence" and his "brilliancy and wit."

4 WHEATLEY, H[ENRY] B. "The Strawberry-Hill Press." Bibliographica 3 (May):83-98.
   Studies Walpole's productions at the Strawberry Hill Press, surveys previous bibliographies of the Press, and appends a "short list" of Strawberry Hill books and pamphlets.

1898

1 HALE, SUSAN. "Horace Walpole and Gray." In Men and Manners of the Eighteenth Century. Meadvill, Pa.: Flood & Vincent,

pp. 203-32.
A survey of Walpole's life, with copious extracts from his letters. Finds the letters memorable, but his other writings dull. Approves of his views on American independence, and believes that Walpole was unpopular in his own time.

2   HALL, EVELYN BEATRICE [S.G. Tallentyre]. "Horace Walpole."
    Living Age 219 (24 December):851-60.
        Reprint of 1898.3.

3   HALL, EVELYN BEATRICE [S.G. Tallentyre]. "Horace Walpole."
    Longman's Magazine 33 (November):54-67.
        Emphasizes the witty, eccentric side of Walpole. Dismisses all his writings as trivial with the exception of his letters, which "are for all time." Reprinted: 1898.2, 1899.6, and 1900.3.

4   MUS. "Horace Walpole's Letters to Madame du Deffand." Notes and Queries, 9th ser. 1 (26 March):247.
        Enquires about the whereabouts of Walpole's letters to Mme du Deffand.

5   PRIDEAUX, W[ILLIAM] F[RANCIS]. "Walpoliana." Notes and Queries, 9th ser. 2 (8 October):287-88.
        Enquires about the whereabouts of Walpole's annotated copy of "Letters written by the late Right Honourable Lady Luxborough to William Shenstone."

6   TOYNBEE, HELEN. "Horace Walpole and his Editors." Notes and Queries, 9th ser. 1 (29 January):91; 9th ser. 2 (23 July): 75; (22 October):332-33; (31 December):531-32.
        Continuation of 1897.2.

7   VADE-WALPOLE, H.S. "Notes on the Walpoles, With Some Account of a Junior Branch." Genealogical Magazine 2 (October):235-44; (November):300-306.
        A genealogical study of the Walpoles, pointing out Walpole's surprising ignorance of his own family and his "dislike of all his relations on his father's side." When he attempted, in 1776, to construct a Walpole pedigree, he made numerous errors.

                                    1899

1   B., H.T. "Prior's Parentage." Notes and Queries, 9th ser. 3 (10 June):449.
        Enquires about the accuracy of a remark on Matthew Prior's parentage in a letter from Walpole to Mann of 17 May 1749.

2   BADDELEY, ST. CLAIR. "Horace Walpole and his Editors." <u>Notes
    and Queries</u>, 9th ser. 3 (6 May):354.
        Corrects a slight error in Toynbee (1899.12).

3   [CROUCH, ARCHER P.] "The Earlier Letters of Horace Walpole."
    <u>Temple Bar</u> 116 (April):562-71.
        Studies the first twenty years of Walpole's correspon-
    dence, from 1736 to 1756. Criticizes Walpole's poor taste
    in contemporary literature, but commends his wit, his de-
    tailed accounts of social entertainments and his opposition
    to the slave trade, in which he was "in advance of his age."

4   DAVEY, SAMUEL. "The Letters of Horace Walpole." <u>Transactions
    of the Royal Society of Literature</u>, 2d ser. 20:261-95.
        An enthusiastic study of Walpole's letters, epitomizing
    the late-nineteenth-century revival of interest in Walpole.
    Rejects Macaulay's hostile judgments and believes that the
    letters will continue to increase in interest. Walpole "has
    given the best <u>surface</u> history of his time."

5   DOBSON, AUSTIN. "Walpole, Horatio or Horace." In <u>Dictionary
    of National Biography</u>. Edited by Sir Sidney Lee. Vol. 59.
    London: Spottiswoode, pp. 170-76.
        A careful, balanced account of Walpole's life and works
    by his first accurate biographer. Summarizes late-nine-
    teenth-century attitudes to Walpole.

6   HALL, EVELYN BEATRICE [S.G. Tallentyre]. "Horace Walpole."
    <u>Eclectic Magazine</u> 132:190-99.
        Reprint of 1898.3.

7   HODGSON, F[RANCIS] C[OTTERELL]. "Horace Walpole." <u>Gentleman's
    Magazine</u> 286 (March):229-53.
        A comprehensive account of Walpole's life and writings.
    Defends his character from Macaulay's strictures, notes the
    breadth of his interests, and evaluates his works, rating
    first the letters and second the memoirs as his most signif-
    icant achievements. Revised: 1913.7.

8   MARSHALL, GEORGE. "Prior's Parentage." <u>Notes and Queries</u>, 9th
    ser. 4 (8 July):32-33.
        Replies to H.T.B. (1899.1), denouncing Walpole's remarks
    on Prior as absurd and malignant. Walpole found birth a
    "tender subject," and wished to "sully as many beginnings as
    possible."

9   PICKFORD, JOHN. "Horace Walpole and his Editors." <u>Notes and
    Queries</u>, 9th ser. 4 (7 October):284-85.
        Corrects an error in Toynbee (1899.12).

10 PRIDEAUX, WILLIAM FRANCIS. "Gray and Walpole." <u>Notes and</u>

Queries, 9th ser. 4 (30 December):531–32.
     Describes a manuscript collection of "Graiana" compiled
by John Mitford, containing some new information on Walpole
and Gray.

11   STREET, G[EORGE] S[LYTHE].   "After Reading Horace Walpole."
     Fortnightly Review 71 (January):124–28.
     Contends that Walpole wrote his letters not for posterity
but to amuse his friends.   With their wit and humour, the
letters vividly convey the atmosphere of eighteenth-century
English society.   Reprinted: 1900.8, 1902.8.

12   TOYNBEE, HELEN.   "Horace Walpole and his Editors."   Notes and
     Queries, 9th ser. 3 (21 January):54–55; (18 February):131–
     32; (1 April):257–58; (6 May):353–54; (10 June):451–52; 9th
     ser. 4 (26 August):165; (23 September):243–44; (7 October):
     284; (21 October):323–24; (11 November):392–93; (30 Decem-
     ber):532–33.
     Continuation of 1898.6.

13   YARDLEY, E.   "Horace Walpole and his Editors."   Notes and
     Queries, 9th ser. 3 (6 May):354.
     Expands a comment on Walpole and La Fontaine in Toynbee
(1899.12).

                              1900

1   B., H.T.   "Extent of St. Martin's Parish."   Notes and Queries,
     9th ser. 5 (19 May):397.
     Queries Walpole's reference to St. Martin's Parish
reaching to "the other end of the globe."

2   B., W.C.   "Gray and Walpole."   Notes and Queries, 9th ser. 5
     (20 January):51.
     Responds to one of Toynbee's queries (1899.12), supplying
information on William Aislabie, mentioned in Walpole's
correspondence.

3   HALL, EVELYN BEATRICE [S.G. Tallentyre].   "Horace Walpole."
     Book Lover 1 (Summer):463–69.
     Reprint of 1898.3.

4   LONSDALE, T.   "Gray and Walpole."   Notes and Queries, 9th ser.
     5 (20 January):51.
     Responds to Toynbee (1899.12), confirming that one of
Cunningham's notes (1857.7) is inaccurate.

5   O.   "Gray and Walpole."   Notes and Queries, 9th ser. 5 (20
     January):51.
     Responds to one of Toynbee's queries (1899.12),

identifying the purchasers of one of the lots at the 1842 Strawberry Hill Sale.

6   P., H.B. "Extent of St. Martin's Parish." <u>Notes and Queries</u>, 9th ser. 5 (16 June):479.
    Responds to H.T.B. (1900.1), asking for a precise reference to the letter in which Walpole refers to St. Martin's Parish.

7   RICHTER, HELENE. "Horace Walpole." In <u>Thomas Chatterton</u>. Vienna and Leipzig: Wilhelm Braunmüller, pp. 145-60.
    In German. A balanced account of Walpole's dealings with Chatterton, regarding Chatterton as the deceiver. Blames Walpole not for his treatment of Chatterton but for his gullibility.

8   STREET, GEORGE SLYTHE. "After Reading Horace Walpole." <u>Book Lover</u> 1 (Spring):286-88.
    Reprint of 1899.11.

9   TOYNBEE, HELEN. "Horace Walpole and his Editors." <u>Notes and Queries</u>, 9th ser. 5 (27 January):61-62; (17 February):122-24; (14 April):282-83; (12 May):371; (9 June):451; 9th ser. 6 (7 July):2-4; (4 August):81-83; (15 September):201-3; (3 November):344-46; (22 December):483-84.
    Continuation of 1899.12.

10 TOYNBEE, HELEN. "The Mutilation of Horace Walpole's Letters." <u>Athenaeum</u>, 8 December, pp. 759-60.
    Discusses the alterations and bowdlerizations of Walpole's letters to Hannah More, performed by More and by Mary Berry.

1901

1   HAVENS, MUNSON ALDRICH. <u>Horace Walpole and the Strawberry Hill Press, 1757-1789</u>. Canton, Pa.: Kirgate Press, 86 pp.
    A useful study of the foundation and operation of Walpole's press. Contains several inaccuracies about the printing of individual items, corrected by Hazen (1942.5).

2   ROTTEN, J.F. "Horace Walpole's Letters to Mann." <u>Notes and Queries</u>, 9th ser. 7 (23 March):229-30.
    Enquires whether Walpole's letters to Mann survive in manuscript, or, if only in transcript, in whose transcript.

3   TOYNBEE, HELEN. "Horace Walpole and his Editors." <u>Notes and Queries</u>, 9th ser. 7 (9 February):103-4.
    Continuation of 1900.9.

4   TOYNBEE, HELEN. "Horace Walpole's Correspondence with Madame
    du Deffand." Athenaeum, 13 July, pp. 62–63.
        Traces the history of the manuscript of Walpole's corre-
    spondence with Mme du Deffand, and announces a forthcoming
    edition of her letters to Walpole (1912.2).

5   TOYNBEE, HELEN. "The 'Charles' of Horace Walpole's Triumvi-
    rate." Athenaeum, 16 February, pp. 212–13.
        Identifies the "Charles" mentioned in Walpole's letter to
    Montagu of 6 May 1736 as Charles Lyttleton, and discusses
    Walpole's friendship with Lyttleton at Eton.

                               1902

1   FLETCHER, W[ILLIAM] Y[OUNGER]. "Horace Walpole, Fourth Earl of
    Orford, 1717–1797." In English Book Collectors. London:
    Kegan Paul, pp. 209–15.
        A brief account of Walpole's life, focusing on his col-
    lections at Strawberry Hill and especially on his library.
    Describes a few of the principal works, including Pope's
    Homer. Walpole's "literary reputation now rests mainly on
    his letters."

2   LOBBAN, J.H. "Horace Walpole, Earl of Orford (1717–1797).
    Change of Style." In English Essays. London: Blackie,
    pp. 142–47.
        Reprints an essay by Walpole in the World, number ten,
    with annotations.

3   LOUNSBURY, THOMAS R[AYNESFORD]. "The Voltaire–Walpole Corre-
    spondence." In Shakespeare and Voltaire. New York:
    Charles Scribner's Sons, pp. 258–80.
        Examines the correspondence between Walpole and Voltaire
    and their dispute over the merits of Shakespeare, noting the
    highly devious nature of the letters. Believes that Wal-
    pole's "complimentary mendacities" surpassed Voltaire's, and
    that his expressions of admiration for Voltaire were "utter-
    ly insincere."

4   MILLAR, J[OHN] H[EPBURN]. "Horace Walpole." In Periods of
    European Literature. Edited by George Saintsbury. Vol. 9,
    The Mid-Eighteenth Century. New York: Charles Scribner's
    Sons, pp. 306–8.
        Defends Walpole from the charges of moralizing critics,
    arguing that his attitudes were pleasingly independent and
    that his correspondence provides an incomparable picture of
    his age. Finds his other works insignificant.

5   MOBIUS, HANS. "Walpoles Castle of Otranto." In The Gothic
    Romance. Leipzig: Grimme & Trömel, pp. 19–43.

In German. Criticizes several aspects of <u>Otranto</u>, including its weak ending, in which many facile solutions are provided, the inaccuracy of historical details, the absurdity of various events, and the failure to combine romance with realism, as Walpole had intended. Commends <u>Otranto</u>'s concise structure, elegant style and lively dialogue, and acknowledges its originality and influence on other writers.

6 MOULTON, CHARLES WELLS, ed. "Horace Walpole. Earl of Orford. 1717-1797." In <u>The Library of Literary Criticism of English and American Authors</u>. Vol. 4. Buffalo: Moulton, pp. 309-23.

Provides a chronology of Walpole's life and writings and extracts from works discussing Walpole, under the headings "Personal," "Strawberry Hill," "Royal and Noble Authors," "Castle of Otranto," "The Mysterious Mother," "Letters," and "General." Revised: 1966.10.

7 "New Letters of Horace Walpole." <u>Times Literary Supplement</u>, 7 March, p. 58.

Review of 1902.11. Discusses Walpole's dealings with his family, his diminishing enthusiasm for France, his literary criticism, and his politics. Regards his correspondence of over sixty years as an "admirable social chronicle."

8 STREET, G[EORGE] S[LYTHE]. "After Reading Horace Walpole." In <u>A Book of Essays</u>. Westminster: Archibald Constable, pp. 120-32.

Reprint of 1899.11.

9 "The King of Worldlings." <u>Academy and Literature</u> 62 (29 March):339-40.

Review of 1902.11. Finds the letters charming, witty, and informative: "never did a man know more about his own age or convey more of his knowledge to the next." Criticizes the empty rhetoric of Macaulay's portrait of Walpole.

10 "The Strawberry Hill Press." <u>Athenaeum</u>, 12 April, pp. 468-69.

Describes a collection of Strawberry Hill books and detached pieces left by Walpole to Anne Seymour Damer, several containing his marginalia.

11 WALPOLE, HORACE. <u>Some Unpublished Letters of Horace Walpole</u>. Edited by Sir Spencer Walpole. London: Longmans, 113 pp.

A brief introduction describes the life of Walpole's cousin, Thomas Walpole, to whom these letters are addressed; Walpole regarded him with affection. The letters are lightly annotated.

1903

1   CRAWFORD, JOHN N.   "Horace Walpole."   In Chats on Writers and
    Books.   Edited by Horatio Seymour.   Vol. 1.   Chicago:
    Charles H. Sergel, pp. 216-24.
        A hostile survey of Walpole's life and works.   Admires
    Macaulay's essay: "there is not a sentence in it that can-
    not be supported from Walpole's writings."

2   GOSSE, EDMUND.   "Horace Walpole."   In English Literature: An
    Illustrated Record.   Edited by Richard Garnett and Edmund
    Gosse. Vol. 3, From Milton to Johnson. London: Heinemann,
    pp. 364-68.
        A brief biographical and critical sketch.   Enjoys the
    charm and wit of Walpole's letters, which form his "main and
    immortal work."

3   HEBB, JOHN.   "Madame du Deffand's Letters." Notes and Queries,
    9th ser. 12 (7 November):366.
        Enquires about the location of Mme du Deffand's letters
    to Walpole.   The editor replies by referring to Toynbee's
    announcement of their recovery (1901.4).

4   WALPOLE, HORACE.   The Letters of Horace Walpole Fourth Earl of
    Orford.   Edited by Mrs. Paget Toynbee.   Oxford: Clarendon
    Press, vols. 1-4.
        The fullest edition of Walpole's letters until the defin-
    itive Yale Edition (1937.15), but marred by the bowdleriza-
    tion of passages "unfit for publication" and by many inaccu-
    racies in transcription.   The chronological ordering pro-
    vides a useful alternative to Yale's arrangement by corre-
    spondent.   Contains a bibliographical preface, Walpole's
    "Short Notes of my Life," and letters from 1732 to 1760.
    Continued: 1904.19, 1905.11, and, by Paget Toynbee, 1918.9,
    1925.19.

1904

1   BARRINGTON, MICHAEL.   "Some Aspects of Horace Walpole." Temple
    Bar 129 (February):155-63.
        Defends Walpole against Macaulay, praising the wit, ele-
    gance and grace of the letters.   His other works are origi-
    nal and ingenious, but much less significant.

2   BENNETT, EDWARD.   "Horace Walpole's Letters." English Illus-
    trated Magazine 31 (July):424-26.
        Walpole is "the author for all bored people," charming
    them with the brilliance and wit of his letters.   He is also
    "the most modern of all eighteenth century writers," with an
    outlook and preoccupations surprisingly close to those of

the present age: "we are almost cured of our melancholy by his analysis of his own world weariness."

3   [GARNETT, RICHARD.] "Mrs. Paget Toynbee's Edition of Walpole's Letters." Nation 78 (24 March):233-34; 79 (8 September): 201-3.
    Review of 1903.4. Emphasizes the originality of Walpole's writings, and compares him with the younger Pliny and Mme de Sévigné as one of three writers "who have gained great celebrity in the world of letters by familiar correspondence alone."

4   "Gray and Horace Walpole." Athenaeum, 5 March, p. 306.
    Summarizes four unpublished letters of the Quadruple Alliance. The Walpole letter is to Ashton, written on the Grand Tour and "chiefly concerned with gossip about the Conclave of Cardinals."

5   HAZLITT, WILLIAM. "Letters of Horace Walpole." In The Collected Works of William Hazlitt. Edited by A[lfred] R[ayney] Waller and Arnold Glover, introduction by W.E. Hensley. Vol. 10. London: J.M. Dent, pp. 159-72, 421-22.
    Reprint of 1818.2, with annotations.

6   "More Walpole." Academy and Literature 67 (16 July):46.
    Review of 1904.19. Discusses Walpole as an antiquary: his "lordly book-making and collecting supply a thousand pleasant passages in his letters."

7   PRIDEAUX, W[ILLIAM] F[RANCIS]. "Antiquary v. Antiquarian." Notes and Queries, 10th ser. 1 (23 April):325.
    Walpole and his age used the term "antiquary," not "antiquarian," as a substantive.

8   Review of The Letters of Horace Walpole, vols. 1-8. Athenaeum, 13 February, pp. 199-200; 25 June, pp. 807-8.
    Defends Walpole from charges of petulance, insincerity and inconsistency, emphasizing the warmth of his friendships and the good humour of his letters.

9   SECCOMBE, THOMAS. "Walpole's Letters." Speaker, 23 April, pp. 98-100.
    Review of 1903.4, treating Walpole's letters as the epitome of aristocratic literature. Regards Walpole as a great raconteur, but criticizes his lack of seriousness and feeling. Compares Walpole with other aristocratic writers such as Halifax, Chesterfield and Byron, for all of whom "the first law of life seems laughter."

10 STRACHEY, G[ILES] L[YTTON]. "Horace Walpole." Independent Review 2 (May):641-46.

Review article on 1903.4. Rejects Macaulay's portrait of
Walpole, which is rhetorically brilliant but shows not "the
remotest understanding of the subject." Regards Walpole as
superficial but affectionate and sincere, within the limits
of aristocratic propriety. Reprinted: 1933.7 and 1948.7.

11   "The Champagne of History." Academy and Literature 66 (2 Janu-
      ary):11.
          Review of 1903.4. Walpole "wrote to build up memoirs in
      the manner of Saint Simon." His letters display a "singular
      mind."

12   "The Letters of Horace Walpole." Edinburgh Review 199 (April):
      432-56.
          Review article on 1903.4 and 1902.11. Also draws atten-
      tion to Walpole's other writings, especially the Memoirs and
      Anecdotes of Painting. Finds the letters "essentially
      sincere," showing sympathy, understanding, and an "elemental
      human quality." Reprinted: 1904.13.

13   "The Letters of Horace Walpole." Living Age 242 (23 July):205-
      23.
          Reprint of 1904.12.

14   "The Oxford Horace Walpole." Saturday Review 97 (5 March):
      302-3; 98 (13 August):204-5.
          Review of 1903.4 and 1904.19. Compares the renown of
      Walpole's letters with those of Cicero, and admires his
      "astonishing combination of curiosity, seriousness and
      levity."

15   VINCENT, LEON H. "Walpole and Chesterfield." Methodist Review
      64 (July):597-613.
          Compares Walpole and Chesterfield as aristocratic writ-
      ers, both despising professional authors. Finds Historic
      Doubts and Otranto trivial, but the letters "incomparable."

16   WALPOLE, HORACE. Essay on Modern Gardening. Edited by L[ewis]
      Buddy, introduction by Alice Morse Earle. Canton, Pa.:
      Kirgate Press, 94 pp.
          Contains Walpole's essay and the Duc de Nivernois' French
      translation. An introduction discusses Walpole's high opin-
      ion of the translation and studies the essay's influence in
      England and France. Walpole exposed the "poor flimsy whim-
      sies of the formal garden of his day," and founded the
      "natural school" of gardening.

17   WALPOLE, HORACE. Horace Walpole's Letters. A Selection.
      Edited by Stuart J. Reid. Cassell's National Library.
      London: Cassell, 192 pp.
          An introduction claims that Walpole was the greatest

English letter writer. His correspondence combines literary criticism, political insight, gossip, and observations on society. His conduct, however, was often reprehensible: he was "a spoiled child of fortune."

18 WALPOLE, HORACE. Letters of Horace Walpole. Edited by C.B. Lucas. London: Simpkin, 849 pp.
    A lightly annotated selection of Walpole's letters, in which frequent omissions and alterations are made without indication. A sketchy introduction depicts Walpole as a curious and archaic figure, but "a characteristic product of his age."

19 WALPOLE, HORACE. The Letters of Horace Walpole Fourth Earl of Orford. Edited by Mrs. Paget Toynbee. Oxford: Clarendon Press, vols. 5-12.
    Continuation of 1903.4, with letters from 1760 to 1783.

20 "Walpole Re-edited." Independent 56 (16 June):1389-90.
    Review of 1903.4. Contends that Walpole's letters are "the most interesting and the most important in the English language." Regards Walpole as both a "privileged histori-ographer of the eighteenth century" and a commentator on the English character.

21 "Walpole's Letters." Spectator 92 (30 January):184-86.
    Review of 1903.4. Defends Walpole from Macaulay's censures and contends that his letters give "a most graphic and various picture" of his age. Regrets, however, the "dirt and coarseness which stain too many of Walpole's pages," of which the worst, fortunately, is omitted in Mrs. Toynbee's edition.

22 "Walpole's Letters." Times Literary Supplement, 8 January, pp. 1-2.
    Review article on 1903.4, contending that Walpole's letters are among the greatest in English. Finds several unattractive elements in Walpole's personality but believes that his malice was crucial to the fascination of his work, supplying "the salt and seasoning."

1905

1 BLEACKLEY, HORACE. "A New Light on the Douglas Cause." Notes and Queries, 10th ser. 4 (29 July):85-86.
    Confirms the accuracy of a passage in Walpole's Memoirs of George III, stating that the principal witness for the Douglas cause was subsequently convicted of perjury in a French court.

2   "Exit Horace Walpole." <u>Academy and Literature</u> 69 (16 Decem-
    ber):1310-11.
        Review of 1905.11, studying the letters of Walpole's old
    age. Considers his interest in aeronauts and aeronautics,
    his continuing dislike of Johnson and the Johnson circle,
    his relationship with Mary and Agnes Berry, and his comments
    on the growing size and congestion of London. Despite his
    age and illnesses, Walpole was still a perceptive observer
    of his times.

3   [GARNETT, RICHARD.] "Horace Walpole's Letters." <u>Nation</u> 80 (23
    March):231-33.
        Review of 1904.19. Discusses the letters written from
    1774 to 1783, "one of the most inglorious periods of English
    history," and defends Walpole from the charge of ill-treat-
    ing Chatterton.

4   MOYER, REED.   "The Letters of Gray, Walpole and Cowper."
    <u>Sewanee Review</u> 13 (July):367-71.
        Compares Gray, Walpole and Cowper as letter writers.
    Walpole's letters have the widest appeal, but are often
    concerned mainly with gossip and scandal. Their charm "is
    one for which the English language has no native turn."

5   PROTHERO, ROWLAND E.   "Horace Walpole and William Cowper."
    <u>Quarterly Review</u> 202 (January):35-60.
        Review article on 1903.4. Compares the respective merits
    of Walpole's and Cowper's letters, finding Walpole less sym-
    pathetic as a man but more brilliant as a stylist. Depicts
    Cowper as the master of the English school of letter writ-
    ing, whereas Walpole is the only English rival to the French
    school.

6   RELTON, FRANCIS H.   "Horace Walpole's Letters." <u>Notes and
    Queries</u>, 10th ser. 3 (20 May):386.
        Enquires about the apparent absence of a letter from Wal-
    pole to the Countess of Ailesbury from Toynbee's edition.

7   Review of <u>The Letters of Horace Walpole</u>, vols. 9-12. <u>Athenae-
    um</u>, 14 June, pp. 40-41.
        Admires the style, wit, and grace of the letters of Wal-
    pole's middle period.

8   SILLARD, P.A. "Horace Walpole." <u>Month</u> 106 (October):382-93.
        Concentrates on Walpole's humour, quoting and discussing
    many comical passages in his correspondence. Finds his oth-
    er works, such as <u>Otranto</u>, <u>Historic Doubts</u>, and the <u>Memoirs</u>,
    of much less value than his letters, which provide an
    "inexhaustible fund of entertainment." Walpole is unique in
    English literature, but his Epicurean philosophy resembles
    that of Montaigne; both writers are "delightful companions."

9   "The Letters of Horace Walpole." Academy and Literature 68 (4
     March):195-96.
          Treats Walpole as a valetudinarian and studies his gout.
     His letters are always brilliant, yet he is "everything but
     lovable."

10   "The Oxford Horace Walpole." Saturday Review 99 (18 February):
     208-9.
          Review of 1904.19. Emphasizes Walpole's close involve-
     ment with contemporary politics in the late 1770s and early
     1780s, despite his claims to be living in idle seclusion at
     Strawberry Hill.

11   WALPOLE, HORACE. The Letters of Horace Walpole Fourth Earl of
     Orford. Edited by Mrs. Paget Toynbee. Oxford: Clarendon
     Press, vols. 13-16.
          Continuation of 1904.19. Contains letters from 1783 to
     1797, an appendix of undated letters, addenda and corri-
     genda, genealogical tables, a list of correspondents with
     Walpole's letters to them arranged in chronological order,
     and separate indexes of persons, places, and subjects. The
     editor dissociates herself from errors in the indexes, pre-
     pared by other hands.

12   WALPOLE, HORACE. The Wisdom of Horace Walpole. Edited by
     L[ewis] B[uddy] III. Cambridge, Mass.: Kirgate Press, 41
     pp.
          Reprints Walpole's "Detached Thoughts" from his Works
     (1798.7), with a prefatory note. The thoughts are fragments
     but they show Walpole's "fine appreciation of human nature,"
     contradicting the common idea of Walpole as a dilettante.

13   Y. "Horace Walpole's Letters." Notes and Queries, 10th ser. 4
     (19 August):158.
          Replies to Relton (1905.6), pointing out that Toynbee's
     edition does include Walpole's letter to the Countess of
     Ailesbury under the date 8 June 1784.

                              1906

1   BOYNTON, H.W. "Walpole Letters, Old and New." Dial 40 (16
     May):320-22.
          Review of 1905.11. Finds Walpole more attractive in his
     old age than in his youth, as "gradually the mask of cyni-
     cism slips away from him." His letters, however, are all
     invaluable for a study of eighteenth-century life; their
     expurgation in the Toynbee edition is regrettable.

2   BRADFORD, GAMALIEL, JR. "The Letters of Horace Walpole."
     Atlantic Monthly 97 (March):350-58.

Review article on 1903.4, 1904.19, and 1905.11. Finds
Otranto of some interest because of its originality, but
Walpole's letters alone have kept his name alive. He was
completely immersed in his age: his letters are "nothing
but eighteenth century." Revised: 1932.1.

3   MORE, PAUL ELMER. "The Letters of Horace Walpole." In Shel-
burne Essays, 4th ser. New York: G.P. Putnam's Sons, pp.
254-83.
An eloquent review article on 1904.19, focusing on Walpole's portraiture of eighteenth-century society. Rebukes
critics of Walpole, such as Macaulay and Wordsworth: "this
apparent trifler has his own philosophy of life." Quotes
several passages from the letters to illustrate Walpole's
incisive and witty depictions of his contemporaries.

4   RELTON, FRANCIS H. "Horace Walpole's Letters." Notes and
Queries, 10th ser. 5 (17 February):133-34.
Enquires about the apparent absence of two letters from
Mrs. Toynbee's edition and corrects one of her annotations.

5   Review of The Letters of Horace Walpole, vols. 13-16. Athenaeum, 20 January, pp. 69-70.
Suggests that Walpole is "a little sweetened with old
age" in his later letters, and notes the importance of his
friendship with the Berrys.

6   S., A. "'Anecdotes of Polite Literature,' 1764." Notes and
Queries, 10th ser. 6 (15 September):201-3.
Rejects Halkett and Laing's attribution of the anonymous
Anecdotes of Polite Literature to Walpole.

7   SECCOMBE, THOMAS, and NICOLL, W. ROBERTSON. "Horace Walpole."
In The Bookman Illustrated History of English Literature.
Vol. 2. London: Hodder & Stoughton, pp. 295-96.
A brief survey of Walpole's life and writings. Walpole
himself was "rather selfish and mean," but his letters are
always fascinating and re-create a complete period of
English history. Of his other works, only the Memoirs are
comparable to the letters; Otranto and The Mysterious Mother
have a merely historical interest.

8   "The Complete Walpole." Saturday Review 101 (2 January):110-
11.
Review of 1905.11, discussing Walpole in his old age.
Notes that Walpole had to travel no longer: "it is the
world that goes to Strawberry."

9   WALPOLE, HORACE. The Castle of Otranto. In Classic Tales.
Introduction by C[harles] S[cott] Fearenside. The York
Library. London: George Bell, pp. 391-497.

An introduction criticizes <u>Otranto</u>'s wooden characterization, but claims that it "deserves the praise of being the outcome of a vision" beyond the everyday world.

10 Y. "Horace Walpole's Letters." <u>Notes and Queries</u>, 10th ser. 5 (3 March):173.
Replies to Relton (1906.4), pointing out that the two supposedly missing letters are in fact by Walpole's uncle, also named Horace Walpole.

1907

1 MERRITT, EDWARD PERCIVAL. <u>Horace Walpole: Printer</u>. Boston: Riverside Press, 67 pp.
Discusses the history of private presses in England, the establishment of Walpole's at Strawberry Hill, and his difficulties with his printers. Studies the most significant publications of Walpole's press and those in which he took a special interest. It is "the best eighteenth century private press both in its typographical work and in the character of its productions."

2 MERRITT, E[DWARD] P[ERCIVAL]. "The 'Strawberry Hill' Catalogue." <u>Notes and Queries</u>, 10th ser. 7 (15 June):461-62.
Corrects an error in Bates's account of the Strawberry Hill Sale Catalogues (1882.1), and adds a preliminary description of the various editions.

3 RUSSELL, F.A. "The 'Strawberry Hill' Catalogue." <u>Notes and Queries</u>, 10th ser. 7 (29 June):517.
Responds to Merritt (1907.1), drawing attention to a copy of the 1842 Strawberry Hill Catalogue currently on sale.

4 WALPOLE, HORACE. <u>The Castle of Otranto</u>. Preface by Caroline [F.E.] Spurgeon, introduction by Sir Walter Scott. The King's Classics. London: Chatto & Windus, 136 pp.
Spurgeon's preface contends that <u>Otranto</u> cannot now be taken seriously, yet this "crude story" played a seminal role in the romantic revival. Walpole's interests in antiquarianism, Gothic architecture and the Gothic tale of chivalry are all characteristic of the romantic movement. <u>Otranto</u> contains three commonplaces of romantic literature: the Gothic castle, the accompanying climatic conditions, and the Byronic hero. Scott's introduction to <u>Otranto</u> (1811.5) is also reprinted.

1908

1 H., S.F. "Walpole and the Duchess of Devonshire." <u>Notes and</u>

Queries, 10th ser. 9 (6 June):449.
Enquires about the whereabouts of a manuscript stanza by
Walpole on the Duchess of Devonshire.

2   NOBLE, PERCY.   Anne Seymour Damer: A Woman of Art and
Fashion. London: Kegan Paul, 220 pp.
Discusses Walpole's relations with Mrs. Damer throughout,
blandly eliminating any tensions. Describes her as "irre-
proachable in moral character," ignoring her strong amorous
interest in Mary Berry.

3   WALPOLE, HORACE.   Earlier Letters.   Edited by A[rthur] T.
Quiller-Couch. Select English Classics. Oxford: Clarendon
Press, 48 pp.
Extracts from letters by Walpole on six major topics,
including the Rebellion of 1745, the earthquake of 1750, and
the death of George II. A brief introduction outlines Walpole's life, emphasizing the superiority of his letters to
his other writings.

4   WALPOLE, HORACE.   Letters on the American War of Independence.
Edited by W[illiam] H[enry] D[enham] Rouse.   London:
Blackie & Son, 125 pp.
Prints Walpole's letters on the American Revolution with
a glossary and brief notes, using the text of Mrs. Toynbee's
edition. A brief introduction surveys Walpole's life, stating that his letters "contain a vast deal of information on
the events of the time."

1909

1   ABRAHAMS, ALECK.   "The 'Strawberry Hill' Catalogue."   Notes and
Queries, 10th ser. 12 (11 September):216-17.
Corrects and expands Merritt (1907.1), supplying further
details about the 1842 Sale Catalogue.

2   ABRAHAMS, ALECK.   "The 'Strawberry Hill' Catalogue."   Notes and
Queries, 10th ser. 12 (18 December):491-92.
Replies to Merritt (1909.6), acknowledging some errors in
his own note (1909.1) and adding further information on the
Sale Catalogue and on Walpole's Description of the Villa.

3   BENJAMIN, LEWIS SAUL [Lewis Melville].   "Walpole's Last Journals." Bookman, November, pp. 95-96.
Review of 1910.7. Discusses Walpole's treatment of the
American War of Independence and believes that he was "un-
necessarily depreciatory of his journal," which is informative and important.

4   CURIOUS.   "The   'Strawberry   Hill'   Catalogue."   Notes   and

<u>Queries</u>, 10th ser. 12 (18 December):492.
Enquires about the locations of copies of Walpole's <u>Aedes Walpolianae</u> (1747).

5 FAIRFAX, J.G. "Horace Walpole's Views on Literature." In <u>Eighteenth Century Literature: An Oxford Miscellany</u>. Oxford: Clarendon Press, pp. 103-26.
A vigorous defence of Walpole against Macaulay, using his comments on literature as evidence of his good judgment and taste. When Walpole's views seem extraordinary, they can be attributed to the prejudices of his age. Provides numerous unidentified quotations from Walpole's letters to illustrate his opinions of literature, ancient and modern. His criticism, "if it cannot always inform, will never cease to delight."

6 MERRITT, E[DWARD] P[ERCIVAL]. "The 'Strawberry Hill' Catalogue." <u>Notes and Queries</u>, 10th ser. 12 (27 November): 430-32.
Replies to Abrahams and Roberts (1909.1, 10), expanding his own comments in 1907.1.

7 PEARSON, NORMAN. "Some Neglected Aspects of Horace Walpole." <u>Fortnightly Review</u> 92 (1 September):482-94.
Rejects Macaulay's portrait of Walpole, suggesting that Walpole's self-depiction as a "brilliant trifler" has had a misleading influence. His letters and memoirs are "valuable historical works," while <u>Otranto</u> and Strawberry Hill began new trends in fiction and architecture. He expressed strong opinions on such subjects as animal rights, warfare, slavery, religion, republicanism, and superstitions of all kinds; only in his political machinations is he seen in a bad light. He was honest, often loveable, and "almost great." Revised: 1911.6.

8 RAPHAEL, HERBERT H. <u>Horace Walpole. A Descriptive Catalogue of the Artistic and Literary Illustrations Collected by Herbert H. Raphael . . . for the Extension of the Original Edition of Walpole's Letters into Eighteen Folio Volumes.</u> Bristol: Edward Everard, 659 pp.
Lists, in alphabetical order, a large number of prints owned by Raphael that could be used to extra-illustrate Walpole's letters. Each print is described and indexed to the appropriate volume of Cunningham's edition (1857.7). A brief introduction states that Walpole's letters were selected for the project because they mention almost everyone of note from 1735, when they began, until Walpole's death in 1797.

*9 RIGGS, BLANCHE. "The Place of Horace Walpole in the Gothic Revival." Ph.D. dissertation, University of Chicago.

Source: Lévy (1968.11), p. 677.

10   ROBERTS, W. "The 'Strawberry Hill' Catalogue." Notes and Queries, 10th ser. 12 (9 October):294-95; (30 October):353.

Mentions the withdrawal and recataloguing of the works in the Strawberry Hill Sale, citing the "Names of Purchasers and the Prices" as his authority.

1910

1   DOBSON, AUSTIN. Horace Walpole: A Memoir. With an Appendix of Books Printed at the Strawberry Hill Press. 3d ed. London: Harper, 328 pp.

Slightly revised edition of 1893.1.

2   INGRAM, JOHN H. "A Patron Wanted," and "Walpole." In The True Chatterton. A New Study from Original Documents. London: T. Fisher Unwin, pp. 157-78, 305-7.

Condemns Walpole for his "cowardly, mean, untruthful attack" on Chatterton's reputation after his death. Believes that Walpole "hated men of genius" and regards his letter to Rousseau from the King of Prussia as one of his many "despicable crimes."

3   MERRITT, E[DWARD] P[ERCIVAL]. "Strawberry Hill Catalogue: 'Aedes Walpolianae.'" Notes and Queries, 11th ser. 1 (12 March):214-15.

Provides further information on the 1842 Sale Catalogues and on Walpole's Description of the Villa.

4   STRAUSS, RALPH. "Dodsley, Gray and Horace Walpole." In Robert Dodsley: Poet, Publisher & Playwright. London: John Lane, pp. 153-68.

Studies Walpole's and Gray's dealings with Dodsley over the publication of Gray's poems, noting that Walpole was "genuinely attached" to Dodsley.

5   TUPPER, JAMES W. Review of The Last Journals of Horace Walpole. Sewanee Review 18 (January):113-16.

Regards Walpole as representative of his time: "to understand him is to understand the age." His journal shows him as an astute commentator on events, but his judgments of his contemporaries are superficial.

6   W., L.A. "Strawberry Hill Catalogue: 'Aedes Walpolianae.'" Notes and Queries, 11th ser. 1 (8 January):34.

Informs Curious (1909.4) that Aedes Walpolianae is "easily to be found" in any public library.

7   WALPOLE, HORACE. The Last Journals of Horace Walpole during

the Reign of George III from 1771-1783. Edited by A. Francis Steuart. London: Bodley Head, 2 vols.

Reproduces the corrupt text of Doran's edition (1859.10), correcting some misprints while adding new ones. Contains annotations based on Doran's, with corrections, deletions, and additions. An introduction dwells inordinately on the marriage of Walpole's niece, Maria Walpole, to the Duke of Gloucester, while admitting that the journal also contains "invaluable comments on Parliamentary debates, foreign news, and court gossip."

1911

1   BECKER, CARL. "Horace Walpole's Memoirs of the Reign of George the Third." American Historical Review 16 (January):255-72; (April):496-507.

A detailed study of Walpole's Memoirs, questioning "to what extent are they contemporaneous with the events they chronicle." Shows that Memoirs was revised after its original completion in 1772, with several insertions made in 1784 expressing theories about the reign of George III that Walpole developed only after the outbreak of the American War in 1775. These insertions are generally "interpretative, discursive, speculative in nature." In his revisions of the Memoirs Walpole changed his attitude not only to George III but also towards "the function of the historian, and towards his own Memoirs and the function they might serve."

2   COURTNEY, WILLIAM PRIDEAUX. "Walpole, Horatio." In Encyclopaedia Britannica, 11th ed. Vol. 28. New York: Encyclopaedia Britannica, pp. 288-90.

A biographical and critical sketch. Walpole's letters are "the crowning glory of his life," but his Memoirs, Anecdotes of Painting, Historic Doubts and Catalogue of Royal and Noble Authors are also of interest. Otranto and The Mysterious Mother, however, are "now all but forgotten."

3   MERRITT, E[DWARD] P[ERCIVAL]. "Strawberry Hill: 'Description of the Villa,' 1774." Notes and Queries, 11th ser. 4 (9 September):207.

Enquires about the location of an edition of Walpole's Description of the Villa used by Walpole's servants in showing the house.

4   MOBIUS, H[ANS]. "H. Walpole. The Castle of Otranto." In Die englischen Rosenkreuzerromane und ihre Vorläufer. Eine Studie über die Entwicklung der phantastisch-romantischen Erzählungsart in England während des 18. und 19. Jahrhunderts. Hamburg: Lütcke & Wulff, pp. 5-10.

In German. Otranto is not a successful work of litera-

ture, and comes close to being ridiculous. Walpole did,
however, create a new kind of novel and found a new school
of writing: Otranto has an important place in literary
history.

5   NORTHRUP, CLARK S.   "A Critique of Horace Walpole."   Modern
    Language Review 6 (July):387-89.
        Correcting Mrs. Toynbee (1905.11), notes that Walpole, in
    a letter to Mason of 22 March 1796, attacks a poem by
    Richard Payne Knight entitled The Progress of Civil Society
    (1796), which contains hostile references to Gray.

6   PEARSON, NORMAN.   "The Serious Side of a Worldly Man."   In
    Society Sketches in the Eighteenth Century.   London:
    Edward Arnold, pp. 191-209.
        Revision of 1909.7.

7   PRIDEAUX, W[ILLIAM] F[RANCIS].   "Strawberry Hill: 'Description
    of the Villa,' 1774."   Notes and Queries, 11th ser. 4 (23
    September):251-52.
        Replies to Merritt (1911.3) with some information on Wal-
    pole's Description of the Villa.

8   RICHTER, HELENE.   "Horace Walpole."   In Gesichte der englischen
    Romantik. Vol. 1. Halle: Max Niemeyer, pp. 172-91.
        In German.   Surveys Walpole's life and writings and
    studies the influence of Otranto, which combines romance and
    realism in a masterly fashion.   Walpole's other works, how-
    ever, are largely superficial: he had many interests but
    was always a dilettante.

                              1912

1   AYNARD, JOSEPH.   "Horace Walpole et Madame du Deffand."   Jour-
    nal des débats, 30 November, feuilleton.
        Criticizes Walpole for the selfishness of his attitude
    towards Mme du Deffand, whom he regarded primarily as a
    means of enlarging his own fame. Analyzes the qualities in
    Walpole that made him attractive to the Marquise.

2   du DEFFAND, MARQUISE. Lettres de la Marquise du Deffand à Hor-
    ace Walpole (1766-1780).   Edited by Mrs. Paget Toynbee.
    Preface by Paget Toynbee. London: Methuen, 3 vols.
        An extensive introduction discusses the previous editions
    of Mme du Deffand's letters, the finding of new letters, and
    Walpole's relationship with the Marquise.   Considers Wal-
    pole's popularity in France, his increasing conservatism,
    and his conflicting emotions for Mme du Deffand. The intro-
    duction, preface, and annotations are in French.

3 "Madame du Deffand and Horace Walpole." <u>Times Literary Supplement</u>, 21 November, pp. 521–22.
Review of 1912.2. Explains Mme du Deffand's fascination with Walpole by noting that her salon lacked a distinguished man. Sees Walpole as "the typical dilettante of his period" and feels more sympathy for the Marquise, the pursuer in their relationship, than for Walpole, the pursued.

4 STILLWELL, MARGARET B. "Horace Walpole: Printer and Gallant." <u>Brown Alumni Weekly</u>, December, pp. 123–26.
Surveys Walpole's life and writings, concentrating on his activities at Strawberry Hill. Discusses some of the major productions of the press and notes that John Baskerville considered employment there, before the arrival of Thomas Kirgate.

5 STROWSKI, FORTUNAT. "Madame du Deffand et Horace Walpole." <u>Correspondent</u> 249 (10 December):887–902.
Review article on 1912.2. Contends that Walpole's prohibition on Mme du Deffand's expressions of emotion had an inhibiting effect on her epistolary style. Regards Walpole as cruel, and undeserving of her friendship.

1913

1 BELLOC-LOWNDES, MARIE. "Madame du Deffand and Horace Walpole." <u>Quarterly Review</u> 218 (April):513–31.
Review article on 1912.2. Analyzes Walpole's relationship with Mme du Deffand, censuring his fear of ridicule and his aloofness.

2 BETTANY, F.G. "Horace Walpole's World." <u>Bookman</u> 44 (August): 214–15.
Review of 1913.6. Walpole's letters contain a "veritable mine of information," but his affectation becomes tiresome. He is "excellent enough company for short spells of time."

*3 CHURCH, ELIZABETH. "Walpole and <u>Otranto</u>." In "The Gothic Romance: Its Origin and Development." Ph.D. dissertation, Harvard University.
Summarized by McNutt (1975.7): "devotes over 80 percent of its space to biography and Strawberry Hill. Says [Walpole] had no literary source for <u>Otranto</u>" (p. 81).

4 DAVRAY, HENRY-D. "Lettres anglaises." <u>Mercure de France</u> 102 (16 March):431–34.
Review of 1912.2. Studies the publication history of Walpole's correspondence with Mme du Deffand in the nineteenth century, commenting on the various editions. Finds Walpole a timorous correspondent, afflicted with a strange

fear of ridicule, but his letters in French, despite their
stylistic errors, possess the charm and spirit of his
letters in English.

5   EDGE, J.H. Horace Walpole, the Great Letter Writer: Samuel
     Johnson, the Great Talker. Dublin: privately printed, 62
     pp.
         "Full justice" has never been done to Walpole as a man or
     as a writer. Compares the lives and writings of Walpole and
     Johnson, criticizing Otranto as a "feeble attempt at a tale
     of the Middle Ages." Finds Walpole's letters and journals
     invaluable, however, and rejects Macaulay's unflattering
     portrait.

6   GREENWOOD, ALICE DRAYTON. Horace Walpole's World: A Sketch of
     Whig Society Under George III. London: G. Bell, 257 pp.
         Chapter one is an uncritical portrait of Walpole, empha-
     sizing his fondness for children, dogs and servants, and
     glossing over his shortcomings. Two subsequent chapters
     discuss his writings, primarily the letters, and his col-
     lecting. The remainder of the work depicts English society
     as seen by Walpole.

7   HODGSON, F[RANCIS] C[OTTERELL]. "Horace Walpole." In Thames-
     Side in the Past: Sketches of its Literature & Society.
     London: George Allen, pp. 146-83.
         Revision of 1899.7.

8   "Horace Walpole." Spectator 111 (12 July):62.
         Review of 1913.6. Praises Walpole highly: he is the
     finest English letter writer, one of the most important
     English authors, and "the best guide to the history and
     society of the eighteenth century."

9   SEGUR, MARQUIS de. "Madame du Deffand et Horace Walpole." In
     Vieux dossiers, petits papiers. Paris: Calmann-Lévy, pp.
     1-42.
         Reprint of 1913.10.

10   SEGUR, [MARQUIS de]. "Madame du Deffand et Horace Walpole."
     Revue hebdomadaire 22 (January):301-27.
         Review article on 1912.2. Tells the story of Walpole's
     relationship with Mme du Deffand, reproaching him for a
     self-control and frigidity that does little honour to the
     male sex. Reprinted: 1913.9.

11   STRACHEY, [GILES] LYTTON. "Madame du Deffand." Edinburgh
     Review 217 (January):61-80.
         Review article on 1912.2. Deplores Walpole's treatment
     of Mme du Deffand, analyzes the attractions he held for her,
     and suggests that midway through their correspondence her

"indomitable spirit was broken." Reprinted: 1922.5, 1948.7.

12 TOYNBEE, PAGET. "Unpublished Letters of Horace Walpole." *Times* (London), 25 August, p. 8.

Prints two unpublished letters by Walpole, one to James Bindley and one to an unidentified correspondent, with brief commentaries.

13 WALPOLE, HORACE. Letters on France and the French Revolution. Edited by W[illiam] H[enry] D[enham] Rouse. London: Blackie & Son, 127 pp.

A companion volume to 1908.4, with a brief introduction, notes, and glossary. The text is based on Mrs. Toynbee's.

14 WHEATLEY, HENRY B. "Letter Writers I: Horace Walpole." In The Cambridge History of English Literature. Edited by A[dolphus] W[illiam] Ward and A[lfred] R[ayney] Waller. Vol. 10, The Age of Johnson. Cambridge: Cambridge University Press, pp. 242-55.

Rejects Macaulay's view of Walpole, regarding him instead as the greatest of English letter writers. Finds his other works insignificant, and regrets that Anecdotes of Painting has prevented the publication of a more trustworthy history of English painting.

1914

1 BENJAMIN, LEWIS SAUL [Lewis Melville], ed. The Berry Papers. Being the Correspondence Hitherto Unpublished of Mary and Agnes Berry (1763-1852). London: John Lane, 448 pp.

Discusses Walpole's relations with the Berrys and Mrs. Damer throughout, with copious extracts from the Berrys' correspondence. Emphasizes Walpole's close friendship with the sisters, denying that he was in love with either one.

2 CLARK, RUTH. "Horace Walpole and Mariette." Modern Language Review 9 (October):520-23.

Studies an unpublished translation of Walpole's Anecdotes of Painting by Pierre Jean Mariette, a collector and friend of Mme du Deffand, an unpublished letter from Walpole to Mariette, and an anonymous manuscript translation of Walpole's Historic Doubts.

3 "Gray and Walpole. Discovery of Unpublished Letters." *Times* (London), 6 March, p. 9.

Announces Paget Toynbee's discovery of more than one hundred letters from Gray to Walpole and of various letters by Walpole. Summarizes the collection and prints some extracts, with commentary.

4   MORNET, D. Review of <u>Lettres de la Marquise du Deffand à Hor-
     ace Walpole (1766-1780)</u>. <u>Revue d'histoire littéraire de la
     France</u> 21:207-8.
          Discusses the tensions in Walpole's relationship with Mme
     du Deffand, without apportioning blame. Regards their
     friendship as a tragi-comedy, made inevitable by their
     utterly different temperaments.

5   TOYNBEE, PAGET. "Gray and Walpole. The Pseudonym 'Celadon.'"
     <u>Times</u> (London), 9 March, p. 9.
          Identifies an ode signed "Celadon," printed in Gosse's
     edition as a doubtful poem of Gray's, as one by Walpole,
     addressed to Richard West in a letter of 3 December 1736.

6   TOYNBEE, PAGET. "Gray and Walpole. An Unfounded Inference."
     <u>Times</u> (London), 23 March, p. 9.
          Rejects Tovey's theory (1890.17) that Gray slighted Wal-
     pole shortly after their reconciliation. The assumption
     rests on a letter, supposedly from Walpole to Gray, shown
     here to be from Walpole to Pinkerton and written not in the
     1740s but in 1784.

7   TOYNBEE, PAGET. "Horace Walpole and 'Mrs. G.' Suggested Solu-
     tion of an Enigma." <u>Times</u> (London), 13 April, p. 9.
          Suggests that a "Mrs. G." mentioned in Walpole's early
     correspondence was not, as had previously been supposed, the
     mother of Thomas Gray, but a Mrs. Gravener or Grosvenor who
     was a companion, housekeeper or nurse in Lady Walpole's
     household.

8   TOYNBEE, PAGET. "Rowwaggon." <u>Times Literary Supplement</u>, 30
     July, p. 369.
          Enquires about the meaning of the term "rowwaggon," used
     by Walpole in a letter to Lady Ailesbury.

9   TOYNBEE, PAGET. "Rowwaggon." <u>Times Literary Supplement</u>, 15
     October, p. 460.
          Answers his own query (1914.8): "rowwaggon" is a corrup-
     tion of "roll-waggon," a "low-wheeled vehicle for conveying
     goods."

10   WALPOLE, HORACE. <u>Select Letters of Horace Walpole</u>. Edited by
     Alice D[rayton] Greenwood. Bohn's Popular Library. London:
     H.G. Bohn, 385 pp.
          A selection of Walpole's letters, with brief annotations
     and an extremely inaccurate introduction. Attempts to study
     Walpole's friendships, but is ill-informed about the char-
     acters concerned.

1915

1   CLARK, RUTH. "Walpole and the 'Mémoires de Grammont.'" <u>Modern</u>
    <u>Language Review</u> 10 (January):58-63.
        Studies Walpole's "infinite admiration" for Hamilton's
    <u>Mémoires de Grammont</u>, and discusses the Strawberry Hill
    edition of 1772.

2   "Horace Walpole and his Friends." <u>Nation</u> 18 (24 December):
    482-86.
        Review of 1915.9. Surveys Walpole's relationships with
    the other members of the Quadruple Alliance, concentrating
    on Gray. Praises Walpole's letters highly, but feels that
    he is not at his best in his correspondence with Gray.

3   KILLEN, ALICE M. "Les pionniers: Horace Walpole et Clara
    Reeve." In <u>Le roman "terrifiant" ou roman "noir" de Walpole</u>
    <u>à Anne Radcliffe et son influence sur la littérature fran-</u>
    <u>çaise jusqu'en 1840</u>. Paris: Georges Crès, pp. 9-23.
        Regards Walpole as the founder of the <u>roman noir</u> and
    studies the influence of <u>Otranto</u> on subsequent writers, de-
    spite its exaggerations and despite Walpole's lack of knowl-
    edge of the Middle Ages. Revised: 1923.2.

4   MERRITT, [EDWARD] PERCIVAL. <u>An Account of Descriptive Cata-</u>
    <u>logues of Strawberry Hill and of Strawberry Hill Sale Cata-</u>
    <u>logues Together With a Bibliography</u>. Boston: privately
    printed, 72 pp.
        Still the fullest study of the Strawberry Hill Sale Cata-
    logues of 1842. Includes a discussion of Walpole's <u>Descrip-</u>
    <u>tion of the Villa</u> and of the 1842 sale, and a detailed de-
    scription of the various catalogues issued by Robins.

5   PATERNA, WILHELM AD. "Horace Walpole." In <u>Das Ubersinnliche</u>
    <u>im englischen Roman. (Von Horace Walpole bis Walter Scott.)</u>
    Hamburg: Berngruber & Hennig, pp. 19-31.
        In German. Criticizes the frequent absurdity of <u>Otranto</u>,
    but believes that it improves towards the end. Praises Wal-
    pole's effective use of the castle background and his abili-
    ty to keep the reader in suspense. Walpole does not succeed
    entirely in combining the various elements of the super-
    natural, yet on balance <u>Otranto</u> is a fine novel.

6   TINKER, CHAUNCEY BREWSTER. "Walpole and Familiar Correspon-
    dence." <u>Yale Review</u>, n.s. 4 (April):578-89.
        An elegant essay on the familiar letter as a literary
    genre. Regards Walpole's love of gossip as the key to his
    success as a letter writer, and contends that his prose
    style prefigures that of the Romantics. Revised: 1915.7.

7   TINKER, CHAUNCEY BREWSTER. "Walpole and the Art of Familiar

Correspondence." In <u>The Salon and English Letters</u>. New York: Macmillan, pp. 236-53.
Revision of 1915.6.

8   TOYNBEE, PAGET. "A Misprint in Gray." <u>Times Literary Supplement</u>, 22 April, p. 135.
Quotes a letter from Gray to Walpole of 10 August 1757, pointing out two misprints in the Strawberry Hill "Odes by Mr. Gray."

9   TOYNBEE, PAGET, ed. <u>The Correspondence of Gray, Walpole, West and Ashton (1734-1771)</u>. Oxford: Oxford University Press, 2 vols.
Prints all the letters known to Toynbee exchanged among the Quadruple Alliance, with brief annotations. An extensive introduction studies the lives and interconnections of the four correspondents, and a useful chronological table lists important dates for their lives and works, from the births of Gray, West and Ashton (1716) to the death of Walpole (1797).

1916

1   BLEACKLEY, HORACE. "Mrs. Quon." <u>Notes and Queries</u>, 12th ser. 1 (1 April):272-73.
Replies to Q.N. (1858.9), identifying Mrs. Quon as an actress who gained her fame through playing the part of Desdemona.

2   SQUIRE, JOHN C. [Solomon Eagle]. "Books in General." <u>New Statesman</u> 6 (8 January):329.
Review of 1915.9. Walpole's letters are "unsurpassable of their kind," but Gray's are more natural. Reprinted: 1918.6.

3   "The New Letters of Gray and Walpole." <u>Spectator</u> 116 (22 April):528-29.
Review of 1915.9. Both Gray's and Walpole's letters "have a perennial charm," and are written with "the lightest of touches."

4   TOYNBEE, PAGET. "Horace Walpole's Alleged Use of 'N.E.' for 'N.S.'" <u>Times Literary Supplement</u>, 6 July, p. 321.
Walpole did not, as had previously been supposed, write "N.E." ("New Era") in dating a letter to Ashton; he wrote the orthodox "N.S." ("New Style").

1917

1 "Horace Walpole." <u>Times Literary Supplement</u>, 4 October, pp. 469-70.

A bicentenary essay, emphasizing Walpole's versatility but regarding his correspondence as paramount: "his Letters have a hundred readers for one that reads 'The Castle of Otranto.'" Because of the letters we know Walpole better than any other eighteenth-century figure, apart from Boswell and Johnson. Believes that Mrs. Toynbee's edition (1903.4) is "final and complete."

2 TOYNBEE, PAGET. "Horace Walpole." <u>Times Literary Supplement</u>, 11 October, p. 491.

Responds to 1917.1, pointing out that Mrs. Toynbee's edition is not, in fact, complete, and announcing his own forthcoming supplementary volumes (1918.9). Observes that Walpole wrote his earliest surviving letter at eight, not fifteen, and that the suppression of indecorous passages in his letters was performed not by Walpole himself but by his editors.

1918

1 GOAD, CAROLINE. "The Letter-Writers: Lord Chesterfield and Horace Walpole," and "Horace Walpole's Letters." In <u>Horace and the English Literature of the Eighteenth Century</u>. New Haven: Yale University Press, pp. 271-89, 605-20.

Although Walpole dreaded pedantry, he expresses an admiration for Horace throughout his letters and was fond of playing on the name. Several of his pet phrases have their origin in Horace, and many of his letters contain Horatian quotations or allusions. An appendix lists all such allusions found in Walpole's letters.

2 GOSSE, EDMUND. "The Text of Gray's Poems." <u>Times Literary Supplement</u>, 23 May, p. 245.

An ode, "Seeds of Poetry and Rhime," dated December 1736, signed in Gray's hand "Celadon" and previously attributed to Gray, was in fact by Walpole.

3 LESSER, ERNEST. "Louis XVI and Horace Walpole." <u>Times Literary Supplement</u>, 26 December, p. 657.

Enquires about the authenticity of the translation of <u>Historic Doubts</u>, supposedly by Louis XVI, published in Paris (1800.5).

4 NICHOLSON, F.L. "Walpole and Aeronautics." <u>Times Literary Supplement</u>, 9 May, p. 221.

Quotes a letter from Walpole to Seymour Conway on ballooning, declaring that Walpole's "fooleries" have become almost the "commonplaces" of the war of 1914.

5   SPURGEON, C[AROLINE] F.E.   "The Charm of Walpole's Letters." *Transactions of the Royal Society of Literature*, 2d ser. 36:137-59.
      Locates the charm of Walpole's letters in their constant variety, astuteness, and combination of wit and gravity. Believes that Walpole was not merely a trifler: "his wisdom, courage, and sincerity stand out repeatedly."

6   SQUIRE, JOHN C.   [Solomon Eagle].   "Gray and Walpole."   In *Books in General*. 1st ser. London: Heinemann, pp. 143-49.
      Reprint of 1916.2.

7   THOMSON, SHERIFF A.S.D.   "Horace Walpole's Letters."   *Proceedings of the Royal Philosophical Society of Glasgow* 49 (1917-18):157-77.
      Compares Walpole with Evelyn and Pepys. Illustrates his views on various subjects by undocumented selections from his letters, which are "undoubtedly a classic" and which characterize his age. Walpole was not a man of action but a fastidious aristocrat and an accomplished scholar.

8   TOYNBEE, PAGET.   "The Text of Gray's Poems."   *Times Literary Supplement*, 6 June, p. 264.
      The attribution to Walpole made by Gosse (1918.2) had already been made by Toynbee (1914.5).

9   WALPOLE, HORACE.   *Supplement to the Letters of Horace Walpole Fourth Earl of Orford*.   Edited by Paget Toynbee.   Oxford: Clarendon Press, 2 vols.
      Supplements Mrs. Toynbee's edition (1903.4) with new letters, additions and corrections to her text and notes, a list of missing letters, a supplementary list of correspondents, and indexes of persons, places, and subjects.

10   WEAD, MARY EUNICE.   "Horace Walpole and the Strawberry Hill Press."   *Printing Art* 32 (September):17-24.
      Describes the productions of the Strawberry Hill Press and evaluates its significance. Considers its influence on subsequent private presses, such as Lee Priory, and believes that it throws much light on Walpole's taste and character.

1919

1   BEATTY, H.M.   "Louis XVI and Horace Walpole."   *Times Literary Supplement*, 30 January, p. 57.
      Not, despite the title, on Louis XVI and Walpole, but on Louis XVI as translator of Gibbon.

2   BETTANY, LEWIS. "Letters from Horace Walpole (Earl of Orford) (1717-1797)." In <u>Edward Jerningham and his Friends</u>. London: Chatto & Windus, pp. 44-51.
Prints eight letters from Walpole to Jerningham, with useful annotations.

3   ELGAR, EDWARD. "Gray, Walpole, West and Ashton - The Quadruple Alliance." <u>Times Literary Supplement</u>, 4 September, p. 473.
Suggests that Walpole's designation as "Celadon" in the Quadruple Alliance at Eton derived not from an amorous shepherd but from a courtier in Dryden's <u>Secret Love</u>.

4   LESSER, ERNEST. "Louis XVI and Horace Walpole." <u>Times Literary Supplement</u>, 9 January, p. 21.
Replies to Toynbee (1919.9), giving some reasons for accepting Louis XVI's authorship of the French translation of <u>Historic Doubts</u>.

5   LYND, ROBERT. "Horace Walpole." <u>London Mercury</u> 1 (November): 52-61.
Review article on 1918.9. Finds Walpole's formal works insignificant, but his letters "the greatest work of their kind." Admires Walpole's charm and wit.

6   STRACHEY, [GILES] LYTTON. "Some New Letters of Horace Walpole." <u>Living Age</u> 302 (27 September):788-91.
Reprint of 1919.8.

7   STRACHEY, [GILES] LYTTON. "Suppressed Passages in Walpole's Letters." <u>Athenaeum</u>, 5 September, p. 853.
Replies to Toynbee (1919.11), insisting that neither Walpole's letters nor Rousseau's <u>Confessions</u> should be bowdlerized.

8   STRACHEY, [GILES] LYTTON. "Walpole's Letters." <u>Athenaeum</u>, 15 August, pp. 744-45.
Review of 1918.9. Analyzes the qualities that make Walpole the most important English letter writer, regarding his achievement as "greater than the man." Emphasizes the feminine quality found in other great letter writers. Reprinted: 1919.6, 1933.7, 1948.7.

9   TOYNBEE, PAGET. "Louis XVI. and Horace Walpole." <u>Times Literary Supplement</u>, 2 January, p. 9.
Replies to Lesser (1918.3). Doubts that the translation is by Louis XVI, arguing that had the editor possessed the original manuscript, as he claimed, he would have published a facsimile. If the translation were by Louis XVI, Walpole would have heard of it and "would have left some record of the fact."

10   TOYNBEE, PAGET. "Louis XVI. and Horace Walpole." <u>Times Liter-</u>
     <u>ary Supplement</u>, 23 January, p. 44.
          Casts further doubts on the authenticity of Louis XVI's
     authorship of the translation of <u>Historic Doubts</u> (1800.5).

11   TOYNBEE, PAGET.   "Suppressed Passages in Horace Walpole's
     Letters." <u>Athenaeum</u>, 29 August, p. 823.
          Replies to Strachey (1919.8), defending his own and Mrs.
     Toynbee's bowdlerization of Walpole in their edition of the
     letters. Compares the deleted passages to the "grossest of
     the avowals" in Rousseau's <u>Confessions</u>.

12   WHITLEY, WILLIAM T. "Horace Walpole." <u>Times Literary Supple-</u>
     <u>ment</u>, August 14, p. 437.
          Quotes an advertisement of November 22-24 1753, in which
     Walpole posts a reward of fifty pounds for information on
     the robbers of his goldfish pond. The culprits were subse-
     quently found to be herons.

13   [WOOLF, VIRGINIA.] "Horace Walpole." <u>Times Literary Supple-</u>
     <u>ment</u>, 31 July, p. 411.
          Review article on 1918.9. An elegant character study,
     emphasizing Walpole's mastery of English prose, the accuracy
     of his observations, and the attractiveness of his personal-
     ity. Reprinted: 1958.4 and 1966.14.

                                1920

1   ANTROBUS, R.L. "The Text of Walpole's Letters." <u>Times Liter-</u>
     <u>ary Supplement</u>, 24 June, p. 403.
          Provides more information on Lady John Sackville, dis-
     cussed by Sackville and Sargeaunt (1920.8-10).

2   FINCH, M.B., and PEERS, E. ALLINSON. "Walpole's Relations with
     Voltaire." <u>Modern Philology</u> 18 (August):15-24.
          A detailed, careful study of Walpole's dealings with Vol-
     taire. Discusses their disagreement over the greatness of
     Shakespeare and the intermediary role of Mme du Deffand,
     concluding that despite Voltaire's much greater status
     "their motives and their methods of controversy are amusing-
     ly similar and equally questionable."

*3   DRAPER, JOHN W. "The Life and Works of William Mason." Ph.D.
     dissertation, Harvard University.
          Revised for publication: 1924.3.

4   GWYNN, STEPHEN. "Memories and a Market Garden." <u>Englishwoman</u>
     48 (October):16-24; (November):98-105.
          A rambling, affectionate essay, primarily concerned with
     Walpole's (and the author's) dogs and with Walpole's picture
     of a society in time of war. Revised: 1921.2.

                                116

5   LYND, ROBERT. "Horace Walpole." In The Art of Letters. London: T. Fisher Unwin, pp. 49–64.

      Depicts Walpole as a "dainty rogue," whose first instinct was to disparage. Discusses his sharp comments on many of his contemporaries and some of his various interests. Believes that he always shrank from public life and that he took himself lightly as a writer, "doing little things in a little age."

6   ROBERTSON, W[ALFORD] G[RAHAM]. "Horace Walpole's Correspondence." In Neglected English Classics. Aberdeen: D. Wyllie, pp. 3–72.

      Copious quotations from Walpole's letters with a laudatory commentary. Discusses Walpole's literary criticism, noting his violent prejudices against Scots and Catholics, and commends his insights into both English and European social life and politics.

7   RYE, WALTER. "Horace Walpole." In The Later History of the Family of Walpole of Norfolk. Norwich: H.W. Hunt, pp. 21–22.

      A brief summary of Walpole's life, with some strong opinions. Historic Doubts was "far in front of any historical criticism of the period"; Walpole's treatment of Chatterton was fair; but Strawberry Hill was an "incredibly poor thing."

8   SACKVILLE, S.G. STOPFORD. "The Text of Walpole and Gray's Letters." Times Literary Supplement, 27 May, p. 335.

      Replies to Sargeaunt (1920.9), stating that Walpole could well have written of Lady John Sackville as Lady Sackville.

9   SARGEAUNT, JOHN. "The Text of Walpole's and Gray's Letters." Times Literary Supplement, 13 May, p. 302.

      Proposes several emendations and corrections in the text and notes of Mrs. Toynbee's edition of Walpole's letters. Notes that the mysterious "Pam," who appears in the index of persons (1905.11), is not in fact a person but the Knave of Clubs.

10   SARGEAUNT, JOHN. "The Text of Walpole's Letters." Times Literary Supplement, 10 June, p. 368.

      Confirms one of his proposed emendations in the text of Walpole's letters (1920.9) and withdraws another.

11   TAYLOR, G.R. STIRLING. "The Walpoles." In Modern English Statesmen. London: George Allen & Unwin, pp. 69–103.

      Primarily concerned with the career of Robert Walpole, who can best be understood through the writings of Horace. Contends that "Horace was Robert in mufti, living in retirement" and that "they are part of the same picture." Pro-

vides few examples of Horace's articulations of his father's
ideas, however.

12   TOYNBEE, PAGET. "Horace Walpole and 'Mrs. G.'" Times Literary
      Supplement, 16 December, p. 858.
           Confirms that the "Mrs. G." mentioned in Walpole's corre-
      spondence with Ashton is not Mrs. Gray, mother of the poet,
      as had been conjectured, but Anne Grosvenor, housekeeper at
      Somerset House.

13   TOYNBEE, PAGET. "Horace Walpole's Adventures with Highwaymen."
      Times Literary Supplement, 5 February, p. 86.
           Discusses newspaper reports and Walpole's letters on a
      highway robbery by James Maclean and an apothecary named
      Plunket, in which Walpole was shot at and almost wounded.
      The event took place on 8 November 1749, not 7 November as
      Toynbee states in 1915.9.

14   TOYNBEE, PAGET. "Mme du Deffand, Hume, and Rousseau." Times
      Literary Supplement, 3 June, p. 352.
           Prints an unpublished letter from Hume to Mme du Deffand,
      which throws light on Hume's quarrel with Rousseau.

15   TOYNBEE, PAGET. "The Text of Horace Walpole's Letters." Times
      Literary Supplement, 20 May, p. 320.
           Replies to Sargeaunt (1920.9), accepting his emendations
      and corrections but pointing out that Mrs. Toynbee was not
      responsible for the index volume. The index of persons
      lists not only "Pam" but also Walpole's dogs, Patapan,
      Rosette, and Tonton.

                                1921

1   BOLTON, ARTHUR T. "Horace Walpole and Robert Adam." Times
      Literary Supplement, 1 September, p. 564.
           Like Toynbee (1921.6), suggests that the letter from Wal-
      pole to Robert Adam was written in 1766.

2   GWYNN, STEPHEN. "An Eighteenth Century Gardener." In Garden
      Wisdom. London: T. Fisher Unwin, pp. 126-49.
           Revision of 1920.4. Believes that gardening interested
      Walpole "only in the most amateurish way."

3   "Horace Walpole's Letters. Important Collection for Sale."
      Times (London), 10 November, p. 13.
           Announces the sale of a large collection of Walpole let-
      ters, many unpublished. Compares Walpole with Boswell, "the
      two greatest (literary) portrait-painters of the times,"
      emphasizing the informativeness of Walpole's letters.

4   TOYNBEE, PAGET. "A Walpole Allusion Explained." Times Liter-

ary Supplement, 20 October, p. 680.
Identifies the anonymous poet mentioned in a letter from
Walpole to George Montagu of 8 September 1757 as Richard
Bentley. Includes a sonnet by Bentley, "To the Printing
Press at Strawberry Hill," enclosed with the original letter
but not in the Toynbees' edition.

5   TOYNBEE, PAGET. "Horace Walpole and M. de Castellane." Times
    Literary Supplement, 4 August, p. 499.
        The index to 1912.2 misidentifies M. de Castellane, who
    is frequently mentioned in Walpole's and Mme du Deffand's
    letters and whose correct title is Joseph-Jean-Baptiste de
    Castellane, Marquis d'Esparron.

6   TOYNBEE, PAGET. "Horace Walpole and Robert Adam." Times
    Literary Supplement, 1 September, p. 564.
        Replies to Whitley (1921.8), suggesting that the letter
    from Walpole to Robert Adam was "probably written in the
    latter half of September 1766."

7   TOYNBEE, PAGET. "Horace Walpole and the Brothers Adam." Times
    Literary Supplement, 8 September, pp. 579-80.
        Prints a note by Walpole of 1779 on Mason's "Heroic Epis-
    tle to Sir William Chambers," which reveals Walpole's low
    opinion of the Adam brothers.

8   WHITLEY, WILLIAM T. "A Walpole Letter." Times Literary Sup-
    plement, 25 August, p. 548.
        Prints an undated letter from Walpole to Robert Adam,
    previously published (1866.2) but not included in the Toyn-
    bees' edition.

                              1922

1   B., C.W. "Walpole and Gray." Times Literary Supplement, 23
    March, p. 196.
        Finds an allusion to Gray's Eton College Ode in a letter
    from Walpole to Mason of 8 November 1783.

2   BICKLEY, FRANCIS. "Horace Walpole's Dogs." Nineteenth Century
    and After 92 (December):962-69.
        Describes the lives and deaths of Walpole's dogs: Tory,
    killed by a Swiss wolf in 1739; Patapan, died in 1745; the
    little known Fanny; Rosette, celebrated in an epitaph of
    1773; and Tonton, bequeathed by Mme du Deffand, who died in
    1789. Walpole's "dogmanity" was among his best qualities.

3   CONSTANT READER. "Looking Backward: The Castle of Otranto."
    Literary Review, 25 February, p. 451.
        Regards Otranto as "one of the most amusing stories" in

English and contends that a book can possess different char-
acteristics for different ages. In the eighteenth century
Otranto was a chilling romance; in the twentieth century it
is a comic masterpiece.

4   SAINTSBURY, GEORGE, ed. "Horace Walpole (1717-1797) [And W.M.
    Thackeray]." In A Letter Book. London: G. Bell, pp. 187-
    94.
        Prints a letter from Walpole to the Countess of Upper
    Ossory, together with Thackeray's imitation of Walpole in
    The Virginians and a brief introduction. Contends that Wal-
    pole was "not merely a 'trifler.'"

5   STRACHEY, [GILES] LYTTON. "Madame du Deffand." In Books and
    Characters: French and English. London: Chatto & Windus,
    pp. 76-103.
        Reprint of 1913.11.

                              1923

1   JAMES, M.R. "The Strawberry Hill Shrine." Times Literary Sup-
    plement, 27 September, p. 636.
        Parts of a shrine constructed by Pietro Cavallani in
    1256, acquired by Walpole in 1768, are now in Wilton Church.

2   KILLEN, ALICE M. "Les pionniers du roman 'noir': Horace Wal-
    pole et Clara Reeve." In Le roman terrifiant ou roman noir
    de Walpole à Anne Radcliffe et son influence sur la littéra-
    ture française jusqu'en 1840. Paris: E. Champion, pp. 1-
    10.
        Revision of 1915.3.

3   LUBBOCK, PERCY. "The Castle of Otranto." Nation and Athenaeum
    33 (26 May):267-68.
        A lukewarm appreciation of Otranto, which is "a neat
    exercise in an artificial tone" and "rather dull." Believes
    that Otranto will never again be a popular work but will
    retain its place in textbooks, "for ever heralding an his-
    toric movement."

4   MEYERSTEIN, E[DWARD] H[ARRY] W[ILLIAM]. "Horace Walpole's
    Marginalia in Dean Milles's Edition of the Rowley Poems."
    Times Literary Supplement, 18 January, p. 45.
        Walpole's marginalia on Milles's edition of Rowley (1782)
    reveal his admiration for some of Chatterton's poems and his
    contempt for the pedantic editor, Milles. The views ex-
    pressed "almost induce one to reconsider the most painful
    chapter in literary history."

5   NEWBOLT, FRANCIS. "History and Lord Orford." Nineteenth Cen-

tury and After 94 (July):57-67.
A disorganized, undocumented account of some events of 1714, partly based on Walpole's Reminiscences.

6 OLIVER, EDITH. "The Strawberry Hill Shrine." Times Literary Supplement, 4 October, p. 652.
Responds to James (1923.1). Confirms that the remains of Walpole's shrine are in Wilton Church, as the rector of Wilton noted in "A Short Description of Wilton Church" (1881).

7 RIDLEY, H.M. "Great Friendships V. Thomas Gray and Horace Walpole." Canadian Magazine 60 (February):328-32.
Studies the development of Gray and Walpole's friendship, emphasizing the difference in temperament between the "quiet, fastidious" Gray and the self-complacent, worldly-wise Walpole. Values Walpole primarily for his efforts in publicizing Gray's Elegy.

8 RUSSELL, CHARLES. "Dr. Johnson and Walpole." Fortnightly Review, n.s. 114 (1 October):658-66.
Discusses Walpole's antipathy towards Johnson and Johnson's indifference to Walpole. Suggests that Walpole's attitude was formed in 1771, when he feared that Johnson might ridicule him for having been deceived by Chatterton. Walpole's antipathy was exacerbated by Johnson's "Life of Gray" and by the numerous differences in attitude and conduct between himself and Johnson. Provides a useful list of hostile remarks on Johnson in Walpole's letters.

9 "The Castle of Otranto." Times Literary Supplement, 17 May, p. 336.
Prefers the "elegant mystery-mongering" of Otranto to Mrs. Radcliffe's earnestness, but denies its influence on the Romantic movement.

10 TOYNBEE, PAGET. "Horace Walpole and Pitt." Times Literary Supplement, 15 March, p. 179.
Prints an unpublished letter from Pitt to Walpole of 20 November 1759, in which Pitt graciously acknowledges Walpole's eulogistic letter of the previous day.

11 TOYNBEE, PAGET. "Horace Walpole and the Term 'Hannah.'" Times Literary Supplement, 4 January, p. 12.
"Hannah," a term that Walpole repeatedly uses in letters to Montagu to mean "mistress," is an allusion to Hannah Lightfoot, the reputed mistress of George III.

12 TOYNBEE, PAGET. "Horace Walpole's Type-Founder." Times Literary Supplement, 10 May, p. 321.
Describes Walpole's purchases of type from the firm of William Caslon.

13   TOYNBEE, PAGET. "The Strawberry Hill Shrine." <u>Times Literary</u>
      <u>Supplement</u>, 4 October, p. 652.
                Responds to James (1923.1). Prints an extract from an
      unpublished letter from Walpole to Sir William Hamilton of
      22 September 1768, showing that Walpole originally intended
      to use the materials of his shrine as a chimney-piece.

14   TOYNBEE, PAGET. "Walpole and Caslon Type." <u>Times</u> (London), 8
      November, p. 13.
                Walpole used the type of William Caslon in his printing
      press. In 1768 he purchased 282 pounds of Caslon's "Eng-
      lish" type for the projected edition of his own works, and
      made further purchases until he abandoned the project in
      1787.

15   WALPOLE, HORACE. <u>Journal of the Printing Office</u>. Edited by
      Paget Toynbee. London: Constable, 150 pp.
                Transcribes Walpole's unpublished journal of his printing
      activities. Includes extensive annotations, an index, and
      appendices with miscellaneous writings by Walpole relating
      to the Strawberry Hill press.

16   "Walpole's Press." <u>Times</u> (London), 29 January, p. 16.
                A brief account of the establishment of Walpole's print-
      ing press at Strawberry Hill and of a few of its publica-
      tions.

                                    1924

1   BRADFORD, GAMALIEL. "Bare Souls III: Horace Walpole." <u>Har-</u>
      <u>per's Monthly Magazine</u> 149 (June):114-24.
                A speculative portrait of Walpole's personality and char-
      acter. Notes his interest in everyday affairs but deplores
      his lack of spirituality, concluding that "persons of Wal-
      pole's type trifle away existence and do not live at all."
      Reprinted: 1924.2.

2   BRADFORD, GAMALIEL. "Horace Walpole." In <u>Bare Souls</u>. New
      York: Harper, pp. 97-132.
                Reprint of 1924.1.

3   DRAPER, JOHN W. <u>William Mason. A Study in Eighteenth-Century</u>
      <u>Culture</u>. New York: New York University Press, 397 pp.
                Revision of 1920.3. Studies Walpole's dealings with
      Mason throughout, with a chapter on their collaboration on
      Mason's satires. Defends Mason's character at the expense
      of Walpole's, supporting Croker's "serious charges" against
      Walpole but refuting those made against Mason.

4   GOSSE, EDMUND. "Making our Flesh Creep." <u>Sunday Times</u> (Lon-

don), 2 November, p. 8.

Review article on 1924.13. Contrasts the responses to
Otranto in the eighteenth and twentieth centuries: it ter-
rified Walpole's contemporaries but only amuses modern
readers. Finds the tale itself "a poor affair" but admires
the preface to the second edition, "an elegant and serious
piece of writing." Also criticizes The Mysterious Mother,
but believes that both it and Otranto inspired Walpole's
more important successors in the Gothic. Reprinted:
1925.7.

5   HODGSON, J.E. "Horace Walpole (1717-97)." In The History of
Aeronautics in Great Britain from the Earliest Times to the
Latter Half of the Nineteenth Century. London: Humphrey
Milford, pp. 199-203.

Traces the development of Walpole's attitude to ballooning from 1783 to 1785, showing that his "detached contempt"
gave way to condescending interest. Provides the fullest
account of the subject, with several useful quotations from
Walpole's letters.

6   SARGENT, GEORGE H. "Books Old and Rare. Literary Treasures of
Sir Horace Walpole." Antiques, October, pp. 207-9.

Discusses the books printed at Strawberry Hill, their
sale in 1842, and their high reputation in the twentieth
century: they are "the delight of collectors." Also
praises Walpole as a letter writer: he was "vivacious,
interesting and often brilliant."

7   TIPPING, H. AVRAY. "Strawberry Hill, Middlesex." Country Life
56 (5 July):18-25; (12 July):56-64.

A richly illustrated, highly critical account of Strawberry Hill, particularly contemptuous of Richard Bentley's
contributions. Reprinted: 1926.10.

8   TOYNBEE, PAGET. "Horace Walpole in Paris. Journals of Five
Visits. A New Discovery." Times (London), 16 August, pp.
11-12.

Describes Walpole's journals of his five visits to Paris
in 1765-66, 1767, 1769, 1771, and 1775. Discusses the first
journal in detail, stating that the others are of lesser
interest. Provides brief quotations from the second and
fifth journals, but none from the third or fourth.

9   TOYNBEE, PAGET. "Horace Walpole's Niece and the Duke of
Gloucester." Times Literary Supplement, 24 January, p. 53.

Prints an unpublished letter of 3 May 1764 from Walpole's
niece, Lady Waldegrave, to the Duke of Gloucester, in which,
acting on Walpole's advice, she discourages the Duke's
advances. Shortly afterwards, however, the liaison was
resumed.

10   TOYNBEE, PAGET. "Letters of Horace Walpole." <u>Times Literary</u>
      <u>Supplement</u>, 19 June, p. 388.
          Calls attention to letters from Walpole to Lady George
      Lennox, which will be printed in the forthcoming continua-
      tion of the supplement to Mrs. Toynbee's edition (1925.19).

11   TOYNBEE, PAGET. "Strawberry Hill. 50 Years' Spending by Hor-
      ace Walpole." <u>Times</u> (London), 29 January, p. 15; 30 Janu-
      ary, p. 13.
          Describes Walpole's account book of his expenditures at
      Strawberry Hill, which he began in 1747 and continued until
      1795. The book records his expenditures on the house and
      its contents, but not on the printing press.

12   WALPOLE, HORACE. <u>Reminiscences Written by Mr. Horace Walpole</u>
      <u>in 1788</u>. Edited by Paget Toynbee. Oxford: Clarendon
      Press, 174 pp.
          Transcribes Walpole's <u>Reminiscences</u> from the original
      manuscript, restoring many passages deleted by Mary Berry in
      the <u>Works</u> (1798.7). Includes historical and textual annota-
      tions, an index, and a transcript of Walpole's unpublished
      "Notes of his Conversations with Lady Suffolk."

13   WALPOLE, HORACE. <u>"The Castle of Otranto" and "The Mysterious</u>
      <u>Mother."</u> Edited by Montague Summers. London: Constable,
      306 pp.
          The first annotated edition of either work, with both
      textual and explanatory notes. The reliability of the text
      of <u>The Mysterious Mother</u>, however, is severely criticized by
      Dolan (1970.6). An extensive introduction treats <u>Otranto</u> as
      "the parent of the romantic novel," but considers <u>The Mys-</u>
      <u>terious Mother</u> a greater work. Includes Mason's proposed
      alterations to <u>The Mysterious Mother</u>, criticizing them as
      "generally superfluous and sometimes distinctly for the
      worse."

14   YVON, PAUL. <u>La vie d'un dilettante: Horace Walpole (1717-</u>
      <u>1797); essai de biographie psychologique et littéraire</u>.
      Paris: Les presses universitaires de France, 872 pp.
          The longest, most detailed, and most fully documented
      study of Walpole. Contends that Walpole's dilettantism was
      a pose and that his writings are of lasting importance.
      Contains six sections, each a book-length study: Walpole's
      early life and writings; his major works, including the
      letters, memoirs, <u>Royal and Noble Authors</u>, and <u>Anecdotes of</u>
      <u>Painting</u>; Walpole and politics; Walpole and the Gothic,
      including discussions of Strawberry Hill and of <u>Otranto</u>;
      Walpole and France; and Walpole's final years. Includes
      accounts of minor writings by Walpole neglected by almost
      all other critics. Supplemented by 1924.15.

15 YVON, PAUL. <u>The Poetical Ideals of a Gentleman Author in the</u>
    <u>XVIIIth Century: Horace Walpole as a Poet</u>. Paris: Les
    presses universitaires de France, 217 pp.
        The only full-length study of Walpole's poetry. Studies
    the verse in relation to light and occasional poetry of
    Walpole's time, Walpole's theories of poetry and opinions of
    individual poets, and the development of his own poetry.
    Also discusses Walpole's attitude towards drama and examines
    his comedy, <u>Nature Will Prevail</u>, as well as <u>The Mysterious</u>
    <u>Mother</u>. Finds the poetry, in general, light and superfi-
    cial, but with "a strength and grace of its own."

                              1925

1   "A Horace Walpole Cabinet." <u>Times</u> (London), 5 September, p.
    13.
        Describes a hanging cabinet that Walpole designed for
    himself in 1743.

2   BENSLY, EDWARD. "Strawberry Hill: Mr. Hindley." <u>Notes and</u>
    <u>Queries</u> 148 (14 February):121.
        Replies to Drake (1925.6), identifying Mr. Hindley.

3   BENSLY, EDWARD. "'The Ape and the Tiger.'" <u>Notes and Queries</u>
    149 (12 September):181.
        Replies to F.E.H.R. (1925.12), tracing Walpole's phrase
    to Voltaire's <u>Candide</u>.

4   CHANCELLOR, E[DWIN] BERESFORD. "Horace Walpole's Marginalia."
    In <u>Literary Diversions</u>. New York: Edgar H. Wells, pp. 40-
    46.
        Studies the marginalia in a copy of Bubb Dodington's
    <u>Diary</u> (1784), apparently transcribed from those in Walpole's
    own copy. The marginalia provide biographical details of
    persons mentioned, and add anecdotes about them.

5   DOBREE, EDWARD H. "Strawberry Hill: Mr. Hindley." <u>Notes and</u>
    <u>Queries</u> 148 (21 February):140-41.
        Describes a bow window at Strawberry Hill.

6   DRAKE, WILFRED. "Strawberry Hill: Mr. Hindley." <u>Notes and</u>
    <u>Queries</u> 148 (31 January):82.
        Enquires about a Mr. Hindley, mentioned in a letter by
    Walpole.

7   GOSSE, EDMUND. "Making our Flesh Creep." In <u>Silhouettes</u>.
    London: Heinemann, pp. 113-19.
        Reprint of 1924.4.

8   KER, W[ILLIAM] P. "Horace Walpole." In <u>Collected Essays</u>.

Edited by Charles Whibley.   Vol. 1.   London: Macmillan, pp. 109-27.
    Disputes Macaulay's judgment of Walpole, recommending his letters as an informal history of the eighteenth century. There were wiser commentators than Walpole, but none more eloquent.

9   "Memorabilia."   Notes and Queries 149 (12 September):181.
    Comments on Walpole's hanging cabinet, described by Toynbee (1925.18).

10   POTTLE, FREDERICK A.   "The Part Played by Horace Walpole and James Boswell in the Quarrel Between Rousseau and Hume." Philological Quarterly 4 (October):351-63.
    Explores the repercussions of Walpole's spurious letter to Rousseau from the King of Prussia, observing that Walpole admired Rousseau's works but despised the man. Ascribes to Walpole three other pseudonymous letters in French addressed to Rousseau; these attributions are withdrawn in a greatly revised and expanded version of the article (1967.18).

11   QUARRELL, W.H.   "Strawberry Hill: Mr. Hindley."   Notes and Queries 148 (14 February):121.
    Replies to Drake (1925.6), identifying Mr. Hindley.

12   R., F.E.H.   "'The Ape and the Tiger.'"   Notes and Queries 148 (30 May):338.
    Enquires whether Walpole was the first to note the existence of ape and tiger in the human composition, and whether Tennyson borrowed the phrase from him.

13   SQUIRE, J[OHN] C.   "Books of the Day.   Walpole's Memories." Observer, 1 February, p. 4.
    Review of 1924.12.   Admires both Walpole's Reminiscences and his "Notes on his Conversations with Lady Suffolk," comparing their artistry with that of Walpole's letters.

14   STRACHEY, [GILES] LYTTON.   "Mary Berry."   Nation and Athenaeum 36 (21 March):856-58.
    Review article on 1924.12.   Compares Walpole's passion for the Berrys with Mme du Deffand's for Walpole.   Believes that he was in love with both sisters, and that he was "by far the most feminine of the three."   Reprinted: 1925.15, 1931.10, and 1948.7.

15   STRACHEY, [GILES] LYTTON.   "Mary Berry."   New Republic 42 (1 April):152-54.
    Reprint of 1925.14.

16   STRACHEY, J. ST. LOE.   "A Book of the Moment.   Horace Walpole." Spectator, 14 March, pp. 406-7.

Reviews Walpole's Reminiscences (1924.12), which shows "the same engaging features" as his letters and which has "long been among the chief monuments in our polite literature." Also discusses Walpole's "Notes on his Conversations with Lady Suffolk," which gives "a remarkable picture of this wonderful woman." Reprinted: 1925.17.

17 STRACHEY, J. ST. LOE. "Horace Walpole's 'Reminiscences' Appear in Full." New York Times Book Review, 22 March, p. 13.
    Reprint of 1925.16.

18 TOYNBEE, PAGET. "A Horace Walpole Cabinet." Times (London), 9 September, p. 13; 14 September, p. 8.
    Provides more information on Walpole's hanging cabinet (1925.1), including an account by Walpole of Verskovis, the carver of the figures on the cabinet.

19 WALPOLE, HORACE. Supplement to the Letters of Horace Walpole Fourth Earl of Orford. Edited by Paget Toynbee. Vol. 3. Oxford: Clarendon Press, 451 pp.
    Continuation of 1918.9. Includes a selection of letters to Walpole and supplementary letters by Walpole, bringing the total of Walpole's letters in the Toynbees' edition to 3,424.

20 WINSHIP, GEORGE. "From Mr. Horatio Walpole's Library." Harvard Library Notes 14 (March):23-29.
    Describes twenty-two volumes from Walpole's library, entitled "A Collection of the most remarkable Poems Published in the Reign of King George the Third." The volumes contain 342 poems issued from 1762 to 1789, many with annotations by Walpole. Also describes four pamphlet poems by Mason with Walpole's notes, and some other annotated books from Walpole's library.

1926

1   ALSOP, JOSEPH W., JR. "Walpole." Grotonian 42 (Christmas): 85-87.
    Walpole's revival of the Gothic form in architecture had both positive and negative consequences, but the Gothicisms of Otranto "opened the public mind to a proper appreciation of the Romantics." He was "the greatest of all English letter-writers," and among the most interesting characters of the eighteenth century.

2   CHAPMAN, R.W. "Walpole's Anecdotes of Painting." Bodleian Quarterly Record 5, no. 51:55-56.
    Lists the volumes and page numbers at which the plates of

Anecdotes of Painting should be placed, according to printed
overlines on the plates.

3   DOUGHTY, OSWALD.   "Horace Walpole's Opinions on Architecture."
    Architecture, 5th ser. (July), pp. 74-76.
        Considers Walpole's views on Gothic and classic architec-
    ture, arguing that his enthusiasm for Gothic contributed to
    its increasing predominance over classic in the late eigh-
    teenth century.

4   KING, WILLIAM, and LONGHURST, M.   "A Relic of Horace Walpole."
    Burlington Magazine 48 (February):98-102.
        Describes and illustrates a hanging cabinet designed and
    owned by Walpole, as well as some ivories he acquired in
    Italy.

5   "Nonsense Tales."   Times Literary Supplement, 9 December, p.
    907.
        Review of 1926.14.   Compares the Hieroglyphic Tales to
    extempore variety stage monologues, emphasizing the elements
    of nonsense and satire.

6   ROE, F.C.   "Le voyage de Gray et Walpole en Italie."   Revue de
    littérature comparée 6:189-206.
        An account of Gray and Walpole's Italian tour of 1739-41,
    with an analysis of their contrasting reactions to Italy.
    Sees the influence of Italy on Walpole reflected on his
    sensibility, rather than on his works.   Despite its title,
    there is nothing Italian about Otranto.

7   SMITH, HORATIO E.   "Horace Walpole Anticipates Victor Hugo."
    Modern Language Notes 41 (November):458-61.
        Compares Walpole's views on the grotesque in his second
    preface to Otranto with those of Hugo in his preface to
    Cromwell.   Does not suggest that Hugo had read Walpole's
    preface but notes Hugo's interest in Voltaire, whom Wal-
    pole's preface attacks.

8   STRACHEY, [GILES] LYTTON.   "The Eighteenth Century."   Nation
    and Athenaeum 39 (29 May):205-6.
        Review article on 1925.19.   Discusses Walpole's superfi-
    ciality and indifference to the impending changes of the
    industrial revolution.   His letters are delightful but triv-
    ial.   Reprinted: 1926.9, 1948.7.

9   STRACHEY, [GILES] LYTTON.   "The Eighteenth Century."   New
    Republic 47 (16 June):110-12.
        Reprint of 1926.8.

10 TIPPING, H. AVRAY.   "Strawberry Hill, Middlesex."   In English
    Homes.   Period 6, vol. 1, Late Georgian, 1760-1820.   London:

Country Life, pp. 97–116.
Reprint of 1924.7.

11 TOYNBEE, PAGET. "Horace Walpole on Gray." Times (London), 30
    July, p. 15.
        Prints an unpublished letter from Walpole to Richard
    Stonhewer, written a few weeks after Gray's death in July
    1771, in which Walpole describes Gray as "a Genius of the
    first rank."

12 TOYNBEE, PAGET, ed. Satirical Poems Published Anonymously by
    William Mason, with Notes by Horace Walpole. Oxford:
    Clarendon Press, 158 pp.
        Contains a preface, introduction, notes, and an index.
    Transcribes Walpole's notes on Mason's poems from Walpole's
    manuscript, and discusses his dealings with Mason in detail.

13 WALPOLE, HORACE. A Selection of the Letters of Horace Wal-
    pole. Edited by W[ilmarth] S[heldon] Lewis. New York:
    Harper, 2 vols.
        Contains 149 letters in Mrs. Toynbee's text (1903.4),
    with illustrations, index, and Walpole's "Short Notes of My
    Life." Includes some of Toynbee's and some new annota-
    tions. A brief introduction contends that Walpole has been
    "unfairly treated," and quotes, in his defence, a claim by
    Saintsbury that Walpole's letters make an apt trio with the
    Bible and Shakespeare.

14 WALPOLE, HORACE. Hieroglyphic Tales. London: Elkin Matthews,
    85 pp.
        Reprints Walpole's Strawberry Hill edition of 1785, in-
    cluding the annotations made by Walpole "in his copy of the
    first-sheets of the first edition."

15 WALPOLE, HORACE. Letters of Horace Walpole. Edited by Dorothy
    M[argaret] Stuart. London: George G. Harrap, 207 pp.
        Contains 147 letters by Walpole, without annotations. An
    introduction surveys the major events of Walpole's life and
    evaluates his works: Otranto is "lurid, unconvincing, and
    stilted" but influential; The Mysterious Mother is "grue-
    some." Walpole's letters are his primary achievement.

16 WALPOLE, HORACE. Selected Letters of Horace Walpole. Edited
    by William Hadley. Everyman's Library. London: Dent, 535
    pp.
        Contains a brief introduction, comparing Walpole and
    Cowper as letter writers, a bibliography, and notes taken
    primarily from nineteenth-century editors. The text is
    Cunningham's (1857.7). Distinguished from other selections
    of Walpole's letters by its division of the letters into
    topics, such as "literary criticism," "France and the French

Revolution," and "Social History Illustrated," with prefaces
to each section.

17   YVON, PAUL. "En relisant Horace Walpole." Revue de l'enseigne-
     ment des langues vivantes 43 (December):456-61.
          A review article on 1926.16, considering the advantages
     and disadvantages of a thematic selection of Walpole's
     letters. Believes that Strawberry Hill has had a negative
     effect on Walpole's reputation: he was a dilettante, but
     also a major writer.

                                1927

1   CARLTON, W.N.C. "Horace Walpole's Edition of DeGrammont's
     [sic] Mémoires." American Collector 4:206-8.
          Describes Walpole's copy of Anthony Hamilton's Mémoires
     du Comte de Grammont, printed in one hundred copies at
     Strawberry Hill in 1772. Discusses Walpole's special inter-
     est in the Mémoires, which was one of his favourite books:
     in 1775 he claimed to know it almost by heart.

2   CLYNE, ANTHONY. "Strawberry Hill." Bookman 64 (June):609-11.
          Regards Strawberry Hill as Walpole's "greatest creation."
     His letters, journals and "reminiscences" are valuable for
     the historian and Otranto was the forerunner of Gothic fic-
     tion, although an "absurd concoction of horrors and myster-
     ies."

3   DOBSON, AUSTIN. Horace Walpole: A Memoir. With an Appendix
     of Books Printed at the Strawberry Hill Press. 4th ed.
     Revised and enlarged by Paget Toynbee. London: Humphrey
     Milford, 395 pp.
          An extensively revised edition of 1910.1, with correc-
     tions and additions to both text and notes, a fuller index,
     and new material based on the Toynbees' publications since
     the previous edition.

4   EARL, H.L. "Horace Walpole." Transactions of the Torquay
     Natural History Society 5, pt. 1:6-11.
          A highly inaccurate account of Walpole's involvement in
     eighteenth-century politics. Believes that Walpole's Mem-
     oirs and Reminiscences [sic] is the work by which he is best
     known.

5   LEWIS, WILMARTH S[HELDON]. "Association Items." Saturday
     Review of Literature 3 (7 May):797-98.
          Describes a number of books and paintings once owned by
     Walpole and now in the author's possession, including an
     edition of Otranto presented by Walpole to Cole and a por-
     trait of his sister, Lady Mary Churchill. Reprinted in

part: 1951.6.

6 MAUROIS, ANDRE. "La société sous Louis XV: Madame du Deffand et Horace Walpole." *Conferencia* 21 (15 February):197-209.
Discusses Walpole's relationship with Mme du Deffand. Suggests that her love for him caused him much embarrassment but that, despite his reprimands, it brightened the last years of her life. Reprinted: 1927.7.

7 MAUROIS, ANDRE. "Madame du Deffand et Horace Walpole." In *Etudes anglaises. Dickens, Walpole, Ruskin et Wilde.* Paris: Bernard Grasset, pp. 169-208.
Reprint of 1927.6.

8 PETRIE, CHARLES. "Revaluations V. Horace Walpole." *Outlook* 60 (15 October):509-10.
Compares Walpole to Pepys; he lacks Pepys's "freshness" and "infectious love of life," but he is "second to him alone." Praises the erudition and liveliness of Walpole's letters.

9 RAILO, EINO. *The Haunted Castle. A Study of the Elements of English Romanticism.* London: George Routledge, 388 pp.
Discusses *Otranto* throughout, under such headings as "The Haunted Castle," "The Byronic Hero," "Incest and Romantic Eroticism," "The Young Hero and Heroine and Other Characters," and "Suspense and Terror." Primarily concerned with Walpole's influence on other writers; includes a brief account of *The Mysterious Mother.* The lack of an index makes the book difficult to use.

10 SAINTSBURY, GEORGE. "Walpole Revisited." *Dial* 82 (February): 145-52.
A discursive review article on 1925.19, 1926.13, 15-16. Discusses *Otranto,* which has "always been something of a puzzle," and the letters, which are entertaining and informative. Believes that Walpole "knew nothing" about politics.

11 STUART, DOROTHY MARGARET. *Horace Walpole.* English Men of Letters. New York: Macmillan, 229 pp.
An undocumented study of Walpole's life and writings. Attempts no detailed analysis but touches on almost all of his works, including several scarcely considered by other critics. Rates the letters well above Walpole's other works, is unimpressed by *Otranto* and revolted by *The Mysterious Mother.*

12 TOYNBEE, PAGET. "Horace Walpole's *Delenda est Oxonia.*" *English Historical Review* 42 (January):95-108.
The first publication of a suppressed pamphlet by Wal-

pole, written in 1749 in defence of the liberty of Oxford
University, printed "from Walpole's own transcript of the
original." Includes annotations by Walpole and by Toynbee.

13 TOYNBEE, PAGET.   "Walpoliana."   Blackwood's Magazine 231
    (April):454-63.
        Transcribes and briefly annotates five unpublished manu-
    scripts by Walpole: "A Dream of Horace Walpole," "Reminis-
    cences of Speaker Onslow," "From Mr. Hobart, Brother and
    Secretary of Lord Buckingham, Embassador in Russia," "At the
    Scotch College in Paris," and "Anecdotes Relating to Sir
    Robert Walpole and His Time, and Family."

14 WALPOLE, HORACE.   A Note Book of Horace Walpole, 1780-1783.
    Edited by W[ilmarth] S[heldon] Lewis. Miscellaneous Antiq-
    uities, no. 3. New York: William E. Rudge, 54 pp.
        Transcribes, with a brief introduction, Walpole's note-
    book for 1780-83, which shows his interest in painting,
    architecture, gardening, and collecting. Includes a fac-
    simile of the manuscript and extensive annotations. The
    printed text is inaccurate, as Lewis observes in 1951.6, p.
    219. Revives the series of "Miscellaneous Antiquities"
    founded by Walpole, who printed only two.

15 WALPOLE, HORACE. Strawberry Hill Accounts: A Record of Expen-
    diture in Building, Furnishing, etc. Kept by Mr. Horace Wal-
    pole from 1747 to 1795. Edited by Paget Toynbee. Oxford:
    Clarendon Press, 213 pp.
        Transcribes, with a brief introduction, Walpole's note-
    book of his expenditures on Strawberry Hill from 1747 to
    1795. Contains copious annotations, numerous illustrations,
    several related appendices, and a comprehensive index.
    Points out Walpole's difficulties with financial calcula-
    tions and notes several errors in his accounting.

                            1928

1   BRAUCHLI, JAKOB.   "Der gotische Roman."   In Der englische
    Schauerroman um 1800 unter Berücksichtigung der unbekannten
    Bücher. Weida: Thomas & Hubert, pp. 15-29.
        Contends that the true hero of Otranto is the castle, and
    that subsequent Gothic novelists took this structural device
    from Walpole. In Otranto and in later Gothic novels, the
    term "Gothic" signifies the creation of fear in the reader:
    it is not intended to signify Gothic architecture.

2   CLARK, KENNETH.   "Ruins and Rococo: Strawberry Hill." In The
    Gothic Revival. An Essay in the History of Taste. London:
    Constable, pp. 50-75.
        A well known, influential essay on Strawberry Hill,

studying the question of Walpole's originality and considering "to what extent he influenced, not merely exemplified,
the Gothic Revival." Strongly criticizes Walpole's taste
and deplores his influence. Strawberry Hill is "not merely
absurd; it is a ghastly portent." Associates Walpole with
artificiality, quaintness, and fraudulence. Revised: 1950.2.

3   ELTON, OLIVER. "Horace Walpole." In A Survey of English Lit-
    erature 1730-1780. Vol. 1. London: Edward Arnold, pp. 23-
    38.
         A survey of Walpole's life and writings. The Mysterious
    Mother is "the most ambitious and singular of Walpole's
    inventions"; Otranto is remarkable for its originality.
    Also discusses several of Walpole's minor writings, criti-
    cizing Hieroglyphic Tales and Royal and Noble Authors while
    commending Anecdotes of Painting and the Reminiscences. A
    brief study of Walpole's verse singles out The Entail for
    its "delicacy of image."

4   HUGHES, HELEN SARD. "Another Letter by Horace Walpole."
    Modern Language Notes 43 (May):319-20.
         Prints an unpublished letter from Walpole to the Duchess
    of Northumberland of 2 April 1760, noting that its friendly
    tone differs from Walpole's satirical account of the Duchess
    in his Memoirs of George III.

5   LEWIS, W[ILMARTH] S[HELDON]. "Walpole's Xo Ho." Times Liter-
    ary Supplement, 30 August, p. 617.
         Discusses Walpole's source for his Letter from Xo Ho and
    the number of editions printed.

6   PEOPLES, MARGARET HILL. "La querelle Rousseau-Hume." Annales
    de la société Jean-Jacques Rousseau 18 (1927-28):1-331.
         Discusses the consequences of Walpole's spurious letter
    to Rousseau from the King of Prussia throughout. Suggests
    that Walpole was surprised by the fame of his letter, which
    was not intended to be widely publicized. Considers the
    effect of the letter on Walpole's relationship with Hume,
    and Walpole's embarrassment about the whole affair.

7   WALPOLE, HORACE. "Horace Walpole's Journals of Visits to
    Country Seats." Edited by Paget Toynbee. Walpole Society
    16 (1927-28):9-80.
         Transcribes Walpole's journals of his visits to country
    seats from 1751 to 1784. Provides a prefatory note, list of
    seats visited, index of places, and annotations. Reprinted:
    1982.8.

8   WANKLYN, C. "Artificial Stone." Notes and Queries 154 (14
    April):268.
         In the remodelling of Strawberry Hill Walpole used

Coade's Patent Stone, an artificial stone much employed in the eighteenth century.

9   WHITLEY, WILLIAM T. "Notes on the Catalogues of Eighteenth-Century Exhibitions." In Artists and their Friends in England 1700–1799. Vol. 2. London: The Medici Society, pp. 366–97.
      An account of catalogues of art exhibitions held in London between 1760 and 1799, based on an inaccurate transcript of notes by Walpole.

10 WINDLE, SIR BERTRAM C.A. "Horry." Catholic World 126 (February):646–53.
      A gossipy account of Walpole and his circle. Declares that Walpole was "the most consummate writer of letters that the world has ever known," but that his other works have all been forgotten.

1929

1   AUVRAY, L[UCIEN]. "Horace Walpole et la Bibliothèque du roi (1766–1792)." Bibliothèque de l'école des chartes 90:229–32.
      Expands and clarifies Toynbee (1929.5–6), showing that Walpole presented fifteen volumes to the Bibliothèque du roi and providing further information on their delivery and reception.

2   de KOVEN, ANNA. Horace Walpole and Madame du Deffand: An Eighteenth Century Friendship. New York: D. Appleton, 199 pp.
      An undocumented, inaccurate study of Walpole and Mme du Deffand, without notes or index. Includes biographical chapters, a study of their backgrounds and a discussion of their friendship, which has a "poignant sadness" and a "strangely moving psychological interest." Walpole's treatment of the Marquise has been unfairly criticized.

*3 HANAWALT, LESLIE LYLE. "The Rise of Gothic Drama, 1765–1800." Ph.D. dissertation, University of Michigan.
      Source: Comprehensive Dissertation Index 1861–1972. Vol. 34. Ann Arbor: Xerox University Microfilms, p. 867.

4   HOLZKNECHT, KARL J. "Horace Walpole as Dramatist." South Atlantic Quarterly 28 (April):174–89.
      A highly appreciative essay on The Mysterious Mother. Contends that Walpole's talents were designed for drama, and that The Mysterious Mother is much superior to both Otranto and to the Gothicisms of Strawberry Hill. Walpole handles the incest theme with "fine restraint and dignity and a full

appreciation of dramatic possibilities."

5 TOYNBEE, PAGET. "Books of Horace Walpole – A Gift to Paris."
   Times (London), 23 August, p. 15.
   An account of twelve volumes, all by or printed by Wal-
   pole, that he donated to the Bibliothèque nationale in
   Paris.

6 TOYNBEE, PAGET. "Horace Walpole's Gift to Paris." Times (London), 26 August, p. 8; 29 October, p. 17.
   Two more volumes by Walpole, his Catalogue of Royal and
   Noble Authors, have come to light as a result of 1929.5; his
   original gift of fourteen volumes is now thought to be complete. A second letter, however, announces the discovery of
   yet another volume printed by Walpole, also part of his
   original gift, which thus totalled fifteen volumes.

7 WALPOLE, HORACE. The Castle of Otranto. Edited by Oswald
   Doughty. London: Scholartis Press, 111 pp.
   An extensive introduction provides an unreliable biographical sketch of Walpole, an account of the publication
   and reception of Otranto, and a critical discussion of the
   novel. Believes that Otranto is unsuccessful, but of interest because of the insights into Walpole it affords and
   because of its influence on the romantic revival. Contains
   brief notes and a bibliography.

8 "Walpole's Gothic." Times Literary Supplement, 12 September,
   p. 699.
   Review article on 1929.7. Regards Walpole as "a man of
   modern sensibility," but finds Otranto "an agreeable absurdity." Also discusses Strawberry Hill and its influence on
   the romantic revival.

1930

1 BENJAMIN, LEWIS SAUL [Lewis Melville]. Horace Walpole (1717–
   1797): A Biographical Study. London: Hutchison, 288 pp.
   An undocumented, inaccurate biography, based on copious
   extracts from Walpole's letters. Largely avoids discussion
   of his works. Contends that Walpole was "one of the outstanding figures of the eighteenth century" because of his
   invaluable correspondence; his other writings and his
   collecting are of minor importance.

2 BENJAMIN, LEWIS SAUL [Lewis Melville]. "Horace Walpole's
   England." Bookman 78 (September):355–56.
   Review of 1930.7. Emphasizes Walpole's familiarity with
   the people and events of his age: he "knew everyone and
   went everywhere." His letters are a guide to the eighteenth

century.

3   BENSLY, EDWARD. "A Gray Query." Times Literary Supplement, 25
     September, p. 758.
          Replies to Toynbee (1930.10). The oriental tale is in
     the Spectator, no. 94, and in several earlier works.

4   FOX, JOHN C. "A Strawberry Hill North Briton." Times Literary
     Supplement, 11 December, p. 1066.
          Responds to Needham (1930.9), with more information on
     the Strawberry Hill issue of the North Briton.

5   Horace Walpole and his Printing Office at Strawberry Hill. New
     Rochelle, N.Y.: Walpole Printing Office, 8 pp.
          An unsigned pamphlet. Notes that Walpole's printing was
     not especially ornate, and that he printed both privately
     and commercially. His was the first important private press
     in England; his printer, Kirgate, was "unusually intelligent
     and capable."

6   LEWIS, W[ILMARTH] S[HELDON]. "A Library Dedicated to the Life
     and Works of Horace Walpole." Colophon 1, pt. 3: unpagi-
     nated.
          Describes the author's collection of works by and relat-
     ing to Walpole (since greatly expanded) and explains his
     admiration for Walpole, whose wide range of interests make
     him an ideal guide to the eighteenth century.

7   MASON, ALFRED BISHOP, ed. Horace Walpole's England as his
     letters picture it. Boston: Houghton Mifflin, 398 pp.
          Brief extracts from numerous letters by Walpole, in the
     Toynbees' text, with illustrations but without notes.   A
     short preface draws heavily on Cunningham's introduction
     (1859.11), stating that Walpole "lives for us most vividly
     in his inimitable letters."

8   MEYERSTEIN, E[DWARD] H[ARRY] W[ILLIAM]. "Dodsley and Walpole."
     In A Life of Thomas Chatterton. London: Ingpen & Grant,
     pp. 250-84.
          A scrupulously balanced, meticulous account of Walpole's
     dealings with Chatterton. Criticizes Walpole's later re-
     marks on Chatterton but defends his actions during Chatter-
     ton's lifetime.

9   NEEDHAM, FRANCIS. "A Strawberry Hill North Briton." Times
     Literary Supplement, 27 November, p. 1014.
          Believes that a "soi-disant" copy of the North Briton
     printed at Strawberry Hill in 1763 was also written by
     Walpole.

10   TOYNBEE, PAGET. "A Gray Query." Times Literary Supplement, 18

September, p. 735.

Enquires about the source of an oriental tale mentioned in letters by Gray and Walpole. Notes that they "make diametrically opposite applications of the tale."

11 TOYNBEE, PAGET. "Horace Walpole in Mayfair." Times (London), 26 July, p. 13.

A brief account of Walpole's house at Berkeley Square, now about to be destroyed. Quotes two letters by Walpole to show his liking of the house.

12 WALPOLE, HORACE. The Castle of Otranto. In Shorter Novels: Eighteenth Century. "Rasselas," "The Castle of Otranto," "Vathek." Edited by Philip Henderson. London: J.M. Dent, pp. 97-192.

An introduction contends that Otranto was written "in conscious reaction against the domesticities of Richardson," and paved the way for the romantic novel. It has lost its power to terrify and now seems close to a parody of medieval romance, yet it has something of the "sweep of tragedy."

13 WHIBLEY, LEONARD. "'The Candidate: By Mr. Gray.'" Times Literary Supplement, 21 August, pp. 667-68.

Identifies a rare copy of Gray's satirical poem, "The Candidate," as a Strawberry Hill production, printed by Walpole seven years after Gray's death.

14 WHIBLEY, LEONARD. "The Foreign Tour of Gray and Walpole." Blackwood's Magazine 227 (June):813-27.

Describes Walpole and Gray's European tour and considers the consequences of their quarrel. It "made a profound change in Gray's life," contributing to his characteristic melancholy.

1931

1 BELSHAW, HARRY. "An Eighteenth-Century Wit and Methodism." London Quarterly Review 156 (July):50-60.

Quotes several passages on Methodism from Walpole's letters, admiring his wit but deploring his hostile views. Contends that Walpole's attitude to Methodism became more bitter and cynical after 1760, and believes that his shallowness made him incapable of understanding "the Methodist experience."

2 DASENT, ARTHUR. "Arlington-Street. Horace Walpole's Birthplace." Times (London), 16 March, p. 8.

Corrects an assertion by Paget Toynbee that Walpole was born at 17 Arlington Street, suggesting that the house was in fact number 22.

3   DASENT, ARTHUR. "Horace Walpole's Birthplace." <u>Times</u> (London), 30 March, p. 8.
     Continues to insist that Walpole was born at 22 Arlington
     Street, disagreeing with Toynbee's view (1931.14) that the
     house was formerly numbered 17.

4   ESDAILE, KATHERINE A. "A Vertue Drawing." <u>Times Literary Supplement</u>, 10 December, p. 1006.
     Walpole's plates for his <u>Anecdotes of Painting</u> were taken
     from Vertue's collection.

5   ESDAILE, MRS. [KATHERINE A.]. "Walpole's <u>Anecdotes of Painting</u>." <u>Times Literary Supplement</u>, 19 March, p. 224.
     Studies the publishing history of Walpole's <u>Anecdotes of
     Painting</u> both during and after his lifetime. Deplores the
     removal of Walpole's plates and the substitution of new ones
     in the editions of Dalloway (1826.2) and Wornum (1849.5) and
     calls for a new, standard edition of the work, "a masterly
     summary of a great subject."

6   JOHNSTON, MARY. "Horace Walpole in Italy." <u>Classical Weekly</u>
     24 (19 January):93-94.
     Briefly discusses some remarks on classical topics in
     Walpole's letters from Italy in 1739 and 1740.

7   LEWIS, W[ILMARTH] S[HELDON]. <u>The Forlorn Printer: Being Notes
     on Horace Walpole's Alleged Neglect of Thomas Kirgate</u>. Miscellaneous Antiquities, no. 6. New Rochelle, N.Y.: Walpole
     Printing Office, 24 pp.
     Studies Walpole's dealings with his printer, Kirgate,
     whose poem "The Printer's Farewell to Strawberry-Hill" was
     written for him by Silvester Harding. Defends Walpole's
     apparent ungenerosity in bequeathing Kirgate only one hundred pounds, since Kirgate was withholding valuable copies
     of Strawberry Hill publications for his own use.

8   LEWIS, W[ILMARTH] S[HELDON]. "Walpole's <u>Anecdotes</u>." <u>Times
     Literary Supplement</u>, 7 May, p. 367.
     Describes an unrecorded advertisement to the fourth volume of Walpole's <u>Anecdotes of Painting</u>, printed by Walpole
     in 1773. He published the volume only in 1780, the delay
     being caused by his concern that the essay on Hogarth might
     displease Hogarth's widow.

9   MARTIN, ROGER. "Oeuvres de la 'Quadruple Alliance'" and
     "Chronologie des oeuvres anglaises." In <u>Chronologie de la
     vie et de l'oeuvre de Thomas Gray</u>. London: Humphrey Milford, pp. 118-20, 122-31.
     Two useful chronological tables. The first lists the
     major publications of Gray, Walpole and West, the three publishing members of the Quadruple Alliance, from 1734 to

1742; the second lists those of Gray, Walpole and Mason from 1742 to 1769.

10 STRACHEY, [GILES] LYTTON. "Mary Berry." In Portraits in Miniature and Other Essays. London: Chatto & Windus, pp. 108-19.
Reprint of 1925.14.

11 "Strawberry Hill." Twickenham Public Library Quarterly Bulletin, n.s. 1 (November):1-2.
A brief account of Walpole's life and work at Strawberry Hill, which he made "the 'show house' of the eighteenth century." Also traces the history of Strawberry Hill after Walpole's death.

12 SUMMERS, MONTAGUE. "Architecture and the Gothic Novel." Architectural Design 2 (December):78-81.
Regards the castle as the protagonist of Otranto and Walpole as the father of the school of literary Gothicism, in which buildings figure larger than persons. Deplores critics who dismiss Otranto, a "very notable landmark" in English taste and English literature.

13 SYKES, W.J. "Horace Walpole's England." Dalhousie Review 11 (October):325-48.
Uses Walpole's letters to illustrate London life in the second half of the eighteenth century. Rejects Macaulay's judgment of Walpole, regarding him as the leading English letter writer.

14 TOYNBEE, PAGET. "Horace Walpole's Birthplace." Times (London), 18 March, p. 12; 27 March, p. 10.
Replies to Dasent (1931.2), contending that Walpole was born at what is now 22 Arlington Street, which was formerly numbered 17. Cites Walpole's "Short Notes of my Life" in confirmation.

15 VAUGHAN, HERBERT M. "Horace Walpole (Fourth Earl of Orford)." In From Anne to Victoria. Fourteen Biographical Sketches Between 1702 and 1901. London: Methuen, pp. 90-105.
A survey of Walpole's life and works, concentrating on the letters. Regards Otranto as influential in the romantic revival, and hence as a literary landmark. Walpole is an "admirable counterfoil" to Johnson, and his letters are incomparable.

16 WALPOLE, HORACE. Horace Walpole's "Fugitive Verses." Edited by W[ilmarth] S[heldon] Lewis. Miscellaneous Antiquities, no. 5. New York: Oxford University Press, 188 pp.
Attempts to include all of Walpole's verses, published and unpublished, although many more have since been discov-

ered. A brief introduction suggests that while Walpole
wrote verse all his life, much of it has "more biographical
interest than poetic." Provides annotations and a chronological table.

17   WALPOLE, HORACE. On Modern Gardening. Edited by W[ilmarth]
     S[heldon] Lewis. New York: Young Books, 80 pp.
          A preface considers the influence and aims of Walpole's
     essay, a protest against formal gardens and a "plea to re-
     turn to the 'natural.'" Also contains a bibliographical
     note on the essay's publication history.

18   WALPOLE, HORACE. The Castle of Otranto. In Three Eighteenth
     Century Romances. "The Castle of Otranto," "Vathek," "The
     Romance of the Forest." Edited by Harrison R. Steeves. New
     York: Charles Scribner's Sons, pp. 1-123.
          An introduction claims that it is difficult to take
     Otranto seriously today: "its portentous mysteries and
     exaggerated terrors seem to us both cheap and trivial."
     Briefly outlines Walpole's career and considers the influ-
     ence of Otranto, although Walpole "wrote it with his tongue
     in his cheek."

19   WHITELY, EMILY STONE. "Horace Walpole - Early American."
     Virginia Quarterly Review 7 (April):212-24.
          A gossipy, undocumented account of Walpole's support for
     America in the Revolutionary War.

                                1932

1   BRADFORD, GAMALIEL. "The Letters of Horace Walpole." In
     Biography and the Human Heart. Boston: Houghton Mifflin,
     pp. 213-36.
          Revision of 1906.2.

2   FELD, ROSE C. "Walpole, the Mirror of his Time." New York
     Times Book Review, 8 May, p. 11.
          Review of 1932.3. Compares Walpole with Pepys and Mme de
     Sévigné, finding him a "precious dilettante" but "always
     interesting."

3   GWYNN, STEPHEN. The Life of Horace Walpole. Boston: Houghton
     Mifflin, 286 pp.
          An interpretation of Walpole's life, rather than a formal
     biography or critical study. Assumes that Walpole was the
     son of Carr, Lord Hervey and emphasizes his dilettantism,
     but finds him likable and amusing. Admires the letters but
     is indifferent to Walpole's other writings.

4   IRVINE, LYN LL. "Walpole" and "Walpole and Madame du Deffand."

In <u>Ten Letter Writers</u>. London: Hogarth Press, pp. 31-65.
Concerned mainly with Walpole's relationship with Mme du
Deffand but also with his letters as a whole, which "lay
clear the whole life of a century." His lack of intellec-
tual integrity and humanity "widened rather than narrowed
Walpole's scope as a chronicler."

5   REILLY, JOSEPH J.   "The Gossip of Strawberry Hill." In <u>Dear
    Prue's Husband and Other People</u>. London: Macmillan, pp.
    307-19.
        An informal account of Walpole's letters, "among the most
    fascinating ever written." Considers "Horry's" views on
    various topics, and finds some of his interests surprisingly
    modern.

6   TOYNBEE, PAGET.   "Horace Walpole and Sir Robert." <u>Times Liter-</u>
    <u>ary Supplement</u>, 14 April, p. 271.
        Rejects a conjecture by Gwynn (1932.3) that Walpole was
    once critical of his father in a letter to Mann. The pas-
    sage in question, omitted from Mrs. Toynbee's edition, con-
    tains a bawdy anecdote unconnected with Robert Walpole.

7   TOYNBEE, PAGET.   "Horace Walpole's Memoirs of the Poet Gray."
    <u>Modern Language Review</u> 27 (January):58-60.
        Prints a memoir of Gray in Walpole's "Commonplace Book,"
    with notes and a brief introduction. Reprinted: 1935.13.

8   WALPOLE, HORACE.   <u>Anecdotes Told me by Lady Denbigh</u>. Edited by
    W[ilmarth] S[heldon] Lewis.   Miscellaneous Antiquities, no.
    7. Windham, Ct.: Hawthorn House, 10 pp.
        The anecdotes, printed from Walpole's unpublished manu-
    script, "illustrate Walpole's delight in lively old ladies
    who could give him familiar glimpses of the glamorous past."
    Lady Denbigh was part of Walpole's "circle of animated dowa-
    gers." Does not contain annotations.

                              1933

1   AIMERY de PIERREBOURG, MARGUERITE [Claude Ferval].   "Un gentil-
    homme bourru." In <u>Madame du Deffand, l'esprit et l'amour au</u>
    <u>XVIIIe siècle</u>. Paris: Arthème Fayard, pp. 198-232.
        Mme du Deffand's love for Walpole did not prevent her
    from being remarkably lucid about his character, especially
    about his egotism and concern for public opinion. Walpole,
    when sure of being protected from ridicule, had a deep
    affection for the Marquise.

2   B., H.   "Horace Walpole's Letters: Rumbold." <u>Notes and</u>
    <u>Queries</u> 164 (3 June):388.
        Explains a passage concerning Sir Thomas Rumbold in a

letter from Walpole to Mason of May 1780.

3   HAZLITT, WILLIAM. "Letters of Horace Walpole." In <u>The Com-</u>
     <u>plete Works of William Hazlitt</u>. Edited by P.P. Howe. Vol.
     16. London: J.M. Dent, pp. 138-52, 428.
         Reprint of 1818.2, based on the text in 1904.5, with some
     additional notes.

4   JALOUX, EDMOND. "L'ami de Madame du Deffand." <u>Le Temps</u>, 26
     May, p. 3.
         Review article on 1933.1. Defends Walpole from his
     critics, who have disliked his treatment of Mme du Deffand.
     Regards him as a sensitive man, afraid of being hurt by
     friendship, and emphasizes the significance of <u>Otranto</u>.

5   LEWIS, W[ILMARTH] S[HELDON]. <u>Horace Walpole's Letter from</u>
     <u>Madame de Sévigné</u>. Miscellaneous Antiquities, no. 8.
     Windham, Ct.: Hawthorn House, 22 pp.
         An account of the snuff box and letter sent from Mme du
     Deffand to Walpole as if from Mme de Sévigné, and of
     Walpole's failure to recognize the author of the hoax.
     Includes a facsimile and transcript of the letter. A prefa-
     tory note discusses the history of Walpole's and Lewis's
     Miscellaneous Antiquities.

*6   RECKERBERGER, ROSINA. "August Wilhelm Schlegels Interesse für
     Horace Walpole." Ph.D. dissertation, University of Vienna.
         Source: Thiergard (1959.6), p. 103. Studies both
     Schlegel's interest in Walpole and Walpole's reception in
     Germany.

7   STRACHEY, [GILES] LYTTON. "Horace Walpole," "Horace Walpole,"
     "Walpole's Letters," and "The Eighteenth Century." In <u>Char-</u>
     <u>acters and Commentaries</u>. Edited by James Strachey. London:
     Chatto & Windus, pp. 32-44, 87-95, 263-68, 297-302.
         The first essay, written in 1905 and now first published,
     studies four aspects of Walpole revealed in his letters:
     the politician, the man of letters, the antiquary and the
     gossip. The other essays are reprints of 1904.10, 1919.8,
     and 1926.8.

8   WHITLEY, WILLIAM T. "A Letter of Horace Walpole." <u>Times</u>
     <u>Literary Supplement</u>, 23 March, p. 200.
         Prints parts of an unpublished letter by Walpole of
     November 1779, addressed to "a lady of high Rank."

1934

1   BRUNOT, F[ERDINAND]. "Lord Chesterfield et Walpole." In <u>His-</u>
     <u>toire de la langue française des origines à 1900</u>. Vol. 8.

Paris: Armand Colin, p. 286.

Asserts, erroneously, that both Walpole and Chesterfield wrote the majority of their letters in French and sees Walpole as an important figure in French literature, close behind the great writers.

2 CRICK, REV. WALTER. "Horace Walpole and Lunardi." Times (London), 29 September, p. 8.

Cites a letter by Walpole stating that he saw a balloon carrying a passenger on 30 June 1784. This predates Lunardi's first balloon ascent on 15 September 1784.

3 HUTCHISON, ROBERT. "Medicine in Horace Walpole's Letters." Annals of Medical History, n.s. 6 (January):56-68.

Discusses Walpole's low opinion of doctors, which reflects the backward state of eighteenth-century medicine. Surveys Walpole's views on gout, innoculation, epidemics, nerves, the illnesses of eminent persons, prominent medical men, and quacks.

4 LEWIS, W[ILMARTH] S[HELDON]. "The Genesis of Strawberry Hill." Metropolitan Museum Studies 5, pt. 1:57-92.

Still the fullest, most accurate account of the development of Strawberry Hill, illustrated with numerous sketches by Bentley, Chute, and Walpole. Acknowledges that these amateur architects made numerous errors, but points out that their work had an enormous influence in Europe and North America. Compares Strawberry Hill with Otranto, showing which rooms could have been used in Walpole's novel.

5 LUCAS, E.V. "A Wanderer's Note Book. Strawberry Hill." Sunday Times (London), 25 November, p. 16.

A brief comparison between Walpole's and the present-day Strawberry Hill. Finds the exterior ugly and unwelcoming and the interior worse; it is an "amusing frippery."

6 MARTIN, ROGER. "La 'Quadruple alliance,'" "Les confidents," and "Les jeunes hommes." In Essai sur Thomas Gray. London: Humphrey Milford, pp. 70-124.

A detailed study of Walpole's relationship with Gray. Suggests that Gray's feelings for Walpole were much stronger than those of Walpole for Gray: Walpole was rather contemptuous of his friend. After their quarrel in Italy, Walpole and Gray were reconciled, but their friendship never fully recovered.

7 MEHROTRA, K[EWAL] K[RISHNA]. Horace Walpole and the English Novel. A Study of the Influence of "The Castle of Otranto" 1764-1820. Oxford: Basil Blackwell, 197 pp.

Studies the influence of Otranto, with a general introduction to the novel and chapters on its creation of a

"School of Walpole," the decline of this school, and the
reputation of Otranto up to 1820. Ascribes to Otranto the
principal part in the development of literary Gothicism. An
appendix lists some editions of the novel from 1765 to 1820.

8   STEIN, JESS M.   "Horace Walpole and Shakespeare."   Studies in
    Philology 31 (January):51–68.
        A detailed study of Walpole's attitude to Shakespeare,
    his attack on Voltaire over Shakespeare, and of Shake-
    speare's influence on The Mysterious Mother and Otranto.
    Contends that while Walpole thought highly of Shakespeare,
    he "was not centrally influenced by him."

9   THANE, ELSWYTH.   "Tonton Remembers."   English Review 59 (Au-
    gust):201–8.
        Portrays life at Mme du Deffand's salon and at Strawberry
    Hill from the viewpoint of Tonton, first Mme du Deffand's
    and then Walpole's dog.

                                1935

1   ASKEW, H.   "Yale Edition of Horace Walpole's Correspondence."
    Notes and Queries 169 (24 August):140.
        Answers one of Lewis's queries (1935.11).

2   BENSLY, EDWARD.   "Yale Edition of Horace Walpole's Correspon-
    dence." Notes and Queries 169 (17 August):124.
        Answers one of Lewis's queries (1935.11).

3   COYKENDALL, FREDERICK.   "Publication Dates."   Times Literary
    Supplement, 10 October, p. 361.
        Questions the practice in reference works of giving 1764
    as Otranto's date of publication when, although it was first
    published in December 1764, its title page is dated 1765.

4   GARTE, HANSJORG.   Kunstform Schauerroman.   Eine morphologische
    Begriffsbestimmung des Sensationsromans im 18. Jahrhundert
    von Walpoles "Castle of Otranto" bis Jean Pauls "Titan."
    Leipzig: Carl Garte, 179 pp.
        Discusses Otranto throughout under numerous headings,
    such as "messengers," "characters," and "events." A morpho-
    logical approach, surveying Otranto and its successors from
    various viewpoints.

5   GUTTMACHER, MANFRED S.   "Walpole's Journals."   Times Literary
    Supplement, 8 August, p. 501.
        Enquires about the whereabouts of Walpole's Journals of
    1788, in published or in manuscript form.

6   HEAL, AMBROSE.   "Yale Edition of Horace Walpole's Correspon-

dence: Maredant's Drops." Notes and Queries 169 (21 September):209.
Answers one of Lewis's queries (1935.11).

7 LEWIS, R.H. "Crossing the Channel by Balloon." Times (London), 12 January, p. 8.
Quotes a letter to the Countess of Upper Ossory in which Walpole describes the first channel crossing by balloon. His letter reflects the widespread contemporary interest in this new form of travel.

8 LEWIS, W[ILMARTH] S[HELDON]. "Horace Walpole." Times Literary Supplement, 24 January, p. 48.
Describes the manuscripts of essays by Walpole published in Old England and the Remembrancer in 1743 and 1747-49. Contrary to Walpole's claim, the published versions were not heavily edited.

9 LEWIS, W[ILMARTH] S[HELDON]. "Horace Walpole's Correspondence." Times Literary Supplement, 20 June, p. 399.
A progress report on the forthcoming Yale Edition, and an enquiry about the location of manuscript letters.

10 LEWIS, W[ILMARTH] S[HELDON]. Le triomphe de l'amitié; ou, l'histoire de Jacqueline et Jeanneton. Miscellaneous Antiquities, no. 10. Windham, Ct.: Hawthorn House, 19 pp.
Discusses an account of two poor women, Jacqueline Pourblé and Jeanneton Milet, by Mme de Menières, a friend of Mme du Deffand, which Walpole considered publishing at Strawberry Hill. Provides an abridged translation of the account.

11 LEWIS, W[ILMARTH] S[HELDON]. "Yale Edition of Horace Walpole's Correspondence." Notes and Queries 169 (20 July):45-46; (27 July):63; (3 August):84-85; (10 August):99; (17 August):118; (24 August):136.
Explains the objectives of the forthcoming Yale Edition, and poses fifty queries concerning Walpole's correspondence with William Cole and Michael Lort.

12 PARKS, MERCEDES GALLAGHER. "Mainly Baroque." In Shadows on the Road. London: George Allen & Unwin, pp. 37-45.
Describes Walpole's house in Berkeley Square (since destroyed), and wonders why a museum of the "greatest letter writer in English" is not established. Discusses Walpole's relationship with Mme du Deffand, the French interest in Walpole, and his life at Strawberry Hill.

13 TOYNBEE, PAGET, and WHIBLEY, LEONARD, eds. Correspondence of Thomas Gray. Oxford: Clarendon Press, 3 vols.
Includes Walpole's letters to Gray, with extensive anno-

tations, and two appendices relating to Walpole. Appendix
D, "The Quarrel Between Gray and Walpole and their Reconcil-
iation," suggests that an unknown letter of Gray's might
have been the cause of their dispute. Appendix Y, "Walpole's Memoir of Gray," is a reprint of 1932.7. Revised:
1971.11.

14   TUCKER, MILDRED M. "The Merritt Walpole Collection." Harvard
      Library Notes 3 (June):41-45.
          Describes the collection of Walpoliana given by Mrs. Per-
      cival Merritt to Harvard University: Strawberry Hill items,
      Walpole's works not printed at Strawberry Hill, association
      volumes, and two Walpole manuscripts – the Strawberry Hill
      visitor's book and the Paris journals. The collection also
      contains the only perfect copy known of the unfinished edi-
      tion of Walpole's Works of 1770.

15   W., E.G. "Yale Edition of Horace Walpole's Correspondence."
      Notes and Queries 169 (10 August):101.
          Answers one of Lewis's queries (1935.11).

                                  1936

1   ANDREWS, IRENE DWEN. "Walpoliana." In Owners of Books: The
      Dissipations of a Collector. Washington: Bruin Press, pp.
      59-76.
          A gossipy account of Walpole's parentage and his rela-
      tions with women, including Mme du Deffand, the Berry sis-
      ters, Anne Damer, Betty Germain, and Henrietta, Countess of
      Pomfret. Illustrated with the bookplates of each lady and
      of the "old dilettante," Walpole.

2   BRYCE, JOHN C. "Anecdotes of Polite Literature." Times Liter-
      ary Supplement, 18 April, p. 340.
          Enquires about the authorship of an anonymous work, Anec-
      dotes of Polite Literature, published in 1764. Walpole
      observed, in a letter to Cole, that it contained a hostile
      reference to himself.

3   CARTER, JOHN. "Gray: Odes (1757)." Bibliographical Notes and
      Queries 2 (May):4-6.
          Suggests that two editions of Gray's Odes were published
      in 1757: one, on thick paper, at Strawberry Hill in one
      thousand copies; the second, on ordinary paper, printed for
      Dodsley in London in two thousand copies. In 1938.3 Carter
      retracts this theory.

4   LEWIS, W[ILMARTH] S[HELDON]. Bentley's Designs for Walpole's
      "Fugitive Pieces." Miscellaneous Antiquities, no. 12.
      Windham, Ct.: Hawthorn House, 22 pp.

Describes and reproduces the unpublished drawings for Walpole's <u>Fugitive Pieces in Verse and Prose</u> (1758) made by Richard Bentley before his quarrel with Walpole in 1760. Bentley's drawings are lively, although they fall short of "Gray's and Walpole's extravagant praise."

5 PERKINSON, RICHARD H. "Walpole and a Dublin Pirate." <u>Philological Quarterly</u> 15 (October):391-400.
A detailed study of the text of <u>The Mysterious Mother</u>, correcting several errors in Summers (1924.13). Observes that Walpole, despite his ostensible disapproval of his own play, was fascinated by it and eager for it to be published.

6 SMITH, WARREN HUNTING. "Strawberry Hill and Otranto." <u>Times Literary Supplement</u>, 23 May, p. 440.
Quoting a letter to Mme du Deffand in which Walpole discusses similarities between the castle in <u>Otranto</u> and a Cambridge college, contends that Otranto was modelled on Trinity College as well as on Strawberry Hill.

7 STEEGMAN, JOHN. "Strawberry Hill and Fonthill." In <u>The Rule of Taste from George I to George IV</u>. London: Macmillan, pp. 72-92.
Depicts Walpole less as an idle dilettante than as a professional scholar, as shown by his <u>Anecdotes of Painting</u> and <u>Journals of Visits to Country Seats</u>. Studies Walpole's serious interest in the Gothic, and his insistence on "fidelity to the original models."

8 STREETER, HAROLD WADE. "The Gothic Romance in France: Walpole, Reeve, Lewis, Radcliffe." In <u>The Eighteenth Century English Novel in French Translation</u>. New York: Publications of the Institute of French Studies, pp. 117-23.
Contends that <u>Otranto</u> attracted little attention in France, despite Walpole's "social prestige," and that it exerted little influence on French literature.

9 VAN PATTEN, NATHAN. "Gray: <u>Odes</u> (1757)." <u>Bibliographical Notes and Queries</u> 2 (October):2.
Corrects and supplements Carter (1936.3), but supports his hypothesis.

10 WALPOLE, HORACE. <u>The Duchess of Portland's Museum</u>. Edited by W[ilmarth] S[heldon] Lewis. Miscellaneous Antiquities, no. 11. New York: The Grolier Club, 11 pp.
Transcribes Walpole's manuscript account of the Duchess of Portland's collection of antiquities and curiosities. An introduction describes the manuscript and discusses Walpole's relationship with the Duchess.

1937

1   ALLEN, B[EVERLY] SPRAGUE. "Strawberry Hill, Vauxhall, and
    Chippendale's Furniture." In Tides in English Taste (1619-
    1800). A Background for the Study of Literature. Cam-
    bridge, Mass.: Harvard University Press, pp. 74-86.
        Strawberry Hill is "mean and paltry," a glamorous sham.
    Its importance has been much exaggerated; it was merely a
    stage in the evolution of Gothicism. Walpole's own loquaci-
    ty about Strawberry Hill helped create its influential repu-
    tation.

2   BACON, LEONARD. "The Delicate Hercules." Saturday Review of
    Literature 17 (20 November):7.
        Review of 1937.15. Compares Walpole and Boswell; despite
    their differences both are deeply concerned with their age,
    and their writings encapsulate eighteenth-century England.

3   [CHAPMAN, R.W.] "The Walpole Correspondence: Portrait of an
    Age." Times Literary Supplement, 30 October, pp. 789-90.
        Review of 1937.15. Regards Cole as an "obscure plodder"
    and Walpole as a "universal amateur." Contemplates the vast
    scope of the Yale Edition and believes that it will eventu-
    ally eclipse the Variorum Shakespeare as an editorial pro-
    ject.

4   CHEW, SAMUEL C. "The Glancing Firefly and the Sober Mole."
    New York Herald Tribune, 17 October, pp. 1-2.
        Review of 1937.15. Compares the personalities and poli-
    tics of Walpole and Cole, whose friendship was "without a
    cloud," despite their political differences.

5   GRAY, W. FORBES. "Horace Walpole: Two Unpublished Letters."
    Times Literary Supplement, 11 September, p. 600.
        Transcribes and discusses two unpublished letters from
    Walpole to William Robertson, Historiographer Royal of Scot-
    land, whose writings Walpole greatly admired.

6   HAYWARD, JOHN. "Aedes Walpolianae." Spectator 159 (17 Decem-
    ber):1111-12.
        Review of 1937.15. Applauds the Yale Edition but finds
    the Cole volumes the least interesting of Walpole's corre-
    spondence, "unless you happen to be deeply interested in
    British antiquities and the gout."

7   JOHNSON, EDGAR. "Glass of Fashion." In One Mighty Torrent:
    The Drama of Biography. New York: Stackpole, pp. 183-88.
        Emphasizes the wit and informativeness of Walpole's let-
    ters: "he knew everybody, went everywhere, and commented on
    everything." Finds his judgments on public affairs "humane
    and sound," although his views are sometimes supercilious

and affected. The letters provide "incomparable entertainment."

8 KIRBY, JOHN P.   "A Strawberry Hill Piece." Times Literary
Supplement, 14 August, p. 592.
Enquires about the authorship of a ballad printed at
Strawberry Hill in 1764, ascribed by Walpole to "Sr Charles
Sidley."

9 [KNOWLES, J.A.] "Horace Walpole and his Collection of Stained
Glass at Strawberry Hill." Journal of the British Society
of Master Glass-Painters 7 (October):45-49.
Briefly considers Walpole's acquisition of stained glass,
and reprints part of the 1842 Sale Catalogue of his stained
glass collection. The remainder of the catalogue is reprinted in 1938.5 and 1939.12.

10 RAGEOT, GASTON. "Sur la voie du salut: Horace Walpole." In
Madame du Deffand. Collection les grandes pécheresses.
Paris: Albin Michel, pp. 179-222.
Walpole took advantage of Mme du Deffand's social posi-
tion. He was snobbish and superficial; their relationship
was much less important for him than for her.

11 SEDGWICK, ROMNEY. "Horace Walpole (1717-1797)." In From Anne
to Victoria: Essays by Various Hands. Edited by Bonamy
Dobrée. London: Cassell, pp. 265-78.
Deplores the censorship of Walpole's letters and memoirs
by several nineteenth and twentieth-century editors. Believes that Walpole's "facts are first-class and his gener-
alizations worthless," and much prefers his letters to his
memoirs.

12 STUART, DOROTHY MARGARET.   "Horace Walpole in Kensington."
English 1, no. 5:389-99.
Studies Walpole's many links with Kensington, including
posthumous ones (Macaulay died there) and conjectural ones,
such as Walpole's journeys through Kensington on his way
between Picadilly and Strawberry Hill.

13 WALCUTT, CHARLES CHILD. "The Ghost of Jemmy Twitcher." Notes
and Queries 173 (24 July):56-62.
Questions Walpole's statement in Memoirs of George III
that the name Jemmy Twitcher was spontaneously applied to
the Earl of Sandwich by the audience during a performance of
Gay's Beggar's Opera. Shows that the name had, in fact,
been applied to Sandwich on many occasions before the performance took place.

14 WALPOLE, HORACE. Anecdotes of Painting in England. Vol. 5.
Edited by Frederick W. Hilles and Philip B. Daghlian. New

Haven: Yale University Press, 262 pp.
A supplementary volume to Walpole's Anecdotes, compiled
from his "Book of Materials": three literary scrapbooks begun in 1759, 1771, and 1786. An introduction contends that
the Anecdotes is Walpole's most significant work. The present volume allows him, for the first time, to "appear as
historian of the arts in England during the latter part of
the eighteenth century."

15   WALPOLE, HORACE.   Horace Walpole's Correspondence with the
     Rev. William Cole. Edited by W[ilmarth] S[heldon] Lewis and
     A. Dayle Wallace. The Yale Edition of Horace Walpole's
     Correspondence, edited by W[ilmarth] S[heldon] Lewis, vols.
     1-2. New Haven: Yale University Press, 2 vols.
        The first of forty-eight volumes of the definitive edi-
     tion of Walpole's correspondence, completed 1983.3.   In-
     cludes a general introduction, with an analysis of the
     shortcomings of previous editions of Walpole's letters, an
     account of Walpole's relationship with Cole, several appen-
     dices, two of which contain accounts by Cole of visits to
     Strawberry Hill, and an index. There are copious annota-
     tions, many useful illustrations, and a highly accurate
     text, as in all the subsequent volumes.

16   WALPOLE, HORACE. Memorandia Walpoliana. Edited by W[ilmarth]
     S[heldon] Lewis. Miscellaneous Antiquities, no. 13. Wind-
     ham, Ct.: Hawthorn House, 21 pp.
        Transcribes notes made by Walpole on a variety of sub-
     jects, probably between 1761 and 1779, collected in a scrap-
     book after his death. An introduction observes that while
     these notes are ephemeral, they illustrate the wide range of
     Walpole's interests. A few, containing "four-letter words,"
     are omitted.

17   WRIGHT, WALTER F. "Walpole's Introduction of Terror and Horror
     into English Prose Fiction."   In Sensibility in English
     Prose Fiction 1760-1814. Urbana: University of Illinois,
     pp. 96-101.
        Although Walpole introduced "superstitious fear" into the
     English novel, he was restricted by the dictates of proba-
     bility and moral earnestness. He admired the supernatural
     but was restrained in its deployment.

18   YOUNG, G.M. "Horace Walpole and the Gothic Revival." Observ-
     er, 5 December, p. 4.
        Review of 1937.15. Commends the Yale Edition but dis-
     likes Walpole, who is effeminate and spiteful. Criticizes
     Walpole's egoism and rootlessness, and finds Cole of greater
     worth as an antiquary.

1938

1 BOURNE, GEOFFREY. "The Aerial Prophecies of Horace Walpole." St. Bartholomew's Hospital Journal, September, pp. 300-301.
Quotes several passages on balloons in Walpole's letters of 1783 and 1784, concluding that Walpole foresaw many "aerial exploits which are commonplace today."

2 CARTER, JOHN. "Gray: Odes. 1757." Bibliographical Notes and Queries 2 (April):2-3.
Corrects and expands 1936.3.

3 CARTER, JOHN. "Gray: Odes. 1757." Bibliographical Notes and Queries 2 (November):2-3.
Retracts Carter's earlier hypothesis about the printing of Gray's Odes (1936.3), suggesting, correctly, that the "thick-paper" Odes postdates the thin-paper edition.

*4 CHASE, ISABEL WAKELIN URBAN. "Horace Walpole: Gardenist. An Edition of Walpole's The History of the Modern Taste in Gardening with an Estimate of Walpole's Contribution to Landscape Architecture." Ph.D. dissertation, University of Cincinatti.
Revised for publication: 1943.2.

5 [KNOWLES, J.A.] "Horace Walpole and his Collection of Stained Glass at Strawberry Hill." Journal of the British Society of Master Glass-Painters 7 (April):100-101; (October):131-33.
Continuation of 1937.9.

6 "More Walpole 'Anecdotes.'" Times Literary Supplement, 26 February, p. 136.
Review of 1937.14. Walpole is seen here as a historian, rather than as Vertue's editor, and his achievement is impressive.

7 QUARRELL, W.H. "Horace Walpole: St. Peter's Church, Bexhill." Notes and Queries 175 (10 December):421.
The window of Bexhill Church, formerly owned by Walpole and containing portraits that he used as the frontispiece for volume one of Anecdotes of Painting, has now been restored to the Church.

8 SHEPPERSON, ARCHIBALD B[OLLING]. "Letters for Posterity." Virginia Quarterly Review 14 (Autumn):607-10.
Review article on 1937.15. Contends that the self-consciousness of Walpole's letters, written for posterity, increases rather than diminishes their value.

9 SHERBURN, GEORGE. "Walpole's Marginalia in Additions to Pope

(1776)." <u>Huntington Library Quarterly</u> 1 (July):473-81.
Transcribes, with an introduction and annotations, Walpole's marginalia in his copy of <u>Additions to the Works of Alexander Pope</u> (1776). Points out several errors in Walpole's annotations, many of which are "pure gossip."

10   SMITH, WARREN HUNTING, ed. <u>Letters to and from Madame du Deffand and Julie de Lespinasse</u>. Miscellaneous Antiquities, no. 14. New Haven: Yale University Press, 97 pp.
Transcribes thirty-one letters, most unpublished, to and from Mme du Deffand and her companion and later rival, Julie de Lespinasse. A useful introduction discusses Walpole's relationship with and attitude to the two women. Provides comprehensive notes and an index.

11   SUMMERS, MONTAGUE. "Historical Gothic." In <u>The Gothic Quest. A History of the Gothic Novel</u>. London: Fortune Press, pp. 153-201.
Resembles Summers's earlier evaluation of <u>Otranto</u> (1924.13), insisting that Strawberry Hill is identical with the castle and repeating that Walpole's novel, although highly influential, was not "the one and only source of the Gothic novel."

12   WALPOLE, HORACE. <u>The Letters of Horace Walpole</u>. Edited by M. Alderton Pink. Scholar's Library. London: Macmillan, 287 pp.
Contains an introduction, noting the appeal of Walpole's letters to both the "serious historian" and the "common reader," a biographical sketch, annotated selections from the letters, often abridged, essay questions for students, and an index.

13   WHIBLEY, LEONARD. "Gray: Odes. 1757." <u>Bibliographical Notes and Queries</u> 2 (April):3-4.
Questions Carter's assumption (1936.3) that copies of Gray's <u>Odes</u> were printed elsewhere than at Strawberry Hill in 1757.

1939

1   ARRIETA, RAFAEL ALBERTO. "La estatua de greda. Al margen de algunas cartas de Horacio Walpole." In <u>Estudios en tres literaturas</u>. Buenos Aires: Editorial Losada, pp. 45-103.
Emphasizes the wide range of Walpole's interests and activities. Studies his letters, collecting, history of gardening, development of Strawberry Hill, printing, and friendships. Responds to Macaulay's portrait, which does little justice to Walpole.

2 AUSTEN LEIGH, R.A. "Problems in Horace Walpole's Correspondence with George Montagu." Notes and Queries 177 (11 November):356-57.

Responds to one of Lewis's problems (1939.13).

3 BACON, LEONARD. "Walpole's 'Dear Old Frenchwoman.'" Saturday Review of Literature 21 (23 December):3-4, 15.

Review of 1939.21. Suggests that Mme du Deffand saw in Walpole "a lucid oracle, a teacher, a father-confessor," whereas Walpole was afraid "of being eaten up alive." Sees Walpole's side of the relationship as, at times, "repellent and stupid."

4 BRYANT, DONALD CROSS. "Horace Walpole - Miscellaneous Writers." In Edmund Burke and his Literary Friends. Washington University Studies, Language and Literature, n.s. no. 9. St. Louis: Washington University, pp. 275-88.

Studies Walpole's dealings with Burke, from their first meeting in 1761 to Walpole's enthusiastic reading of Burke's Reflections on the Revolution in France in 1790. Shows that Walpole and Burke were never close friends but that in general Walpole approved of Burke's writings.

5 CATALANI, G. "Problems in Horace Walpole's Correspondence with George Montagu." Notes and Queries 177 (4 November):337; (23 December):463.

Two notes, with responses to two of Lewis's problems (1939.13).

6 de BEER, E.S. "Problems in Horace Walpole's Correspondence with George Montagu." Notes and Queries 177 (16 December): 445.

Responds to one of Lewis's problems (1939.13).

7 EDWARDS, RALPH. "Cabinets Made for Horace Walpole and Thomas Brand." Burlington Magazine 74 (March):128-31.

Describes the hanging cabinets owned by Walpole and Thomas Brand, observing that Brand's is virtually a replica of Walpole's.

8 GATTY, HUGH. "Notes by Horace Walpole, Fourth Earl of Orford, on the Exhibitions of the Society of Artists and the Free Society of Artists, 1760-1791." Walpole Society 27 (1938-39):55-89.

Transcribes Walpole's annotations to the catalogues of art exhibitions, with a list of contents of the catalogues. An introduction discusses the significance of the catalogues and of Walpole's commentaries.

9 HOOVER, ANDREW GRAHAM. "The Correspondence of Horace Walpole and Sir David Dalrymple, Lord Hailes." Ph.D. dissertation,

Yale University, 214 pp.
An annotated edition of the correspondence between Walpole and Hailes, with an introduction discussing their relationship. An appendix, "Horace Walpole and the Old Age of
Rizzio," discusses "a slight skirmish between Lord Elisbank,
on one side, and Dalrymple and Walpole, on the other."

10   JOHNSTON, G.D.   "Problems in Horace Walpole's Correspondence
      with George Montagu." Notes and Queries 177 (4 November):
      337; (16 December):445.
           Two notes, with responses to two of Lewis's problems
      (1939.13).

*11   KILBY, CLYDE S.   "Horace Walpole as Literary Critic."   Ph.D.
      dissertation, New York University.
           Source: Comprehensive Dissertation Index 1861-1972.
      Vol. 35.   Ann Arbor: Xerox University Microfilms, p. 403.

12   [KNOWLES, J.A.] "Horace Walpole and his Collection of Stained
      Glass at Strawberry Hill." Journal of the British Society
      of Master Glass-Painters 7 (April):192.
           Conclusion of 1938.5.

13   LEWIS, W[ILMARTH] S[HELDON].   "Problems in Horace Walpole's
      Correspondence with George Montagu." Notes and Queries 177
      (26 August):155; (2 September):173-74; (9 September):192-93;
      (16 September):208-9; (23 September):226; (30 September):
      247; (7 October):263-64; (14 October):280; (21 October):296;
      (28 October):315; (4 November):331-32; (11 November):350;
      (18 November):367-68; (25 November):386; (2 December):404;
      (9 December):423-24; (16 December):441-42; (23 December):
      459; (30 December):480.
           A total of 186 problems in 19 installments, concerning
      such matters as allusions, quotations, and obscure persons
      in the forthcoming Yale Edition of Walpole's correspondence
      with Montagu.

14   LEWIS, W[ILMARTH] S[HELDON].   "Problems in Horace Walpole's
      Correspondence with George Montagu." Notes and Queries 177
      (23 December):463; (30 December):483.
           Two responses to three of his own problems in 1939.13.

15   LEWIS, W[ILMARTH] S[HELDON], ed. The Impenetrable Secret,
      Probably Invented by Horace Walpole. Miscellaneous Antiqui-
      ties, no. 15. Windham, Ct.: Hawthorn House, 15 pp.
           Reproduces the playing cards that constituted the game,
      "The Impenetrable Secret," and transcribes Walpole's "Expla-
      nation of the Secret." A brief introduction suggests that
      the game was probably composed by Walpole, shortly after
      1760, when another "Impenetrable Secret," based on Richard-
      son's novels, was issued in playing card form.   Hazen

(1942.5, p. 145) rejects the attribution to Walpole.

16 M., G.   "Problems in Horace Walpole's Correspondence with
    George Montagu." Notes and Queries 177 (11 November):356-
    57; (25 November):390-91.
        Two notes, with responses to two of Lewis's problems
    (1939.13).

17 PERKINSON, RICHARD H. "Walpole and the Biographia Dramatica."
    Review of English Studies 15 (April):204-6.
        In the 1782 edition of Biographia Dramatica (1782.2)
    George Steevens's intended article on The Mysterious Mother
    was cancelled at Walpole's request, and replaced with one by
    Isaac Reed.   In the 1812 edition (1812.1), Steevens's and
    Reed's articles are combined and edited by Stephen Jones.

18 ROBERTS, W. "Problems in Horace Walpole's Correspondence with
    George Montagu." Notes and Queries 177 (21 October):302;
    (18 November):373; (9 December):427.
        Three notes, with responses to four of Lewis's problems
    (1939.13).

19 SETON-ANDERSON, JAMES.   "Problems in Horace Walpole's Corre-
    spondence with George Montagu." Notes and Queries 177 (18
    November):373.
        Responds to one of Lewis's problems (1939.13).

20 TOBIN, JAMES E. "Horace Walpole (1717-1797)."   In Eighteenth
    Century English Literature and its Cultural Background.   New
    York: Fordham University Press, pp. 171-73.
        Lists some nineteenth and twentieth-century editions and
    studies of Walpole's writings.

21 WALPOLE, HORACE.   Horace Walpole's Correspondence with Madame
    du Deffand and Wiart.   Edited by W[ilmarth] S[heldon] Lewis
    and Warren Hunting Smith.   The Yale Edition of Horace Wal-
    pole's Correspondence, edited by W[ilmarth] S[heldon] Lewis,
    vols. 3-8. New Haven: Yale University Press, 6 vols.
        An extensive introduction studies previous editions of
    Mme du Deffand's letters to Walpole, her life, and her rela-
    tionship with Walpole, suggesting that she was a "surrogate"
    for his mother.   Includes Walpole's unpublished journals of
    his five visits to Paris, Mme du Deffand's journal from 1779
    to 1780, many appendices, one of which is a formal "por-
    trait" of Walpole by Mme du Deffand, and a comprehensive
    index.

22 WASSERMAN, EARL R.   "The Walpole-Chatterton Controversy."
    Modern Language Notes 54 (June):460-62.
        Prints an unpublished account of Walpole's dealings with
    Chatterton by Isaac Reed, as told him by Walpole in 1777,

which "serves to substantiate Walpole's later account."

23   WECTER, DIXON.   "Horace Walpole and Edmund Burke."   Modern
     Language Notes 54 (February):124-26.
          Prints and annotates an unpublished letter from Walpole
     to Burke of 3 December 1777, and a letter from Burke to
     Walpole of 7 July 1782. Observes that Walpole's attitude to
     Burke was partly ironic and partly admiring.

24   WHITMORE, J.B.   "Problems in Walpole's Correspondence with
     George Montagu." Notes and Queries 177 (9 September):197;
     (23 September):230.
          Two notes, with responses to two of Lewis's problems
     (1939.13).

25   WITHYCOMBE, E.G.   "Problems in Horace Walpole's Correspondence
     with George Montagu." Notes and Queries 177 (14 October):
     285-86; (28 October):318-19; (4 November):337; (25 Novem-
     ber):390; (9 December):427.
          Five notes, with responses to twenty-five of Lewis's
     problems (1939.13).

26   WOOLF, VIRGINIA.   "Two Antiquaries: Walpole and Cole."   Yale
     Review 28 (March):530-39.
          Review article on 1937.15. Contrasts the dedicated anti-
     quary Cole with the aristocratic Walpole, who loved antiqui-
     ties but loathed most antiquaries. Emphasizes Walpole's
     dilettantism, but contends that he "wrote the best letters
     in the language." Reprinted: 1942.10 and 1966.14.

                                  1940

1   BALDENSPERGER, FERNAND.   "Mme du Deffand and Walpole."   Vir-
     ginia Quarterly Review 16 (Spring):308-11.
          Review article on 1939.21. Believes that Walpole, "the
     strutting lord of Strawberry Hill," was unable to take Mme
     du Deffand quite seriously.

2   BATE, H.N.   "A Prophecy of the Air."   Times (London), 28 Novem-
     ber, p. 5.
          Quotes Walpole's letter to Seymour Conway of October 1784
     in which he envisages aeronautics of the future, inspired by
     the sight of Blanchard's balloon.

3   CATALANI, G.   "Problems in Horace Walpole's Correspondence with
     George Montagu." Notes and Queries 178 (20 January):46.
          Responds to one of Lewis's problems (1939.13).

4   CLARKE, A.H.T.   "Strawberry Hill."   Times Literary Supplement,
     25 May, p. 255.

Replies to M.L.D. (1940.5), stating that Rowlandson included monks in his drawing of Strawberry Hill to emphasize its Gothic, medieval spirit.

5   D., M.L. "Strawberry Hill." Times Literary Supplement, 11 May, p. 231.
    Enquires about the incongruous presence of monks or friars in a drawing by Rowlandson of Strawberry Hill.

6   de BEER, E.S. "Problems in Horace Walpole's Correspondence with George Montagu." Notes and Queries 178 (13 January): 34.
    Responds to one of Lewis's problems (1939.13).

7   DODDS, M.H. "Problems in Horace Walpole's Correspondence with George Montagu." Notes and Queries 178 (28 January):67.
    Responds to one of Lewis's problems (1939.13).

8   FELLOWES, E.H. "Prophecies of the Air." Times (London), 30 November, p. 5.
    Quotes Walpole's letter to Sir Horace Mann of December 1783 in which he predicts that aeronautics might be used, in the future, to destroy the human race.

9   GRIGSON, GEOFFREY. "The Gentleman-Usher." John O'London's Weekly, 7 June, p. 278.
    A hostile review of 1940.10. Supports Macaulay's view of Walpole as a "gentleman-usher," and finds Walpole's life and writings meretricious, mannered, and dull. Deplores his corrupt literary taste, his false modesty, and his lack of any original abilities.

10 KETTON-CREMER, R[OBERT] W[YNDHAM]. Horace Walpole: A Biography. London: Duckworth, 368 pp.
    The standard English biography: accurate, judicious, and comprehensive, although less detailed than Yvon's (1924.14). Acknowledging the lasting influence of Macaulay's essay, attempts to counter prejudice against Walpole by showing him as "a kindlier, wiser, more consistent and straightforward man." A chronological survey of Walpole's life includes chapters on his early years, his Grand Tour, Strawberry Hill, his literary and political writings, his relationships with Mme du Deffand and Chatterton, and his final years. The discussions of Walpole's literary works are pedestrian, but the correspondence is well treated throughout. Includes a useful bibliography and a genealogical table. Revised: 1946.3, 1964.5 and 1966.9.

*11 "Khronika: Pis'ma Uolpola" [Chronicle: Letters of Walpole]. Internatsional'naia literatura, no. 2, p. 226.
    Source: J.S.G. Simmons list, Lewis Walpole Library.

12   KRUTCH, JOSEPH WOOD. "The Master of Strawberry Hill." Nation
     151 (12 October):337-38.
          Review article on 1940.10. Considers Walpole's strengths
     and weaknesses, balancing his dilettantism against his orig-
     inality. His letters are informal and delightful, leaving
     "a carefully planned epistolary record of his age."

13   [LEWIS, WILMARTH SHELDON.] "A Strawberry Hill Forgery." Times
     Literary Supplement, 30 March, p. 164.
          Announces that in his forthcoming Strawberry Hill bibli-
     ography (1942.5), Hazen shows that the thick-paper edition
     of Gray's Odes, although dated 1757, was not printed until
     about 1790.

14   LEWIS, W[ILMARTH] S[HELDON], ed. Notes by Horace Walpole on
     Several Characters of Shakespeare. Miscellaneous Antiqui-
     ties, no. 16. Windham, Ct.: Hawthorn House, 21 pp.
          Concludes Lewis's series of "Miscellaneous Antiquities,"
     begun with 1927.14. Transcribes Walpole's manuscript notes
     on Shakespeare in his three "Books of Materials." A brief
     introduction contends that Walpole "read Shakespeare with
     perhaps the greatest insight of his time." Revised:
     1979.13.

15   "The Genius of Horace Walpole. Mme du Deffand and her Pas-
     sion. A Prince of English Letter-Writers." Times Literary
     Supplement, 4 May, pp. 218, 221.
          Review article on 1939.21 and 1940.10. Justifies Wal-
     pole's treatment of Mme du Deffand, and regards him as the
     greatest of English letter-writers.

16   TROUBRIDGE, ST. VINCENT. "Problems in Horace Walpole's Corre-
     spondence with George Montagu." Notes and Queries 178 (27
     January):67.
          Responds to one of Lewis's problems (1939.13).

17   WHIBLEY, LEONARD. "The Correspondence of Horace Walpole."
     Cambridge Review 62 (25 October):56-57.
          Review of 1937.15 and 1939.21. Considers the utility of
     Walpole's correspondence to students of eighteenth-century
     politics, society and literature.

18   WITHYCOMBE, E.G. "Problems in Horace Walpole's Correspondence
     with George Montagu." Notes and Queries 178 (6 January):
     15.
          Responds to five of Lewis's problems (1939.13).

19   WOOLF, VIRGINIA. "The Humane Art." New Statesman and Nation
     19 (8 June):726.
          Review article on 1940.10. Disagrees with Ketton-
     Cremer's view that Walpole is writing for posterity, as a

historian in disguise; he addresses the private individual
through the "humane art" of letter writing.   Reprinted:
1942.10 and 1966.14.

1941

1   C[HAPMAN], R.W.   "The Castle of Otranto."   Notes and Queries
    180 (22 March):209.
        Suggests that the name William Marshall, the purported
    translator of Otranto, derives from the Marshall whose por-
    trait of Milton was engraved for the 1645 Poems and whom
    Walpole criticizes in his Catalogue of Engravers (1763).

2   HAZEN, ALLEN [TRACY].   "Watermarks and Forgeries: The Role of
    Watermarks in the Examination and Condemnation of Certain
    Eighteenth-Century Productions."   Print 2, no. 2:21-31.
        Studies the authenticity of some of the Strawberry Hill
    detached pieces.   Shows that the thick-paper edition of
    Gray's Odes was not, like the thin-paper edition, printed in
    1757, but by Kirgate in 1789 or the early 1790s.

3   KILBY, CLYDE S.   "Horace Walpole on Shakespeare."   Studies in
    Philology 38 (July):480-93.
        Uses the passages on Shakespeare in Walpole's notebooks
    (1940.14) to revaluate Walpole as a Shakespearian critic.
    Shows that Walpole was concerned primarily with Shake-
    speare's skill in character description and with his "tem-
    pering language to nature."

4   LEWIS, W[ILMARTH] S[HELDON].   "Horace Walpole, Earl of Orford
    (1717-1797)."   In The Cambridge Bibliography of English
    Literature.   Edited by F[rederick] W. Bateson.   Vol. 2.
    Cambridge: Cambridge University Press, pp. 836-41.
        Primarily a list of works by Walpole, with a brief
    section on biography and criticism.   Expanded by Hazen:
    1957.3.

5   WALPOLE, HORACE.   Horace Walpole's Correspondence with George
    Montagu.   Edited by W[ilmarth] S[heldon] Lewis and Ralph S.
    Brown, Jr.   The Yale Edition of Horace Walpole's Correspon-
    dence, edited by W[ilmarth] S[heldon] Lewis, vols. 9-10.
    New Haven: Yale University Press, 2 vols.
        Includes an introduction discussing Walpole's letters to
    Montagu, which "are of more general interest than are those
    written to any other correspondent," some unpublished verses
    by Walpole, and an index.

1942

1   ALTICK, RICHARD D. "Mr. Cambridge Serenades the Berry Sisters." Notes and Queries 183 (12 September):158–61.
    Compares Walpole's and Richard Cambridge's friendships with the Berry sisters. Cambridge, six months older than Walpole, also greatly admired the Berrys and wrote them many verse tributes, here transcribed. Unlike Walpole, however, he had been happily married for fifty years.

2   CARSWELL, CATHERINE. "Walpole, Hume and Home." Times Literary Supplement, 25 April, p. 211.
    The "Mr. Hume" in a letter from Walpole to William Robertson (1942.4) is not David Hume but Walpole's misspelling for John Home.

3   DAVIS, HERBERT. "New Walpole Correspondence." Yale Review 31 (March):611–13.
    Review of 1941.5. Admires Walpole's letters but finds Montagu's mediocre, in contrast with Lewis who suggests that Montagu influenced Walpole's style.

4   GRAY, W. FORBES. "Horace Walpole & Wm. Robertson." Times Literary Supplement, 14 March, p. 132.
    Extracts from several letters from Walpole to William Robertson, mostly on Robertson's History of Scotland, with annotations.

5   HAZEN, A[LLEN] T[RACY]. A Bibliography of the Strawberry Hill Press. With a Record of the Prices at which Copies have been Sold. Together with a Bibliography and Census of the Detached Pieces by A.T. Hazen and J.P. Kirby. New Haven: Yale University Press, 300 pp.
    The definitive study of Strawberry Hill productions, as W.S. Lewis's laudatory preface suggests. Contains full bibliographical descriptions of each book and detached piece printed at Strawberry Hill, including Walpole's own writings, together with a facsimile of the title page of every item. An introduction discusses the history of Strawberry Hill collecting and the difficulties caused by the forgeries of Walpole's printer, Kirgate. Regarded as a classic of bibliography since its first publication; revised: 1973.8.

6   KRONENBERGER, LOUIS. "Horace Walpole." In Kings and Desperate Men: Life in Eighteenth–Century England. New York: A.A. Knopf, pp. 309–20.
    Walpole was a fop with poor taste, yet he is "the greatest social historian of his age and the most constantly diverting letter–writer in English literature." Otranto is stale and mechanical, but it produced the medieval strain that culminates in Scott.

7 QUENNELL, PETER. "Walpole, the Man of the World." <u>Observer</u>, 4
October, p. 3.
Review of 1941.5, emphasizing Walpole's unusual combina-
tion of dilettantism and diligence. Finds his letters to
Montagu on London society interesting but "not always edi-
fying."

8 ROSS, MARVIN CHAUNCEY. "A Gothic Lock from Strawberry Hill."
<u>American Collector</u> 11 (September):5.
Describes and illustrates the ornate Gothic lock presented by Thomas Astle to Walpole in 1788. Walpole's ability to date the lock reveals his knowledge of Gothic art.

9 "The Friend of Horace Walpole. Correspondence with George Montagu. Plums of Humour and Gossip." <u>Times Literary Supple-
ment</u>, 11 July, pp. 342, 345.
Review of 1941.5. Discusses Walpole's friendship and
correspondence with Montagu, who received "some of the very
finest Walpolian plums." Disagrees with Lewis's view that
Walpole's style was heavily influenced by Montagu's.

10 WOOLF, VIRGINIA. "The Humane Art" and "Two Antiquaries: Wal-
pole and Cole." In <u>The Death of the Moth and Other Essays</u>.
London: Hogarth Press, pp. 41-51.
Reprints of 1940.19 and 1939.26.

1943

1 BENNETT, CHARLES [H.]. "Horace Walpole: 'Visitors Book.'"
<u>Notes and Queries</u> 185 (23 October):258.
Asks for assistance in identifying verses in Walpole's
"Visitors Book," and confirms de Castro's correction
(1943.3).

2 CHASE, ISABEL WAKELIN URBAN. <u>Horace Walpole: Gardenist. An
Edition of Walpole's "The History of the Modern Taste in
Gardening" with an Estimate of Walpole's Contribution to
Landscape Architecture</u>. Princeton: Princeton University
Press, 285 pp.
Revision of 1938.4. The definitive edition of Walpole's
<u>The History of the Modern Taste in Gardening</u>, with extensive
textual and explanatory notes. Also contains informative
accounts of Walpole's ideas on landscape design and garden-
ing and on the gardens of his day, including that of Straw-
berry Hill.

3 de CASTRO, J. PAUL. "A Misdated Walpole Letter." <u>Notes and
Queries</u> 185 (3 July):15.
Suggests that a letter from Walpole to Mary Berry, dated
6 October 1795, should in fact be dated 6 November 1795, the

date of a great storm in Twickenham. The corrected date is confirmed by Bennett (1943.1).

4   de CASTRO, J. PAUL. "Torrington Diaries." <u>Notes and Queries</u> 185 (4 December):351.
        Asks for the source of a couplet in an epitaph that Walpole had fixed on St. Ann's Church, Soho, to commemorate the death of Theodore, King of Corsica, in 1756.

5   GREENBERG, HERBERT.   "Dating a Letter by Horace Walpole." <u>Modern Language Notes</u> 58 (December):624.
        Establishes the date of a letter from Walpole to Mason, describing a performance of Mason's play <u>Elfrida,</u> as 19 November 1773.

6   LINDHARD, ANNELIESE. "Walpole, Strawberry Hill og <u>The Castle of Otranto</u>" [Walpole, Strawberry Hill and <u>The Castle of Otranto</u>]. In <u>Det "Gothiske" Element i Engelsk Kultur i det 18. Aarhundrede</u> [The Gothic element in 18th century English culture]. Copenhagen: Povl Branners Forlag, pp. 69–74.
        In Danish. Surveys Walpole's career, his remodelling of Strawberry Hill, and his place in the Gothic renaissance. He lacked the originality he sought to achieve, but rather revived what was previously obscure or unknown. He was much indebted to the more scholarly Gray, whose influence on Walpole should be the subject of further academic research.

7   SEELEY, L[EONARD] B[ENTON]. <u>La época de los tres Jorges a través de la correspondencia de Horace Walpole.</u> Translated with an introduction by Pedro Elias. Barcelona: Collección Historia, 162 pp.
        Abridged translation of 1884.3. An introduction states that because of his position in society, Walpole was ideally placed to reveal everyday eighteenth–century life in his correspondence. Compares Walpole's role in England to that of Pliny in Rome and Mme de Sévigné in France.

8   "The Strawberry Hill Press. Walpole and his Age." <u>Times Literary Supplement</u>, 11 September, p. 444.
        Review of 1942.5. Finds the Strawberry Hill books "curious and entertaining," although technically amateurish.

9   W., F.P. "Crabb Robinson, Mrs. Barbauld, Macaulay, and Horace Walpole." <u>Notes and Queries</u> 185 (18 December):375.
        Traces the "curious traveller from Lima" image in Walpole's letter to Mann of 24 November 1774 through a poem by Mrs. Barbauld of 1812 to an essay by Macaulay of 1840.

10 WAGENKNECHT, EDWARD. "Horace Walpole and <u>The Castle of Otranto.</u>" In <u>The Cavalcade of the English Novel</u>. New York: Henry Holt, pp. 112–14.

Otranto is not the first Gothic novel – it is anticipated
by Leland's Longsword and Smollett's Ferdinand Count Fathom
– but Walpole was the first to develop the form. He was
right to prefer authentic supernaturalism; Clara Reeve and
Ann Radcliffe mistakenly preferred the sham.

11   WALPOLE, HORACE. Le Château d'Otrante: histoire Gothique.
Translated with an introduction by Dominique Corticchiato,
preface by Paul Eluard. Collection romantique, no. 4.
Dijon: José Corti, 154 pp.
A translation of Otranto, with a preface on Walpole as
the founder of the Gothic novel. An introduction regards
Walpole's letters as among the greatest in English literature, and Otranto as a major influence on both the English
and French novel.

1944

1   GOOCH, G[EORGE] P[EABODY]. "Horace Walpole and George II," and
"Horace Walpole and George III." In Courts and Cabinets.
London: Longmans, Green, pp. 171-97.
An informative study of Walpole's Memoirs, focusing on
the portraits of politicians and providing much historical
background. The Memoirs are inferior to the letters as literature, but they contain a "mass of first-hand information"
on eighteenth-century politics.

2   ROWSE, A.L. "Horace Walpole and George Montagu." In The English Spirit: Essays in History and Literature. London:
Macmillan, pp. 202-7.
Review essay on 1941.5. Finds Walpole "at his best, his
gayest and most spontaneous" in his letters to Montagu.
Compares Walpole's aestheticism with Proust's, but observes
that Walpole was also an active politician.

3   THOMSON, MABLE S. "Horace Walpole." In Grist from My Mill.
London: printed for the author, pp. 34-37.
Walpole's letters depict everyday life in the late
eighteenth century, but he "shrank from looking too closely
into the hidden causes" of events. Otranto, often under-
rated, "started the movement which eventually led to the
Waverly Novels." Reprinted from an unlocated issue of the
Christian Science Monitor of 1917; commemorates the bicentenary of Walpole's death.

4   WALPOLE, HORACE. Horace Walpole's Correspondence with Mary and
Agnes Berry and Barbara Cecilia Seton. Edited by W[ilmarth]
S[heldon] Lewis and A. Dayle Wallace, with the assistance of
Charles H. Bennett and Edwine M. Martz. The Yale Edition of
Horace Walpole's Correspondence, edited by W[ilmarth]

S[heldon] Lewis, vols. 11-12. New Haven: Yale University Press, 2 vols.

Includes an introduction, denying that Walpole was in love with the Berrys and discussing Mary Berry's spirited rejoinder to Macaulay (1840.1), a transcript of Walpole's unpublished "Book of Visitors at Strawberry Hill, 1784-1796," and an index.

5   [WELCH, CAROL.] "Life Explores World's Finest Walpole Library." Life 17 (23 October):116-20.

A richly illustrated account of W.S. Lewis's Walpole collection, with conventional remarks on Walpole's life and works. Considers the importance of his letters and the influence of Strawberry Hill and Otranto.

6   WHITE, FREDERICK CONNETT. "Torrington Diaries." Notes and Queries 186 (1 January):25-26.

Replies to de Castro (1943.4), suggesting that the couplet was Walpole's own.

1945

1   BENNETT, CHARLES H. "Horace Walpole." Notes and Queries 188 (24 March):124.

Six queries about allusions and names in Walpole's correspondence with West and Gray.

2   [CONANT, KENNETH J.] "Horace Walpole and the Gothic Revival." Old Wedgwood 12:62-69.

Summarizes a paper contending that Walpole gave "aristocratic respectability" to the Gothic style; Strawberry Hill was among the best known places of the eighteenth century.

3   DORAN, J[OHN]. "Crabb Robinson, Mrs. Barbauld, Macaulay, and Horace Walpole." Notes and Queries 188 (21 April):171.

Reprint of 1857.1a.

4   EASTWOOD, SIDNEY K. "Horace Walpole." Notes and Queries 189 (28 July):40.

Responds to one of Bennett's queries (1945.1).

5   FISCHER, EARL K. "Sidelights on Science: Serendipity." Interchemical Review 4 (Spring):26-28.

Quotes and discusses Walpole's letter to Mann of 28 January 1754, defining "serendipity," and reproduces part of Walpole's copy of the letter. Believes that "serendipity" will continue to be a useful term in modern science.

6   "Foolish, Fond Old Man. Horace Walpole's 'Darlings.'" Times Literary Supplement, 14 April, p. 174.

Review article on 1944.4. Disagrees with the Yale editors' view that Walpole was not really in love with the
Berry sisters, contending that his emotions for Mary Berry,
especially, were stronger than any others in his life. Walpole's letters to the Berrys are anxious bids for attention,
"the devices of an old sick man."

7   LEWIS, WILMARTH S[HELDON]. "Horace Walpole Reread." Atlantic
    Monthly 176 (July):48-51.
        A general essay, considering Walpole's fluctuating repu-
    tation and the significance of his correspondence. Revised:
    1951.6.

8   LEWIS, WILMARTH S[HELDON]. "Searching for Manuscripts."
    Atlantic Monthly 176 (September):67-72.
        Describes the author's search for manuscripts of Wal-
    pole's correspondence. Revised: 1951.6.

9   "Rococo Gothic: Walpole, Bentley and Strawberry Hill." Archi-
    tectural Review 98 (December):150-54.
        Reproduces a selection of Bentley's drawings for Straw-
    berry Hill, owned by W.S. Lewis, with remarks based on
    Lewis's study (1934.4).

10 WRIGHT, AUSTIN. "Prince of Letter Writers." Carnegie Magazine
    19 (November):151-53.
        A review essay on the Yale Edition. Walpole is "the his-
    torian of his own time"; his grace, wit and shrewdness make
    him the greatest of English letter writers.

11 WRIGHT, JOHN. "A Famous 18th Century Visitor: Horace Wal-
    pole." Sussex County Magazine, June, pp. 135-38.
        An indignant survey of the largely uncomplimentary refer-
    ences to Sussex in Walpole's letters. Prefers the mansions
    and castles of Sussex to "the pseudo-Gothic shams" of Straw-
    berry Hill, and deplores Walpole's condescending attitude to
    Sussex edifices.

                            1946

1   COLGATE, WILLIAM. "Russia in 1710: A Diplomatic Incident."
    Queen's Quarterly 53 (Summer):236-40.
        Describes a Strawberry Hill publication, Charles Whit-
    worth's An Account of Russia as it Was in the Year 1710
    (1758). Discusses the quality of the bookmaking and Wal-
    pole's preface, commending Walpole for rescuing Whitworth's
    work from obscurity.

2   FINBERG, H[ILDA] F. "Mrs. Metheglin." Notes and Queries 190
    (4 May):193.

Queries the identity of a Mrs. Metheglin mentioned in a
letter from Walpole to Montagu of 11 August 1748.

3   KETTON-CREMER, R[OBERT] W[YNDHAM].   Horace Walpole: A Biog-
    raphy. 2d ed. London: Faber & Faber, 333 pp.
    Revision of 1940.10.

4   LEWIS, WILMARTH S[HELDON].   "The Start of a Collection."
    Atlantic Monthly 177 (April):128–32.
         Records the beginnings of a lifelong interest in Walpole,
    pointing out the attractions of Walpole's style, wit, un-
    expectedness, and energy. Revised: 1951.6.

                                1947

1   ALLEN, TREVOR.   "'Horry' of Strawberry Hill."   John O'London's
    Weekly, 4 April, p. 323.
         Review of 1946.3, defending Walpole from such critics as
    Macaulay and Croker. Admires his humanity and family loyal-
    ty.

2   "At Strawberry Hill."   Times (London), 17 May, p.5.
         Summarizes Ketton-Cremer's bicentennial lecture (1947.13)
    and discusses Walpole's connection with Strawberry Hill.
    Compares Walpole with Pepys and Boswell: all three were
    "invincible egoists," who illuminated their age through
    vivid accounts of their own lives.

3   BENNETT, CHARLES H.   "Horace Walpole."   Notes and Queries 192
    (15 November):500.
         Five queries, the most significant of which enquires why
    Sir Robert Walpole chose the title of Orford on being
    created a peer in 1742.

4   CAPETANAKIS, DEMETRIOS.   "Thomas Gray and Horace Walpole (A
    Chapter from an Unfinished Study)."   In Demetrios Capeta-
    nakis: A Greek Poet in England. Edited by John Lehmann.
    London: John Lehmann, pp. 117–24.
         Studies Gray's life at Cambridge and his unhappy letters
    to Walpole during their separation. Believes that while
    Walpole felt merely friendship for Gray, Gray "experienced
    all the sufferings of unrequited love." Reprinted: 1949.4.

5   CRAIG, J.D.   "Epilogue."   In 1947.20, p. 20.
         Claims that Walpole is a household name. Eighteenth-
    century soldiers and politicians are forgotten, but the
    writers live on.

6   DAHL, INGEBORG.   "Die englische Gesellschaft des 18. Jahrhun-
    derts im Spiegel von Horace Walpoles Briefen."   Ph.D. dis-

sertation, University of Heidelberg, 182 pp.
Uses Walpole's letters as a guide to eighteenth-century
England, discussing such topics as domestic and foreign politics, social life in London and at country estates, literature, art, and religion. Also studies Walpole's attitudes
to France, regarding him throughout as representative of his
age.

7   DIGEON, AURELIEN. "Horace Walpole." In Histoire illustrée de
la littérature anglaise. Paris: Didier, pp. 176-77.
Walpole's reputation rests on his correspondence, which
contains valuable information on his age. Otranto is also
significant as the foundation of the Gothic novel.

8   EVANS, BERTRAND. "The Mysterious Mother" and "The First Adaptation of Otranto: The Count of Narbonne." In Gothic Drama
from Walpole to Shelley. California University Publications
in English, no. 18. Berkeley: University of California
Press, pp. 32-39, 49-61.
Walpole's The Mysterious Mother initiates the school of
Gothic drama, and his skill was unequalled by his successors. Robert Jephson's adaptation of Otranto, The Count of
Narbonne, omits the "grossest elements" of the novel but
retains its essential qualities.

9   HAZEN, A[LLEN] T[RACY]. "Strawberry Hill Sale Catalogues,
1842." Notes and Queries 192 (25 January):33-35.
Supplements Merritt (1915.4), distinguishing seven "editions" of the Strawberry Hill Sale Catalogues.

10 HOPKINS, MARY ALDEN. "Bishop Porteus and Horace Walpole." In
Hannah More and her Circle. New York: Longmans, pp. 136-
42.
Discusses More's friendship with "that sacrilegious
charmer Horace Walpole," regarding it as "a credit to both."
Studies the printing of Bishop Bonner's Ghost at Strawberry
Hill and More's poem dedicated to Walpole, Florio: A Tale,
for Gentlemen and Ladies.

11 "Horace Walpole." Times Literary Supplement, 24 May, p. 253.
Commemorates the bicentenary of Walpole's acquisition of
Strawberry Hill, which was "the right expression of his
intellectual resolution" and "a challenge to materialism."

12 JUDD, GERRIT PARMELE, IV. "Horace Walpole's Journal 1783-91."
Ph.D. dissertation, Yale University, 947 pp.
Contains an extensive introduction to all of Walpole's
memoirs and journals (revised for publication 1959.2), and a
very thoroughly annotated text of the journal for 1783-91.
Contends that this journal lacks literary merit, and that it
is less valuable than the previous memoirs as Walpole had

little knowledge of political affairs in his later years.

13   KETTON-CREMER, R[OBERT] W[YNDHAM].   "Horace Walpole."   In
      1947.20, pp. 5-13.
            A general essay on Walpole's life and works. Defends
      Strawberry Hill as an individual fantasy; Walpole did not
      advocate the Gothic style for large public buildings. His
      letters create an "incomparable panorama" of eighteenth-
      century England.

14   KETTON-CREMER, R[OBERT] W[YNDHAM].   "Horace Walpole in Fifty
      Volumes." *Listener* 38 (17 July):103-5.
            Walpole's letters create a matchless panorama of the
      eighteenth century and deserve the editorial cares of the
      Yale Edition, the most elaborate ever of an English author.

15   LEWIS, WILMARTH SHELDON.   "Collector's Progress." *Atlantic
      Monthly* 179 (April):82-85.
            Using Walpole's works as examples, discusses four stages
      in a book collector's development: an interest in binding,
      in association items, in condition, and in provenance.
      Revised: 1951.6.

16   LEWIS, W[ILMARTH] S[HELDON].   "Horace Walpole's Library."
      Library, 5th ser. 2 (June):45-52.
            Describes Walpole's library at Strawberry Hill, the
      arrangement of his books, their dispersal at the Strawberry
      Hill Sale of 1842, and their subsequent history. Revised:
      1947.17.

17   LEWIS, WILMARTH SHELDON.   "The Books at Strawberry Hill."
      Atlantic Monthly 180 (September):109-13.
            Revision of 1947.16.

18   RADICE, SHEILA. "Horace Walpole." *Times Literary Supplement*,
      21 June, p. 309.
            Quotes a letter from Croker to Lord Liverpool of 1824,
      expressing intense dislike of Walpole for "poisoning the
      sources of history."

19   RICHARDSON, A.E.   "Strawberry Hill Gothic."   In 1947.20, pp.
      15-19.
            Studies Strawberry Hill as the precursor of the nine-
      teenth-century Gothic revival. Walpole stimulated interest
      in medievalism at a time when classicism was predominant.

20   SHANNON, REV. DR.   Introduction to *Bicentenary of Strawberry
      Hill: A Reprint of the Proceedings at St. Mary's College on
      May 16th, 1947*. London: The Georgian Group, p. 3.
            Introduces three essays commemorating the bicentennial of
      Walpole's acquisition of Strawberry Hill, which was "the

life of Horace Walpole." Regards Walpole's combination of detachment and enthusiasm as quintessentially eighteenth century.

1948

1   HAZEN, ALLEN T[RACY]. A Bibliography of Horace Walpole. New Haven: Yale University Press, 189 pp.
    The definitive bibliography of Walpole's own writings. Includes a brief preface by W.S. Lewis, an introduction discussing the variety and significance of Walpole's works, and sections on books by Walpole, books with editorial contributions by Walpole, Walpole's contributions to periodicals, books dedicated to Walpole, apocrypha, and unprinted manuscripts. For writings by Walpole printed at Strawberry Hill, refers throughout to Hazen's previous bibliography (1942.5): "the two books together form in effect a two-volume Walpolian bibliography."

2   ILCHESTER, EARL OF. "Madame du Deffand to Walpole." Times Literary Supplement, 19 June, p. 348.
    Transcribes and annotates an unpublished letter from Mme du Deffand to Walpole of 26 December 1770, describing the fall of the Duc de Choiseul.

3   KETTON-CREMER, R[OBERT] W[YNDHAM]. "George Walpole, Third Earl of Orford." In A Norfolk Gallery. London: Faber & Faber, pp. 162-87.
    The fullest account of Walpole's dealings with his highly eccentric and sometimes insane nephew, George Walpole.

4   KETTON-CREMER, R[OBERT] W[YNDHAM]. "Samuel Johnson and Horace Walpole." New Rambler, no. 12 (January), pp. 8-15.
    Discusses Johnson's disdain for Walpole and his circle, and Walpole's antipathy for Johnson. Walpole's hostility was aroused by Johnson's Toryism, his bad manners, and his criticism of Gray.

5   McKILLOP, ALAN DUGALD. "Horace Walpole (1717-1797)." In English Literature from Dryden to Burns. New York: Appleton-Century-Crofts, pp. 356-59.
    A survey of Walpole's life and works. Stresses the influence of Otranto and the significance of the letters, which combine "literary value and social documentation."

6   NEVILL, JOHN CRANSTON. "In Search of a Patron." In Thomas Chatterton. London: Frederick Muller, pp. 78-107.
    Studies Walpole's dealings with Chatterton, finding Walpole generally culpable. Deplores Walpole's spurious letter to Rousseau from the King of Prussia and is baffled by the

success of <u>Otranto</u>.

7   STRACHEY, [GILES] LYTTON.   "Madame du Deffand," "Horace Wal-
     pole," "Walpole's Letters," "The Eighteenth Century," and
     "Mary Berry."   In <u>Biographical Essays</u>.   Edited by James
     Strachey.   London: Chatto & Windus, pp. 165-210.
         Reprints of 1922.5, 1931.10, and 1933.7.

8   TAYLOR, FRANCIS HENRY.   "Horace Walpole and the Rule of Many
     Tastes," and "Houghton and Strawberry Hill."   In <u>The Taste
     of Angels: A History of Art Collecting from Rameses to
     Napoleon</u>.   Boston: Little, Brown, pp. 420-42.
         An informative study of Walpole as art collector and art
     historian.   Regards <u>Aedes Walpolianae</u> as the most important
     work of English art criticism of the eighteenth century,
     before Reynolds's <u>Discourses</u>.   Strawberry Hill, <u>Anecdotes of
     Painting</u> and the essay on gardening all grew out of Wal-
     pole's conviction of "the greatness of England's past."

9   WALPOLE, HORACE.   <u>Horace Walpole's Correspondence with Thomas
     Gray, Richard West and Thomas Ashton</u>.   Edited by W[ilmarth]
     S[heldon] Lewis, George L. Lam and Charles H. Bennett.   The
     Yale Edition of Horace Walpole's Correspondence, edited by
     W[ilmarth] S[heldon] Lewis, vols. 13-14.   New Haven: Yale
     University Press, 2 vols.
         Includes a brief study of the Quadruple Alliance at Eton
     and after, a survey of the reception of previous volumes of
     the Yale Edition, Walpole's "Short Notes of my Life," pub-
     lished from the manuscript with extensive annotations and
     described as "the most important Walpole document in exis-
     tence," Walpole's unpublished "Anecdotes of Lady Mary Wort-
     ley Montagu and Lady Pomfret," and an index.

                                1949

1   BARRINGTON, MICHAEL.   "'Historic Doubts' Concerning Perkin War-
     beck."   <u>Notes and Queries</u> 194 (28 May):229-32.
         Compares Walpole's <u>Historic Doubts</u> with George Buck's
     <u>History of the Life and Reigne of Richard the Third</u> (1647).
     Finds Walpole's major contentions plausible, though disput-
     able.   Both he and Buck believed that Richard III had been
     maligned by Tudor historians, and that Perkin Warbeck was
     the true Prince.

2   BRANDENBURG, ALICE STAYERT.   "The Theme of <u>The Mysterious
     Mother</u>."   <u>Modern Language Quarterly</u> 10 (December):464-74.
         Discusses the incest theme in Walpole's play, and its
     occurrence in several eighteenth-century plays and novels.
     Believes that the Countess of Narbonne's incest was shocking
     because it was committed deliberately; incest was normally

involuntary. Walpole used incest as a tragic subject, not merely as "cheap sensationalism."

3 BUTTERFIELD, HERBERT. "Horace Walpole and the Yorkshire Movement." In George III, Lord North and the People 1779-80. London: G. Bell, pp. 388-91.
Walpole, a Whig of the old type, welcomed the Yorkshire movement, of which he was well informed by Mason, but gradually turned against it. This change epitomizes Walpole's career.

4 CAPETANAKIS, DEMETRIOS. "Thomas Gray and Horace Walpole (A Chapter from an Unfinished Study)." In The Shores of Darkness: Poems and Essays. New York: Devin-Adair, pp. 117-24.
Reprint of 1947.4.

5 COHEN, WALTER. "Serendipity." New York Times Book Review, 2 October, p. 44.
A note on Walpole's invention of the word, and on its source in The Three Princes of Serendip.

6 FORMAN, R.S. "Sir Horace Mann." Notes and Queries 194 (16 April):160-61.
The Dictionary of National Biography entry on Mann is incorrect in stating that Mann and Walpole were not related.

7 HALSBAND, ROBERT. "An Irresistible Epistolary Style." New York Times Book Review, 2 January, p. 11.
Review of 1948.9. Considers the importance of Walpole's correspondence with Gray, and suggests that the Yale Edition will show Walpole to be "the greatest memoirist of English literature."

8 HELLMAN, GEOFFREY T. "The Steward of Strawberry Hill." New Yorker 25 (6 August):26-37; (13 August):31-37.
A lively, informative essay on W.S. Lewis, his collection of Walpoliana, and the progress of the Yale Edition of Walpole's correspondence. Draws attention to its immensely detailed annotation and indexing, "one of the prodigies of the scholarly world."

9 HUMPHREYS, ARTHUR R. "'Spirits of Hartshorn.'" Cambridge Journal 2 (May):474-84.
An enthusiastic survey of Walpole's letters, with numerous quotations. Emphasizes their charm and wit, rather than their substance.

10 LEWIS, WILMARTH SHELDON. "Relics." Atlantic Monthly 184 (December):74-78.
Discusses various relics of Walpole, including furniture,

art, and parts of Strawberry Hill itself, now in the author's collection. Revised: 1951.6.

11   LEWIS, WILMARTH SHELDON.   "The Last Word."   New Colophon 2
      (June):163-66.
            Considers the problems involved in annotating Walpole's
      correspondence, using his letter to William Cole of 7 April
      1773 as an example.

12   "Records of Friendship."   Times Literary Supplement, 22 July,
      p. 472.
            Review of 1948.9.   Notes that Walpole recognized Gray's
      genius "long before anyone else," and traces the development
      and temporary interruption of their friendship.

13   SHEPPERSON, ARCHIBALD B[OLLING].   "The Quadruple Alliance."
      Virginia Quarterly Review 25 (Spring):290-93.
            Review article on 1948.9.   Considers the significance of
      Walpole's correspondence with Gray and of Walpole's influ-
      ence on Gray's style: he is "almost as much present in
      Gray's letters as Gray is himself."

14   SMITH, WARREN HUNTING.   "Horace Walpole and Two Frenchwomen."
      In The Age of Johnson: Essays Presented to Chauncey
      Brewster Tinker. Edited by Frederick W. Hilles. New Haven:
      Yale University Press, pp. 341-48.
            One of Mme du Deffand's great attractions for Walpole was
      her link with Mme de Sévigné, Walpole's "saint" and one of
      his favourite authors. Both he and Mme du Deffand compared
      their letters with those of Mme de Sévigné: "the eternal
      triangle assumes a new aspect when one member of the trio is
      a deceased authoress whom both the other members are thought
      to resemble."

1950

1   [BREDVOLD, LOUIS I.]   "Letter Writers: Chesterfield and Wal-
      pole." In A History of English Literature. Edited by Har-
      din Craig. New York: Oxford University Press, pp. 417-18.
            Discusses the French influence on Walpole and the impor-
      tance of his letters, which record a "whole era in the
      social history of England." Reprinted: 1962.1.

2   CLARK, KENNETH.   "Ruins and Rococo: Strawberry Hill."   In The
      Gothic Revival. 2d ed. London: Constable, pp. 60-86.
            Revision of 1928.2.

3   DOBRÉE, BONAMY.   "Books and Writers."   Spectator, 23 June, p.
      859.
            Strawberry Hill has almost passed away, but Otranto lives

on. It is "beautifully done," compelling reading, and deeply thought out. Reprinted in part: 1963.2.

4 LEWIS, WILMARTH SHELDON. "'You Know All About Books.'" Atlantic Monthly 186 (July):77-80.
    Shows how knowing "all about books" aids in accumulating the world's largest Walpole collection. Revised: 1951.6.

5 O'DOWD, D. "Horace Walpole and Strawberry Hill." In Centenary Record of St. Mary's College. London: St. Mary's College, pp. 57-65.
    Studies Walpole's links with Catholicism, both through some Jesuit ancestors and through his interest in the Gothic architecture of the Catholic Church. Regards Otranto as absurd but seminal; the letters "give a very full picture of the period."

6 RODDIER, HENRI. "Le séjour de Rousseau en Angleterre: asile ou exile?" In J.-J. Rousseau en Angleterre au XVIIIe siècle. Paris: Boivin, pp. 259-306.
    Describes Walpole's spurious letter to Rousseau from the King of Prussia and its effect on Hume's relations with Walpole and Rousseau, without taking sides in the controversy.

7 SIREN, OSVALD. "Horace Walpole, the Garden Patriot." In China and the Gardens of Europe of the Eighteenth Century. New York: The Ronald Press, p. 52.
    Discusses Walpole's disapproval of the "fantastic sharawadgis" of the Chinese style in gardening, and his aspirations for an English tradition. Describes Walpole as "the final authority in this sphere."

8 WHITE, T.H. "Men, Women and Herveys." In The Age of Scandal. London: Jonathan Cape, pp. 97-112.
    Supports the theory that Walpole was the son of Lord Hervey, comparing his personality with that of the Hervey family. Also discusses Walpole's life at Strawberry Hill; he was "a skillful antiquary and virtuoso midwife."

1951

1 BOULTON, J[AMES] T. "Burke and Walpole." Times Literary Supplement, 20 April, p. 245.
    Transcribes an unpublished letter from Walpole to Burke of 4 November 1790, thanking Burke for a copy of his Reflections on the Revolution in France.

2 BROWN, JOHN MASON. "Horace Walpole Moves to Conn." Saturday Review of Literature 34 (22 September):26-29.
    Review of 1951.6. Commends Lewis's collection of Walpol-

iana, which will assure Walpole's place in history.

3   CONNOLLY, CYRIL. "Strawberry Hill." Sunday Times (London), 8 July, p. 2.

        Review of 1951.11. Compares Walpole's letters to harpsichord music; "there are times when they sound unimaginably lovely and moments when they sound intolerably monotonous." Reprinted: 1963.1.

4   GOOCH, G[EORGE] P[EABODY]. "Four French Salons. IV: Mme du Deffand and Horace Walpole." Contemporary Review 180 (September):148–57.

        An account of Walpole's relationship and correspondence with Mme du Deffand, contending that his letters to his friends show a deeper affection for her than do his few surviving letters to her. Criticizes Walpole for "obstinately suppressing" his emotions. Revised: 1954.2.

5   HEWSON-SMITH, ROBERT. "A Little Journey to Strawberry Hill Near Twickenham, Middlesex, England." In Rambling Over Strawberry Hill. Long Island: Strawberry Hill Press, pp. 3–4.

        An account of the architecture and furnishings of Strawberry Hill, emphasizing the "exceptional excellence" of the printing press.

6   LEWIS, WILMARTH [SHELDON]. Collector's Progress. New York: Knopf, 253 pp.

        An account of Lewis's connections with Walpole, begun in 1923. Describes his search for works by, about and related to Walpole, and the foundation of the Yale Edition of Walpole's correspondence. Includes revisions of 1945.7–8, 1946.4, 1947.15, 1949.10 and 1950.4.

7   PEVSNER, NIKOLAUS. "Strawberry Hill." In Middlesex. Harmondsworth: Penguin, pp. 161–66.

        Traces the history and describes the architecture of Strawberry Hill, which is "both amusing and awful, both Rococo and romantic."

8   SMITH, WARREN HUNTING. "Cipher and Code in Horace Walpole's Correspondence." Yale University Library Gazette 25 (January):117–19.

        Studies the cipher used by Walpole and Mann in some of their correspondence. In the surviving examples it is seen to be elementary, and unlikely to pose problems for the authorities who regularly intercepted eighteenth-century letters.

9   WALPOLE, HORACE. Horace Walpole's Correspondence with Sir David Dalrymple. Edited by W[ilmarth] S[heldon] Lewis,

Charles H. Bennett and Andrew G[raham] Hoover. The Yale Edition of Horace Walpole's Correspondence, edited by W[ilmarth] S[heldon] Lewis, vol. 15. New Haven: Yale University Press, 395 pp.

Contains Walpole's correspondence with Dalrymple and ten other antiquaries. An introduction to this volume and to 1951.10 studies Walpole's place in the antiquarian world, considering his dealings with Pinkerton and Chatterton and defending him vigorously from pro-Chattertonian attacks. There are several appendices, including anecdotes of Walpole in Farington's diary, 1793-97, and an index.

10 WALPOLE, HORACE. Horace Walpole's Correspondence with Thomas Chatterton, Michael Lort, John Pinkerton, John Fenn and Mrs. Fenn, William Bewley, Nathaniel Hiller. Edited by W[ilmarth] S[heldon] Lewis and A. Dayle Wallace. With Henry Zouch. Edited by W[ilmarth] S[heldon] Lewis and Ralph M. Williams. The Yale Edition of Horace Walpole's Correspondence, edited by W[ilmarth] S[heldon] Lewis, vol. 16. New Haven: Yale University Press, 439 pp.

Continuation of 1951.9, Walpole's correspondence with antiquaries. Includes, as an appendix, Walpole's marginalia in his collection of Chattertoniana, and an index.

11 WALPOLE, HORACE. Letters of Horace Walpole. Edited by W[ilmarth] S[heldon] Lewis, introduction by R[obert] W[yndham] Ketton-Cremer. London: Folio Society, 283 pp.

Contains seventy-three letters by Walpole, of which sixty-nine were published in Lewis's previous selection (1926.13). The text and notes are based on those of the Yale and the Toynbees' editions. An introduction discusses Walpole's various correspondents and notes the value of the letters for a study of both Walpole and his century.

1952

1 ANDERSEN, JORGEN. "Giant Dreams: Piranesi's Influence in England." English Miscellany 3:49-60.

Considers Piranesi's influence on English writers, primarily on Walpole and Beckford. Discusses Walpole's references to Piranesi, and compares parts of Otranto to a Piranesi vision.

2 BARRINGTON, MICHAEL. "The Prince of Connoisseurs. Horace Walpole and Strawberry Hill." Notes and Queries 197 (7 June): 253-58.

Discusses Walpole as a collector, with extensive quotations from his Description of the Villa. Believes that no private collector in England will ever again be as lavish.

3   BENNETT, CHARLES H.   "Horace Walpole and Hannah More."   <u>Notes</u>
    <u>and Queries</u> 197 (24 May):238.
          Asks for the sources of five literary allusions in Wal-
    pole's correspondence with Hannah More.

4   BENNETT, CHARLES H.   "The Text of Horace Walpole's Correspon-
    dence with Hannah More."   <u>Review of English Studies</u>, n.s. 3
    (October):341-45.
          Studies the alterations and expurgations made by More in
    Walpole's letters to her.   Revised: 1961.10.

5   CHAPMAN, R.W.   "Strawberry Hill in New England."   <u>Listener</u> 48
    (24 July):148-49.
          Review of 1951.6.   Discusses Lewis's collecting and edit-
    ing of Walpole, applauding the Yale Edition of Walpole's
    correspondence, which forms an "encyclopaedia of the age."

6   CONNOLLY, CYRIL.   "Squire of Otranto."   <u>Sunday Times</u> (London),
    15 June, p. 11.
          Review of 1951.6.   Walpole "nursed a grand design: to
    present a complete picture of his time through a planned
    exchange of letters with an ambassador, an antiquary, a don,
    a field-marshal, a man of the world and a series of intelli-
    gent and fashionable women."   Reprinted: 1963.1.

7   FINBERG, HILDA F.   "Jewish Residents in Eighteenth-Century
    Twickenham."   <u>Transactions of the Jewish Historical Society</u>
    <u>of England</u> 16:129-35.
          Walpole's letters, with their "extraordinary gossip,"
    provide much information about Jewish residents of Twicken-
    ham, and show that he was on friendly terms with several of
    them.

8   GEORGE, MARY S.F.   "Horace Walpole's Letters to Ampthill."
    <u>Bedfordshire Magazine</u> 3, no. 23:294-300.
          Studies Walpole's friendship and correspondence with the
    Countess of Upper Ossory, and his admiration for her home at
    Ampthill, Bedfordshire.

9   JONES, M.G.   "The Literati."   In <u>Hannah More</u>.   Cambridge:
    Cambridge University Press, pp. 66-73.
          Regards More's relationship with Walpole as "the most
    interesting and diverting" of her friendships.   Suggests
    that Walpole chose More as a correspondent in his later
    years because she "shared his elderly interests and preju-
    dices," despite their religious differences.

10 [KETTON-CREMER, ROBERT WYNDHAM.]   "The Yale Edition of Wal-
    pole."   <u>Times Literary Supplement</u>, 3 October, p. 644.
          Review of 1951.9-10.   Discusses Walpole's relations with
    various antiquaries, including Pinkerton, Beloe, and Conyers

Middleton. Justifies Walpole's dealings with Chatterton, observing that he "sincerely admired" Chatterton's poetry.

11 KUNITZ, STANLEY J., and HAYCRAFT, HOWARD. "Walpole, Horace (Horatio) (Fourth Earl of Orford)." In British Authors Before 1800. New York: H.W. Wilson, pp. 541–43.
     An inaccurate biographical sketch, with some comments on Walpole's works. His letters constitute a "history of their time," surpassing those of Mme de Sévigné "in pure wit and as pure art."

12 PEVSNER, NIKOLAUS. "Strawberry Hill, Twickenham." Listener 48 (10 July):55–56.
     A lively account of the architecture of Strawberry Hill. Walpole did not invent "domesticated medievalism," but no other building was as influential in spreading the vogue. Otranto, similarly, caused a virulent growth of Gothic novels.

*13 SAITO, BISHU. "Preliminary Notes on The Castle of Otranto." Rising Generation 98:56–58; 108–9.
     Source: Annual Bibliography of English Language and Literature 30 (1952):419.

1953

1 BROWN, T.J. "English Literary Autographs: VIII. Horace Walpole: 1717–1797." Book Collector 2 (Winter):274–75.
     Three examples of Walpole's handwriting (1765, 1779, and 1796) show the difficulties caused by his gout. An example of Kirgate's hand shows that it "is not really very like his master's."

2 CHURCHILL, R[EGINALD] C[HARLES]. "Walpole and the 'Gothic' Novel." In English Literature of the Eighteenth Century. London: University Tutorial Press, pp. 235–38.
     The fame of Otranto in Europe was exceeded only by that of Clarissa. It had an immense influence on German romantic literature, and a smaller but still important influence in Britain. Walpole's letters, however, "make up a better novel than his 'Gothic' story."

3 COLGATE, WILLIAM. Horace Walpole on Milton. A Summary of his Annotations on the Work of Thomas Warton Concerning the Poems of John Milton from the London Edition of James Dodsley 1785. Toronto: privately printed, 18 pp.
     Transcribes and summarizes Walpole's marginalia on Warton's edition of Milton. Most of the marginalia correct or expand Warton's notes, rather than commenting on Milton's poetry.

4   LEWIS, WILMARTH SHELDON. "Editing Familiar Letters." <u>Listener</u>
     49 (9 April):597-98.
          Uses the Yale Edition of Walpole's correspondence to
     illustrate the problems and challenges involved in editing
     familiar letters. Reprinted: 1955.8; revised: 1979.12.

5   SUMMERSON, JOHN. "The Amateurs: Sanderson Miller and Horace
     Walpole."   In <u>Architecture in Britain 1530 to 1830</u>.   Har-
     mondsworth: Penguin, pp. 241-45.
          Studies the development of Strawberry Hill, emphasizing
     the architectural contributions of William Robinson.   Con-
     tends that Strawberry Hill was "<u>not</u> the source of Georgian
     Gothic in general," but that it exerted a strong influence
     at the end of the eighteenth century.

                                     1954

1   CHRISTIE, IAN [R.]. "Horace Walpole: The Gossip as Histori-
     an." <u>History Today</u> 4 (May):291-300.
          Evaluates Walpole's letters and memoirs as historical
     works.   The letters provide a running commentary on eigh-
     teenth-century society; the memoirs "have a greater coher-
     ence and completeness of form," although they also reveal
     Walpole's personal prejudices. Together, they both enlight-
     en and entertain posterity. Reprinted: 1970.3a.

2   GOOCH, GEORGE PEABODY. "Mme du Deffand and Horace Walpole."
     In <u>Catherine the Great and Other Studies</u>.   London: Long-
     mans, pp. 167-79.
          Revision of 1951.4.

3   HACKENBROCH, YVONNE. "A Limoges Enamel Hunting Horn."   <u>Con-
     noisseur</u> 133 (June):249-51.
          Describes and illustrates a sixteenth-century hunting
     horn owned by Walpole, who pursued his collecting with
     "amazing gusto." The horn was a special feature of the 1842
     Strawberry Hill Sale, and was burlesqued in several satires.

4   ILCHESTER, EARL OF. "Some Pages Torn from the Last Jour-
     nals of Horace Walpole." In <u>Studies in Art and Literature
     for Belle da Costa Greene</u>.   Edited by Dorothy Miner.
     Princeton: Princeton University Press, pp. 449-58.
          Transcribes a violent attack on Charles James Fox, writ-
     ten by Walpole as part of his <u>Last Journals,</u> but omitted
     from Doran's edition (1859.4).   An introduction considers
     the reasons for the attack and for its omission.   Also
     transcribes an indignant response by Fox's nephew, Henry
     Vassall.

5   ROHDE, H[ERMANN] P[ETER]. "De etruskiske Bogbind. A propos en

Gave fra Horace Walpole" [A Gift of books in Etruscan bind-
ings from Horace Walpole]. Bogvennen. Aarbog for Bogkunst
og Boghistorie 9:1-28.

In Danish, with English summary. Describes Walpole's
gift of a collection of books to the Royal Library, Copenhagen, in 1788 and notes that Walpole complained, in a
letter of 1792, that the Danish monarch had never acknowl-
edged the gift.

6   ROTHSCHILD, LORD. "Odes by Mr. Gray," "Horace Walpole, Fourth
Earl of Orford," and "The Strawberry Hill Press." In The
Rothschild Library: A Catalogue of the Collection of
Eighteenth-Century Printed Books and Manuscripts Formed by
Lord Rothschild. 2 vols. Cambridge: Cambridge University
Press, 1:266-68; 2:669-79, 727-30.

The section on Gray's Odes contains a complete transcript
of Walpole's annotations on his copy. The sections on Walpole and Strawberry Hill list books by and printed by Walpole in the Rothschild Library, with useful commentaries.

7   WELCHER, JEANNE KATHRYN. "The Literary Opinions of Horace Walpole." Ph.D. dissertation, Fordham University, 469 pp.

The fullest study of Walpole's views on literature.
Examines all of Walpole's writings to show the range of his
literary opinions, and places them in their contemporary
critical context. Includes an extensive introduction and
sections on Walpole's formal writings, his opinions on
drama, verse and prose, and his views on literary and aesthetic theory. His literary commentary is both "useful for
an understanding of the age and thoroughly enjoyable in
itself."

                                1955

1   CLIFFORD, JAMES L. "Epistolary Peak." Saturday Review 38 (15
January):21-22.

Review of 1955.12. Notes the early maturity of Walpole's
crisp style and ironic attitude. Regrets the "arid
stretches" in his correspondence with Mann, but finds that
as a whole it offers "the most substance and entertainment"
of all Walpole's correspondences.

2   HAZEN, A[LLEN] T[RACY]. "The Booksellers' 'Ring' at Strawberry
Hill in 1842." Studies in Bibliography 7:194-98.

Demonstrates that the many very low prices of Walpole's
books at the Strawberry Hill Sale of 1842 were artificially
created by a group of cooperating booksellers. These low
prices, however, apply only to the miscellaneous lots; the
prices of other items were generally satisfactory and sometimes inflated.

3   HUSSEY, CHRISTOPHER. "Strawberry Hill, Middlesex." In English
     Country Houses, Early Georgian. 1715-1760. London:
     Country Life, pp. 211-16.
          A well-illustrated account of Walpole's remodelling of
     Strawberry Hill. Walpole's was not the first eighteenth-
     century experiment in Gothic architecture, but Strawberry
     Hill is "the outstanding example of the style's develop-
     ment." Revised: 1965.5.

4   IRVING, WILLIAM HENRY. "Walpole and Cowper." In The Provi-
     dence of Wit in the English Letter Writers. Durham, N.C.:
     Duke University Press, pp. 328-59.
          Regards Walpole and Cowper as the greatest eighteenth-
     century letter writers. Notes the influence of Mme de
     Sévigné and George Montagu on Walpole's style, and finds
     "all England of the eighteenth century" revealed in his
     letters.

5   KETTON-CREMER, R[OBERT] W[YNDHAM]. Thomas Gray: A Biography.
     Cambridge: Cambridge University Press, 310 pp.
          The standard English biography of Gray, by the author of
     the standard English biography of Walpole (1940.10). Dis-
     cusses Walpole's relationship with Gray throughout, with
     scrupulous accuracy and fairness.

6   [KETTON-CREMER, ROBERT WYNDHAM.] "Walpole and Horace Mann."
     Times Literary Supplement, 8 July, p. 380.
          Review of 1955.12. Suggests that Walpole's letters to
     Mann on the Jacobite rising of 1745 reach a level which he
     never excelled: "they were the first of his great 'set-
     pieces' of historical writing." Mann is often trivial and
     long-winded, but remains a likable personality.

7   KRONENBERGER, LOUIS; LEWIS, WILMARTH [SHELDON]; and BRYSON,
     LYMAN. "Horace Walpole. Correspondence." In The Invita-
     tion to Learning Reader. Self-Revelation. Edited by Ralph
     Backlund. Vol. 5, no. 2. New York: Herbert Muschel, pp.
     193-201.
          Transcribes a broadcast conversation on the value of
     Walpole's letters. Kronenberger considers the "set pieces,"
     such as the funeral of George II, while Lewis emphasizes the
     accounts of everyday life. Other writings by Walpole are
     also briefly mentioned.

8   LEWIS, W[ILMARTH] S[HELDON]. "Editing Familiar Letters."
     Daedalus 86 (May):71-77.
          Reprint of 1953.4.

9   RAYMOND, JOHN. "Herculean Weakness." New Statesman 49 (12
     March):360-61.
          Review of 1955.12. Depicts Walpole conducting the

eighteenth century, "as though it were some great Mozartian symphony." Commends his "dazzling magpie mind," and finds him surprisingly modern in outlook.

10   SHERBURN, GEORGE. "Walpolian Pageant." Yale Review 44 (June): 592-96.
      Review article on 1955.12, "one of the most impressive and entertaining correspondences ever printed." Sees Walpole's and Mann's letters as akin to historical novels, each with a public and a personal plot. Considers Walpole's wit, lightness of touch, and occasional indecency.

11   WAIN, JOHN. "A Kind of History." Spectator, 11 February, pp. 159-60.
      Review of 1955.12. Finds Walpole unattractive, but believes that his "silliness and indolence" were, paradoxically, the characteristics that made him the ideal chronicler of his age.

12   WALPOLE, HORACE. Horace Walpole's Correspondence with Sir Horace Mann. Edited by W[ilmarth] S[heldon] Lewis, Warren Hunting Smith and George L. Lam. The Yale Edition of Horace Walpole's Correspondence, edited by W[ilmarth] S[heldon] Lewis, vols. 17-19. New Haven: Yale University Press, vols. 1-3.
      An introduction discusses Walpole's and Mann's almost entirely epistolary friendship, pointing out the variety of their correspondence, which "quickens and slows according to the pulse of national affairs." Contains letters from 1740 to 1748; continued: 1960.10, 1967.25, 1971.13.

13   WALPOLE, HORACE. Horace Walpole's Correspondence with William Mason. Edited by W[ilmarth] S[heldon] Lewis, Grover Cronin, Jr. and Charles H. Bennett. The Yale Edition of Horace Walpole's Correspondence, edited by W[ilmarth] S[heldon] Lewis, vols. 28-29. New Haven: Yale University Press, 2 vols.
      An introduction discusses the cynical, sometimes savage tone of the correspondence, observing that Mason is "the least attractive" of Walpole's correspondents. Includes several appendices and an index.

1956

1   [KETTON-CREMER, ROBERT WYNDHAM.] "Walpole and Mason." Times Literary Supplement, 4 May, p. 268.
      Review of 1955.13. Agrees with the Yale editors that Mason is the least attractive of Walpole's correspondents, and that he "brought out many of the less engaging qualities in Walpole." Walpole greatly over-estimated Mason's writings, but in the case of Mason's Memoirs of Gray there was

"some justification for his raptures."

2   LEWIS, WILMARTH S[HELDON].   "Horace Walpole Antiquary."   In
    Essays Presented to Sir Lewis Namier. Edited by Richard
    Pares and A.J.P. Taylor. London: Macmillan, pp. 178-203.
        An authoritative study of Walpole's antiquarian inter-
    ests, revealed in his collecting, his visits to country
    seats and churches, his redesigning of Strawberry Hill, and
    his writings.   Devotes a section to each of these four
    aspects of Walpole's antiquarianism, with emphasis on his
    writings and especially on Anecdotes of Painting and Histor-
    ic Doubts. Concludes that despite the "stupidity and taste-
    lessness of some of its practitioners, 'antiquities' ab-
    sorbed him until he died."

3   MILLS, JACK.   "Horace Walpole as a Critic of British Public
    Address."   Ph.D. dissertation, University of Illinois, 224
    pp.
        Uses Walpole's correspondence and memoirs to study the
    nature of eighteenth-century oratory.   Includes chapters on
    Walpole's life, on his criteria for judging speeches, and on
    his reliability and impartiality as a critic.   Contends that
    his writings shed new light on the great eighteenth-century
    speakers, and also acquaint us with significant speakers
    little known today.

4   SHEPPERSON, ARCHIBALD BOLLING.   "More Letters for Posterity."
    Virginia Quarterly Review 32 (Spring):300-302.
        Review of 1955.12-13.   Emphasizes the care with which
    Walpole selected his correspondents, and the "passionate
    assiduity" with which he recorded his age for posterity.

5   SHERBURN, GEORGE.   "Walpole Turns Serious."   Yale Review 45
    (March):455-58.
        Review of 1955.13.   Finds Walpole's correspondence with
    Mason relatively dull, and believes that Walpole's literary
    criticism and political views depend largely on his personal
    prejudices.

                                1957

1   BUTTERFIELD, HERBERT.   "Horace Walpole's Memoirs."   In George
    III and the Historians.   London: Collins, pp. 108-18.
        Since Walpole's memoirs embody his afterthoughts on
    political events, as well as his immediate responses, they
    possess qualities quite distinct from those of his letters.
    They are important works, but best read in conjunction with
    Walpole's correspondence.   Walpole has provided the histori-
    an with "two great bodies of material and two imposing sets
    of opinions and reactions."

2   CARNIE, R[OBERT] H[AY]. "A Missing Hailes-Walpole Letter."
    Notes and Queries 202 (February):75-76.
        Transcribes and annotates an unpublished letter from Lord
    Hailes to Walpole of 17 April 1764, omitted from the Yale
    Edition of Walpole's correspondence.

3   HAZEN, A[LLEN] T[RACY]. "Horace Walpole, Earl of Orford (1717-
    1797)." In The Cambridge Bibliography of English Litera-
    ture. Vol. 5, Supplement: A.D. 600-1900. Edited by George
    Watson. Cambridge: Cambridge University Press, pp. 489-90.
    Supplements Lewis (1941.4). Revised: 1971.3.

4   HONOUR, HUGH. Horace Walpole. Writers and Their Work, no.
    92. London: Longman, 44 pp.
        A useful short introduction to Walpole, with chapters on
    Walpole as antiquary, Strawberry Hill, Otranto, the corre-
    spondence, and Walpole's politics. Harshly critical of
    Otranto and The Mysterious Mother, "a distasteful little
    piece." Includes a bibliography of works by and about Wal-
    pole. Revised: 1970.8.

5   KETTON-CREMER, R[OBERT] W[YNDHAM]. "Some New Letters of Horace
    Walpole." Times Literary Supplement, 15 March, p. 164.
        Transcribes, with an introduction and annotations, some
    unpublished correspondence between Walpole and the Norfolk
    antiquary, John Fenn.

6   LAYTON, T.B. "Horace Walpole's Quinsy." Guy's Hospital
    Gazette 71 (12 October):399-403; (19 October):419-21.
        A detailed study of the type of quinsy that Walpole con-
    tracted in Reggio in 1741. Believes that it was a strepto-
    coccal disease, rather than quinsy "in our modern acceptance
    of the term."

7   ROHDE, H[ERMANN] P[ETER]. Strawberry Hill: i Tohundredaaret
    for Oprettelsen af Trykkeriet paa Strawberry Hill [Straw-
    berry Hill: the two hundredth anniversary of the foundation
    of the printing press at Strawberry Hill]. Odense: Andels-
    bogtrykkeriet, 172 pp.
        In Danish, with English summary. Discusses Walpole's
    activities at Strawberry Hill, and the foundation and opera-
    tion of his printing press. Studies the history of Straw-
    berry Hill after Walpole's death and his posthumous reputa-
    tion: he was "excessively praised by Byron and abused
    beyond reason by Macaulay." The Yale Edition of Walpole's
    letters has now secured his "definitive rehabilitation."
    Also treats in detail Walpole's presentation of books to
    Prince Frederick of Denmark.

8   SHIPLEY, JOHN B. "Horace Walpole: Some Mistaken Identifica-
    tions." Notes and Queries 202 (November):475-77.

In his "Short Notes of My Life" Walpole admitted to the
authorship of three pamphlets, Three Letters to the Whigs,
written in response to A Letter to the Tories, which he
wrongly attributed to George Lyttleton. It was in fact
written by Styan Thirlby.

9   SMITH, ALBERT. "Nichol's [sic] Anecdotes of Hogarth." Notes
     and Queries 202 (August):352-53.
          Discusses the revisions in successive editions of John
     Nichols's Anecdotes of Hogarth, in which severe criticisms
     of Walpole, probably written by George Steevens, were con-
     siderably modified in later editions. The changes were pro-
     duced by "editorial tact on the part of Nichols rather than
     a change of opinion in Steevens."

10   VARMA, D[EVENDRA] P[RASAD].   "The First Gothic Tale: Its
     Potentialities." In The Gothic Flame. Being a History of
     the Gothic Novel in England: Its Origins, Efflorescence,
     Disintegration, and Residuary Influences. London: Arthur
     Barker, pp. 42-73.
          A laudatory study of Otranto, its origins, and its influ-
     ence on subsequent writers. Refuting the various criticisms
     made of the novel, finds it a "bold and amazingly successful
     experiment." Emphasizes Walpole's industry as a writer and
     his serious intentions in Otranto, in which the characteris-
     tic features of Gothic fiction originate. It is "a towering
     achievement of art and beauty."

11   WAITE, HAROLD E. "Strawberry Hill Press." Gutenberg Jahrbuch,
     pp. 217-20.
          Explains why Walpole, an "eighteenth-century playboy,"
     wished to print his works in limited editions, and discusses
     his difficulties with printers. The Strawberry Hill Press
     did not influence subsequent British printing; it was merely
     "a means of satisfying a fancy."

12   WAITE, HAROLD E. "The Strawberry Hill Press." Printing World,
     July 10, p. 34; July 17, p. 66.
          Although Walpole printed some works for commercial pur-
     poses, Strawberry Hill was a private press with which he
     "followed his own fancy." The press gave a wider audience
     for Walpole's writings, and issued rare and attractive
     books.

                                1958

*1   HORWITZ, SYLVIA. "A Study of the Nature and Function of De-
     vices Used in Gothic Fiction in England (1764-1820)."
     Ph.D. dissertation, University of Virginia.
     Source: Lévy (1968.11), p. 669.

2   LEWIS, W[ILMARTH] S[HELDON]. <u>Horace Walpole's Library</u>. Cambridge: Cambridge University Press, 74 pp.
     An elegant, highly informative study, with sections on Walpole's books, his reading, and the dispersal and partial recovery of his library. Discusses the various categories into which Walpole classified his collection, the nature and extent of his marginalia and their reappearance in his letters and published works, and the history of the library from the Strawberry Hill Sale of 1842 to the present. Revised: 1969.4.

3   LEWIS, WILMARTH SHELDON. "Horace Walpole: Collector." <u>The Third Annual Wedgwood International Seminar</u>. Boston: Museum of Fine Arts, pp. 18-23.
     Classifies Walpole's collections under nine headings: classical antiquities; English coins; prints and drawings (his greatest collection); paintings; miscellaneous small items (such as snuff-boxes); ancient furniture and armour; glass; curiosities (such as Dr. Dee's speculum); and china and ceramics. Contends that Walpole was not a book-collector, since his was a working library: "he bought books to read."

4   WOOLF, VIRGINIA. "Horace Walpole." In <u>Granite and Rainbow</u>. London: Hogarth Press, pp. 181-86.
     Reprint of 1919.13.

                              1959

1   HELLMAN, GEOFFREY T. "Onward and Upward with the Arts. Farmington Revisited." <u>New Yorker</u> 35 (31 October):144-60.
     A sequel to 1949.8, surveying the progress of the Yale Edition and of the Lewis Walpole Library. Notes that Lewis's "loyalty to his subject" remains unchanged.

2   JUDD, GERRIT P[ARMELE], IV. <u>Horace Walpole's Memoirs</u>. New York: Bookman Associates, 119 pp.
     Revision of the introduction to 1947.12, evaluating Walpole's memoirs as a historical source. Studies their composition, Walpole's "philosophy of history" and his style of historical writing, his character sketches, and the accuracy of his memoirs. Concludes with a consideration of Walpole's contribution to the "Whig Myth."

3   KRUTCH, JOSEPH WOOD. "Walpole on Gardening." In <u>The Gardener's World</u>. New York: G.P. Putnam's Sons, pp. 260-68.
     Introduces a passage from Walpole's "Essay on Modern Gardening" (1770) with the comment that Walpole was "the most literate and articulate historian-defender" of landscape gardening in the eighteenth century.

4   LUCAS, F[RANK] L.   "Horace Walpole."   In The Art of Living:
    Four Eighteenth-Century Minds.   London: Cassell, pp. 79-
    128.
        An elegant, incisive essay on Walpole's life and writ-
    ings, with numerous well-chosen quotations from the corre-
    spondence.   Admires Walpole's ability to create a portrait
    of his age through his masterful prose style.   Finds his
    other writings, especially Otranto and The Mysterious
    Mother, of little worth; the core of his work is the corre-
    spondence with his innermost circle.

5   SAUNDERS, BEATRICE.   "Horace Walpole 1717-1797."   In Portraits
    of Genius.   London: John Murray, pp. 67-74.
        An archaic, undocumented portrait of Walpole as dilet-
    tante and gossip.   Finds his formal works insignificant, but
    admires the man and his letters.

6   THIERGARD, ULRICH.   "Schiller und Walpole.   Ein Beitrag zu
    Schillers Verhältnis zur Schauerliteratur."   Jahrbuch der
    Deutschen Schillergesellschaft 3:102-17.
        Both Schiller and Goethe knew Otranto and had a plan to
    continue it, which was never fulfilled.   Goethe was at-
    tracted by its mystery and fairy-tale elements; Schiller
    made a dramatic sketch, entitled "Narbonne," related to
    Jephson's dramatic adaptation of 1781.   Schiller's play The
    Bride of Messina might have been influenced by The Mysteri-
    ous Mother, to which it has several similarities.

7   WARE, MALCOLM R., JR.   "The New Taste for Gothic and its Ex-
    pression in The Castle of Otranto."   In "Sublimity in the
    Major British Gothic Novelists of the Eighteenth and Early
    Nineteenth Centuries: A Study of Contemporary Taste Re-
    flected in the Novel of the Period."   Ph.D. dissertation,
    University of Tennessee, pp. 36-63.
        Studies Otranto as "a reflection of contemporary taste,"
    contending that the elements Walpole "uses to produce terror
    are the things enumerated in the aesthetic treatises of the
    period as productive of the sublime."

                              1960

1   HALSBAND, ROBERT.   "Eighteenth-Century Tastemaker.   Horace Wal-
    pole's Letters Reflect the Life and Manners of his Time."
    New York Times Book Review, 4 September, pp. 1, 14.
        Review of 1960.10.   There is some falling off in Wal-
    pole's correspondence with Mann.   As the forty-five year se-
    quence of letters progresses, it becomes more dutiful and
    less affectionate.

2   LA GORCE, AGNES de.   "Horace Walpole chez Madame du Deffand."

<u>Miroir de l'histoire</u> 131 (November):549–55.
An undocumented account of Walpole's travels in France and his relationship with Mme du Deffand. Also considers Walpole's attitude towards the French Revolution, which transformed his liberal views into the conservatism of his old age.

3   LEWIS, WILMARTH SHELDON.   <u>Horace Walpole</u>.   The A.W. Mellon Lectures in the Fine Arts, no. 9. Bollingen Series, no. 35. New York: Pantheon Books, 215 pp.
Richly illustrated, lucid and remarkably compressed: perhaps the single most useful work on Walpole. Contains chapters on Walpole's family, his friends, his politics, Strawberry Hill, his formal works and his letters, drawing on the author's unique collection of Walpoliana and on his intimate knowledge of Walpole's life and works. Attempts to explain the "contradictions and complexities" of Walpole's "character, behaviour, and achievement."

4   NICHOLSON, HAROLD.   "Dilettante (Horace Walpole, 1717–1797)." In <u>The Age of Reason</u>. London: Constable, pp. 247–65.
Surveys Walpole's life and writings, regarding him as gifted, likable, and original. Notes the influence exerted by <u>Otranto</u> and by the <u>Essay on Modern Gardening,</u> and finds the letters "the most informative and amusing of any in the language." Strawberry Hill was "an architectural experiment of great importance."

5   PARREAUX, ANDRÉ.   "Horace Walpole et William Beckford; ou, de l'origine de quelques erreurs." In <u>William Beckford: auteur de "Vathek" (1760–1844). Etude de la création littéraire</u>. Paris: A.G. Nizet, pp. 18–19.
Contrasts Strawberry Hill with Fonthill Abbey and <u>Otranto</u> with <u>Vathek</u>. The purity and grandeur of Fonthill are completely different from the amusing originality of Strawberry Hill. <u>Vathek</u>, likewise, owes little to <u>Otranto</u>.

6   PLUMB, J.H.   Review of <u>Horace Walpole's Correspondence with Sir Horace Mann</u>. <u>Listener</u> 65 (15 December):1111.
Believes that "we know more about the facts of Horace Walpole's life than we know about any other human being." The Yale Edition of his correspondence has become "one of the most precious works of reference for eighteenth-century British history."

7   REA, ROBERT.   "Mason, Walpole, and That Rogue Almon." <u>Huntington Library Quarterly</u> 23 (February):187–93.
Defends John Almon, publisher of Mason's satirical poems, from Walpole's accusations of corruption. Walpole's remarks on Almon present "the misleading picture of a hapless author betrayed by a rascally bookseller."

8   SCHAAR, BERNARD E.   "'Serendipity.'"   Notes and Queries 205
     (October):387-89.
          Compares Walpole's remarks on The Three Princes of Seren-
     dip with the tale itself, which he read carelessly. His use
     of the term "serendipity" rests on an erroneous interpreta-
     tion of the tale, and dictionaries have perpetuated his mis-
     reading. The use of the term in scientific investigations
     "does not have validity."

9   SHEPPERSON, ARCHIBALD BOLLING.   "Journal of an Age." Virginia
     Quarterly Review 36 (Autumn):652-55.
          Review of 1960.10. Questions whether the letters them-
     selves or the footnotes in the Yale Edition will ultimately
     be of more value to social and political historians.

10   WALPOLE, HORACE. Horace Walpole's Correspondence with Sir Hor-
     ace Mann. Edited by W[ilmarth] S[heldon] Lewis, Warren
     Hunting Smith and George L. Lam. The Yale Edition of Horace
     Walpole's Correspondence, edited by W[ilmarth] S[heldon]
     Lewis, vols. 20-22. New Haven: Yale University Press,
     vols. 4-6.
          Continuation of 1955.12, with letters from 1748 to 1768.

11   WHITE, ERIC WALTER. "The Rehearsal of an Opera." Theatre
     Notebook 14 (Spring):79-90.
          Studies a painting, "The Rehearsal of an Opera," owned by
     Walpole and attributed by him to Sebastiano and Marco Ricci,
     uncle and nephew. Shows that the painting was in fact by
     Marco Ricci alone, and corrects other errors made by Walpole
     about the painting.

                              1961

1   CECIL, LORD DAVID. "Walpole's Way of Life." Sunday Telegraph
     (London), 22 October, p. 6.
          Review of 1960.3. Prefers the Gothicism of Strawberry
     Hill to that of Otranto, which is ridiculously unconvinc-
     ing. Admires Walpole's life and letters, each "a conscious-
     ly designed work of art on a given theme."

2   CLIVE, JOHN. "Born with Pen and Silver Spoon. 1. The Man."
     Saturday Review 44 (26 August):29.
          Review of 1960.3. Compares Walpole's world with the
     "neo-Gothic splendor" of Yale and notes his desire for fame;
     he would be delighted, but not surprised, to have achieved
     it.

3   CONNOLLY, CYRIL. "Horace Walpole and Posterity." Sunday Times
     (London), 8 October, p. 31.
          Review of 1960.3 and 1961.9-10. Dislikes Walpole's triv-

iality and snobbery, but believes that he is of value to "the scholar and social historian." Reprinted: 1963.1.

4   GOODMAN, LEO A. "Notes on the Etymology of Serendipity and Some Related Philological Observations." Modern Language Notes 76 (May):454-57.
     Discusses the source of Walpole's term "serendipity," its etymology, and its correct definition.

5   "In Arts Reposed." Times Literary Supplement, 17 November, p. 822.
     Review article on 1961.9-10 and 1960.3. Discusses Walpole's relations with George Selwyn, Lord Lincoln, Henry Fox, Lady Mary Coke, and Hannah More. Finds the youthful letters to Lord Lincoln "rather attractive," and dismisses the suggestion of Walpole's homosexuality.

6   NICHOLSON, HAROLD. "Spirit of Strawberry Hill." Observer, 15 October, p. 30.
     Review of 1960.3. Contrasts the malice of Walpole's Memoirs with the charm of Strawberry Hill. Regards Otranto and The Mysterious Mother as immensely influential but of no present interest. The letters, however, are "among the best in our literature."

7   PLUMB, J.H. "Born with Pen and Silver Spoon. 2. His Works." Saturday Review 44 (26 August):30.
     Review of 1961.9-10. Regards the "warmth of affection" in Walpole's letters to Lord Lincoln as evidence of Walpole's homosexuality, and the ribald poem "Little Peggy" as a sign of the "darker side" of his nature.

8   PLUMB, J.H. "Horace Walpole's Century." Listener 65 (26 October):663.
     Review of 1960.3 and 1961.9-10. Raises the question of Walpole's homosexuality, citing the "highly amorous letters to Lord Lincoln" that W.S. Lewis sees simply as expressions of friendship.

9   WALPOLE, HORACE. Horace Walpole's Correspondence with George Selwyn, Lord Lincoln, Sir Charles Hanbury Williams, Henry Fox, Richard Edgcumb. Edited by W[ilmarth] S[heldon] Lewis and Robert A. Smith. The Yale Edition of Horace Walpole's Correspondence, edited by W[ilmarth] S[heldon] Lewis, vol. 30. New Haven: Yale University Press, 479 pp.
     Contains Walpole's correspondence with young men about town; the rakish letters constitute "not the pleasantest volume of the Correspondence." Includes an introduction, denying that Walpole's extravagant letters to Lord Lincoln indicate homosexual attitudes, several appendices - with unpublished verses by Walpole, an account of his relationship

with Fox, and a transcript of his will – and an index.

10   WALPOLE, HORACE.   Horace Walpole's Correspondence with Hannah
      More, Lady Browne, Lady Mary Coke, Lady Hervey, Mary Hamil-
      ton (Mrs. John Dickenson), Lady George Lennox, Anne Pitt,
      Lady Suffolk.   Edited by W[ilmarth] S[heldon] Lewis, Robert
      A. Smith and Charles H. Bennett.   The Yale Edition of Horace
      Walpole's Correspondence, edited by W[ilmarth] S[heldon]
      Lewis, vol. 31.   New Haven: Yale University Press, 528 pp.
          A brief introduction stresses the special importance of
      Walpole's correspondence with Hannah More, and suggests that
      the volume might be "the pleasantest" of the entire Yale
      Edition.   Includes a revision of Bennett (1952.4), several
      appendices and an index.

1962

1   BREDVOLD, LOUIS I.   "Letter Writers: Chesterfield and Wal-
      pole."   In The Literature of the Restoration and the Eigh-
      teenth Century 1660–1798.   A History of English Literature,
      edited by Hardin Craig, vol. 3.   New York: Collier, pp.
      125–26.
          Reprint of 1950.1.

2   GREGORY, HORACE.   "A Bloomsbury Ancestor."   Commonweal 76 (11
      May):173–75.
          Review article on 1960.3.   Contrasts the Bloomsbury
      group, especially Lytton Strachey and Virginia Woolf, un-
      favourably with their "ancestor" Walpole.   Emphasizes the
      clarity of his insight into his age: he was the tireless
      "observer of human events and motives."

1963

1   CONNOLLY, CYRIL.   "Letters of Horace Walpole," "Collector's
      Progress," and "Horace Walpole and Posterity."   In Previous
      Convictions.   New York: Harper & Row, pp. 140–49.
          Reprints of 1951.3, 1952.6, and 1961.3.

2   DOBRÉE, BONAMY.   "Horace Walpole."   In Restoration and Eigh-
      teenth-Century Literature.   Essays in Honor of Alan Dugald
      McKillop.   Edited by Carroll Camden.   Chicago: University
      of Chicago Press, pp. 185–200.
          Responds to Macaulay's essay with a fresh analysis of
      Walpole's character and personality.   Includes an appreci-
      ative discussion of Strawberry Hill and Otranto, "a seminal
      work," and brief comments on Walpole's other imaginative
      writings.   Walpole's letters are his "enduring monument."

3 DUISIT, LIONEL. "Portrait de Walpole," "Walpole et la révéla-
tion de l'amitié," and "L'ascendant tyrannique de Walpole."
In Madame du Deffand: épistolière. Geneva: Droz, pp. 88-
91, 99-102, 106-8.
"Portrait de Walpole" studies Mme du Deffand's formal
portrait of Walpole presenting him as an original, fanciful
and diversified in his interests. Subsequent sections con-
sider the attractions that Walpole held for Mme du Deffand,
and his exploitation of the ascendancy he held over her by
setting rules for her life and letters.

4 LEWIS, WILMARTH SHELDON. "Editing Private Correspondence."
Proceedings of the American Philosophical Society 107 (August):289-93.
Considers the problems of collecting, transcribing and
editing private correspondence, using the Yale Edition of
Walpole's correspondence as the primary example. Emphasizes
the significance of private letters, citing Walpole's remark
that they are "genuine history" and "more satisfactory than
formal premeditated narratives." Revised: 1979.12.

*5 SANDY, STEPHEN. "A Rhetoric of Suspense: The Castle of
Otranto." In "Studies in the Form of the Romantic Novel:
Otranto to Waverly." Ph.D. dissertation, Harvard Univer-
sity.
Revised for publication: 1980.11.

6 SHERWIN, OSCAR. "Strawberry Hill." In A Gentleman of Wit and
Fashion: The Extraordinary Life and Times of George Selwyn. New York: Twayne, pp. 102-23.
A gossipy, undocumented and disorganized account of Walpole's dealings with George Selwyn. Depicts Walpole as Selwyn's Boswell, jotting down his witticisms.

7 VICTOR, SISTER M. "Three Princes of Serendip." American Notes
and Queries 1 (February):87.
Enquires about the source of Walpole's term "serendipity."

8 WALPOLE, HORACE. Memoirs and Portraits. Edited by Matthew
Hodgart. New York: Macmillan, 264 pp.
Presents well-selected extracts from Walpole's Memoirs of
George II and George III, from 1751 to 1771, in more accurate texts than those of the nineteenth-century editions.
Contains a useful introduction, evaluating the memoirs and
discussing the complex history of their publication, several
illustrations, notes on the text, explanatory notes, and an
index.

9 WALPOLE, HORACE. The Castle of Otranto. Introduction by Marvin Mudrick, with Sir Walter Scott's introduction. New

York: Macmillan, 128 pp.

Contains Scott's introduction to Otranto (1811.5), a
brief biographical sketch, and an enthusiastic survey of
Walpole's works by Mudrick, who finds Walpole possibly the
best letter writer in English. Commends the Memoirs and
Hieroglyphic Tales, but regards The Mysterious Mother as "a
very bad play." Otranto, despite the weakness of its characterization and plot, is a seminal work, announcing the
breakup of the Augustan age. Introduction revised:
1979.14.

10   WALPOLE, HORACE. The Castle of Otranto. In Seven Masterpieces
of Gothic Horror. Edited by Robert Donald Spector. New
York: Bantam Books, 465 pp.

An introduction contends that Walpole's defensive prefaces to Otranto show his reluctance to acknowledge his own
irrationality. Otranto initiated the Gothic novel, "an
awakening response to a coldly rational world." Also
admires Walpole's letters, which provide a "record of the
history and personality of his times."

11   WALPOLE, HORACE. The Castle of Otranto. In "The Castle of
Otranto" by Horace Walpole; "The Mysteries of Udolpho" by
Ann Radcliffe; "Northanger Abbey" by Jane Austen. Edited by
Andrew Wright. New York: Holt, Rinehart & Winston, 543 pp.

An introduction declares that Otranto, the first Gothic
novel, possesses "the rare merit of brevity." Walpole's
other works are more substantial than he himself pretended,
and his letters are "monuments of both assiduity and deter-
mination."

1964

1   BROOKE, JOHN. "Walpole, Hon. Horatio." In The House of Com-
mons 1754-1790. By Sir Lewis Namier and John Brooke. Vol.
3. London: History of Parliament Trust, pp. 595-97.

Studies Walpole's parliamentary career and revaluates his
Memoirs, which "have been unjustly deprecated by historians." Finds the Memoirs of George II inferior both histori-
cally and artistically to the Memoirs of George III, "a historical document of the highest importance." Warns, however, against three types of error that occur in Walpole's
historical writings: conscious bias, lack of information,
and unconscious fantasy.

2   DREW, ELIZABETH. "Horace Walpole 1717-1797." In The Literature of Gossip. Nine English Contemporaries. New York:
W.W. Norton, pp. 91-112.

An undocumented survey of Walpole's correspondence,
emphasizing its more trivial aspects. Finds Walpole "the

best company in the world."

3   DUNNING, PATRICK J.   "Horace Walpole as an Historian."   Histor-
     ian, St. Mary's College, 1:19-25.
          Briefly considers Walpole's stature as political and
     social historian in his letters and Memoirs: he was not a
     "scientific historian," but his works are "invaluable
     sources of history."   Appends an annotated bibliography of
     works by and about Walpole concerning Strawberry Hill.

4   EADS, KATHLEEN.   "Three Princes of Serendip."   American Notes
     and Queries 2 (February):87-88.
          Replies to Victor (1963.7), providing some information on
     the many editions and translations of Walpole's source for
     "serendipity."

5   KETTON-CREMER, R[OBERT] W[YNDHAM].   Horace Walpole: A Biogra-
     phy.   3d ed.   London: Methuen, 335 pp.
          Revision of 1946.3, including "some further corrections
     and adjustments, but no substantial alterations."

6   KETTON-CREMER, R[OBERT] W[YNDHAM].   "William Cole, Friend of
     Walpole and Gray."   New Rambler, no. 14 (January), pp. 5-10.
          Although Cole was a high church Tory, his friendship with
     Walpole endured until the end of his life.   Their correspon-
     dence, beginning in 1762, throws much light on Walpole, and
     their discussions of antiquarian topics are of "the greatest
     human interest."

7   "The Connoisseur's Diary: A Set of Sèvres Vases Bought in
     Paris by Horace Walpole."   Connoisseur 157 (October):102.
          Describes three Sèvres vases bought in Paris by Walpole
     during a visit with William Cole, in Autumn 1765.   One of
     the vases, preserved at the Vyne, is illustrated.

8   WALPOLE, HORACE.   The Castle of Otranto.   Edited by W[ilmarth]
     S[heldon] Lewis.   London: Oxford University Press, 110 pp.
          Contains a chronology and a valuable introduction, dis-
     cussing the genesis and reception of Otranto and accounting
     for the artificiality of its style.   Revised: 1969.14;
     reprinted: 1975.12.

9   WOLFF, ERWIN.   "Die Ambivalenz des Fabulösen: Walpole, Dr.
     Johnson und Goldsmith."   In Der englische Roman im 18.
     Jahrhundert: Wesen und Formen.   Göttingen: Vandenhoeck &
     Ruprecht, pp. 123-39.
          Walpole chose a medieval setting for Otranto because of
     the dissatisfaction with his own time he expressed in his
     letters: he turned towards the past in both architecture
     and fiction.   Unlike Scott, who wrote realistic fiction,
     Walpole wrote a fable.   Otranto is dreamlike, in contrast to

the idyllic <u>Vicar of Wakefield</u> and the exotic <u>Rasselas</u>.

1965

1   DUNNING, P[ATRICK] J.   "Horace Walpole and the Building of
     Strawberry Hill." <u>Historian</u>, St. Mary's College, 2 (Septem-
     ber):81-95.
          Describes the alterations made by Walpole to Strawberry
     Hill, with illustrations. Believes that visitors can still
     experience "something of the magic and make-believe that
     Walpole tried to achieve."

2   GILL, BRENDAN.   "Literary Industry." <u>New York Review of Books</u>
     5 (28 October):40.
          Replies to Plumb (1965.8), declaring that his indictment
     of the Yale Walpole is inaccurate and grotesque.

3   "Horace Walpole's Tiepolo Drawings." <u>Illustrated London News</u>
     246 (20 February):27.
          An illustrated account of an album of 150 Tiepolo draw-
     ings owned by Walpole.

4   HOWES, VICTOR.   "Walpole the Collector." <u>Christian Science
     Monitor</u>, 2 September, p. 10.
          Studies Walpole's collections and their dispersal at the
     Strawberry Hill Sale of 1842. Believes that he collected
     out of loneliness, to rescue history, to found a museum, and
     simply from love of old things.

5   HUSSEY, CHRISTOPHER. "Strawberry Hill, Middlesex." In <u>English
     Country Houses. Early Georgian. 1715-1760</u>. Rev. ed. Lon-
     don: Country Life, pp. 213-18.
          Revision of 1955.3.

6   KRONENBERGER, LOUIS.   "Horace Walpole's Career." <u>Encounter</u> 24
     (March):36-40.
          A discursive survey of Walpole's life and works.
     Stresses the literary qualities of the letters and the
     influence exerted by Strawberry Hill and <u>Otranto</u> on the
     Gothic Revival in architecture and fiction. Reprinted:
     1969.7.

7   LIEBERT, VERA.   "Walpoliana." <u>New York Review of Books</u> 5 (9
     December):41.
          Replies to Plumb (1965.8), suggesting that his disbelief
     in Walpole's historical importance is based on "contempt for
     his private character."

8   PLUMB, J.H.   "Horace Walpole at Yale." <u>New York Review of
     Books</u> 5 (30 September):9-10.

Review of 1965.15. Believes that the Yale Edition has had a pernicious effect on eighteenth-century studies, since Walpole is of little historical importance. His correspondence "touches practically no aspect of eighteenth-century life at a serious level." He wrote as a literary artist; hence his letters are "nearer to imaginative literature than historical record."

9 PLUMB, J.H. "Replies." New York Review of Books 5 (9 December):42.

Responds to Gill and Liebert (1965.2, 7). Claims that the study of Walpole "obscures rather than reveals" the politics and society of eighteenth-century England.

10 REMER, THEODORE G., ed. Serendipity and the Three Princes. From the "Peregrinaggio" of 1557. With a preface by W[ilmarth] S[heldon] Lewis. Norman: University of Oklahoma Press, 199 pp.

Contains chapters on Walpole's remarks on "serendipity" in his letters and its current usage, and a translation of The Three Princes of Serendip, in which Walpole first encountered the word. Corrects the errors of previous commentators but introduces several new ones, listed by Cammann (1967.2). Lewis's preface reports on the recurrence of enquiries about the term "serendipity."

11 ROSE, EDWARD J. "'The Queenly Personality': Walpole, Melville and Mother." Literature and Psychology 15 (Fall):216-29.

Compares The Mysterious Mother to works by Melville, who links the play with Sophocles's Oedipus Tyrannus in White-Jacket. Both The Mysterious Mother and Melville's novels, especially Pierre, are concerned with sexual transgressions. Walpole's play is a major work, deserving more critical attention than it has yet received.

12 STEEVES, HARRISON R. "The Gothic Romance. Walpole, Ann Radcliffe, Lewis." In Before Jane Austen. The Shaping of the English Novel in the Eighteenth Century. New York: Holt, Rinehart & Winston, pp. 243-71.

Takes the same approach to Otranto as in 1931.18. Regards the novel as the foundation of Gothic romance but worthless in itself, lacking "literary charm or grace," absurd, implausible, and puerile.

13 WALPOLE, HORACE. "Exhumations II: Horace Walpole's 'Thoughts on Comedy.'" Edited by F[rederick] W. B[ateson]. Essays in Criticism 15 (April):162-70.

Reprints Walpole's "Thoughts on Comedy" from his Works (1798.7). A brief introduction questions the date of composition: 1775-76, according to the Works, yet the essay contains references to productions of 1777 and 1786.

14   WALPOLE, HORACE. <u>Historic Doubts on the Life and Reign of King</u>
      <u>Richard III</u>. In <u>Richard III: The Great Debate</u>. Edited by
      Paul Murray Kendall. New York: W.W. Norton, pp. 147-244.
          Reprints Walpole's <u>Historic Doubts</u>, with a brief intro-
      duction evaluating the strengths and weaknesses of Walpole's
      history and tracing its critical reputation.

15   WALPOLE, HORACE. <u>Horace Walpole's Correspondence with the</u>
      <u>Countess of Upper Ossory</u>. Edited by W[ilmarth] S[heldon]
      Lewis and A. Dayle Wallace, with the assistance of Edwine
      M. Martz. The Yale Edition of Horace Walpole's Correspon-
      dence, edited by W[ilmarth] S[heldon] Lewis, vols. 32-34.
      New Haven: Yale University Press, 3 vols.
          Contains an introduction, considering the importance of
      Walpole's correspondence with Lady Ossory in illuminating
      the social life of his time, several appendices, including
      Walpole's notes on Lady Mary Wortley Montagu's letters, and
      an index.

16   WOOF, R.S. "Some Horace Walpole Letters." <u>Notes and Queries</u>
      210 (January):24-26.
          Prints three unpublished letters by Walpole, with brief
      comments.

                                    1966

1   BINFORD, JOSEPH NEWBILL. "The Politics of Horace Walpole."
      Ph.D. dissertation, University of Kentucky, 286 pp.
          A detailed study of Walpole's political views, taking a
      chronological approach. Includes chapters on Walpole's
      attitude to his father's political successors, the Pelhams
      and Pitt, George III, and the American and French Revolu-
      tions. There are also separate studies of Walpole's <u>Memoirs</u>
      and of his views on the constitution. Regards Walpole as a
      matchless source of information on eighteenth-century
      England.

2   BLAIR, CLAUDE. "The Most Superb of all Royal Locks." <u>Apollo</u>
      84 (December):493-94.
          Illustrates and provides further information on the lock
      discussed by Ross (1942.8).

3   BLUNDEN, EDMUND. "Horace Walpole's Young Poet." In <u>Renais-</u>
      <u>sance and Modern Essays</u>. Edited by G[eorge] R. Hibbard.
      New York: Barnes & Noble, pp. 95-99.
          Discusses Walpole's dealings with the Reverend Thomas
      Pentycross, who wrote "Verses to Horace Walpole" in 1780.
      Walpole considered the poem "by no means despicable."

4   COLEY, W.B. "Henry Fielding and the Two Walpoles." <u>Philologi-</u>

cal Quarterly 45 (January):157-78.

A detailed, informative study of Fielding's relations with Robert Walpole and of Horace Walpole's attitude to Fielding. Draws on Walpole's correspondence and on several of his unpublished writings to show his antipathy towards Fielding, and believes that Fielding could never have "sold out" to Robert Walpole, since Horace nowhere records such an occurrence.

5   FRANCON, MARCEL.   "Horace Walpole, Mme du Deffand et Montaigne." Bulletin de la société des amis de Montaigne, 4th ser. 7:99-101.

Contrasts Walpole's disdain for Montaigne with Mme du Deffand's enthusiasm, quoting several passages from their letters. Walpole's attitude was unusual for his time.

6   FREE, WILLIAM N.   "Walpole's Letters: The Art of Being Graceful."   In The Familiar Letter in the Eighteenth Century. Edited by Howard Anderson, Philip B. Daghlian and Irvin Ehrenpreis.   Lawrence: University of Kansas Press, pp. 165-85.

Regards "grace" as the characteristic feature of both Walpole's career and his letters, which "describe life as a mid-eighteenth-century gentleman ought to know it." Analyzes the tone and style of some familiar passages from the letters, which Walpole's "buoyant wit" elevated to an art.

7   GERSON, J.H.C.   "The 1796 Edition of Walpole's Anecdotes: A Fifth Volume." Book Collector 15 (Winter):484.

Supplements Hazen's comments on an unpublished fourth edition of Anecdotes of Painting (1942.5, p. 66) by describing the hitherto unknown title-page of volume five of this edition.

8   HOWES, VICTOR.   "Walpole's Correspondence." Christian Science Monitor, 29 April, p. 12.

Walpole writes on a small scale, yet his letters as a whole form a "grand design" and provide "a full-length portrait of his age."

9   KETTON-CREMER, R[OBERT] W[YNDHAM].   Horace Walpole: A Biography. 4th ed. Ithaca: Cornell University Press, 317 pp.

First American edition of the standard biography. Reprints 1964.5 with a new "author's note."

10   MOULTON, CHARLES WELLS.   "Horace Walpole.   Earl of Oxford [sic]."   In Moulton's Library of Literary Criticism of English and American Authors Through the Beginning of the Twentieth Century. Abridged, revised, and with additions by Martin Tucker.   Vol. 2.   New York: Frederick Ungar, pp. 436-46.

Revision of 1902.6. Includes fewer but longer extracts from studies of Walpole, omitting the sections on Royal and Noble Authors and The Mysterious Mother.

11   UNDERDOWN, DAVID.   "Posterity Behind the Chair."   Virginia Quarterly Review 42 (Spring):328–32.
Review of 1965.15. Walpole's letters to the Countess of Upper Ossory are "among the most polished compositions of the greatest correspondent of his age." Walpole's outlook was metropolitan and reactionary; he looked back to "a more spacious, tranquilly aristocratic time."

12   "Walpole and the Countess."   Times Literary Supplement,   21 April, p. 343.
Review of 1965.15. Agrees with the Yale editors that Walpole's letters to the Countess of Upper Ossory are among his best, although her side of the correspondence was undistinguished.

13   WALPOLE, HORACE.   The Castle of Otranto.   In Three Gothic Novels. Edited by E[verett] F[ranklin] Bleiler. New York: Dover, pp. 1–106.
Includes Scott's introduction to Otranto (1811.5) and an introduction by Bleiler surveying Walpole's career, with particular emphasis on Strawberry Hill, "a monstrosity with charm." Admires Walpole's letters more than Otranto, a highly influential but mediocre work of literature.

14   WOOLF, VIRGINIA.   "The Humane Art," "Horace Walpole," and "Two Antiquaries: Walpole and Cole."   In Collected Essays of Virginia Woolf. Edited by Leonard Woolf. 3 vols. London: Hogarth Press, 1:102–5; 3:105–17.
Reprints of 1942.10 and 1958.4.

1967

1   BROOKE, JOHN.   "Horace Walpole and the Politics of the Early Years of the Reign of George III."   In 1967.22, pp. 3–23.
Studies Walpole's role as an active politician in the early part of George III's reign, ending with the resignation of Conway in 1767. Regards Walpole's memoirs as an invaluable guide to eighteenth-century politics, and defends him from the "sneers of Macaulay."

2   CAMMANN, SCHUGLER V.R.   "Christopher the Armenian and the Three Princes of Serendip."   Comparative Literature Studies 4, no. 3:229–58.
Discusses Walpole's source for the term "serendipity" and notes many errors in Remer's account (1965.10).

3   FOORD, ARCHIBALD S.   "'The Only Unadulterated Whig.'"   In
     1967.22, pp. 25-43.
         Examines Walpole's remarks on Whiggism in an attempt to
     distinguish between Whig and Tory doctrines in the eigh-
     teenth century. Concludes, after considering numerous types
     of Whig, that almost all, including Walpole, were united by
     one basic principle: retention of the monarchy and reduc-
     tion of "the rôle of the Crown in politics."

*4   GARRIGAN, KRISTINE OTTESEN.   "Horace Walpole and Strawberry
     Hill: An Expression of Self." Ph.D. minor thesis, Univer-
     sity of Wisconsin-Madison, 69 pp.
         Source: Kristine Ottesen Garrigan, Ruskin on Architec-
     ture: His Thought and Influence (Madison: University of
     Wisconsin Press, 1973), p. 8. Contains "a detailed discus-
     sion of Walpole's attitudes toward classical and Gothic
     architecture."

5   HALSBAND, ROBERT.   "Walpole versus Lady Mary," and "Walpole's
     Annotations to Lady Mary's Poems." In 1967.22, pp. 215-26,
     339.
         Contrasts Walpole's "supercilious contempt" for Lady Mary
     Wortley Montagu with his admiration for her writings. Con-
     siders the reasons for Walpole's harshness, contending that
     his enthusiasm for Lady Mary's poems and letters is ample
     recompense. An appendix transcribes Walpole's annotations
     to Lady Mary's poems.

6   HAZEN, ALLEN T[RACY].   "The Earlier Owners of Walpole's Books."
     In 1967.22, pp. 167-79.
         Contends that Walpole was not a bibliophile, but bought
     his books to read. The significance of his library is due
     to the importance of the books themselves and to their
     associational interest, not to their rarity, splendour, or
     antiquity.

7   HILLES, FREDERICK W.   "Horace Walpole and the Knight of the
     Brush." In 1967.22, pp. 141-66.
         A detailed study of Walpole's relations with Joshua Rey-
     nolds, and of their views of each other's works. Walpole's
     admiration for Reynolds's paintings, which he considered the
     greatest of the age, belies the idea that he was indifferent
     to major contemporaries.

8   HOGAN, CHARLES BEECHER.   "The 'Theatre of Geo. 3.'"   In
     1967.22, pp. 227-40.
         Discusses Walpole's interest in contemporary drama and
     his collection of some 550 plays, under the title of "thea-
     tre of Geo. 3." Also studies his two plays, The Mysterious
     Mother and Nature Will Prevail, preferring the comedy to the
     tragedy, Robert Jephson's adaptation of Otranto, The Count

of Narbonne, and <u>Otranto</u> itself, treated as a five-act drama
and as the "grandfather of the Gothic play."

9   HOWES, VICTOR. "Walpole, Man of Paradox." <u>Christian Science
    Monitor</u>, 9 May, p. 14.
        Considers the reasons for Walpole's "curiously mixed"
    reputation, concluding that his multi-faceted personality is
    responsible. As a man of paradox, he invites paradoxical
    responses.

10 JOHNSON, JAMES WILLIAM. "Horace Walpole and W.S. Lewis."
    <u>Journal of British Studies</u> 6 (May):64-75.
        Surveys Walpole's contemporary and posthumous reputation,
    noting the constant emphasis on his triviality and eccen-
    tricity, and regards one of Lewis's articles (1930.6) as a
    turning point. Studies the progress of the Yale Edition,
    detecting a shift in emphasis beginning with volume thirteen
    (1948.9); hereafter the edition itself, rather than Wal-
    pole's letters, is offered as a guide to the eighteenth cen-
    tury. Walpole's letters reveal only a third-rate mind, but
    "what Walpole lacked, Lewis has supplied."

11 KETTON-CREMER, R[OBERT] W[YNDHAM]. "The Elizabethan Walpoles."
    In 1967.22, pp. 131-40.
        Despite Walpole's interest in his ancestry, he knew lit-
    tle of an Elizabethan generation of Walpoles who converted
    to Catholicism. Walpole had "little genuine interest in
    religious matters" and would not have understood his ances-
    tors' desire for martyrdom.

12 KNOLLENBERG, BERNARD. "Walpole: Pro-American." In 1967.22,
    pp. 85-90.
        Discusses Walpole's support of the colonists in the 1760s
    and 1770s, and considers to what extent his views were
    shared by other Englishmen. Admires Walpole for "his forti-
    tude in outspokenly maintaining" his position.

13 LAM, GEORGE L. "Walpole and the Duke of Newcastle." In
    1967.22, pp. 57-84.
        Studies Walpole's lifelong detestation of Newcastle,
    expressed in his letters, memoirs, political essays and
    marginalia, considering the parts played by personal dislike
    and political differences. Despite a temporary rapproche-
    ment in the mid-1760s, Walpole's "amiable attitude" did not
    survive Newcastle's death in 1768.

14 LEWIS, WILMARTH SHELDON. <u>One Man's Education</u>. New York:
    Knopf, 488 pp.
        Walpolian sections in this autobiography include chapters
    on the beginnings and development of the Lewis Walpole
    Library, the foundation, methods and progress of the Yale

Edition of Walpole's correspondence, and the future of Walpole studies at Yale in Farmington.

15 LIEBERT, HERMAN [W.]. "Walpole and Pearch." In 1967.22, pp. 293-97.

Walpole was one of three authors whose poems were cancelled in the second issue of the first edition of George Pearch's Collection of Poems (1768). Suggests that James Dodsley, rather than the three authors, was responsible for the poems' cancellation.

16 MAYOR, A. HYATT. "A Note on the Prints at Strawberry Hill." In 1967.22, pp. 181-83.

Walpole was one of the first private collectors to organize his prints according to a system devised by Carl von Heinecken in a treatise of 1771. This treatise contains "the basic assumptions that govern most public print collections today."

17 OSBORN, JAMES M[ARSHALL]. "Horace Walpole and Edmond Malone." In 1967.22, pp. 299-324.

Studies Walpole's dealings with Malone, noting that their "relationship was far from central in the life of either, but was valued by both." Discusses their involvement over The Count of Narbonne, the Chatterton controversy, Malone's edition of Shakespeare, and, after Walpole's death, Malone's vigorous response to Pinkerton's Walpoliana in 1800.1.

18 POTTLE, FREDERICK A. "The Part Played by Horace Walpole and James Boswell in the Quarrel Between Rousseau and Hume: A Reconsideration," and "Reply to Walpole's Letter to Rousseau." In 1967.22, pp. 255-91, 341-42.

Presents the material of 1925.10 in "a radically revised and chastened form." Withdraws several conjectures made in the earlier version and contributes much new material bearing on the quarrel. An appendix transcribes an anonymous "pretended reply by Rousseau to Walpole's pretended letter to him from the King of Prussia."

19 SEDGWICK, ROMNEY. "Horace Walpole's Articles 1747-49." In 1967.22, pp. 45-55.

Discusses eighteen political essays that Walpole contributed to two opposition weeklies: fifteen in Old England (1747-49), and three in the Remembrancer (1748-49). The essays are anti-government propaganda although Walpole ostensibly supported the government, headed by Henry Pelham, his father's political heir. The explanation offered is that Walpole was working for the reward of a reversionary office from the Prince of Wales.

20 SMITH, ROBERT A. "Walpole's Reflections on the Revolution in

France." In 1967.22, pp. 91-114.
Contends that Walpole's horror at the French Revolution,
rather than Wordsworth's and other sympathizers' enthusiasm,
expressed the national mood. Points out the similarity between Walpole's views and those of Burke in his Reflections
of 1790, and regards Walpole as a spokesman for, as well as
a chronicler of, the English governing class.

21   SMITH, WARREN HUNTING.   "'Horatius Italicus.'"   In 1967.22,
      pp. 117-29.
      Explains why Walpole did not return to Italy after his
      youthful Grand Tour, despite his continuing interest in the
      country, and believes that his decision to remain resident
      in England was essential to the success of his writings.
      Studies Walpole's correspondence with Mann, his dealings
      with his sister-in-law, who resided in Italy, and the influ-
      ence of Italian works on his own publications.

22   SMITH, WARREN HUNTING, ed.   Horace Walpole: Writer, Politi-
      cian, and Connoisseur. Essays on the 250th Anniversary of
      Walpole's Birth. New Haven: Yale University Press, 358 pp.
      The only collection of essays on Walpole. Contains nine-
      teen essays in three sections: "Walpole as politician and
      political commentator," "Walpole as connoisseur and anti-
      quarian," and "Walpole as a literary figure." A brief in-
      troduction observes that "Victorian disapproval and Edwardi-
      an enthusiasm" in Walpole studies have now been replaced by
      a more balanced assessment. Acknowledges the writings, edi-
      tions and collection of W.S. Lewis, to whom the volume is
      dedicated.

23   TAIT, HUGH.   "'The Devil's Looking-Glass': The Magical Specu-
      lum of Dr John Dee," and "Items Falsely Labelled as Dr
      Dee's." In 1967.22, pp. 195-212, 337-38.
      Describes Dr. John Dee's magic mirror, now in the British
      Museum, and traces its history from Dee's death in 1608
      until its acquisition by Walpole in 1770. An appendix lists
      spurious articles purporting to be Dee's mirror.

24   WALLACE, A. DAYLE.   "Two Unpublished Fairy Tales by Horace Wal-
      pole." In 1967.22, pp. 241-53.
      Transcribes, with brief introductions, two unpublished
      short fictions by Walpole: "A Fairy Tale" (1743) and "The
      Bird's Nest," intended for Hieroglyphic Tales but not
      included. Suggests that Otranto could also be profitably
      read as a fairy tale, but does not develop the idea.

25   WALPOLE, HORACE.   Horace Walpole's Correspondence with Sir
      Horace Mann. Edited by W[ilmarth] S[heldon] Lewis, Warren
      Hunting Smith and George L. Lam, with the assistance of
      Edwine M. Martz.   The Yale Edition of Horace Walpole's

Correspondence, edited by W[ilmarth] S[heldon] Lewis, vols.
23-24. New Haven: Yale University Press, vols. 7-8.
Continuation of 1960.10, with letters from 1768 to 1779.

26   WALPOLE, HORACE. Zamok Otranto [The Castle of Otranto]. In
    Horace Walpole "The Castle of Otranto," Jacques Cazotte "Le
    diable amoureux," William Beckford "Vathek." Translated by
    V.E. Shor, edited by V[iktor] M[aksimovich] Zhirmunskii and
    N.A. Sigal. Leningrad: Nauka, 292 pp.
        Russian translation of Otranto, with a translation of
    Scott's preface (1811.5). An essay by Zhirmunskii and Segal
    summarizes Walpole's life and writings, discussing the
    influence of Strawberry Hill in Europe, which extended to
    Russian art and architecture. Also considers the influence
    of Otranto and The Mysterious Mother in the development of
    Gothicism and romanticism.

27   WATSON, F.J.B. "Walpole and the Taste for French Porcelain in
    Eighteenth-Century England," and "Walpole's Purchases of
    Porcelain." In 1967.22, pp. 185-94, 327-36.
        Describes and illustrates Walpole's collection of French
    porcelain, acquired during his visits to Paris. An appendix
    records all the items of French porcelain and faïence listed
    in Walpole's "Paris Journals" and traced in the Description
    of the Villa or the 1842 Strawberry Hill Sale Catalogues.

1968

1   BROOKE, JOHN. "Horace Walpole." Times Literary Supplement, 15
    August, p. 873.
        Replies to 1968.13. Finds Lord Holland's mutilation of
    the manuscript of Walpole's Memoirs reprehensible even by
    the standards of his time.

2   DRALLE, LEWIS A. "Strawberry Leaves." Studies in Burke and
    his Time 10 (Fall):1060-69.
        Review article on 1967.22, studying Walpole as a politi-
    cian and historian. Concludes that the eighteenth century
    is "epitomized in the figure of one man."

3   HARFST, BETSY PERTEIT. "Horace Walpole and the Unconscious:
    An Experiment in Freudian Analysis." Ph.D. dissertation,
    Northern Illinois University, 264 pp.
        An original, provocative attempt to relate Walpole's
    imaginative works to his unconscious repressions. Includes
    chapters on the "psychical background" of Otranto and The
    Mysterious Mother, analyses of each work in terms of a
    dream, and an extensive study of Hieroglyphic Tales.
    Believes that "the relationship between Walpole's hidden
    dreams and his imaginative creations" is very close and

direct. Published: 1980.4.

4   HARTLEY, LODWICK. "A Late Augustan Circus: Macaulay on John-
    son, Boswell, and Walpole." South Atlantic Quarterly 67
    (Summer):513-26.
       Suggests that Macaulay's vituperative essays on Boswell
    and Johnson were influenced by Walpole's contempt for both
    writers, while Macaulay's essay on Walpole was also influ-
    enced by Walpole's treatment of Boswell. Thus Walpole,
    ironically, is responsible for the most famous attack on
    himself.

5   "Horace Walpole." Times Literary Supplement, 8 August, p. 857.
       The author of 1968.13 replies to Waldegrave (1968.17),
    defending Lord Holland's treatment of Walpole's Memoirs.

6   IKVER, BARRY. "The Persecuted Heroine in a 'Gothic' Setting."
    In "Sexual Perversion in Eighteenth-Century English and
    French Fiction." Ph.D. dissertation, Indiana University,
    pp. 65-86.
       Compares Otranto as Gothic novel with Clarissa as senti-
    mental novel. Both present "a sensuous, virtuous female
    under stress," and both "show the ultimate triumph of Virtue
    over Vice through the agency of Divine Providence."

7   JOHNSON, JAMES W[ILLIAM]. "Walpole Against Burke: Some Ancil-
    lary Speculations." Studies in Burke and his Time 10
    (Fall):1022-34.
       Supplements Kallich (1968.8) by considering the psycho-
    logical reasons for Walpole's hostility to Burke. Suggests
    that their common denunciation of the French Revolution
    brought them closer in the last decade of their lives:
    "Walpole the Englishman and Burke the Irishman came to be
    Britons at last."

8   KALLICH, MARTIN. "Horace Walpole Against Edmund Burke: A
    Study in Antagonism." Studies in Burke and his Time 9
    (Winter):834-63; (Spring):927-45.
       A detailed analysis of Walpole's antagonism towards
    Burke, dealing with financial, religious and political ques-
    tions. Examines numerous letters and passages in Walpole's
    Memoirs to provide a survey of Walpole's comments on Burke
    from 1766 to 1796.

9   KALLICH, MARTIN. "Houghton Hall: The House of the Walpoles."
    Papers in Language and Literature 4 (Fall):360-69.
       Examines Walpole's Aedes Walpolianae (1747) both as a
    guide to Robert Walpole's collection at Houghton Hall and to
    Horace Walpole's taste and attitude to his father. Believes
    that Horace's career as collector and politician parallelled
    that of his father, and considers a possible connection be-

tween Houghton Hall and The Mysterious Mother. Revised:
1971.4.

10   KETTON-CREMER, R[OBERT] W[YNDHAM].   "Horace Walpole."   Yale
     Review 58, no. 1:94-102.
          Review article on 1967.14, 22, and on the Yale Edition of
     Walpole's correspondence. Applauds both Walpole's achieve-
     ment and the editorial labours of W.S. Lewis, "who has pre-
     sented that achievement to us in this unrivaled form."

11   LEVY, MAURICE.   "Le rêve gothique d'Horace Walpole."   In Le
     roman "gothique" anglais 1764-1824. Toulouse: Faculté des
     lettres et sciences humaines de Toulouse, pp. 77-142.
          An extensive study of Otranto, relating Walpole's liter-
     ary Gothicism to his taste for Gothic architecture. Regards
     Otranto as a major work because it breaks completely with
     the literary rules of its time and recognizes the importance
     of dreams and fantasy.

12   LEWIS, WILMARTH S[HELDON].   "The Accords and Resemblances of
     Johnson and Walpole."   Bulletin of the Rocky Mountain Lan-
     guage Association 22 (June):7-12.
          Finds some unexpected resemblances between "two apparent-
     ly antipodal figures," noting the similarities of their
     bibliographies, their productivity and their taste.   Each
     sought to improve the world, and reflected the spirit of his
     time. Reprinted: 1970.9.

13   "Mummy Worship."   Times Literary Supplement, 1 August, p. 821.
          Review of 1967.22. Concurs with Selwyn's view of Walpole
     as "the best preserved mummy in the whole collection" at
     Strawberry Hill, and warns against overpraising Walpole.

14   ROGERS, DONNITA MARLENE LAMB.   "Horace Walpole, Amateur Archi-
     tect and Art Historian." Ph.D. dissertation, University of
     Minnesota, 249 pp.
          Studies Walpole as an antiquary, historian and archi-
     tect.   Includes chapters on his place in the antiquarian
     movement, on his criticism of art and architecture in his
     correspondence and in Anecdotes of Painting, and an exten-
     sive section on Walpole and the Gothic, with an account of
     Strawberry Hill.

15   SCOTT, SIR WALTER.   "Horace Walpole."   In Sir Walter Scott on
     Novelists and Fiction. Edited by Ioan Williams.   London:
     Routledge & Kegan Paul, pp. 84-93, 468.
          Abridgment of Scott's introduction to Otranto (1811.5),
     with annotations.

16   SHIPPS, ANTHONY W.   "Horace Walpole and Hannah More."   Notes
     and Queries 213 (August):304.

Replies to Bennett (1952.3), identifying two quotations in Walpole's correspondence with More.

17   WALDEGRAVE, MARY.   "Horace Walpole."   Times Literary Supplement, 8 August, p. 857.
Replies to 1968.13, deploring Lord Holland's editing of Walpole's Memoirs (1822.9).

18   WALPOLE, HORACE.   The Castle of Otranto.   In Three Gothic Novels.   Edited by Peter Fairclough, introduction by Mario Praz.   Harmondsworth: Penguin, pp. 37-148.
An edition of Otranto, with very sketchy annotations.   An introduction regards the novel, like Strawberry Hill, as "rococo in a Gothic disguise," acknowledges its influence, but finds it inferior in quality to Beckford's Vathek and Mary Shelley's Frankenstein.

1969

1   FREGNAC, CLAUDE.   "Horace Walpole et ses collections à Strawberry Hill."   Plaisir de France 35 (September):50-58.
A profusely illustrated essay, discussing Walpole's relations with Mme du Deffand, his writings, and his collection at Strawberry Hill.   The account is sympathetic to Walpole, but finds him lacking in taste and discernment.

2   GAINES, EDITH.   "Eight Chairs from Strawberry Hill."   Antiques 96 (October):587.
Describes and illustrates a set of eight Gothic chairs from Strawberry Hill, jointly designed by Bentley and Walpole.   Four are now at the Lewis Walpole Library; two are at Bunratty Castle, Ireland.

3   GAINES, EDITH.   "Strawberry Hill and a China Trade Bowl."   Antiques 96 (December):921.
Suggests, on the authority of W.S. Lewis, that the design on a China Trade Bowl was modelled on an early-nineteenth-century engraving of Strawberry Hill.

4   HAZEN, ALLEN T[RACY].   A Catalogue of Horace Walpole's Library.   With Horace Walpole's Library, by Wilmarth Sheldon Lewis.   New Haven: Yale University Press, 3 vols.
The most detailed study of the library of any English author.   Identifies almost all the books, pamphlets and manuscripts owned by Walpole, shows where each item was placed in his collection, traces its history after Walpole's death, and indicates the nature of Walpole's marginalia.   Includes an extensive introduction, discussing Walpole's collecting and arranging of books and the Strawberry Hill Sale of 1842, a revision of Lewis's study of Walpole's

library (1958.2), appendices on false attributions, books given away by Walpole, and books he owned at Eton and Cambridge, and comprehensive indexes, with separate ones of binders and owners. The catalogue follows Walpole's own arrangement, with sections on the Main Library, the Strawberry Hill Press collection, and manuscripts in the Glass Closet, the Offices, and the Round Tower.

5   "H.W.'s Strawberry Hill." The Month at Goodspeed's Book Shop 40, no. 5:99-101.
    A note on Walpole's acquisition and development of Strawberry Hill, and his printing A Description of the Villa of Horace Walpole (1774).

6   KALLICH, MARTIN. Review of Horace Walpole's Correspondence with Sir Horace Mann, vols. 7-8. Studies in Burke and his Time 10 (Winter):1175-79.
    Walpole's correspondence with Mann is "perhaps the longest and most regularly sustained exchange of letters" in English literature. Its interest is "almost exclusively political," and its effect on the reader "must inevitably be that of sadness and despair."

7   KRONENBERGER, LOUIS. "Horace Walpole's Letters." In The Polished Surface: Essays in the Literature of Worldliness. New York: Knopf, pp. 85-98.
    Reprint of 1965.6.

8   LAMBIN, GEORGES. "Louis XVI angliciste." Etudes anglaises 22, no. 2:118-36.
    Discusses Louis XVI's putative authorship of the translation of Walpole's Historic Doubts (1800.5), concluding in his favour. Does not consider the manuscript of the translation in Louis XVI's hand: see Duckworth, 1979.6.

9   MIYOSHI, MASAO. "The Castle of Catatonia: The Gothic Tradition." In The Divided Self: A Perspective on the Literature of the Victorians. New York: New York University Press, pp. 5-14.
    A balanced study of the strengths and limitations of Otranto. Acknowledges the lack of psychological development, but shows that Walpole's use of the Gothic villain, supernatural beings and marvellous events proved highly influential.

10 QUENNELL, PETER. "The Moon Stood Still on Strawberry Hill." Horizon 11 (Summer):113-17.
    Otranto set a pattern for the subsequent Gothic novelists. Like Walpole they drew images from "the darkest recesses of their own subconscious," and like Walpole they were impelled by "some violent secret emotions."

11   SEZNEC, JEAN.   "Madame du Deffand Loves Horace Walpole."   <u>Lis-</u>
     <u>tener</u> 82 (11 December):825-26.
          Traces the fluctuations in Walpole's relationship with
     Mme du Deffand, showing the psychological interest of their
     correspondence and avoiding partisanship with either side.

12   SHIPPS, ANTHONY W.   "Horace Walpole and Hannah More."   <u>Notes</u>
     <u>and Queries</u> 214 (March):107.
          Replies to Bennett (1952.3), identifying a quotation in
     Walpole's correspondence with More.

13   TILLOTSON, GEOFFREY; FUSSELL, PAUL, JR.; WAINGROW, MARSHALL;
     and ROGERSON, BREWSTER, eds.   "Horace Walpole, Fourth Earl
     of Orford."   In <u>Eighteenth-Century English Literature</u>.   New
     York: Harcourt, Brace & World, pp. 1178-1201.
          A selection of Walpole's letters, with annotations.   An
     introduction sketches Walpole's life and writings, taking a
     neutral attitude towards the significance of his formal
     works but emphasizing the importance of his letters.

14   WALPOLE, HORACE.   <u>The Castle of Otranto</u>.   Edited by W[ilmarth]
     S[heldon] Lewis.   Explanatory notes and notes on the text by
     Joseph W. Reed, Jr.   Oxford English Novels.   London: Oxford
     University Press, 115 pp.
          Expanded edition of 1964.8, with brief explanatory notes
     and a note on the text.

                                1970

1   ADAMS, C. KINGSLEY, and LEWIS, W[ILMARTH] S[HELDON].   "The Por-
     traits of Horace Walpole."   <u>Walpole Society</u> 42 (1968-70):
     1-34.
          The standard Walpole iconography.   Includes several con-
     temporary descriptions of Walpole and three lists of por-
     traits, with illustrations: authentic portraits, portraits
     that might be of Walpole, and portraits not of Walpole but
     often thus labelled.   Walpole has always "been a favourite
     name to attach to portraits of elegant, slim, mid-eigh-
     teenth-century young men."

2   BIERWITH, GERHARD.   "Der Mythos der Autorität."   In <u>Die Proble-</u>
     <u>matik des englischen Schauerromans.   Ein kritisches Modell</u>
     <u>zur Behandlung diskriminierter Literatur</u>.   Ph.D. disserta-
     tion, Frankfurt am Main, pp. 98-119.
          Studies the theme of authority in <u>Otranto</u> and the causes
     of fear in the novel.   The relationships among the various
     characters involve either the acceptance or rejection of
     authority.   At the end of the novel, however, authority is
     replaced by self-control, as the hero, Theodore, gains au-
     tonomy.

3   BROWN, HAROLD CLIFFORD, JR. "Horace Walpole as Historiographer and Antiquary: A Study of Enlightenment Anti-Medievalism." Ph.D. dissertation, University of Virginia, 180 pp.

Examines Walpole's historical and antiquarian writings "with attention to what the original author thought them important or interesting for." Includes studies of the letters, Memoirs, Historic Doubts, Royal and Noble Authors, and Anecdotes of Painting. Contends that Walpole can best be understood as a historian.

4   CROOK, J. MORDAUNT. "Horace Walpole." In 1970.7, pp. [41]-[45].

Walpole "killed the freedom of Rococo by popularizing the cult of archaeology." Strawberry Hill is a museum, a "treasure-house of Gothick souvenirs."

5   DOBB, CLIFFORD. "From Strawberry Hill to Gilmorehill: Two Horace Walpole Items in Glasgow University Library." Bibliothek 5 (1967-70):264-67.

Transcribes and discusses a hitherto unknown letter from Walpole to Dr. William Hunter. Also describes an unremarkable volume from Walpole's library discovered in Glasgow University Library.

6   DOLAN, JANET ADELE. "Horace Walpole's The Mysterious Mother: A Critical Edition." Ph.D. dissertation, University of Arizona, 202 pp.

The most reliable edition of The Mysterious Mother. An extensive introduction evaluates the play and studies its complex textual history. Includes an annotated text with a list of variants, and appendices on Mason's proposed alterations to the play, on the various editions, and on the Strawberry Hill printers.

7   EASTLAKE, CHARLES L[OCK]. "Horace Walpole." In A History of the Gothic Revival. Edited with an introduction by J. Mordaunt Crook. Leicester: Leicester University Press, pp. 42-49.

Reprint of 1872.2. Also contains 1970.4.

8   HONOUR, HUGH. Horace Walpole. Writers and Their Work, no. 92. Harlow: Longman, 40 pp.

Revision of 1957.4, with "minor amendments and additions to Bibliography."

9   LEWIS, WILMARTH SHELDON. "The Accords and Resemblances of Johnson and Walpole." In Eighteenth-Century Studies in Honor of Donald F. Hyde. Edited by W.H. Bond. New York: The Grolier Club, pp. 179-86.

Reprint of 1968.12.

10   LIPKING, LAWRENCE. "Horace Walpole's Anecdotes and the Sources
      of English History of Art." In The Ordering of the Arts in
      Eighteenth-Century England. Princeton: Princeton Univer-
      sity Press, pp. 127-63.
          An important study of Walpole as antiquary and art his-
      torian. Discusses his use of Vertue's notebooks in Anec-
      dotes of Painting, his part in the antiquarian movement, his
      theories of the Gothic and his practice at Strawberry Hill,
      the relationship between Walpole's Anecdotes and Vasari's
      Lives of the Painters, and that between Walpole and Beck-
      ford. Believes that "historians of English art must still
      look to Vertue and Walpole."

*11   PINSON, ERNEST RAY. "The Black Sun: A Re-Evaluation of Gothic
      Drama and its Influence." Ph.D. dissertation, Ohio Univer-
      sity, 245 pp.
          Source: Dissertation Abstracts International 31: 4132-
      33A. "The typical Gothic hero-villain was the result of a
      struggle between his passionate nature and individual will
      and the restraints of a stifling authoritarian tradition.
      Horace Walpole, the first to formulate a Gothic play, was
      not certain of his subject matter. Although his methods
      were crude and his perception dim, his devices of terror
      were mild compared to those of M.G. Lewis."

*12   REILLY, DONALD THOMAS. "The Interplay of the Natural and the
      Unnatural: A Definition of the Gothic Romance." Ph.D. dis-
      sertation, University of Pittsburgh, 210 pp.
          Source: Dissertation Abstracts International 31:
      2353A. Demonstrates, through analyses of Otranto and other
      Gothic novels, that "the common denominator of the gothic
      novel is the interplay of the natural and the unnatural
      within and between the cosmic and human spheres of exis-
      tence."

13   SAMOORIAN, VAHE. "The Gray-Walpole Friendship" and "The First
      Gothic Novel: Horace Walpole." In "The Way to Otranto:
      Gothic Elements in Eighteenth-Century English Poetry, 1717-
      1762." Ph.D. dissertation, Bowling Green State University,
      pp. 85-91, 118-33.
          Suggests that despite their early friendship, Gray and
      Walpole had very different temperaments; Walpole was a great
      lover of society, but Gray was basically dull. Regards
      Otranto as an innovative work that prefigured "trends in the
      Romantic Movement," but doubts whether it can be enjoyed by
      twentieth-century readers. Believes that Walpole "did
      little other writing of value."

14   VATSURO, V[ADIM] E. "Uolpol i Pushkin" [Walpole and Push-
      kin]. Vremennik pushkinskoi komisii (1967-68), pp. 47-57.
          An original study, in Russian, of Walpole's influence on

Pushkin. Pushkin drew on Walpole's correspondence and memoirs in writing about the Enlightenment, and on his correspondence with Voltaire concerning Shakespeare in composing Boris Godunov. He had several works by Walpole in his library.

15 WALPOLE, HORACE. "The Prefaces to The Castle of Otranto, A Story, 1764 and 1765." In Novel and Romance 1700-1800: A Documentary Record. Edited by Ioan Williams. London: Routledge & Kegan Paul, pp. 263-69, 464-65.
Prints Walpole's prefaces to the first and second editions of Otranto, with brief annotations.

16 WALPOLE, HORACE. "The Sequel to Gulliver's Travels." In Swift: The Critical Heritage. Edited by Kathleen Williams. London: Routledge & Kegan Paul, pp. 189-91.
Prints Walpole's sequel to Gulliver's Travels from his letter to the Countess of Upper Ossory of 14 December 1771. A prefatory note observes that "the personal and literary differences of Swift and Walpole . . . did not prevent Gulliver's Travels from appealing to Walpole's imagination."

17 WATSON, J.R. "The Individual Experience: Gray and Walpole." In Picturesque Landscape and English Romantic Poetry. London: Hutchison, pp. 50-62.
Compares Walpole's and Gray's reactions to landscapes on their Grand Tour and after. Finds Walpole's responses more conventional, but points out his "love of curiosities" and the originality of Otranto and Strawberry Hill.

1971

1 CONOLLY, L.W. "Horace Walpole, Unofficial Play Censor." English Language Notes 9 (September):42-46.
Transcribes and discusses five letters to Walpole from Francis Seymour Conway, who, as Lord Chamberlain, sought Walpole's advice on censoring new plays. Walpole tended to discourage censorship, although the censorship laws were passed by his father, Robert Walpole.

2 DRURY, MARTIN. "Walpole and Strawberry Hill." Discovering Antiques 2, no. 40:938-41.
A conventional but well illustrated account of Strawberry Hill, "a medieval fantasy and one of the most influential examples of eighteenth-century gothic architecture."

3 HAZEN, A[LLEN] T[RACY]. "Horace Walpole 1717-97." In The New Cambridge Bibliography of English Literature. Edited by George Watson. Vol. 2. Cambridge: Cambridge University Press, pp. 1588-94.

Amalgamates, revises and expands 1941.4 and 1957.3.

4   KALLICH, MARTIN.   Horace Walpole.   Twayne's English Authors
    Series, edited by Sylvia E. Bowman, no. 116.   New York:
    Twayne, 147 pp.
        A concise, highly informative and perceptive critical
    study. Largely avoids the very frequently discussed let-
    ters, concentrating instead on Walpole's memoirs, his criti-
    cism, and his creative works. Includes a brief chronology,
    chapters on Walpole the man, the politician and the connois-
    seur, and analyses of Otranto, The Mysterious Mother and
    Hieroglyphic Tales. Concludes with a judicious evaluation
    of Walpole's achievement, and an annotated bibliography of
    primary and secondary material.

5   KELLY, LINDA. "The Search for a Patron" and "The Embarrassed
    Dilettante." In The Marvellous Boy: The Life and Myth of
    Thomas Chatterton.   London: Weidenfeld & Nicholson, pp.
    23-27, 51-56.
        An undocumented account of Walpole's dealings with
    Chatterton. Exonerates Walpole from causing Chatterton's
    death, but regards his dismissal of the young poet as "a
    tragically lost opportunity."

6   KETTON-CREMER, R[OBERT] W[YNDHAM].   "Walpole, Horace."   In
    Encyclopaedia Britannica. Vol. 23. Chicago: Encyclopaedia
    Britannica, pp. 176-77.
        Replaces Courtney's essay (1911.2). Surveys Walpole's
    life and writings, noting that his most important works
    "were intended for posthumous publication." Regards Walpole
    as the ablest English letter writer, and his correspondence
    as a panoramic study of his age.

7   MALCOLMSON, A.P.W.   "Some New Walpoliana from the Caledon
    Papers, Public Record Office of Northern Ireland."   Irish
    Booklore 1:157-64.
        Transcribes and discusses two hitherto unknown letters
    from Walpole to the second Earl of Hardwicke. One of the
    letters is of special interest, since it deals with Wal-
    pole's "epistolary idol, Mme de Sévigné."

8   ROUSSEAU, G[EORGE] S.   "Colossus on the Hill."   Studies in
    Burke and his Time 12 (Spring):1910-20.
        Review article on 1969.4. Considers the central place
    Walpole's library held in his life, and shows that his
    well-annotated collection belies the stereotype of Walpole
    as dilettante.

9   SOLOMON, STANLEY J.   "Subverting Propriety as a Pattern of
    Irony in Three Eighteenth-Century Novels: The Castle of
    Otranto, Vathek, and Fanny Hill."   Erasmus Review 1 (Novem-

ber):107-16.

Compares <u>Otranto</u> with <u>Vathek</u> and <u>Fanny Hill</u> in terms of their subversion of literary propriety. Regards <u>Otranto</u> as a "stylized comedy," with an ironic preface preparing the reader for an "assault on literary verisimilitude." All three authors were aware of the "disintegrating values" of the late eighteenth century.

10 SPACKS, PATRICIA MEYER, ed. "Walpole" and "Horace Walpole, Fourth Earl of Oxford [sic]." In <u>Late Augustan Prose</u>. Englewood Cliffs, N.J.: Prentice Hall, pp. 24, 269-77.

Notes Walpole's lively interest in both private and public affairs, and his dual role as gossip and historian. Includes a brief bibliography, in which one of the seven items is on Robert, not Horace, Walpole.

11 TOYNBEE, PAGET, and WHIBLEY, LEONARD, eds. <u>Correspondence of Thomas Gray</u>. With corrections and additions by H.W. Starr. Oxford: Clarendon Press, 3 vols.

A corrected, expanded edition of 1935.13.

12 WALPOLE, HORACE. "General Criticism of Dr. Johnson's Writings." In <u>Johnson: The Critical Heritage</u>. Edited by James T. Boulton. London: Routledge & Kegan Paul, pp. 324-26.

Transcribed from the original manuscript, the text differs "at many points" from that published in Walpole's <u>Works</u> (1798.7).

13 WALPOLE, HORACE. <u>Horace Walpole's Correspondence with Sir Horace Mann and Sir Horace Mann the Younger</u>. Edited by W[ilmarth] S[heldon] Lewis, Warren Hunting Smith and George L. Lam, with the assistance of Edwine M. Martz. The Yale Edition of Horace Walpole's Correspondence, edited by W[ilmarth] S[heldon] Lewis, vols. 25-27. New Haven: Yale University Press, vols. 9-11.

Continuation of 1967.25, concluding the correspondence with Horace Mann and also printing Walpole's correspondence with Horace Mann the Younger. Among numerous appendices is one on Walpole's references to "serendipity," which has "inspired more inquiries than all other passages of the Walpolian correspondence put together." An index occupies almost two volumes.

1972

1 ALTICK, RICHARD D. "Crossing the Andean Range." <u>Virginia Quarterly Review</u> 48 (Autumn):613-16.

Review of 1971.13. Compares the Yale Edition of Walpole's correspondence with Besterman's edition of Voltaire's, noting Yale's much more extensive annotation. Both

Walpole and Voltaire provide superb portraits of their soci-
eties, but while Voltaire was a seminal force in shaping the
modern world, Walpole was "a mere spectator."

2   BARRELL, R[EX] A.   "Horace Walpole and France."   Humanities
    Association Bulletin 23 (Spring):33-40.
        Studies several of Walpole's French connections, includ-
    ing his journeys to Paris, his attitude to French language,
    literature and politics, his relationship with Mme du Def-
    fand, and his reputation in France and England. The precur-
    sor of a full-length study (1978.1 and 1979.2).

3   BURNEY, E.L.   "Shakespeare in Otranto."   Manchester Review 12
    (Winter):61-64.
        Despite its reputation for originality Otranto is heavily
    indebted to the later Shakespeare, "with the nobility speak-
    ing in irregular iambic rhythm and the domestics in rustic
    prose."

4   DOYLE, REV. J.   Strawberry Hill.   Twickenham: St. Mary's
    College, 31 pp.
        An illustrated booklet, with descriptions of Twickenham,
    Strawberry Hill and its gardens, Walpole's Gothic remodel-
    ling, his collecting, and his way of life. Also studies the
    history of Strawberry Hill in the nineteenth and twentieth
    centuries.

5   FRANKLIN, COLIN, and FRANKLIN, CHARLOTTE.   "Strawberry Hill."
    In Catalogue Five. Oxford: privately printed, pp. 1-20.
        A bookseller's catalogue of many of the Strawberry Hill
    books, with useful annotations supplementing and sometimes
    correcting Hazen (1942.5). A brief preface contends that
    the books "suggest the habit and sensitivity" of Walpole's
    life.

6   GOLLER, KARL HEINZ.   "Gothic Novel."   In "Romance" und "Novel."
    Die Anfänge des englischen Romans.   Sprache und Literatur.
    Regensburger Arbeiten zur Anglistik und Amerikanistik.
    Regensburg: Verlag Hans Carl, pp. 205-17.
        In German. Regards Otranto as the foundation of the
    Gothic novel. Walpole was interested not in realism or his-
    torical accuracy, but in the creation of archetypal charac-
    ters and symbolic actions.

7   KIELY, ROBERT.   "The Castle of Otranto."   In The Romantic Novel
    in England.   Cambridge, Mass.: Harvard University Press,
    pp. 27-42.
        An elegant, penetrating study of Otranto and the nature
    of Gothic fiction. Regards Walpole's dissatisfaction with
    the present as the primary source of his interest in Gothi-
    cism. Since boredom inspired much Gothic fiction, it often

lacks focus and moral seriousness. Otranto, however, has "an authentic impulse, which is to throw off the current platitudes and clichés of art."

8 MOMBELLO, GIANNI. "J.-M.-L. Coupé e H. Walpole: Gli amori di Christine de Pizan." Studi Francesci 16 (April):5-25.
    Walpole's account, in his Catalogue of Royal and Noble Authors, of the liaison between Christine de Pizan and the Count of Salisbury was not original, but derived from Coupé.

9 MORAN, JAMES. "The Strawberry Hill Sale." In Henry George. Printer, Bookseller, Stationer, and Bookbinder, Westerham 1830- c. 1846. Westerham: Westerham Press, pp. 37-42.
    Discusses the part played by Henry George in the booksellers' "ring" at the Strawberry Hill Sale of 1842. Contradicts Hazen (1955.2), who believes that George did not take part in this ring.

*10 ONOCHIE, B.C. "Changing Expressions of Gothicism in English Fiction from The Castle of Otranto to Wuthering Heights." Ph.D. dissertation, University of Ibadan.
    Source: Annual Bibliography of English Language and Literature 48 (1973):342.

11 SHELDEN, PAMELA J. "The Castle of Otranto." In "American Gothicism: The Evolution of a Mode." Ph.D. dissertation, Kent State University, pp. 49-72.
    Analyzes the virtues and vices of Otranto, which is not "a great work of art" but which is important for its exploration of human psychology. Walpole's pioneering interest in the unconscious was much more fully developed by subsequent writers.

12 SHIPPS, ANTHONY W. "Horace Walpole: 'Visitors Book.'" Notes and Queries 217 (October):386.
    Replies to Bennett (1943.1), identifying a quotation from Horace.

13 STAR, MORRIS. "Melville's Markings in Walpole's Anecdotes of Painting in England." Papers of the Bibliographical Society of America 66 (3d quarter):321-27.
    Records fifteen markings made by Melville in his copy of Walpole's Anecdotes of Painting. There are, however, "no annotations or comments."

1973

1 BROOKE, JOHN. "Horace Walpole and King George III." In Statesmen, Scholars and Merchants. Essays in Eighteenth-Century History Presented to Dame Lucy Sutherland. Edited

by Anne Whiteman, J.S. Bromley and P.G.M. Dickson. Oxford: Clarendon Press, pp. 263-75.

Accounts for Walpole's antipathy to George III, which derived from the prejudices of Walpole's nephew, Lord Waldegrave, the King's embittered tutor. Suggests other reasons for Walpole's dislike of George III, concluding that his portrait is interesting "not for what it tells us of the King, but for what it tells us of Walpole."

2   [CLIFFORD, JAMES L., and MIDDENDORF, JOHN H.]   "The Walpole Jubilee." <u>Johnsonian Newsletter</u> 33 (September):13-14.

Reports on the progress of the Yale Edition of Walpole's correspondence, commending the achievement of both Walpole and the Yale editors.

3   COOPER, GEORGE B.   <u>The Age of Horace Walpole and Wilmarth Sheldon Lewis. An exhibit marking the fortieth jubilee of the Yale Edition of Horace Walpole's Correspondence and the fiftieth of the Lewis Walpole Library at Farmington.</u> Hartford, Ct.: Trinity College Library, unpaginated.

Regards Walpole as "the man best suited to be the central figure around whom to build a collection" illustrating the eighteenth century. Includes sections on Walpole's life, W.S. Lewis's collection and writings on Walpole, and books by, printed by, and owned by Walpole.

4   CORDASCO, FRANCESCO.   "Horace Walpole and Junius." <u>Notes and Queries</u> 218 (January):22-23.

Names as possible candidates for Junius both Walpole's choice, Charles Wolfran Cornwall, and Walpole himself. Draws attention to Walpole's annotated copy of the <u>Letters,</u> now lost, and to his "Hints for Discovering Junius" (1891.6).

5   CROOK, J. MORDAUNT.   "Strawberry Hill Revisited." <u>Country Life</u> 153 (7 June):1598-1602; (14 June):1726-30; (21 June):1794-97; (28 June):1896.

Three richly illustrated essays, discussing Strawberry Hill in Walpole's time, the contributions made by various architects, and its history in the Victorian age. The second essay, studying the work at Strawberry Hill of ten architects, from William Robinson to James Wyatt, provides much information on the development of Walpole's views on architecture.

6   GIBSON, J[EREMY] S.W.   "Horace Walpole and the Hardwicke Marriage Act of 1753." <u>Genealogist's Magazine</u> 17 (September): 367-70.

Walpole opposed the Earl of Hardwicke's Marriage Act in the House, and described the affair in his <u>Memoirs of George the Second.</u> His opposition almost certainly stemmed from personal antipathy to Hardwicke.

7   HALL, H. GASTON.   "French Books in Horace Walpole's Library."
    <u>Australian Journal of French Studies</u> 10 (September-December):254-73.
    Studies Walpole's interest in French literature and discusses some of the 850 French works (out of nearly 4000) in his library. Walpole's active use of his French books "is abundantly testified by markings, marginalia, and frequent references in the letters."

8   HAZEN, A[LLEN] T[RACY].   <u>A Bibliography of the Strawberry Hill Press.   With a Record of the Prices at which Copies have been Sold.   Including a New Supplement.   Together with a Bibliography and Census of the Detached Pieces</u> by A.T. Hazen and J.P. Kirby. Preface by W[ilmarth] S[heldon] Lewis. New York: Barnes & Noble, 300 pp.
    Reprint of 1942.5 with an important supplement, containing an introductory note, a new preface by Lewis, and additions and corrections to many of the original entries.

9   HELLMAN, GEOFFREY T.   "Our Far-Flung Correspondents. The Age of Wilmarth Lewis." <u>New Yorker</u> 49 (15 October):104-11.
    A sequel to 1959.1, surveying the final stages of the Yale Edition of Walpole's correspondence.

10 LEWIS, W[ILMARTH] S[HELDON].   <u>A Guide to the Life of Horace Walpole (1717-1797), Fourth Earl of Orford, as Illustrated by an Exhibition Based on the Yale Edition of his Correspondence.</u> New Haven: Yale University Press, unpaginated.
    The catalogue of an exhibition, with illustrations of fifty-five objects closely associated with Walpole and accompanying descriptions. Includes a brief preface, a survey of Walpole's life, and an account of his chief correspondents.

11 LEWIS, WILMARTH S[HELDON].   "The Yale Edition of Horace Walpole's Correspondence, 1933-1973." <u>Yale University Library Gazette</u> 48 (October):69-83.
    Describes the genesis and progress of the Yale Edition, which answered the need for an accurate text, comprehensive annotations, and the replies from Walpole's correspondents. Walpole's "chronicle has been subjected to microscopic study and found to be seldom wrong."

12 LUCKETT, RICHARD.   "Strawberry Hill for Ever." <u>Spectator</u> 231 (6 October):448-49.
    Review of 1973.23. Presents a balanced view of Walpole, mediating between Macaulay's disparagement and excessive subsequent rehabilitation.

13   MYERS, ROBIN.   "George Henry Robins (1778–1847):   Strawberry
      Hill Auctioneer." Printing Art 1 (Spring):2–10.
            A lively account of Robins's flamboyant handling of the
      Strawberry Hill Sale of 1842, with contemporary accounts of
      his behaviour.

14   [NETHERY, WALLACE.]   "Strawberry Hill–Hoose–Farmington." Cor-
      anto 9, no. 1:36–37.
            An exchange of letters between Nethery and W.S. Lewis
      concerning Walpole's copy of one of Shaftesbury's treatises.

15   PLUMB, J.H.   "Bigness in Scholarship." Horizon 15 (Winter):
      46–47.
            Compares the Yale Edition of Walpole's correspondence
      with such projects as Besterman's Voltaire, the Yale Ben-
      jamin Franklin and the Bollandists' Acta Sanctorum, all
      examples of "scholarly gigantism." The Yale Edition "has
      grown as vast as the Pyramids of Cheops."

16   QUENNELL, PETER.   "Horace Walpole." In A History of English
      Literature. Springfield, Mass.: G. & C. Merriam, pp. 283–
      86.
            A survey of Walpole's life and works, singling out the
      correspondence for special praise. Regards both Otranto and
      The Mysterious Mother as products of Walpole's subcon-
      scious.

17   RIELY, JOHN C.   "The Age of Horace Walpole in Caricature.   An
      Exhibition of Satirical Prints and Drawings from the Collec-
      tion of W.S. Lewis." Preface by Wilmarth S[heldon] Lewis,
      introduction by Dayle R. Roylance. Yale University Library
      Gazette 48 (October):87–134.
            The catalogue of an exhibition commemorating the fortieth
      anniversary of work on the Yale Edition. Includes descrip-
      tions and reproductions of prints and drawings of Walpole
      and Strawberry Hill, and of persons and items associated
      with Walpole. Reprinted: 1973.18.

18   RIELY, JOHN C.   The Age of Horace Walpole in Caricature.   An
      Exhibition of Satirical Prints and Drawings from the Collec-
      tion of W.S. Lewis. Preface by Wilmarth S[heldon] Lewis,
      introduction by Dayle R. Roylance. New Haven: Yale Univer-
      sity Library, 47 pp.
            Reprint of 1973.17.

19   "The Walpologist." Time 102 (29 October):100, 102.
            A gossipy, inaccurate account of W.S. Lewis's collecting
      and editing of Walpole. Includes a "Walpole Sampler," with
      extracts from three of Walpole's letters.

20   VAN LUCHENE, STEPHEN ROBERT.   "The Castle of Otranto."   In

"Essays in Gothic Fiction from Horace Walpole to Mary Shelley." Ph.D. dissertation, University of Notre Dame, pp. 4-41.

Otranto had a threefold influence on subsequent Gothic fiction: it introduced stock character types, established narrative devices, and presented an "idealized reconstruction of the middle ages" within a theological framework. Pays particular attention to the role of Catholicism in the novel, which previous commentators are said to have neglected. Published: 1980.16.

21 WALPOLE, HORACE. Horace Walpole's Correspondence with John Chute, Richard Bentley, The Earl of Strafford, Sir William Hamilton, The Earl and Countess Harcourt, George Hardinge. Edited by W[ilmarth] S[heldon] Lewis, A. Dayle Wallace and Robert A. Smith, with the assistance of Edwine M. Martz. The Yale Edition of Horace Walpole's Correspondence, edited by W[ilmarth] S[heldon] Lewis, vol. 35. New Haven: Yale University Press, 649 pp.

Includes a brief introduction, describing the "virtuosi" and the part played by Chute and Bentley in the redesigning of Strawberry Hill, and, as an appendix, George Hardinge's account of Walpole, a reprint of 1814.1.

22 WALPOLE, HORACE. Horace Walpole's Correspondence with The Walpole Family. Edited by W[ilmarth] S[heldon] Lewis and Joseph W. Reed, Jr., with the assistance of Edwine M. Martz. The Yale Edition of Horace Walpole's Correspondence, edited by W[ilmarth] S[heldon] Lewis, vol. 36. New Haven: Yale University Press, 336 pp.

An introduction observes that Walpole's devotion to his family – with the exception of his uncle Horace and his brother Robert – has been underestimated. Contains Walpole's correspondence with twenty-six family members. Appendices include a study of the dispersal of the manuscripts of all of Walpole's correspondence, and a Walpole genealogy.

23 WALPOLE, HORACE. Selected Letters of Horace Walpole. Edited by W[ilmarth] S[heldon] Lewis. New Haven: Yale University Press, 323 pp.

Contains 112 letters, most of which were in Lewis's first selection (1926.13) but now with a more accurate text and annotations. An introduction considers the originality of Walpole's formal works, and describes his plan to transmit, through his correspondence, "a full and dependable history of the time."

1974

1   ASHE, GEOFFREY. "The Gothic Plunge." In Do What You Will: A
    History of Anti-Morality. London: W.H. Allen, pp. 192-95.
        Otranto grew out of Walpole's dissatisfaction with the
    escapism of Strawberry Hill, during his political campaign-
    ing for Henry Seymour Conway; it is "a dark dream-projection
    of Strawberry Hill housing characters symbolizing Walpole's
    conflicts." Identifies Manfred as the Walpole of Strawberry
    Hill, Alfonso as Sir Robert, and Theodore as "the new polit-
    ical Horace."

2   BASSIN, HENRY ALAN. "The Genesis of Gothic Romance: Horace
    Walpole's The Castle of Otranto." In "The Gothic Transfor-
    mation: Developments in the British Gothic Romance, 1764-
    1887." Ph.D. dissertation, University of Indiana, pp. 19-
    48.
        Emphasizes Otranto's weaknesses, especially its failure
    to connect the natural with the supernatural and the reason-
    able with the inexplicable. This failure, in turn, indi-
    cates an unreconciled dualism in Walpole's "social vision."

3   COOPER, DONALD BRYANT. "Epistolary Virtuoso: A Study of the
    Style of Horace Walpole." Ph.D. dissertation, University of
    South Carolina, 172 pp.
        A thematic and stylistic analysis of Walpole's letters.
    The chapter headings and over a third of the text are taken,
    with slight revisions but without acknowledgment, from the
    headings and prefaces in Hadley's edition (1926.16), which
    also supplies all the letters for discussion. Ascribes
    Walpole's success as a letter writer primarily to his charm
    and lightness of touch.

4   DAVIS, TERENCE. "Twilight on the Thames." In The Gothick
    Taste. Newton Abbot: David & Charles, pp. 65-82.
        A richly illustrated account of the development of Straw-
    berry Hill. Suggests that Walpole wished to make Gothic
    respectable, but in doing so dampened "the charm of Rococo."

5   DRABBLE, MARGARET. "Through Walpole's Window." Listener 91 (6
    June):738-39.
        Review of 1973.21-22. Admires Walpole's letters, despite
    the triviality of his obsessions. He disliked the "horrid
    wildness of nature," and "saw life through the glass of his
    own mind."

6   GIBSON, J[EREMY] S.W. "Travellers' Tales Part 2." Cake and
    Cockhorse, Banbury Historical Society, 5 (Spring):143-45,
    148-50.
        Discusses Walpole's accounts of his visits to George
    Montagu at Greatworth, which throw light "on the life of an

eighteenth-century squire." Also considers Walpole's accounts of visits to other country seats.

7   GRIGSON, GEOFFREY. "The Freedom of Horace Walpole." In The
     Contrary View: Glimpses of Fudge and Gold. London: Mac-
     millan, pp. 146-48.
         Review article on 1967.25. Contrasts Gray's desire to be
     part of the establishment with Walpole's independence and
     pride in speaking his mind. Reprinted from an unlocated
     source of 1967.

8   KARL, FREDERICK R. "Horace Walpole - The Castle of Otranto
     (1764)." In The Adversary Literature. The English Novel in
     the Eighteenth Century: A Study in Genre. New York:
     Farrar, Straus & Giroux, pp. 241-47.
         Studies Walpole's contribution to Gothic fiction by con-
     sidering several elements that originate in Otranto. Sug-
     gests that Otranto should be read as a vision, rather than
     as a traditional novel. Reprinted: 1975.3.

9   McCABE, KEVIN. "Verse in the Gray, Walpole, West and Ashton
     Correspondence." Notes and Queries 219 (December):471.
         Two queries on the sources of quotations in letters from
     Gray to West and from Walpole to Ashton.

10   MORTIMER, RAYMOND. "Letters from Otranto." Sunday Times (Lon-
     don), 27 January, p. 31.
         Review of 1973.21-22. Analyzes Walpole's character,
     finding him, despite some weaknesses, "an uncommonly engag-
     ing fellow with a genius for friendship as well as for
     prose."

11   RAYMOND, JOHN. "Harry and Horry." New Statesman 88 (27 Decem-
     ber):935-36.
         Review of 1974.17. "Three human passions" stand out in
     Walpole's life: his affection for his mother, his infatua-
     tion with Mary Berry, and his "unrequited passion" for his
     cousin, Henry Seymour Conway. Discusses Walpole's relations
     with Conway and the Conway family.

12   RIELY, J[OHN] C. "Horace Walpole, Friend of American Liberty."
     Studies in Burke and his Time 16 (Fall):5-21.
         Examines Walpole's principles as a "True Blue Whig," and
     traces his reactions to American politics from the mid-1760s
     to the early 1780s. Shows that Walpole foresaw the American
     Revolution and consistently deplored English policy, regard-
     ing the colonists as the upholders of Whig principles.

13   ROWSE, A.L. "A Taste for Life." Books and Bookmen 19 (July):
     78-79.
         Review of 1973.23. Walpole is "not only one of the best

eighteenth-century writers but a prime source for its history."

14   SHIPPS, ANTHONY W.   "Source Wanted."   Notes and Queries 219
     (December):471.
          Attributes a quotation to Walpole, but is unable to veri-
     fy the attribution.

15   "Strawberry Hill Mob."   Times Literary Supplement, 3 May, p.
     469.
          Review of 1973.21-22.   Regards the Yale Edition as "a
     vast monument," but avoids commenting on the value of the
     letters it commemorates.

16   TRACY, ANN BLAISDELL.   "Walpole, Horace.   The Castle of Otran-
     to."   In "Patterns of Fear in the Gothic Novel, 1790-1830."
     Ph.D. dissertation, University of Toronto, pp. 431-32.
          A brief plot summary of Otranto.   Published: 1980.15.

17   WALPOLE, HORACE.   Horace Walpole's Correspondence with Henry
     Seymour Conway, Lady Ailesbury, Lord and Lady Hertford,
     Mrs Harris.   Edited by W[ilmarth] S[heldon] Lewis, Lars
     E[leon] Troide, Edwine M. Martz and Robert A. Smith.   The
     Yale Edition of Horace Walpole's Correspondence, edited by
     W[ilmarth] S[heldon] Lewis, vols. 37-39.   New Haven: Yale
     University Press, 3 vols.
          Contains Walpole's correspondence with his cousin and
     closest friend, Conway, Conway's brother, Lord Hertford, and
     their families.   An introduction studies the development of
     Walpole's friendship with Conway and his dealings with
     Conway's family.   Among the many appendices are unpublished
     verses by Walpole.

18   WALPOLE, HORACE.   Zamczysko w Otranto: opowiesc gotycka [The
     Castle of Otranto: A Gothic Story].   Translated with an
     afterword by Maria Przymanowska.   Cracow: Wydawnictwo
     Literackie, 115 pp.
          A Polish translation of Otranto, with an afterword dis-
     cussing Walpole's life, writings and development of Straw-
     berry Hill.   Emphasizes the popularity of Otranto, trans-
     lated into numerous languages, and its influence on subse-
     quent writers.   Strawberry Hill, likewise, was highly influ-
     ential: even the Polish King Jozef Krasinski was inspired
     to rebuild his castle in the Gothic style.

1975

1   CHRISTIE, IAN R.   "The Whimsical Horry."   Times Literary Sup-
     plement, 2 May, p. 485.
          Replies to Sutherland (1975.9), confirming the accuracy

of Walpole's statement about Conway's baptismal date.

2   HUNT, JOHN DIXON, and WILLIS, PETER.   "Horace Walpole (1717-
    97)."   In The Genius of the Place.   London: Paul Elek, pp.
    311-16.
        Excerpts from two Walpole letters and from his History of
    the Modern Taste in Gardening, with a brief introduction on
    Walpole as historian of landscape gardening.

3   KARL, FREDERICK R.   "Horace Walpole - The Castle of Otranto
    (1764)."   In A Reader's Guide to the Development of the
    English Novel in the Eighteenth Century.   London: Thames &
    Hudson, pp. 241-47.
        Reprint, under a different title, of 1974.8.

4   KLEIN, JURGEN.   "Walpoles Prefaces," "'Das altvätterische
    Strawberry Hill des Sir Horace Walpole,'" and "Horace Wal-
    pole (1717-1797): The Castle of Otranto."   In Der Gotische
    Roman und die Asthetik des Bösen.   Impulse der Forschung,
    vol. 20.   Darmstadt: Wissenschaftliche Buchgesellschaft,
    pp. 238-54, 272-77.
        Compares Walpole's two prefaces to Otranto, and considers
    his reasons for revealing his authorship in the second.
    Studies Walpole's remodelling of Strawberry Hill and his
    interest in the supernatural.   Ascribes the low opinion of
    Otranto held by many nineteenth-century critics, with the
    notable exception of Byron, to their incomprehension of Wal-
    pole's interest in the supernatural, in which he was ahead
    of his time.

5   MACAULAY, JAMES.   "Strawberry Hill and Alnwick Castle."   In The
    Gothic Revival 1745-1845."   Glasgow and London: Blackie,
    pp. 56-82.
        Ascribes the influence of Strawberry Hill less to the
    originality of its architecture than to Walpole's gift for
    self-publicity and the fame of his literary activities.   It
    is amateurish and a "personal statement."

6   McCABE, CHARLES.   "'You Will Regret Me. . . .'"   San Francisco
    Chronicle, 11 December, p. 39.
        Discusses Walpole's relationship with Mme du Deffand,
    "one of the most curious affairs of the 18th Century."
    Believes that her passion for Walpole was threatening to
    him, but sometimes "touching in the extreme."

7   McNUTT, DAN J.   "Horace Walpole.   4th Earl of Orford (1717-
    1797)."   In The Eighteenth-Century Gothic Novel: An Anno-
    tated Bibliography of Criticism.   Foreword by Devendra
    P[rasad] Varma and Maurice Lévy.   New York: Garland, pp.
    136-65.
        The fullest bibliography of works on Walpole to date,

with incisive and accurate annotations. Contains sections
on editions, bibliographies, full-length studies, articles,
notices in general works, and early reviews. Primarily
concerned with works dealing with Otranto, The Mysterious
Mother, and Strawberry Hill.

8   RIELY, JOHN C.   "Horace Walpole and 'the Second Hogarth.'"
     Eighteenth Century Studies 9 (Fall):28-44.
          A well-illustrated study of Walpole's dealings with a ne-
     glected late-eighteenth-century caricaturist, Henry William
     Bunbury. Suggests that Walpole's admiration for Bunbury
     derived less from Bunbury's artistic talents than from his
     "personal charm and his status as a polite amateur."

9   SUTHERLAND, JAMES.   "The Whimsical Horry."   Times Literary
     Supplement, 25 April, p. 447.
          Review of 1974.17. Emphasizes the historical value of
     Walpole's letters and studies his relations with Henry Sey-
     mour Conway. Suggests that this was Walpole's most intimate
     friendship, and "almost a love affair."

10   THE DIRECTORS.   "Otranto on the Thames."   Limited Editions Club
     Monthly Letter, no. 490 (August), 8 pp.
          Issued with 1975.12. Discusses Walpole's life at Straw-
     berry Hill, his letters, in which he was the "historian of
     his age," and Otranto, "the first Gothic novel in English."

11   VALENSISE, RACHELE.   "The Castle of Otranto e l'incubo del
     potere."   Siculorum Gymnasium, n.s. 28, no. 2:391-410.
          A psychoanalytic study of Otranto, focusing on the strug-
     gle for power. Regards the novel as veiled autobiography,
     with the characters representing different aspects of Wal-
     pole, and finds signs of both oedipal and castration com-
     plexes.

12   WALPOLE, HORACE.   The Castle of Otranto.   Edited by W[ilmarth]
     S[heldon] Lewis.   Westerham, Kent: Limited Editions Club,
     100 pp.
          Reprints the introduction and text of 1964.8, without the
     notes of 1969.14.

13   WEISS, FREDRIC.   "Walpole's The Castle of Otranto: A Dilet-
     tante's Irony."   In "Satiric Elements in Early Gothic
     Novels."   Ph.D. dissertation, University of Pennsylvania,
     pp. 51-83.
          Considers the seriousness of Walpole's intentions in
     Otranto, with sections on the links between Otranto and
     Strawberry Hill, the two prefaces, the dramatic elements,
     and the novel as satire. Finds Otranto "alternately moving
     and absurd, melodramatic and parodic, tragic and ironic,"
     and immensely influential. Published: 1980.21.

1976

1   DRALLE, LEWIS A.   "The Daily Hum of the Eighteenth Century."
    Studies in Burke and his Time 17 (Spring):127-38.
        Review article on 1971.13, 1973.21-22, and 1974.17.   Con-
    siders the range of Walpole's interests and acquaintances,
    concluding that his letters make the eighteenth century real
    "for those in the twentieth century and beyond."

2   MADOFF, MARK.   "Vitality in Fiction: The Mixed Mode."   In "Am-
    bivalent and Nostalgic Attitudes in Selected Gothic Novels."
    Ph.D. dissertation, University of British Columbia, pp. 80-
    152.
        An extensive analysis of Strawberry Hill and Otranto as
    "parts of a common project," Walpole's recreation of the
    Gothic past.   Compares Otranto with Clara Reeve's The Old
    English Baron, emphasizing the two novelists' mutual dis-
    dain.

3   ROGAL, SAMUEL J.   "Horace Walpole and the Methodists."   Univer-
    sity of Dayton Review 12 (Summer):107-19.
        Studies Walpole's persistent anti-Methodism, examining
    his remarks on John and Charles Wesley, George Whitefield,
    and the Countess of Huntingdon.   Since most of Walpole's
    comments on the Methodist leaders were made in his corre-
    spondence, they were unaware of his hostility.

4   TROIDE, LARS ELEON.   "A Critical Edition of Horace Walpole's
    Miscellany."   Ph.D. dissertation, Yale University, 200 pp.
        An extensively annotated edition of a commonplace book by
    Walpole, with entries from 1786-1795.   Contains a valuable
    introduction, showing that most of Walpole's numerous inter-
    ests are reflected in the Miscellany.   Includes a select
    bibliography, appendices on Walpole's pencilled memoranda in
    the Miscellany and on his characteristic spellings, and an
    index.   Revised for publication: 1978.15.

5   WALPOLE, HORACE.   "Horace Walpole on Shakespeare and French
    Rules, 1765."   In Shakespeare: The Critical Heritage.
    Edited by Brian Vickers.   Vol. 4, 1753-1765.   London: Rout-
    ledge & Kegan Paul, pp. 546-50.
        An excerpt from Walpole's second preface to Otranto, with
    a brief introduction and notes.   Walpole's correspondence
    contains "many (mostly slight) references to Shakespeare."

6   WALPOLE, HORACE.   The Castle of Otranto.   Edited by Devendra
    P[rasad] Varma.   London: Folio Society, 142 pp.
        An enthusiastic introduction declares that Otranto sig-
    nalled a revolt against "cold unemotional Reason and plain
    Common   Sense,"   which   "now made way   for   the   wondrous
    unknown."   Treats Otranto as an articulate, aesthetically

perfect surrealistic novel.

1977

1   ASTLE, RICHARD SHARP.   "The Birth of the Gothic" and "The Cas-
    tle of Otranto."   In "Structures of Ideology in the English
    Gothic Novel."   Ph.D. dissertation, University of Cali-
    fornia, San Diego, pp. 20-42, 261-66.
        A Marxist comparative study of Otranto and The Old Eng-
    lish Baron, stressing the "ideological opposition" between
    the two novels and finding Walpole's the more progressive.
    Otranto reflects Walpole's support for the forthcoming
    American Revolution.   Includes a detailed plot summary of
    Otranto.

*2 BOWMAN, BARBARA.   "The Gothic Novel: A Structuralist Enquiry."
    Ph.D. dissertation, University of Maryland, 431 pp.
        Source: Dissertation Abstracts International 38:4175A.
    "Because The Castle of Otranto associates the good with
    being inside society and being rational, its mileu is a
    highly repressed one into which the supernatural periodical-
    ly erupts."   Its villain "must come to recognize his own
    aggressiveness   and   the   tragic   necessity   that   it   be
    suppressed."

3   di MICHELE, LAURA.   "I canoni del 'Gotico.'"   In L'educazione
    del sentimento.   La crisi del romanzo inglese fra Gotico e
    sentimentale (1750-1800).   Naples: Instituto Universitario
    Orientale, pp. 265-75.
        Discusses Walpole's two prefaces to Otranto, and his use
    of Shakespeare to justify his technique.   Regards Walpole as
    part of a new movement in English literature, and examines
    the connections between the Gothic and the sublime.

*4 EHLERS, LEIGH ANN.   "From Polarity to Perspective: The Devel-
    opment   of   Structure   and   Character   in   Gothic   Fiction."
    Ph.D. dissertation, University of Florida, 312 pp.
        Source: Dissertation Abstracts International 39:294A.
    "Walpole's The Castle of Otranto and Reeve's The Old English
    Baron epitomize the early Gothic romance, particularly the
    established Providential progression through glory-ruin-
    restoration.   Events dominate the externalized characters,
    while a didactic Christian narrator comments on the poetic
    justice of Providential dispositions."   Walpole and Reeve
    "assume a fictional world of dualism or universal good and
    evil, and from that secure basis they subject their char-
    acters to terrors and trials that bring them to salvation
    and poetic justice."

*5 LEWIS, PAUL.   "Fearful Questions, Fearful Answers: The Intel-

lectual Functions of Gothic Fiction." Ph.D. dissertation, University of New Hampshire, 322 pp.
    Source: Dissertation Abstracts International 38:2791-92A. "Chapter II shows how some writers (Walpole, Reeve, Radcliffe, and Lewis) use the resolution of mystery to advance theses and inculcate virtue." Manfred's conversion, in Otranto, supports "a world view that condemns the previous folly of the misguided penitents."

6   LEWIS, WILMARTH S[HELDON]. "A House-Party at Stowe." In Read as You Please. Cleveland: The Rowfant Club, pp. 21-31.
    An elegant account of Walpole's visit to Stowe in July 1770, of his hosts, Lord and Lady Temple, and of the guests, including Princess Amelia. Walpole is used with increasing frequency "as a dependable chronicler of his time." Reprinted: 1978.8.

7   LEWIS, WILMARTH SHELDON. "Geoffrey in Walpoleshire." Book Collector 26 (Spring):36-38.
    A tribute for Geoffrey Keynes's ninetieth birthday, recording his involvement with Lewis's Walpole collection.

*8   MASSARA, G. "Horace Walpole and the Sources of The Castle of Otranto." Ph.D. dissertation, University of Glasgow.
    Source: ASLIB: Index to Theses 29, pt. 1 (1981-82):9.

                            1978

1   BARRELL, REX A. Horace Walpole and France. Vol. 1, Walpole the Francophile. New York: Carlton Press, 224 pp.
    A detailed, thoroughly documented study of Walpole's connections with France. Includes chapters on Walpole and Gray's Grand Tour, Walpole's subsequent visits to Paris, his relations with Rousseau, Voltaire and Mme du Deffand, his involvement with French émigrés, and his response to the French Revolution. This chronological discussion of Walpole's "francophilic activities and interests" is complemented by the thematic approach of 1979.2.

2   BEASLEY, JERRY C. "Horace Walpole (1717-97)." In English Fiction 1660-1800: A Guide to Information Sources. Detroit: Gale Research, pp. 269-73.
    A brief, annotated bibliography of works by and about Walpole. Stresses the importance of the correspondence and of Otranto, erroneously described as Walpole's "only work of fiction."

3   CORNFORTH, JOHN. "The Cowles-Lewis House, Farmington." Country Life 163 (27 April):1150-53; (4 May):1230-33.
    A well-illustrated description of the Lewis Walpole

Library and its matchless collection of books, manuscripts
and prints by, about, printed by and owned by Walpole.

4   ENGLISH, SARAH WARDER.   "The Castle of Otranto: Bombast and
    Irony."   In "The Hunger of Imagination: A Study of the
    Prose Style of Four Gothic Novels."   Ph.D. dissertation,
    University of North Carolina at Chapel Hill, pp. 29–69.
        A stylistic analysis of Otranto, contrasting the novel's
    bombastic language with the narrator's detached irony.
    Although Walpole sought to dissociate himself from his own
    creation, Otranto brought "a broader and darker range of
    passions" to the English novel.

*5 FUJMOTA, YUKIO.   "From Amusement to Quest: The Castle of
    Otranto and Edgar Huntley.   Chu-Shikoku Studies in American
    Literature 14:61–70.
        Source: MLA International Bibliography 1 (1979):177.

6   HENNESSY, BRENDAN.   "Horace Walpole: The Castle of Otranto."
    In The Gothic Novel.   Writers and their Work, no. 267.
    Harlow: Longman, pp. 9–14.
        A routine discussion.   Otranto is "greatly flawed" and
    "hardly readable," but important for its influential innova-
    tions.   Walpole was the first novelist to use the Gothic
    castle, forces of nature for atmospheric effect, and the
    Byronic hero.   Subsequent novelists, notably Ann Radcliffe,
    developed his techniques to greater effect.

7   LEWIS, PAUL.   "The Atheist's Tragedy and The Castle of Otranto:
    Expressions of the Gothic Vision."   Notes and Queries 223
    (February):52–54.
        Compares the plots and morals of Otranto and The Athe-
    ist's Tragedy, concluding that Gothic fiction was based less
    on medieval than on Elizabethan sources.   Acknowledges,
    however, that Walpole might not have known The Atheist's
    Tragedy.

8   LEWIS, W[ILMARTH] S[HELDON].   "A House-Party at Stowe."   In The
    Dress of Words: Essays on Restoration and Eighteenth Cen-
    tury Literature in Honor of Richmond P. Bond.   Edited by
    Robert B. White, Jr. University of Kansas Publications
    Library Series, no. 42.   Lawrence: University of Kansas
    Libraries, pp. 117–25.
        Reprint of 1977.6.

9   LEWIS, WILMARTH S[HELDON].   Rescuing Horace Walpole.   New
    Haven: Yale University Press, 251 pp.
        Describes and illustrates the twenty-six most precious
    items by or associated with Walpole in the Lewis Walpole
    Library; several "runners-up" are also included.   The illus-
    trations are invaluable, but much of the text is repeated

from 1951.6.

10 MARKHAM, SARAH. "Mary Berry on the Death of Horace Walpole." Notes and Queries 223 (February):65-67.
Prints an unpublished letter from Mary Berry to Penelope Benwell, written ten days after Walpole's death and including a list of his legatees.

11 RIELY, JOHN C. "Source Wanted." Notes and Queries 223 (February):71.
Enquires about the source of an anecdote in a letter from Walpole to John Craufurd.

12 RIELY, JOHN [C.]. "The Castle of Otranto Revisited." Yale University Library Gazette 53 (July):1-17.
Examines the composition, contemporary reception, and illustration of Otranto, the latter "a subject which has been almost totally ignored by scholars." Otranto was the "primary model" for the Gothic novel, and caused "a revolution in public taste."

13 SAUERMANN-WESTWOOD, DORIS. "Das Frauenbild in Horace Walpoles The Castle of Otranto." In Das Frauenbild in englischen Schauerroman. Ph.D. dissertation, University of Marburg-Lahn, pp. 76-102.
Surveys Walpole's life and the critical reception of Otranto, pointing out some links between Walpole and Richardson, from whom Walpole takes the theme of persecuted innocence. Studies the female characters in Otranto, concluding that they have a subordinate role but that each has a distinct personality.

14 THORNDIKE, JOSEPH J., JR. "Horace Walpole's Strawberry Hill." In The Magnificent Builders and their Dream Houses. New York: American Heritage Publishing, pp. 243-48.
An informal, illustrated account of Strawberry Hill, with brief comments on the significance of Otranto and Walpole's letters.

15 TROIDE, LARS E[LEON]. Horace Walpole's "Miscellany" 1786-1795. Yale Studies in English, no. 188. New Haven: Yale University Press, 174 pp.
Revision of 1976.4.

16 VAN CLEEF, JOY. "Dance in Horace Walpole's Correspondence." Dance Research Journal 10 (Spring-Summer):55-56.
Quotes a letter from Walpole to the Countess of Upper Ossory of 17 July 1781 to show that the country dance "Hemp-dressers" was still in vogue in the late eighteenth century. No dance historian has yet made use of the hundreds of similar references in Walpole's correspondence.

1979

1   AMES, DIANNE S.   "Strawberry Hill: Architecture of the 'as
    if.'"   Studies in Eighteenth-Century Culture 8, edited by
    Roseann Runte.   Madison: University of Wisconsin Press,
    pp. 351-63.
        Walpole designed Strawberry Hill in the subjunctive mood,
    using artificial materials to create an "architecture of the
    'as if.'"   Strawberry Hill is a scrapbook in which the vari-
    ous items have been pasted down, and which is intended to be
    read.   It is not, as is often argued, a "cheap forgery," but
    rather "visionary architecture."

2   BARRELL, REX A.   Horace Walpole and France.   Vol. 2, Walpole
    the Critic.   Ottawa: Borealis Press, 147 pp.
        Conclusion of 1978.1.   Studies Walpole's "observations on
    the French nation and French culture," with chapters on his
    response to the people and their arts, historical writing,
    fiction, philosophy, and poetry.   A chapter on Walpole and
    his critics surveys Walpole's critical reputation in both
    France and England from the eighteenth century to the pres-
    ent.   Throughout his life, Walpole took an intense interest
    "in almost every aspect of French life."

3   BUTT, JOHN, and CARNALL, GEOFFREY.   "Walpole, Horace, 1711
    [sic]-97."   In The Oxford History of English Literature.
    Vol. 8, The Mid-Eighteenth Century.   Oxford: Clarendon
    Press, pp. 650-51.
        A short bibliography of works by and about Walpole.   The
    volume also contains accounts of Walpole's Memoirs, letters,
    and Otranto.

4   COLEMAN, ANTONY.   "Walpole's Annotations in a Copy of Love of
    Fame, The Universal Passion."   Notes and Queries 224 (Decem-
    ber):551-54.
        Transcribes and annotates Walpole's marginalia in his
    copy of Edward Young's satirical poem Love of Fame, noting
    that Walpole's commentary makes "a small but useful contri-
    bution" to our understanding of the poem.

5   CONGER, SYNDY McMILLEN.   "Faith and Doubt in The Castle of
    Otranto."   Gothic 1:51-59.
        Walpole achieves a balance between faith and doubt in
    Otranto, but the faith is that of "primitive, irrational,
    superstitious tenets," rather than of Christianity.   The
    dreamlike irrationality of the novel is qualified by the
    scepticism of the prefaces.   The dominant message is that
    man should recognize his lack of ultimate knowledge.

6   DUCKWORTH, COLIN.   "Louis XVI and English History: A French
    Reaction to Walpole, Hume and Gibbon on Richard III."

Studies on Voltaire and the Eighteenth Century 176:385-401.
Compares the manuscript of Louis XVI's translation of
Historic Doubts with the faulty published version (1800.5).
Shows that Louis XVI is almost certainly the author of this
translation, despite the claims of authorship made by his
brother Louis XVIII, and that Louis XVI had a strong interest in English and in Richard III. Also compares his translation with that of Gibbon in 1769.2, which the King might
have read.

7   du DEFFAND, MARQUISE. Lettres à H. Walpole, Voltaire et quelques autres. Edited by François Bott and Jean-Claude
Renault. Paris: Plasma, 211 pp.
Contains a selection of Mme du Deffand's letters to Walpole, with brief prefaces by Bott and by Renault and sketchy
annotations.

8   EHLERS, LEIGH A[NN]. "The Gothic World as Stage: Providence
and Character in The Castle of Otranto." Wascana Review 14
(Fall):17-30.
Finds the unity of Otranto in its combination of the
religious and the theatrical. Revealing Walpole's interest
in drama it is also governed by a providential justice,
which finally resolves the "seeming disorder of the Gothic
machinery."

*9   HAGGARTY, GEORGE. "Gothic Fiction from Walpole to James: A
Study of Formal Development." Ph.D. dissertation, University of California, Berkeley, 267 pp.
Source: Dissertation Abstracts International 40:4036A.
"The Gothic novel began as an attempt on the part of Horace
Walpole to create a new kind of fiction - a blend of the
'ancient and modern' romance - in which 'the great resources
of fancy' could enrich the nature-bound conventions of the
novel. This enrichment included both a particular setting
and a particular use of setting." In Otranto "the second of
these concerns is most crucial to its Gothic nature."

10   KALLICH, MARTIN. "Walpole, Horace." In Great Writers of the
English Language. Novelists and Prose Writers. Edited by
James Vinson. New York: St. Martin's Press, pp. 1245-47.
A brief chronology, bibliography and appraisal of Wal-
pole's works, emphasizing the significance of his letters
and of Otranto and The Mysterious Mother.

11   LEVY, MAURICE. "Lecture plurielle du Château d'Otrante." In
La mort, le fantastique, le surnaturel du XVIe siècle à
l'époque romantique. Edited by Michèle Plaisant and Jean-
Claude Dupas. Lille: Université de Lille III, pp. 149-53.
Otranto, of all eighteenth-century English novels, is the
one in which death, the fantastic and the supernatural are

most pervasive. The critical techniques of Northrop Frye, Vladimir Propp and Roland Barthes suggest various ways of reading Otranto, while recognizing the plurality of the text.

12   LEWIS, WILMARTH S[HELDON].   "Editing Familiar Letters."   In Editing Correspondence. Papers Given at the Fourteenth Annual Conference on Editorial Problems, University of Toronto, 3-4 November 1978. Edited by J.A. Dainard. New York: Garland, pp. 25-37.
     Extensive revision of 1953.4 and 1963.4, with new material on the near completion of the Yale Edition of Walpole's correspondence.

13   LEWIS, WILMARTH S[HELDON].   "Edmond Malone, Horace Walpole, and Shakespeare."   In Evidence in Literary Scholarship. Essays in Memory of James Marshall Osborn. Edited by René Wellek and Alvaro Ribeiro. Oxford: Clarendon Press, pp. 353-62.
     Revision of 1940.14.

14   MUDRICK, MARVIN.   "Chamber of Horrors."   In Books Are Not Life But Then What Is? New York: Oxford University Press, pp. 303-9.
     Revision of the introduction to 1963.9.

15   PHELPS, GILBERT.   "The Castle of Otranto: A Gothic Story."   In A Reader's Guide to Fifty British Novels 1600-1900. London: Heinemann, pp. 128-33.
     Contains a biographical sketch of Walpole, a summary of Otranto, and an account of the novel's influence on the romantic revival.

16   PLUMB, J.H.   "Walpole's Knight Errant."   Books and Bookmen 24 (June):20-21.
     Review of 1978.9. Regards W.S. Lewis's prolonged involvement with Walpole as misdirected. Walpole is "lightweight" compared with Boswell, and Macaulay's diatribe, though excessive, "contained a kernel of truth."

17   PRICKETT, STEPHEN.   "The Evolution of a Word."   In Victorian Fantasy. Bloomington: Indiana University Press, pp. 1-38.
     Much of the chapter is concerned with Otranto, Hieroglyphic Tales, and Strawberry Hill. Notes that the Tales, Walpole's "final flowering of fantasy," prefigure subsequent surrealist fiction. Walpole had "in embryo at least, a theory of the unconscious."

18   QUAINTANCE, RICHARD E.   "Walpole's Whig Interpretation of Landscaping History."   Studies in Eighteenth-Century Culture 9, edited by Roseann Runte. Madison: University of Wisconsin Press, pp. 285-300.

An original analysis of the politics of Walpole's essay on gardening, relating it to a "century-long tradition of partisan myth in writing about English gardens." Contends that Walpole's advocacy of the values of landholding Whigs is reflected in his "hortipolitical" essay, and demonstrates its political partisanship through ;lose analysis of the texture of its prose.

19 RIELY, JOHN [C.]. "Horace Walpole's Bookplate." British Journal for Eighteenth-Century Studies 2 (Spring):69.
Corrects a misidentification of one of Walpole's book-plates, and comments on the various book-plates and fleurons that he employed.

20 SHENKER, ISRAEL. "Can he be the real Walpole or is he Wilmarth Lewis?" Smithsonian 10 (May):102-8.
An illustrated account of Lewis's extraordinary involvement with Walpole, of the Lewis Walpole Library, and of the near completion of the Yale Edition of Walpole's correspondence, written a few months before Lewis's death.

21 STEVENS, JOAN. "Jersey through Walpole's Pen." Country Life 166 (22 November):1939-43.
Discusses Walpole's interest in the island of Jersey. His two Jersey connections were Richard Bentley, who took refuge there from 1753 to 1755 when pursued by creditors in England, and Henry Seymour Conway, Governor of Jersey from 1772 until his death in 1795.

22 WALPOLE, HORACE. Die Burg von Otranto. Translated with an afterword by Helmut Findeisen. Leipzig: Insel-Verlag, 147 pp.
A translation of Otranto, with a translation of Scott's introduction (1811.5). An afterword relates Otranto to previous fiction and surveys Walpole's life and works. Regards Otranto as an important influence on Scott and later novelists with effects still felt today, in film as well as in literature. Prefers Otranto to its successors among the Gothic novels.

1980

1 ARNAUD, PIERRE. "The Castle of Otranto et l'éclosion de la littérature fantastique en Angleterre," and "H. Walpole: The Mysterious Mother." In Le préromantisme anglais, by Pierre Arnaud and Jean Raimond. Paris: Presses universitaires de France, pp. 198-204.
A brief account of Walpole's life and works, and of the genesis and influence of Otranto. Also regards The Mysterious Mother as a seminal influence on Gothic drama.

2   CALLOWAY, STEPHEN. "Horace Walpole, Writer and Printer." In
    1980.3, pp. 18-22.
        Discusses Walpole's library, his collection of prints and
    drawings, his printing-press, and several of his works, in-
    cluding the letters, Anecdotes of Painting, Historic Doubts,
    Otranto, Hieroglyphic Tales and The Mysterious Mother. The
    most important Strawberry Hill production was Walpole's A
    Description of the Villa, which secured him some of the
    "immortality which he craved."

3   CALLOWAY, STEPHEN; SNODIN, MICHAEL; and WAINWRIGHT, CLIVE.
    Horace Walpole and Strawberry Hill. Richmond upon Thames:
    Libraries Department, 72 pp.
        The catalogue of a major exhibition on Walpole, tracing
    the progress of his career and the development of Strawberry
    Hill. Includes a chronology of Walpole's life and works, an
    introduction, and three essays: 1980.2, 13, 18.

4   HARFST, BETSY PERTEIT. Horace Walpole and the Unconscious: An
    Experiment in Freudian Analysis. Gothic Studies and Disser-
    tations. New York: Arno Press, 264 pp.
        Publication of 1968.3.

5   HAZEN, ALLEN T[RACY]. "The Strawberry Hill Press." In Ency-
    clopaedia of Library and Information Science. Vol. 29. New
    York: Marcel Dekker, pp. 176-77.
        A brief history of Walpole's press, contending that
    although its productions were not especially brilliant, it
    "marked the beginning of the whole private press movement."

6   JONES, STEPHEN. "Horace Walpole and Strawberry Hill." Bur-
    lington Magazine 122 (November):783-84.
        Describes the Walpole exhibition at Twickenham and its
    catalogue (1980.3). Walpole made a "serious academic con-
    tribution to the documentation of the history of art."

7   KERSLAKE, JOHN. "Robert and Horace Walpole." Antique Collec-
    tor 51 (June):76-79.
        Compares father and son as collectors, with illustrations
    of works from Houghton and Strawberry Hill.

8   LEWIS, WILMARTH S[HELDON]. "Horace Walpole, Collector." Pro-
    ceedings of the Massachusetts Historical Society 92:45-51.
        The revised version of an unpublished paper first read in
    1932, incorporating parts of 1958.3. Suggests that Wal-
    pole's collection, which fetched in thirty-three thousand
    pounds at the Strawberry Hill Sale of 1842, would be worth
    ten million pounds today.

9   LIEBERT, HERMAN W. "Wilmarth Sheldon Lewis (1895-1979)."
    Yale University Library Gazette 54 (April):198-200.

Evaluates Lewis's contribution to Walpole studies, emphasizing the significance of his collection, now the Lewis
Walpole Library, his edition of the correspondence, and his
many writings on Walpole.

10   PUNTER, DAVID. "Horace Walpole." In The Literature of Terror:
      A History of Gothic Fiction from 1765 to the Present Day.
      London: Longman, pp. 49-53.
            Regards Otranto and Smollett's Ferdinand Count Fathom as
      the two sources of Gothic fiction. Otranto is "a fairy-tale
      rather than a nightmare"; its plot is "a joyous compilation
      of absurdities." Walpole is not interested in characteriza-
      tion or in realism, but he is concerned with history, pro-
      viding "an eighteenth-century view of feudalism and the
      aristocracy."

11   SANDY, STEPHEN. "A Rhetoric of Suspense: The Castle of Otran-
      to." In The Raveling of the Novel: Studies in Romantic
      Fiction from Walpole to Scott. Gothic Studies and Disserta-
      tions. New York: Arno Press, pp. 21-44.
            Revision of 1963.5. Examines the threefold influence of
      Otranto on subsequent fiction, considering its combination
      of romance and realism, its liberation of the imagination,
      and its innovative style. Suggests that its sparseness
      might have influenced the dwindling size of novels from the
      1760s until the works of Ann Radcliffe.

12   SHIPPS, ANTHONY W. "Yale Edition of Horace Walpole's Corre-
      spondence." Notes and Queries 225 (February):84.
            Replies to one of Lewis's queries (1935.11).

13   SNODIN, MICHAEL. "Horace Walpole, Builder and Designer." In
      1980.3, pp. 9-13.
            Distinguishes three phases in Walpole's remodelling of
      Strawberry Hill. Considers its links with Elizabethan and
      Jacobean ancestral houses, as well as with the Gothic.

14   TOMPKINS, J.M.S. "The Debt to Horace Walpole." In Ann Rad-
      cliffe and her Influence on Later Writers. Foreword by
      Maurice Lévy, introduction by Devendra P[rasad] Varma.
      Gothic Studies and Dissertations. New York: Arno Press,
      pp. 36-54.
            Revision of a master's thesis of 1921. Studies the
      influence of Otranto on Ann Radcliffe's novels, pointing out
      several similarities. Still the fullest, most penetrating
      comparative study of Walpole and Radcliffe.

15   TRACY, ANN BLAISDELL. "Walpole, Horace. The Castle of
      Otranto." In Patterns of Fear in the Gothic Novel. Gothic
      Studies and Dissertations. New York: Arno Press, pp. 431-
      32.

Publication of 1974.16.

16   VAN LUCHENE, STEPHEN ROBERT.   "The Castle of Otranto."   In
     Essays in Gothic Fiction from Horace Walpole to Mary
     Shelley. Gothic Studies and Dissertations.   New York: Arno
     Press, pp. 4-41.
          Publication of 1973.20.

17   WAINWRIGHT, CLIVE, and WAINWRIGHT, JANE.   "Horace Walpole and
     Strawberry Hill."   Antiques 118 (October):694, 698.
          An account of the Walpole exhibition in Twickenham; see
     1980.3.

18   WAINWRIGHT, CLIVE.   "Horace Walpole and his Collection."   In
     1980.3, pp. 14-17.
          Compares Walpole's collection at Strawberry Hill with his
     proposals for such a collection in an essay of 1746.   The
     collection "constituted an essential part of the interiors
     of his house."

19   WALDEGRAVE, MARY.   "'Lefty' Wilmarth Sheldon Lewis."   Book
     Collector 29 (Summer):239-50.
          An affectionate memoir of Lewis, recording his life as
     Walpole editor and collector.   Regards the Yale Edition of
     Walpole's correspondence as indispensable to eighteenth-
     century scholarship, and the Lewis Walpole Library as "per-
     fection."

20   WALPOLE, HORACE.   Horace Walpole's Miscellaneous Correspon-
     dence.   Edited by W[ilmarth] S[heldon] Lewis and John [C.]
     Riely, with the assistance of Edwine M. Martz and Ruth K.
     McClure.   The Yale Edition of Horace Walpole's Correspon-
     dence, edited by W[ilmarth] S[heldon] Lewis, vols. 40-42.
     New Haven: Yale University Press, 3 vols.
          Includes a memoir of Lewis by Warren H. Smith, discussing
     the development of the Yale Edition and its increasing
     emphasis on Walpole as a serious historian, rather than a
     "mere dispenser of gossip."   Prints Walpole's correspondence
     with 330 persons, with all of whom he exchanged only a few
     letters, including Burke, Boswell, Gibbon, Hume and Vol-
     taire.   Among the appendices is a study of Walpole's Twic-
     kenham, with an annotated map.

21   WEISS, FREDRIC.   "Walpole's The Castle of Otranto: A Dilet-
     tante's Irony."   In The Antic Spectre: Satire in Early
     Gothic Novels.   Gothic Studies and Dissertations.   New York:
     Arno Press, pp. 51-83.
          Publication of 1975.13.

22   WILSHER, ANN.   "Horace Walpole, William Storer and the Accurate
     Delineator."   History of Photography 4 (July):247-49.

Describes Walpole's purchase of an "Accurate Delineator," an improved camera obscura, from its inventor, William Storer, and his introducing the device to Joshua Reynolds.

23   WILT, JUDITH.   "Gothic Fathers: The Castle of Otranto, The Italian, The Monk, Melmoth the Wanderer."   In Ghosts of the Gothic.   Austen, Eliot, & Lawrence.   Princeton: Princeton University Press, pp. 25-61.
       A vigorous analysis of Otranto.   Begins by dismissing the novel as "a rather gormless tale," but goes on to demonstrate the significance of its "tableaux, frozen moments of action," deriving from Walpole's dreams.   Stresses Walpole's lack of artistic accomplishment, but notes his strong influence on subsequent Gothic melodrama and fiction.

1981

1   ASTON, NIGEL.   "Horace Walpole."   Times Literary Supplement, 7 August, p. 909.
       Calls for a paperback edition of Walpole's selected letters.

2   BELL, ALAN.   "Horace Walpole."   Times Literary Supplement, 21 August, p. 958.
       Replies to Aston (1981.1), pointing out that Lewis's paperback edition of Walpole's letters (1973.23) is still in print.

3   CROWDER, WILLIAM.   "Horace Walpole's Correspondence."   Times Literary Supplement, 3 July, p. 757.
       "The eighteenth century is illuminated for us by the meticulous detail" of the Yale Edition of Walpole's correspondence.   Regrets the choice of an American to review the work (1981.5).

4   FRANK, FREDERICK S.   "The Castle of Otranto: A Story" and "The Mysterious Mother."   In Horror Literature: A Core Collection and Reference Guide.   Edited by Marshall B. Tymm, foreword by Peter Haining.   New York: R.R. Bowker, pp. 167-69.
       Plot summaries and laudatory evaluations of Otranto and The Mysterious Mother.   Otranto is "universally influential," displaying all the "fantastic and melodramatic elements that would shortly become standard" in Gothic romance.   The sexual transgressions of The Mysterious Mother also contributed to the development of literary Gothicism.

5   HALSBAND, ROBERT.   "A Collector's Connections."   Times Literary Supplement, 12 June, pp. 681-82.
       Review of 1980.20.   Welcomes the near completion of the Yale Edition of Walpole's correspondence, although "opinions

may differ" over his importance. Lytton Strachey would be
pleased by the edition's ample footnotes and freedom from
bowdlerization. In the Yale Edition, Walpole's letters
constitute "an all-encompassing history of the English scene
during the latter half of the eighteenth century."

6   HALSBAND, ROBERT. "Horace Walpole." Times Literary Supple-
     ment, 17 July, p. 813.
          Replies to Crowder (1981.3), who "betrays a lamentable
     chauvinism" in calling for an English reviewer of Walpole.

7   JESTIN, CATHERINE. "Marginalia." Yale University Library
     Gazette 56 (October):60.
          Describes a work from Walpole's Strawberry Hill collec-
     tion acquired by the Lewis Walpole Library: William Mait-
     land's History of Edinburgh (1753).

8   LAMBERT, ELIZABETH. "Historic Architecture: Strawberry Hill.
     The Eighteenth-Century Beginnings of the Gothic Revival."
     Architectural Digest 38 (June):144-50.
          A lavishly illustrated but unoriginal and undocumented
     account of Walpole's Gothic remodelling of Strawberry Hill.
     The building "looked ahead in its own day, and is a joy to
     look back on in ours."

9   [MIDDENDORF, JOHN H.] "Walpole Triumphant." Johnsonian News-
     letter 41 (September):1-2.
          Review of 1980.20, supporting Halsband's view (1981.5) of
     the importance of the Yale Edition.

*10 PEVOY, JOHN ROGER. "Artificial Terrors and Real Horrors: The
     Supernatural in Gothic Fiction." Ph.D. dissertation, Bran-
     deis University, 312 pp.
          Source: Dissertation Abstracts International 42:714A.
     Chapter one studies Otranto, together with Clara Reeve's The
     Old English Baron and Ann Radcliffe's Gaston de Blondeville,
     showing "that the only actor, the only motivating force, in
     them is the benevolent supernatural. The evil characters
     are impotent; the good, mere instruments of a supernatural
     will."

11   PLUMB, J.H. "Was Walpole Worth It?" New York Times Book
     Review, 19 April, pp. 10-11, 23.
          Review of 1980.20, contending that the Yale Edition has
     buried Walpole in an unreadable "bibliographical monument."
     Walpole himself "lacks stature" and "can never be more than
     a minor figure and a minor source." His letters are enter-
     taining and informative, but not encyclopaedic as the Yale
     Edition suggests.

12   SMITH, WARREN HUNTING. "The Yale Edition of Horace Walpole's Correspondence: An Editorial History." East-Central News letter, American Society for Eighteenth-Century Studies, 4 (November):1-3.

      Surveys the development of the Yale Edition of Walpole's correspondence from its beginnings in 1933 to the present, pointing out some of the various types of annotation. It is appropriate that Walpole, "a man of many diverse interests, has been edited by a succession of people with many different skills and points of view." The edition is "a mine of information" on numerous topics. Reprinted: 1982.4.

1982

1   McCORMICK, THOMAS J. Review of Horace Walpole's Miscellaneous Correspondence. Apollo 116 (August):127.

      Review of 1980.20. Walpole's correspondence with artists and architects, although "by no means his most important," provides "fascinating material about his various interests and activities."

2   SMITH, D. KIMBALL. "There Will Always be a Little Bit of England." Yale Alumni Magazine and Journal, November, pp. 14-15.

      Describes some of the holdings of the Lewis Walpole Library, the life work of W.S. Lewis. The Yale Edition of Walpole's correspondence is "one of the most useful tools for the study of the eighteenth century."

3   SMITH, WARREN HUNTING; assisted by JESTIN, CATHERINE, and PELTIER, KAREN V. "The Manuscript Collection at the Lewis Walpole Library." Yale University Library Gazette 56 (April):53-60.

      Emphasizes the miscellaneous nature of the Lewis Walpole Library's manuscript holdings: "associations with Walpole and his circle often prompted the acquisition of vast collections" of non-Walpolian items.

4   SMITH, WARREN HUNTING. "The Yale Edition of Horace Walpole's Correspondence: An Editorial History." Yale University Library Staff News, May, pp. 1-4.

      Reprint of 1981.12.

5   SVILPIS, J[ANIS] E. "Fantasy and Aesthetic Deformity in The Castle of Otranto." Transactions of the Samuel Johnson Society of the Northwest 13:72-81.

      A structural analysis of Otranto as literary fantasy. Walpole "was never fully in control of his material," which "played an important role in his own unconscious processes." Otranto has, however, been highly influential: it "does not exhibit a successfully achieved form but adumbrates a potential."

6 TAYLOR, MERRILY E. "Horace Walpole." In Encyclopaedia of Library and Information Science. Vol 33. New York: Marcel Dekker, pp. 342-47.

Part of an extensive essay on Yale University Library. Describes W.S. Lewis's collecting and editing of Walpole, issuing in the Lewis Walpole Library and the Yale Edition of Walpole's correspondence. The account draws frequently on Lewis's own writings.

7 WALPOLE, HORACE. Hieroglyphic Tales. Edited with an introduction by Kenneth W. Gross. The Augustan Reprint Society, nos. 212-13. William Andrews Clark Memorial Library, University of California, 55 pp.

A facsimile of the 1785 edition of Hieroglyphic Tales with a transcript of the uncollected tale, "The Bird's Nest," also printed in 1967.24. An introduction discusses the mixture of "historical referent," "fantastic image or event," and "personal anecdote" in the Tales. They are "songs of innocence," leaving us "not simply with doubt, but with delight and self-possession."

8 WALPOLE, HORACE. The History of the Modern Taste in Gardening; Journals of Visits to Country Seats. The English Landscape Garden, edited by John Dixon Hunt, vol. 18. New York: Garland, pp. 233-326, 9-80.

Facsimile reprints of 1827.3 and 1928.7, with a brief preface by Hunt. Walpole's essay on gardening traces "the history of English landscape gardening," stressing "the literary inspiration (notably Milton) and the role of the ha-ha." The journals supplement the essay with a valuable study of the art collections, architecture and gardens of country houses.

1983

1 CALLOWAY, STEPHEN. "Horace Walpole and Strawberry Hill." Victoria and Albert Album 1:151-55.

A brief account of Walpole's career and his collections at Strawberry Hill, with descriptions and illustrations of nine items at the Victoria and Albert Museum.

2 WALPOLE, HORACE. Horace Walpole's Correspondence. Additions and Corrections. Subject Index to Illustrations. Index of Horace Walpole's Correspondents. Chronological List of Letters. Compiled by Edwine M. Martz, with the assistance of Ruth K. McClure and William T. La Moy. The Yale Edition of Horace Walpole's Correspondence, edited by W[ilmarth]

S[heldon] Lewis, vol. 43. New Haven: Yale University Press, 649 pp.

Contains ten previously unpublished letters by Walpole, and many letters printed from recently discovered manuscripts. Updates and corrects the footnotes to the entire Yale Edition, and includes a valuable index of Walpole's correspondents and a chronological list of letters.

3 WALPOLE, HORACE. Horace Walpole's Correspondence. Complete Index. Compiled by Warren Hunting Smith, with the assistance of Edwine M. Martz, Ruth K. McClure and William T. La Moy. The Yale Edition of Horace Walpole's Correspondence, edited by W[ilmarth] S[heldon] Lewis, vols. 44-48. New Haven: Yale University Press, 5 vols.

Completes the series begun with 1937.15. This index to the entire edition is "an index to the eighteenth century," as reflected in Walpole's correspondence and the supporting materials of the Yale Edition. Includes individuals, "events, objects, publications, and the whole fabric of political, social, financial, artistic, military, and literary history." As well as Walpole's correspondence, indexes the appendices and supporting material in the Yale Edition.

4 WELCHER, JEANNE K[ATHRYN]. "Horace Walpole and Gulliver's Travels." Studies in Eighteenth-Century Culture 12, edited by Harry C. Payne. Madison: University of Wisconsin Press, pp. 45-57.

A detailed study of the references to Swift and to Gulliver's Travels in Walpole's letters, and of Walpole's imitations of Gulliver. Discusses four such "Gulliveriana": the first of the Hieroglyphic Tales, An Account of the Giants, "A Sequel to Gulliver's Travels," and a projected but never written Gulliverian fantasy. Walpole read Gulliver with "distinguished perception and appreciation," while his imitations form "a substantial and delightful body of variations on theme and image."

Addenda

1766

5a   Review of An Account of the Giants Lately Discovered. Critical Review 22 (August):156-57.

The author of this anonymous satire is "only accidentally witty." The work fails to live up to its "good selling Title," and little of its "invective and humour . . . is tolerable."

1857

1a   DORAN, J[OHN]. "The Ruins of London, Sketched by Walpole before Macaulay." Notes and Queries, 2d ser. 3 (11 April): 286.

A letter from Walpole to Mason of 27 November 1775 contains a possible source for Macaulay's image of the ruins of London. Reprinted: 1945.3.

1b   DORAN, J[OHN]. "Walpole and Macaulay's Ruins of London." Notes and Queries, 2d ser. 3 (16 May):397.

An earlier letter from Walpole to Mason, of 24 November 1774, "will still more closely remind one of the famous passage in Macaulay."

1910

1a   BENJAMIN, LEWIS SAUL. [Lewis Melville]. "Beckford the Collector." In The Life and Letters of William Beckford of Fonthill (Author of "Vathek"). New York: Duffield, pp. 289-313.

A series of letters from Beckford to H.G. Bohn, strongly criticizing the Strawberry Hill Sale, with useful annotations and commentary. Beckford ridicules George Robins, the auctioneer, but is fascinated by Walpole's collection.

1932

1a   COLLINS, NORMAN. "The Major Minor Novelists." In <u>The Facts of Fiction</u>. London: Victor Gollancz, pp. 82-103.

      Compares <u>Otranto</u> with Johnson's <u>Rasselas</u> and Goldsmith's <u>The Vicar of Wakefield</u>; all three are works by "men of genius" who were not natural novelists. Walpole's achievement in <u>Otranto</u> was to replace the episodic story with "a cat's cradle of ingenious complexity," and "to lay out a plot like a pattern and not merely uncoil it like a rope."

1958

1a   EDWARDS, RALPH. "Walpole Versus Burlington." <u>Country Life</u> 124 (6 November):1062, 1065.

      Rebuking Hussey, prefers the neo-Classical ideals of Burlington to the "nostalgic revivalism of the Walpole set," which bequeathed nothing of lasting importance.

1b   HUSSEY, CHRISTOPHER. "Mr. Hussey Writes." <u>Country Life</u> 124 (6 November):1065.

      Replies to 1958.1a, contending that the "reliance of the Palladians on dogmatic principles" is more remote from modern taste than the "fluid experimentalism initiated by the Walpoleans."

1959

3a   LLOYD-JOHNES, H. "For Walpole's Visitors." <u>Country Life</u> 126 (17 December):1217.

      Provides a photograph of Walpole's rules and instructions for visitors to Strawberry Hill, pasted in a copy of <u>Anecdotes of Painting</u>.

1961

3a   "Friends Apart." <u>Times Literary Supplement</u>, 10 February, p. 90.

      Review of 1960.10. In his letters to Mann, Walpole was "quite consciously and openly writing the history of his own time," while maintaining the intimacy of their friendship. Mann's replies provide a detailed view of eighteenth-century diplomatic life. Of all Walpole's correspondences, this is "the most rewarding to the historian, and possibly even to the general reader."

1963

4 a   REITLINGER, GERALD. "Horace Walpole and William Beckford." In
        The Economics of Taste: The Rise and Fall of the Objets
        d'Art Market since 1750. London: Barrie & Rockliff, pp.
        75-88.

            Examines Walpole's purchases of objets d'art and the
        prices they fetched at subsequent sales, concentrating on
        the Strawberry Hill Sale of 1842. Contends that Walpole did
        not found the "eighteenth-century Gothic cult," and compares
        his career as a collector with that of Beckford: "for a
        very few years their collecting must have overlapped."

1970

3 a   CHRISTIE, IAN R. "Horace Walpole: The Gossip as Historian."
        In Myth and Reality in Late-Eighteenth-Century British Poli-
        tics and Other Papers. Berkeley and Los Angeles: Univer-
        sity of California Press, pp. 359-71.
        Reprint of 1954.1.

1979

13 a   MAGILL, FRANK N. "Horace Walpole (1717-1797)." In Magill's
        Bibliography of Literary Criticism. Selected Sources for
        the Study of more than 2,500 Outstanding Works of Western
        Literature. Edited by Frank N. Magill; associate editors
        Stephen L. Hanson and Patricia King Hanson. Vol. 4, Shake-
        speare - Zola. Englewood Cliffs, N.J.: Salem Press, pp.
        2235-36.

            Lists twenty-four essays, chapters and passages in works
        on The Castle of Otranto, without annotations. All the
        items are in English, and published in the twentieth cen-
        tury.

Indexes

Author Index

The names of all authors, editors, translators, and writers of prefaces, introductions, etc., in the Reference Guide are indexed. Anonymous entries are excluded; "a" and "b" entries refer to the addenda, beginning on page 243. Walpole's works are listed in the subject index.

Beatty, H.M., 1919.1
Becker, Carl, 1911.1
Bedford, Duke of, 1825.1
Bell, Alan, 1981.2
Bell, Robert, 1850.3
Belloc-Lowndes, Marie, 1913.1
Beloe, William, 1817.1
Belsham, William, 1789.1
Belshaw, Harry, 1931.1
Benjamin, Lewis Saul, 1909.3;
    1910.1a; 1914.1; 1930.1-2
Bennett, Charles H., 1943.1;
    1944.4; 1945.1; 1947.3;
    1948.9; 1951.9; 1952.3-4;
    1955.13; 1961.10
Bennett, Edward, 1904.2
Bensly, Edward, 1925.2-3; 1930.3;
    1935.2
Bentley, Richard, 1856.1
Beresford, S.B., 1889.1
Berry, Mary, 1798.7; 1810.2;
    1840.1; 1844.1; 1865.1
Berry, Robert, 1798.7
Bettany, F.G., 1913.2
Bettany, Lewis, 1919.2
Bickley, Francis, 1922.2
Bierwith, Gerhard, 1970.2
Binford, Joseph Newbill, 1966.1
Bisset, Andrew, 1833.1
Blair, Claude, 1966.2
Blakeway, J.B., 1800.1
Bleackley, Horace, 1905.1; 1916.1
Bleiler, Everett Franklin,
    1966.13
Blunden, Edmund, 1966.3
Bohn, Henry G., 1864.1, 5
Bolton, Arthur T., 1921.1
Bond, W.H., 1970.9
Bott, François, 1979.7
Boulton, James T., 1951.1;
    1971.12
Bourne, Geoffrey, 1938.1
Bowman, Barbara, 1977.2
Bowman, Sylvia E., 1971.4
Boynton, H.W., 1906.1
Bradford, Gamaliel, Jr., 1906.2;
    1924.1-2; 1932.1
Brandenburg, Alice Stayert,
    1949.2
Brauchli, Jakob, 1928.1

Braybrooke, 1851.1
Brayley, Edward Wedlake, 1816.1;
    1834.1
Bredvold, Louis I., 1950.1;
    1962.1
Brewer, James Norris, 1816.1
Bridgen, Edward, 1788.1
Bromley, J.S., 1973.1
Brooke, John, 1964.1; 1967.1;
    1968.1; 1973.1
Brown, Harold Clifford, Jr.,
    1970.3
Brown, J. Macmillan, 1894.1
Brown, John Mason, 1951.2
Brown, Ralph S., Jr., 1941.5
Brown, T.J., 1953.1
Brunet, Jacques-Charles, 1839.1;
    1864.2
Brunot, Ferdinand, 1934.1
Bryant, Donald Cross, 1939.4
Bryce, John C., 1936.2
Brydges, Sir Egerton, 1809.1
Bryson, Lyman, 1955.7
Buckley, W.E., 1886.1
Buddy, Lewis, III, 1904.16;
    1905.12
Burke, Edmund, 1758.1; 1762.1
Burn, J.H., 1842.3-4
Burney, Charles, 1798.1; 1800.2
Burney, E.L., 1972.3
Butt, John, 1979.3
Butterfield, Herbert, 1949.3;
    1957.1

C., 1819.1; 1851.2; 1878.1
C., C.T., 1788.1
Calloway, Stephen, 1980.2-3;
    1983.1
Camden, Carroll, 1963.2
Cammann, Schugler V.R., 1967.2
Capetanakis, Demetrios, 1947.4;
    1949.4
Carlton, W.N.C., 1927.1
Carnall, Geoffrey, 1979.3
Carnie, Robert Hay, 1957.2
Carswell, Catherine, 1942.2
Carter, John, 1936.3; 1938.2-3
Catalani, G., 1939.5; 1940.3
Cecil, Lord David, 1961.1
Chalmers, Alexander, 1817.2

Subject Index

The principal subjects of each item are indexed: thus references to Macaulay are to items primarily on Walpole and Macaulay, not to the numerous entries that mention Macaulay in passing. Walpole's writings are indexed under Correspondence and Works; writings printed by Walpole are indexed under Strawberry Hill.

reviews of, 1762.1-2, 5-6;
1764.2-4; 1767.2-3; 1768.8;
1780.1-2; 1781.1, 3; 1782.3;
1783.2; 1827.1-2; 1828.1;
1938.6

Anecdotes Told me by Lady
Denbigh
edition of, 1932.8

Castle of Otranto
criticisms of, 1778.1; 1781.2;
1782.4-5; 1784.2; 1812.6;
1870.2; 1882.3; 1883.1-2;
1894.7; 1902.5; 1911.4, 8;
1913.3; 1915.3, 5; 1922.3;
1923.2-3, 9; 1927.9; 1928.1;
1931.12; 1932.1a; 1934.7;
1935.4; 1936.6, 8; 1937.17;
1938.11; 1943.10; 1947.8;
1950.3; 1952.1; 1953.2;
1957.10; 1959.7; 1963.2, 5;
1964.9; 1965.12; 1968.3, 6,
11, 15; 1969.9-10; 1970.2,
12-13; 1971.9; 1972.3, 6-7,
10-11; 1973.20; 1974.1-2, 8,
16; 1975.3-4, 10-11, 13;
1976.2; 1977.1-5, 8;
1978.4-7, 12-13; 1979.5, 8-9,
11, 13a-15, 17; 1980.1, 4,
10-11, 14-16, 21, 23; 1981.4,
10; 1982.5
editions of, 1810.4; 1811.5;
1817.4; 1830.1; 1834.6;
1840.6; 1886.2; 1906.9;
1907.4; 1924.13; 1929.7;
1930.12; 1931.18; 1963.9-11;
1964.8; 1966.13; 1968.18;
1969.14; 1975.12; 1976.6
prefaces to, Walpole's, 1866.1;
1867.1; 1926.7; 1941.1;
1970.15; 1975.4, 13; 1976.5;
1977.3
reviews of, 1765.1-4; 1767.4;
1774.1; 1804.1; 1924.4;
1925.7; 1929.8
translations of, 1795.3;
1943.11; 1967.26; 1974.18;
1979.22

Catalogue of Engravers
criticism of, 1862.1
review of 1764.3

Catalogue of Royal and Noble
Authors
criticisms of, 1759.1-2, 4-5,
7; 1765.5; 1789.1; 1834.5;
1862.1; 1864.3; 1972.8
edition of, 1806.1
reviews of, 1758.1-3; 1759.3,
6; 1762.3-4; 1807.1
collected
edition of, 1798.7
reviews of, 1798.1-3, 6
translation of, 1800.4

Counter-Address to the Public
criticism of, 1764.1

"Countess of Desmond"
criticism of, 1853.1

Delenda est Oxonia
edition of, 1927.12

Description of the Villa
criticisms of, 1909.2; 1910.3;
1911.3, 7; 1915.4; 1952.2;
1967.27; 1969.5; 1980.2

"Detached Thoughts"
edition of, 1905.12

Dialogue between Two Great
Ladies
review of, 1760.2

Duchess of Portland's Museum
edition of, 1936.10

Essay on Modern Gardening. See
Modern Taste in Gardening

essays
criticisms of, 1935.8; 1957.8;
1967.19; 1980.18
editions of, 1902.2; 1927.12-13

Hieroglyphic Tales
criticisms of, 1967.24; 1968.3;
1979.17; 1980.4; 1983.4
editions of, 1926.14; 1982.7
review of, 1926.5

"Hints for Discovering Junius"
criticism of, 1973.4
edition of, 1891.6

Historic Doubts
criticisms of, 1768.1-2, 4-6,
13; 1770.1; 1771.1; 1772.1;
1789.1; 1791.1; 1914.2;
1918.3; 1919.4, 9-10; 1949.1;
1969.8; 1970.3; 1979.6
editions of, 1860.5; 1965.14

criticisms of, 1852.1; 1883.3;
1908.1; 1914.5; 1918.2, 8;
1924.15; 1936.4; 1943.4;
1944.6; 1961.7
edition of, 1931.16
"Visitors Book"
criticisms of, 1943.1; 1972.12
edition of, 1944.4
Walpoliana

criticisms of, 1799.3; 1800.1,
3; 1851.10
editions of, 1798.4; 1799.1-2
review of, 1800.2
Wisdom of Horace Walpole. See
"Detached Thoughts"
Wyatt, James, 1973.5

Young, Edward, 1979.4